a personal preface

Making a living working with food is a wholly unexpected outcome for a kid who grew up without an iota of interest in either cooking or business.

I know it would be far more romantic to tell a tale of youthful fascination with the ethnic neighborhood eateries in my native Chicago. Or that I ran straight home from school to help my mother prepare old family recipes in our small South Side apartment kitchen. But in truth, I had no clue about what I was going to do when I eventually grew up. When I went off to college in Ann Arbor, I figured something would occur to me.

At the end of my sophomore year at the University of Michigan, I arrived at that dreaded deadline: I had to declare my major.

Having successfully avoided any definitive career decision to date, I opted for what I was interested in, which, at the time, was history. Russian history, to be exact. I was fascinated by the tsars, Soviet dissidents, nineteenth-century anarchists, endless cycles of revolution, rebellion, and reform. Food was most definitely not in the picture—I was bewitched by bomb throwers, not bread bakers; drawn to onion domes, not onion soups; probably pondered the Politburo, but most certainly not pastrami.

The idea for Zingerman's originated in the late 1970s, at a restaurant in which I started my food career as a dishwasher and where my now partner, Paul Saginaw, was the general manager. Despite the disparity in our respective levels of responsibility, we became good

Zingerman's®
guide to good eating

how to choose the best bread, cheeses,
olive oil, pasta, chocolate, and much more

ARI WEINZWEIG

Houghton Mifflin Company · Boston · New York

For information about permission to reproduce selections from this book, write to Permissions, Houghton Mifflin Company, 215 Park Avenue South, New York, New York 10003.

Visit our Web site: www.houghtonmifflinbooks.com.

Library of Congress Cataloging-in-Publication Data

Weinzweig, Ari.
  Zingerman's guide to good eating : how to choose the best bread, cheeses, olive oil, pasta, chocolate, and much more / Ari Weinzweig.
      p. cm.
  ISBN 0-618-41108-9
  ISBN 0-395-92616-5 (pbk.)
      1. Cookery. 2. Food. 3. Zingermans (Restaurant) I. Zingermans
  (Restaurant) II. Title.

  TX652.W384 2003
  641.5—dc21 2003051148

Book design by Melissa Lotfy

Illustrations by Ian Nagy, with help from Phil Stead, Adam Forman, and Kate Uleman

Printed in the United States of America

MP 10 9 8 7 6 5 4 3

in thanks and appreciation

Many thanks to the literally hundreds of friends, family members, partners, and purveyors who've helped me to get all this information together. I'm sure that I'm forgetting to thank dozens of you; please be patient with me if I've omitted some names that ought to be on this list. But here goes:

A thousand thanks to Lex Alexander, Darina Allen, Myrtle Allen, Ed Behr, Alexander Berkman, Carla Capalbo, Holly Firmin, Lance Forman, Mark Furstenberg, Emma Goldman, Joyce Goldstein, Jose Guerra, Randolph Hodgson, Caroline Hostettler, Nancy Harmon Jenkins, Steve Jenkins, Michelle Jordan, Joshua Kaiser, Lynne Rossetto Kasper, Mary Keehn, Sotiris Kitrilakis, Evan Kleiman, Kevin Knox, Aglaia Kremezi, Prince Kropotkin, Corby Kummer, Kim Reick Kunoff, Ann Lofgren, Michael and Wendy London, Jan and Dan Longone, Elizabeth Luard, Mike Maki, Peggy Markel, Bill McAlister, Mary Sue Milliken, Elizabeth Minchilli, Dany Mitzman, Ian Nagy, everyone at Oldways and Slow Food, Mariano Sanz Pech, Nicole Pomaranski, Maricel Presilla, Nancy Radke, Justin Rashid, Glenn Roberts, Judy Schad, Lakshmi Shetty, Mike Spillane, Robert Steinberg, Jeffrey Steingarten, Molly Stevens, Ellen Szita, John and Matt Thorne, Vikram and Meeru Vij, Lisa Walker, Paula Wolfert, Lynn Yates, and Daphne Zepos. Thanks to Janet Campbell, Allison Schraf, and Julie Stanley for help with recipes. In remembrance of Lydia Kitrilakis, Lionel Poilâne, and Patrick Rance, all of whom passed away while this book was in process—the food world is a less joyous place without them.

Special thanks to the writing group: Mort Cohn, Mabelle Hsui, and Deborah Tyman, who've heard more of this book more times than anyone should probably have had to. Thanks to Doe Coover, for being a great agent. Thanks to Beth Crossman for editing help along the way. A note of gratitude to David Swan, who started pushing me to do this book about ten years ago. Thanks to Rux Martin for editing and for first asking me to do a book more years ago than I can remember. Thanks to Jayne Yaffe Kemp for her very fine and very supportive manuscript editing. And thanks to Melissa Lotfy for her lively, readable design.

Thanks to all the partners at Zingerman's: Paul Saginaw, Frank Carollo, Maggie Bayless, Mo Frechette, Jude Walton, Tom Root, Toni Morell, Amy Emberling, John Loomis, Dave Carson, Stas´ Kazmierski, Todd Wickstrom, and Alex Young. Thanks, too, to everyone in our organization for all your support, encouragement, and enthusiasm and for giving me the opportunity to work in such a special group.

About ten thousand thanks to the one and only Jenny Tubbs, without whom much of this book wouldn't exist.

Thanks to Laurel for being so supportive and patient with me while I've worked on this seemingly without end over the past five years.

contents

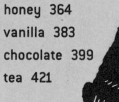

friends. Quickly I moved my way up the organizational ladder from dishwasher to prep person to line cook and kitchen manager, during which time Paul and I spent many an evening discussing what we might do if we had our own place. In 1979 Paul left the restaurant and opened a fish market in a converted feed-and-seed store beside the Ann Arbor farmers' market. Still, we stayed friends, getting together to share strategies about one food business fantasy or another. The idea that stuck was a deli; we'd both grown up eating Jewish food (Paul in Detroit), and we'd been accustomed to enjoying a good corned beef sandwich when we wanted one. Not to mention all the traditional Jewish dishes we'd had the opportunity to eat at home: chicken soup with matzo balls, noodle kugel, potato latkes, chopped liver, none of which was available in Ann Arbor.

Finally, in the fall of 1981, I found myself growing increasingly itchy to move beyond the corporate food world, which paid mere lip service to quality. Without a real plan in mind, I gave two months' notice and started preparing myself for some unknown but hopefully exciting future. Then, in one of those twists of fate that you can never explain, Paul called me. Opportunity beckoned: a building across the street from the fish market was opening up, and he thought it was time for us to launch our deli. In early December, we started meeting regularly to review menus, business plans, pro forma financials, and everything else we thought might be relevant.

For some reason, Ann Arbor had, until then, been anathema to delis—a dozen had opened and closed their doors during the previous decade. Still, no matter how many times we went over our plans, we couldn't figure out any reason why a good one wouldn't succeed. If we sold good food, gave good service, and took care of our crew, we reasoned, people would come back. So we decided to go for it. On March 15, 1982, we opened Zingerman's doors for the first time.

The one question nearly everyone asks us is where we got the name. The short answer: we made it up. The long answer goes like this: we wanted a name that would convey the sense of a good local deli, something that would "sound Jewish," would somehow telegraph that this was a real delicatessen. Because both Paul and I are Jewish, we might have opted to use either his last name or mine. But neither was of any value in Ann Arbor. Weinzweig is unpronounceable—not a great way to go into business. Saginaw is an anglicized version of "Sagin Or," which is Hebrew for "seer of light," but in Michigan, Saginaw is almost immediately associated with either the city of the same name or the Native American tribe after which the city was named. Nobody hears Saginaw and thinks "corned beef sandwich."

Instead we decided to name the deli after Hannah Greenberg, an elderly Jewish woman who was a Saturday regular at the fish market. No more than four feet ten inches tall and about ninety-five pounds, and always with an assortment of pink curlers clipped to her head, she used to stop by to pick up smoked chubs. Each week, like clockwork, she'd complain about how bad the chubs had been the previous week, with lines like, "Oy, you almost killed me with all the bones . . . Give me two more."

We designed our first print ad to run in the local paper, announcing the opening of Greenberg's Delicatessen. We had a neon sign—green, of course—made up for the front window. And then about ten days before we were due to open, the phone rang.

I answered politely, "Good afternoon. Greenberg's. May I help you?"

A pushy-sounding guy on the other end demanded, "Let me talk to Mr. Greenberg."

"There is no Mr. Greenberg," I answered honestly.

Not put off in the least, he went on: "Well, where'd ya get the name, then?"

"Do you like it?" I asked innocently.

"Yeah, I like it," he shot back. "It's mine, and you can't use it."

Turns out Mr. Greenberg had registered the name "Greenberg's Delicatessen" with the secretary of state's office up in Lansing a few weeks before. We pleaded, reasoned, and begged him to let us use it. He was planning to open in the Detroit suburbs; we were adamant about staying only in Ann Arbor. But he was convinced that he was on his way to national fame and franchising.

We retreated to Paul's house to figure out what to do. It was only a week before we were supposed to open. We sat on the floor of his living room, drank a couple of beers, and tested hundreds of names. After a few hours, we'd decided that we wanted a name that began with either an "A" or a "Z" to make us easy to find in the Yellow Pages. Finally we opted for Zinger-

man's. It sounded Jewish. And, as everyone now says with a chuckle, it has "zing."

Because Ann Arbor is a university community of about one hundred thousand, it has a level of cultural activity that you rarely find in a Midwestern town of this size. Even though it's best known nationwide for its sporting activities, the university has attracted lots of good music, dozens of used-book stores, and foreign films. It also has plenty of people of obscure origins who are interested in eating unusual foods from the far corners of the globe.

The town's demographic diversity has certainly helped us to introduce new foods into the Midwest, which has never been known for being on the cutting edge of the culinary world. Who'd have thought that you could sell so much sheep's milk cheese in a small town in the middle of Michigan? At the same time, our Ann Arbor clientele has challenged us. It's hard to get away with poor cheese quality when you're waiting on people who grew up in Paris. And you can't really cut too many corners with your corned beef and pastrami when every tenth customer used to live in Manhattan.

If you come to Ann Arbor, you'll still find the deli on its original site, at the intersection of Detroit and Kingsley streets, a block from the farmers' market and about two blocks from the old train station. The two-story, orange-brick main building, with its mere thousand square feet of selling space, has been in the food business its whole life—it was built as a grocery in 1902. The building is on the historic register. The whole space, including the kitchen, was roughly 1,300 square feet—a tiny spot compared with all the enormous upscale gourmet supermarkets that have sprung up since then.

When we opened for business that first day, we had a total of two employees—one part-time and one full-time. Fortunately, we also had a lot of loyal friends who were willing to help out by busing tables while they were waiting for their sandwiches. We had four spots for customers and four more solo eating places at a counter by the front window. We started with a small but meaningful selection of made-to-order deli sandwiches, much-loved Jewish specialties like chopped liver and chicken soup, traditionally made cheeses, smoked fish, cured and smoked meats, and breads and pastries from various local bakeries. We carried a lot less than we do today, but the basics were all present and accounted for.

The traditional Jewish foods, cheeses, breads, salamis, and sandwiches that got us going are all still here, in force. And what were once obscure ingredients—balsamic vinegar, extra virgin olive oil, goat cheese, and Gorgonzola—have grown enormously popular and have come to be a big part of what we offer.

Today there are seven entities that make up Zingerman's Community of Businesses—each with its unique specialty—with a total workforce of nearly 350.

introduction

This book presents my very strong belief that, despite the standard wisdom to the contrary, anyone who's interested really can tell the difference between mediocre commercial offerings and the many great-tasting traditional foods that are still being made in the world.

Although I long ago left behind my belief in political anarchism, I've remained something of an anarchist in my approach to food. The standard industry perception is that the most flavorful foods should be reserved for an elusive upper-crust gourmet elite. But the way I see it, good food is for everyone. I'm firm in my conviction that you don't have to have been born French or be an insufferable food snob to discern the difference between a well-made farmhouse cheese and a bland, rubbery factory version that bears the same name. Nor do you have to be some kind of connoisseur to tell freshly ground black pepper from the stale, prepacked stuff most restaurants put on their tables. Armed with a little background information, a heightened sense of awareness, and a shopping bag filled with great ingredients, almost anyone who's interested can understand, prepare, and appreciate top-quality food.

Ultimately, I could care less whether or not food is fancy; I just want it to taste good. While I certainly enjoy a slice of fresh foie gras or an occasional eight-course meal in a five-star restaurant, what really gets me going are simple, down-to-earth dishes. Stuff with substance, with solid roots, with history and heritage. Like a bowl of superb spaghetti topped with a full-flavored olive oil and Parmigiano-Reggiano cheese. Or a dark-crusted piece of country bread slathered with cultured butter and topped with a slice of extra-aged mountain Gruyère. Or a spoonful of choice chestnut honey drizzled over a wedge of aged Gorgonzola. You can eat and enjoy these foods almost any time, in almost any setting. And when you knowingly, willingly, consciously, eat better-tasting foods, they add a little zing to your daily routine.

After you've read this book—either in pieces or in its entirety—I hope that you'll put it down knowing a bit more about great food than you did when you bought it. And, perhaps most important, that you'll be further on your way to buying superior ingredients and putting some memorable meals on the table.

become a mindful eater

For those of us fortunate enough not to have to fight for our daily bread, eating presents an opportunity. If we're going to do it two or three times a day for the rest of our lives, we might as well make our meals as enjoyable and interesting as possible. For a modicum of effort, even the least-experienced eater can easily increase eating enjoyment. The key is to become what Buddhists might call a "mindful eater."

It's not that tough to do. Start out your meal as you always do. But then somewhere along the line, stop, teeth suspended. Get in touch with your tongue and all its tiny tasting apparatus. Feel the food. Activate your senses. Savor. Look for a level of enthusiasm, of excited, focused

how to overcome your fear of the guy behind the counter

To me, asking for a taste of any unfamiliar food before buying it is as natural as test-driving a car or trying on a pair of pants. But I know that many shop owners will stare at you as if you're crazy, then refuse your request for a prepurchased sample. What should you do if the store turns you down? Think twice about where you shop. Over time, if enough consumers shift their purchases to places where they can confidently and calmly ask for tastes before buying, the marketplace will respond as it always does, by making that sort of tasting the norm.

Allowing consumers to taste before they buy is part of our effort to get out of the mass-market, superstore mentality and get back to the basics of buying food from small producers, people who are very aware of the fact that they're selling food that others are going to eat.

you really can taste the difference

All too often, retailers offer only average ingredients in the (misheld) view that their customers aren't perceptive enough to identify more flavorful, if more expensive, options. I take the opposite approach: I'm an adamant advocate of the belief that seemingly average eaters can and will be able to tell the difference.

Tasting isn't rocket science. I'll always remember the time a guy was wandering through the deli, looking at the tiny glass flasks of specially aged, traditionally made, authentic balsamic vinegars. Because of their small size (less than 4 ounces a bottle) and high prices (some go for nearly $200), we keep them under lock and key. I could tell he was mystified, wondering what kind of food was so special that it had to be kept locked up. Sensing a challenge, I offered him a taste. "No," he insisted, "it'd be lost on me.

I'm just waiting for my sandwich." Unwilling to give up, I insisted.

He walked away for a minute, then came back with his wife and teenage son in tow. The four of us sat down to sample a quartet of different balsamics ranging from six years up to one that had been aged for more than a century. When we got to the one-hundred-year-old traditional balsamic, their eyes lit up, which happens whenever anyone tastes this vinegar for the first time. It even elicited a "Wow" from the teenage son. Dad smiled and shook his head. "You were right. That's amazing." I don't know if he ever came back to buy balsamic, but I felt good, regardless. What matters most to me is that he got a hint of just how wonderful great vinegar can be. So, to make a long story short, yes, absolutely, 100 percent guaranteed, you *can* tell the difference.

attention to detail, that will carry you to higher levels of culinary consciousness.

Here are some simple steps that will set you on your way to becoming a mindful eater.

1. get to know your food

In the food world, increased knowledge brings increased opportunity for enjoyment. If you learn little or nothing about apples, how can you possibly tell bad from brilliant? Take the apple you bought at the farmers' market last week. Its skin is streaked with brown. Does that mean it's showing signs of excess wear and tear? Or is it supposed to be marked with such russeting?

Ask questions: Where does the item come from? How is it used in its homeland? How long is its shelf life? How was it prepared? What should it look like?

Over the years, I've continued my ongoing food education by combining travel and learning. Anytime I'm on vacation, I squeeze in a few visits to local food producers. These excursions are always eye-opening. The people who grow or craft the food turn out, time and again, to be exceptionally interesting individuals. The cultures, of course, fascinate me, as they always had in history classes. But even more than that, I'm struck by the immediacy of the smells, by the look and feel of the food in its native environment, by how different its flavor is on-site than in the United States. These realizations inevitably set me on a search for the authentic article: wild rice from the lakes of Minnesota (not the cultivated stuff we see in supermarkets); genuine French olive oils (not the ones that were made in Morocco and bottled in France); and really great Mexican vanilla beans (not the cheap brown bottles of "extract" they sell to tourists at the border).

2. look at it

Look at ten loaves of artisan bread from the same bakery. If you make time to do a close visual assessment, you'll quickly notice that each loaf has its own hue. Compare crusts, and what at first appears to be "all brown" will probably become everything from chestnut to cherry wood to chocolate.

Look closely and you'll find colors in your food that will go well beyond the confines of the standard Crayola box: the deep purple-black of an Italian olive paste as you spread it on a golden slice of toasted wheat bread, the nearly Day-Glo emerald green of newly pressed Tuscan olive oil.

External visuals aren't just about color schemes either. The more you look, the more you learn. If it's cheese, check the rind for the coarser-looking handmade farmhouse offerings. If it's tea, look for discernible leaves, usually a sign of something better than the standard shavings and pieces. If it's bread, check the bottom—a random, rough surface says it was baked on a stone hearth. If it's a packaged product, read the label to check the ingredients.

3. smell it

One of my favorite childhood heroes was Curious George, who once stood outside a restaurant "eating the smells," a treat for which the restaurateur tried unsuccessfully to charge him.

Aroma isn't everything, but it's about as close as you can get to flavor without actually eating, since the sense of smell accounts for roughly 90 percent of what you taste. The nose knows what it's doing: it can detect something like ten thousand different scents. Ever notice how hard it is to taste anything when you've got a cold? If you don't stop to smell your food, to appreciate its aroma, you diminish the fullness of the flavor.

Smells alone are often enough to make my day. Break open a loaf of country bread and put your nose against its surface. (Breaking is better than slicing for scent-gathering, since the sliced surface is so flat that it's hard to get your nose into the nooks and crannies.) Test the perfume of a potent new olive oil as it rises up from a hot slice of toast. Experience the astounding aroma of a bottle of well-aged balsamic vinegar. Crack open a well-made croissant and stick your nose right inside to catch a whiff of real butter. Or sample the earthy scent of chanterelles, freshly gathered in the woods, before you drop them into a pot of mushroom soup.

4. taste it

Each of us has about twenty thousand taste buds. Inside each bud, fifty or so cells relay information to a neuron that passes it on to the brain. In general, women have more taste buds (and perhaps better taste?) than men. An infant

has many more taste buds than does an adult. Taste buds tend to wear out every ten days or so, and then we replace them, though in our mid-forties we start to show a net taste bud loss. Consequently, our palate becomes jaded as we age, and older people are predisposed to fuller flavors.

As you eat, notice that you sense different flavor components in different parts of your mouth. You'll detect sweetness primarily in front, toward the tip of your tongue. Sourness starts to show up toward the back, along the sides. Bitter comes in all the way at the back. You can taste saltiness all over.

Pay attention to the feel of the food. Is the sliver of very fresh goat cheese meltingly, velvety soft? Or the bread crust so crackly and crunchy you can't sneak a bite for fear of waking someone? Feel the heat of a habanero chile as it sears and sizzles its way across your tongue and leaves your lips aglow. Savor the creaminess of good chocolate—the kind that's supposed to melt in your hand as well as in your mouth.

Finally, assess the flavor, ultimately the true pleasure of mindful eating. Although I'm probably operating with fewer taste buds than I used to a decade or two ago, I notice so many more flavors in my food now than I ever did as a kid: the intricacies, the complexities, the character of marvelously meaty Serrano ham from Spain; the silky smooth, mild gaminess of oak-smoked, wild Irish salmon; the pleasantly salty, juicy succulence of a great corned beef sandwich. These are the things that get my mental, as well as my salivary, juices flowing.

buy better ingredients

If you were going to make only one meaningful modification to your shopping routine, I'd tell you to buy better-tasting ingredients. For a fairly small amount of additional effort and not much more money, you can improve the flavor of your food enormously.

I should warn you, though, that there is some risk to upgrading. There's some truth to the old saying that "ignorance is bliss." If you've never knowingly partaken of real Parmigiano-Reggiano cheese, then you won't feel as if you're missing much when your aunt automatically pulls one of those now ubiquitous green cans from her refrigerator. I don't mean to embarrass anyone or point fingers. Some of my best friends still keep a cardboard tube of pregrated Parm tucked into their refrigerator doors. But I will tell you with confidence that once you make the move to more flavorful food, you'll never go back. So why run the risk? Because life—my life at least—is just a lot more enjoyable when I'm eating good food than when I'm not.

I can also tell you with conviction that the flavor of the finished food you prepare will never be better than the quality of the stuff you put in. Take a simple recipe for pasta tossed with olive oil, garlic, and cheese, and try it two ways. First pour some cheap oil on a bowl of poorly made, inexpensive pasta, then sprinkle it with powdered garlic and pregrated, cardboard-canned Parmesan. You'll have an inexpensive but, to my taste, pretty unappealing dinner. Then take the exact same recipe, cook up some excellent artisan pasta, toss it with an exceptional, full-flavored olive oil, a touch of chopped fresh garlic, and top it with some real Parmigiano-Reggiano cheese. This time you'll find yourself sitting in front of one of the best meals you'll eat this month. Heck, maybe even this year. The intent, the recipe, the procedures, and the preparation time are almost identical. The difference is all in the ingredients. And also in the final flavor. If you question the validity of this approach, take a week and try using better ingredients yourself. I'm confident that almost overnight you'll notice the improvement.

Then why are so many shoppers willing to start with less-than-good-quality ingredients? Because that's how most of us were raised. Because marketing messages give the (false) impression that factory-made food is just as good (if not better!) than stuff that's still produced on farms. And also because low-end alternatives almost always cost less. In the following chapters, you'll find information and insights into how to identify better ingredients of all sorts. While many will cost more per ounce than their inferior alternatives, I'm convinced that smaller quantities of better-tasting raw materials will buy you more satisfaction for the same, or even less, outlay.

the story of purple popsicles

A few years ago, I stopped over at my three-year-old friend Leo's house just after lunch. It was one of those steaming hot August afternoons in Michigan, and in deference to the heat, his mom pulled a "special dessert" out of the freezer — a box of Popsicles.

"I . . . I want a purple one," Leo said with that sense of urgency kids can get when it comes to selecting sweets. His mom tore off the wrapper for him and carefully handed him the stick. Smiling, he started to take big, long licks. I watched him eat, the deep purple of the Popsicle contrasting nicely with his brightly blond hair. His smile grew even bigger.

"Is it good?" I inquired.

"Mmmmm!" he answered enthusiastically.

"What flavor is it?"

"Purple," he said matter-of-factly as if, of course, purple was one of the world's better-known flavors.

I confess I was a little surprised. "What's it taste like?" I asked.

"Like a purple Magic Marker," he answered without hesitating, and then he went right back to licking. Got me on that one. Certainly gave me a new perspective on food, flavor, and aroma.

Thanks to Leo, two things are clear:

1. We assimilate flavors by comparing them to other flavors we already know. In this context, it was as clear as could be to Leo that, despite the word *grape* on the label, purple Popsicles are obviously from the same plant as purple Magic Markers.

2. Smells and tastes are interwoven in our minds. I'm pretty sure that Leo never actually ate a purple Magic Marker. But I'm even more certain that he'd regularly had the chance to smell some at school. And these days, the pen people make Magic Markers that smell like the fruit of the same color: cherry-scented reds, orange oranges, grape purples.

the quality issue

The renowned psychologist James Hillman has commented that certain words are so overused in our society that they ought to be withdrawn from the English language for a hundred years before they're allowed to return. *Quality* is my number-one nominee for early retirement. How many foods have you found lately that don't claim to be the best? These days even 7-Elevens and Stop & Gos promise great coffee. Bottled industrial salad dressings say they're the best. Not long ago I saw an only slightly better-quality supermarket loaf billed as "the best bread in the universe."

There is no right or wrong definition of quality; it isn't some sort of religious thing. Each of us—food producer, retailer, restaurateur, or home cook—has the option of developing his own definition. Only after we create our criteria for quality can we make any real claim to be meeting them.

McDonald's, for example, has high-quality food. "How can fast food be high-quality?" you may wonder. Because quality—as McDonald's defines it—is about consistency, cleanliness, and quickness. McDonald's doesn't promise the best-tasting hamburger in the world. But you can be sure it's going to taste exactly the same from McDonald's to McDonald's. By its own standards, the chain does an excellent job.

In this book, quality means two things: first, flavor; second, tradition.

Great flavor is something you can understand and appreciate even when you don't personally like the item at hand. A full-flavored food should be like a good essay: it ought to have an intriguing introduction, a good bit of body in the middle to keep you going, and an engaging, memorable finish.

Some of the most complex flavors I've ever had the pleasure of enjoying were found in a single perfectly ripe peach or an incredible sliver of Prosciutto di Parma. The experience starts with an enticing aroma that beckons you to eat. Then, once the introductions are out of the way, it continues with a series of small but succulent little interactions with your taste buds.

But it's the finish that frequently separates the so-so food from the finest. When you eat something really special, enjoyable flavors continue to make their way around in your mouth long after you've swallowed. Great flavors keep on coming, making you marvel at their downright deliciousness. The best cheeses, breads, baked goods, olive oils, vegetables, and vinegars will linger. How do you test this for yourself?

Slow down your eating. And after you've swallowed, count slowly to ten, then take note of the flavors that are still there.

the triumph of tradition

Over and over again, I've found that the raw ingredients and finished dishes that stay true to long-lived techniques are the ones with the fullest and most authentic flavors.

Why? For most of the twentieth century (and a good part of the nineteenth), we've expended enormous effort to make our food more consistent and less costly, all the while increasing its shelf life. Far more often than not, this homogeneity results in uninteresting, unrewarding food, lacking the flavor, character, and finish it had before our overly industrial attitude got in the way.

Foods made with traditional techniques connect us with the past. In the same way that it's important to develop an understanding of the era in which a great artist did her best work, so, too, is it essential to get back to the roots of the foods we eat if we really want to understand and appreciate them. Learning where artisan cheeses and oils and pastas come from, how they fit into their cultures, how they were eaten in days of old, can carry them into our modern-day culinary routines.

By heading back to traditional techniques, we're also often able to get at food made without artificial additives or lab-produced preservatives. Two hundred years ago, these sorts of additives simply didn't exist. Consequently, traditional techniques push us toward simple foods, prepared with simple ingredients, in an all-natural, time-tested way.

practice tasting

Practice may not make a perfect palate, but I guarantee that it will get you awfully close. How do you practice tasting?

taste as part of a group.

It's interesting to see what others taste or experience when they're eating the same things you are. You'll find that you can develop the language you need to describe what you taste when you have to communicate what you're experiencing to others.

try comparative tastings.

Either on your own time, or in some more formal educational forum, make the effort to compare, say, four fresh goat cheeses, half a dozen red wine vinegars, or five brands of dark chocolate.

take notes.

You may feel a bit foolish at first. But if you take a few minutes to jot down your thoughts on what you're eating day after day, you can't help increasing your awareness.

Taste, compare, and chronicle as you go.

get comfortable in the kitchen

Looking back on the past thirty years, I see that my comfort level in kitchens has come only from spending a lot of time in them. The more I cook, the more comfortable I get, the more fun I have, the more flavorful my food. And I'm convinced that the same is going to be true for you and almost anyone else who's even moderately interested in good food. After all, few of us are naturally good at anything. As the writer William Saroyan said, "If you practice an art faithfully, it will make you wise." Cooking is no exception.

adventurous eating

Part of being a mindful eater means adopting a willingness to sample new foods, to overcome a natural reluctance to try sea beans or celeriac, loquats or fresh favas, smoked venison or smoked tea, pistachio paste or periwinkles, and all sorts of other items that we may not have heard of.

There are a few foods — mostly sweets — that are almost always instant winners. Others aren't as easy to get to know. Bitter flavors, for example, take particular getting used to. Hardly anyone is initially attracted to the pronounced bitterness that's characteristic of beer or coffee. And not many ten-year-olds would trade a milky-sweet Hershey bar for a bit of extra-dark French chocolate. Yet as we mature, most of us migrate from the accessible to the complex.

So don't just settle for the status quo. Get out there and start tasting. Life is short. Make it interesting. Be adventurous. Eat on the edge.

Home cooking is as much a craft as any of the traditional agricultural activities or artisan cheesemaking. In both cases—whether you're working with pots and pans or with plows—what's needed is the same blend of hands-on experience, dedication, skill, and healthy respect for and understanding of science.

Many of the recipes in this book come from my travels, learned from the people who make the food I've written about. Almost inevitably these folks seem to cook pretty much the way I do, with a little of this and a little of that. Most of the recipes are fairly simple, requiring minimal time in the kitchen and appealing to longtime food lovers and novices alike, the sort of dishes that you can make on a Wednesday evening when you're in a rush and have no significant reason to cook other than wanting to eat.

Throughout, I've tried to focus on dishes that people can and will be able to reproduce even if they've never traveled to the source. Keep in mind, though, that the integrity and quality of the ingredients used to prepare the recipes are critical. The simpler the dish, the more important the quality of the food that goes into it. After all, if there are only four or five items in play, they'd all better be pretty good.

Most of the recipes I've included are ideas, foundations upon which you can build your own culinary adventures. If I can use them to convince you that great ingredients can make good meals quickly and manageably, so much the better. While each has the requisite Fannie Farmer–style measurements, there are loads of opportunities to improvise because, ultimately, only you know your own taste.

product recommendations

In each chapter, I recommend brands or producers whose wares I'm particularly enthusiastic about. I've based my picks on more than twenty years of extensive tasting at Zingerman's, in stores and restaurants, at trade shows, and throughout my travels around the world. Wherever possible, I've tried to offer names and brands that are avail-

 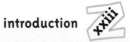

able either in specialty shops across the country or via mail order. These products have proven track records. They're made by folks who've been at it for many years, if not many generations.

But this book isn't a specialty food version of *Consumer Reports*. Artisan foods are ever changing, ever evolving. At best, what these lists give you is a good starting point. Despite my best efforts to search out great food everywhere, I'm sure there are still hundreds of wonderful small producers that I don't yet know about. (Don't hesitate to drop me a line at foodfinds@zingermans.com to let me know of anyone you think is of interest.) I guarantee that the more you learn, the more you pay attention to what you're buying and eating, the more effectively you'll able to evaluate and appreciate the quality of food. Add to my lists by making notes and adding your own favorites. Go wild. Taste early, taste often, and above all have fun.

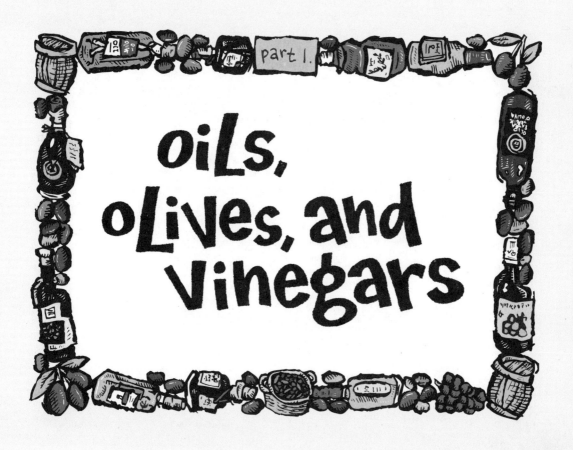

part 1.

oiLs, oLives, and vinegars

OLive OiL

"Without oil, without vinegar, how can we take a trip?"
● Greek proverb

In 1982, when Zingerman's opened, I don't think you could find extra virgin olive oil in Ann Arbor. Today we stock more than forty varieties on any given day. In the intervening years, I've visited dozens of oil producers, traveled hundreds of miles to watch the olive harvest, read about olive oil, written about it, stayed up late at night talking about it. For people like me who love the food of the Mediterranean, having access to great olive oil has been one of the single most significant improvements in the quality of our cuisine in the last two decades. Because olive oil is such an essential element in the cooking of every Mediterranean country, it would be impossible to replicate the authentic flavors of regional cooking without it. Like corn in the Americas, olive oil is the icon of Mediterranean food. It's integral to the area's history, religion, agriculture, economy, and eating. The best oils add complexity and character to any dish in which you use them. When deciding what to buy, remember that you can't replace their fullness of flavor with any amount of low-grade olive oil, or with anything else for that matter.

a quick history

Olive oil is one of the oldest foods, made from the fruit of one of the most ancient trees known to humankind. No one really knows when and where the olive tree originally sank its roots, but it was first cultivated somewhere in the eastern Mediterranean about six thousand years ago. Olives and olive oil get multiple mentions in the Bible, as food and for a long list of religious and ritualistic reasons. For centuries olive oil was the primary fuel for lighting Mediterranean lamps. The ancient Egyptians used it for food and also for perfumes and medicines.

The Greeks first brought olive oil to the commercial and culinary heights from which it has never fallen. It became so essential to their economic and cultural existence that they put a series of laws on the books protecting olive groves and olive trees. A few centuries later, the Romans planted olive trees, cured olives, and pressed olive oil all across southern Europe and North Africa. Before long, their Iberian settlements were exporting large quantities of olive oil back to Rome, and continue to do so to this day: Italy is still the largest buyer of Spanish oil exports.

The Romans also left a technological legacy to the world's olive oil producers. At the ruins at Volubilis in Morocco, I had the chance to see a reconstructed Roman oil press from the third century A.D. I recognized it immediately because it looked just like the "modern" working presses I had seen in Italy. The only real differences were that the stones at Volubilis would have been turned by hand or by donkeys and that the pressure on the olive paste came from a large log instead of mechanical hydraulics.

Olives came to the Western Hemisphere with the Spaniards, who introduced them into Peru and Paraguay in about the sixteenth century. Table olives remain a significant crop in much of South America, but I've yet to taste a great oil produced there. I'm convinced there are some—I just haven't found them yet.

From its southern base, the olive spread north to Mexico and then up the California coast, carried by Franciscan monks as they established their New World missions in the second half of the seventeenth century. To this day you can see olive trees along the Pacific coast. Many native Californians have warm childhood memories of gathering roadside olives to take home and cure. (Unfortunately, 95 percent of California table olives are no longer home-cured: instead they're turned into those pallid, pitted black ones that come in a can.) Although historically little attention was paid to making oil in the States, in recent years a number of Californians have dedicated themselves to producing world-class olive oils. Keep your eye on them; my bet is that the efforts of these producers will pay off in the form of exceptional oils.

I'd say the same for the up-and-coming oils of Australia, New Zealand, and South Africa. Like wine, it takes time to develop the tradition, technique, and rootstock needed to make great oil. But all of these new areas are well on their way.

The use of olive oil began to grow in the United States as large numbers of southern European immigrants arrived in the late-nineteenth and early-twentieth centuries. In the past twenty years, olive oil has gone from immigrant outcast to hot commodity, and imports have increased fivefold. Americans living in households that use olive oil now consume about three liters per person per year. Still small by Italian standards, but headed in the right direction —as of 2003, olive oil sales in the United States are up over 35 percent since 1995.

a guide for the perplexed olive oil buyer

With all the hubbub comes a host of misinformation. There are so many brands that you may feel as though you have to be an expert to figure out which one to buy. On the next few pages, I've endeavored to put together the basics of getting to know good olive oil, knowledge that will help you avoid the overpriced and steer clear of impersonators.

What makes any given oil different from the next? How do you find the perfect oil for your kitchen? The answers to these and other important olive oil questions coming right up.

what is extra virgin anyway?

Traditionally produced extra virgin oils, made from the first pressing of olives, are essentially little more than the juice of the olive. Technically, "extra virgin" is a grade of olive oil—usually indicating higher quality—distinguished by its naturally low levels of free oleic acid. Generally, the lower the level of free oleic acid— meaning that there is almost no oxidation of the oil—the better. To qualify as extra virgin, an olive oil must have a free oleic acid count of less than 1 percent.

Oils made from lesser-quality olives or from the residue of first-pressing oils are significantly less flavorful and have much higher levels of free acidity: "virgin" olive oil has two to three times the free acid of an extra virgin oil. Take note that "free acid" doesn't mean the oil will taste acidic; on the contrary, oils with high levels of free oleic acid tend to be greasy and taste either unpleasantly sweet (as in overripe fruit) or, alternatively, of benzine.

"Olive oil"—the term is somewhat deceptive because it omits the all-important modifier "extra virgin"—is the chemically refined stuff they sell at the supermarket. It's the lowest edible grade and has by far the least flavor. (It used to be known as "pure" olive oil, and you may still see it referred to as such.) "Pomace" oil is even lower on the flavor scale. It's made by blending a bit of better-quality oil with the oil that's extracted from the solids—skin, pulp, and pits—left from earlier pressings. It has almost no flavor and is of little use to anyone who's after the great taste of good olive oil. I've seen gallons on display on the counters of chichi restaurants that apparently fail to grasp the message they're sending.

Unfortunately, in today's high-tech world, it's possible to take a low-quality, essentially flavorless olive oil and chemically remove or reduce its free acidity to a level that technically qualifies it as "extra virgin." Oil of this sort has appeared on the market in the United States and other countries. If you've had real extra virgin olive oil, you'll notice the difference immediately. The low-grade pretender costs about half as much. I've seen gallons of "extra virgin olive oil" on sale for something like $7. First-time buyers may take home this phony product thinking they got a good deal. But after using it, they'll quickly decide that olive oil is just one more example of modern marketing hype with no real redeeming value. And that would be a shame. Other than noticing price, the easiest way to spot this type of oil is to taste it. It will be greasy and have hardly any olive flavor. Next to a good-quality extra virgin olive oil, the difference in taste, texture, and aroma will be overwhelmingly apparent. To be sure, buy from a reputable olive oil seller and, please, taste before you buy.

is cold-pressed olive oil better?

Usually, yes. "Cold-pressed" refers to the technique used to extract the best oil from the olives. To get the highest-quality oil, the presser cannot use any heat. Although some methods work more quickly and yield more oil, the friction created by industrial pressing methods can damage the quality and flavor of the oil. Cold-pressing is one sign that a producer is trying to make good oil. But as with the "extra virgin"

label, the "cold-pressed" label is not a guarantee of flavor. Again, the bottom line is taste.

Quality oil producers typically used to crush their olives with stone wheels (a.k.a. millstones, or *pietre* in Italian). Traditional cold-pressing methods involve spreading the resulting olive mash on mats of rope or nylon, stacking them between metal disks on a large metal spindle, then hydraulically pressing to extract the liquid. A recent twist on the cold-pressing story is the "sinolea" method of extracting the oil. A notable few have switched to this newer technique, which incorporates modern technology while protecting the delicate flavor and character of the oil. After the olives are crushed, small, paper-thin, crescent-shaped steel blades run quickly and continuously through the mash while maintaining temperatures lower than the 100-degree-Fahrenheit maximum allowed for cold-pressing. Only the oil that naturally adheres to the blades is gathered, yielding a top-quality product that has been spared the exertion of high pressure demanded by the traditional method.

More popular than sinolea is the newer "continuous-press" technique. Invented by a Polish-born engineer working for the Italian firm of Pieralisi, this process seems to be the favorite of those who are on the cutting edge of olive oil technology. In this method, the olives are crushed with a series of small hammers in a twelve-foot-long round metal tube with a four-foot opening. It looks a lot like a hot water heater turned on its side. The olive mash is spun inside the machinery in order to separate oil, solids, and water.

Proponents of the continuous-press process are adamant that the oil it produces is far supe-

In Spain, the traditional hand-picking is called *ordeñar,* meaning "to milk" the branches. The name comes from the similarity of motion used in milking cows and in taking ripe olives from the trees. The picker carefully closes her hand around a branch as far as she can get. She then slowly pulls down toward the end of the branch, maintaining a soft but sufficiently firm grip in order to loosen any olives that are ready to be removed. The trick is not to grip so tightly that you don't also take off olives that aren't ready.

rior, especially when it comes to cleanliness. "The old system is very dirty," one quality-conscious producer told me. Those who use the continuous press insist that producers who still stick with the old stone-and-hydraulic methods are living in the dark ages. Not surprisingly, those who use the traditional methods are equally adamant that the new technology is a sham and that the oil it produces is inferior. Since I've tasted good and bad oils produced with each technique, I've found that the true test is still in the taste.

why does one oil taste so different from another?

Although we buy it in bottles, olive oil is an agricultural—not an industrial—product. Much like wine, oil is influenced by a wide range of factors—some controllable, others not. Although most people focus on cold-pressing and extra virgin as indicators of quality, these are but the tip of the iceberg. Jordi Ballbé, who produces high-end oil from Arbequina olives in Catalonia, in northeast Spain, says, "There's so much more to oil quality. Mostly you have to have really good olives to start out with." He's right. Olives are to an oil producer what milk is to a cheesemaker, and the best oil producers will go on for hours about their olives.

There are other important factors that distinguish one oil's flavor from the next.

region matters

The soil content, the weather, the climate, and the vintage will all have an impact. That's why the flavors of olive oils, like those of wines, vary so much. In fact, many experts argue that the soil has an even bigger influence on the flavor of an oil than it does on a wine.

The oil of each of the great growing regions—Tuscany, Catalonia, and Provence, to name just three—has its own distinctive flavor profile. Note that the focus is on regional differences, not, as is often implied, on the borders of modern nation-states. People ask me all the time whether I prefer Spanish oil or Italian oil. But that's an impossible question to answer. An oil from Baena in southern Spain has no more in common with an oil from Catalonia in the north than it does with one from southern France or northern Italy. Part of the fun of learning to appreciate fine olive oil is trying oils from different areas and learning to recognize the differences in taste.

handpicking is important

The best olive oils are made from handpicked olives. Careful picking ensures that the fruit is gathered only when ready and that a minimum of bruising occurs in the process. It takes a lot of work to pick olives by hand. One grower in Spain estimated that "just picking by hand costs about 3 euros [about $3] per liter of oil." Add in the cost of growing, pressing, bottling, labeling, freight, and retailing, and it's obvious that when you see a bottle of olive oil on the shelf for less than $10 or $12 a liter, it can't possibly have been produced from handpicked olives.

Since biblical times, olive growers more interested in cash than quality have used a variety of techniques to knock their olives off the trees, from sticks to tree-shaking machines. Mechanical means do speed up the process and save money. But they also damage the olives. Imagine dropping an apple on the floor. Three hours later it has turned brown and mushy, right? Same idea. Any break in the olive's skin will increase the odds of early arrival of rancidity in the oil. Even less desirable is the southern Italian tradition of waiting until the olives are so ripe they simply fall off the tree. It's a lot less work, but oil pressed from these superripe olives is almost always inferior.

seasonal considerations

One of the most critical decisions an oil producer must make each year is when to press. The flavor of an olive oil changes dramatically depending on the time in autumn in which the olives are harvested. The later the harvest, the riper the olives. Two oils from the same estate pressed from olives harvested at different degrees of ripeness will taste different. Most of the highly prized oils are pressed early in the season, in October or early November. At this point the olives are only partially ripe, but their oils tend to be fruitier, more robust, and more peppery. The typical oils of Tuscany, with their distinctive hints of pepper, green tomato, and artichoke, are representative of this early harvest style. At this stage the olives have a high level of polyphenols (the naturally occurring oxidants in olive oil), which contribute the pepperiness and also add to the shelf life of the oil. Yields for these oils are generally quite low, and prices, consequently, are quite high.

Olives that are allowed to ripen more fully on the tree, into December or even early January, have a higher oil content but generally a milder, softer flavor. The oils of Liguria, on the Italian Riviera, are typical. Generally yields will be higher at this later point in the season, and prices may be somewhat lower. Done well, this later harvest will still produce a flavorful oil.

When considering the season of harvest, it's also important to remember that olives grown in more southerly climates usually ripen earlier in the autumn than those grown in colder areas, so a mill in the southern Italian region of Molise may be pressing very peppery olive oil well before anyone farther north in Tuscany is ready.

The weather will also affect the oil. Drier climates and drier years tend to yield oils with more body. While regular rain is the farmer's friend during the spring and summer, in the fall drier weather is likely to produce a better-quality oil, keeping the pests away and the oil content of the olives high. A very wet autumn, on the other hand, can be disastrous. Too much rain can quickly cause rot, and the fruit can split because its skin stretches tightly over its rapidly increasing water content. Lots of rain makes the oil "more humid," giving it a shorter shelf life. One producer swore to me that this factor could make almost a year's difference in helping the oil retain its quality.

pressing considerations

From the moment an olive is picked, it starts to deteriorate, and the flavor, complexity, and character of the oil drop markedly. The best oils, then, are pressed within hours of picking. Within twenty-four hours is the usual target. This race to get to the press increases costs.

varietal differences

There are dozens of different varieties of the single tree—*Olea europaea*—that produce edible olives. Each growing region uses its own varieties. In Italy more than three dozen types are grown for oil, including Taggiasca in Liguria; Frantoio, Moraiola, and Leccino in Tuscany; Coratina in Puglia; and on Sicily, the one with my favorite olive name, the Giraffa. In Catalonia, the tiny, delicious Arbequina is the dominant oil olive; its nutty sweetness is responsible for the unique flavor of Catalan oil. Some estates blend a number of varieties in the belief that each contributes its flavor and character.

Like a winemaker, each olive oil producer works with his own olives to create a unique oil. No two estate oils will taste exactly alike. The same variety grown in two different regions will yield slightly different flavors in the oil. Even from the same estate, each year's production will have its own quirks. The character and variety of flavor is part of the charm and pleasure of eating these fine olive oils.

why does one olive oil sell for $15 and another for $50?

Everyone is familiar with the decent $5 bottle of wine — tastes pretty good and is fine for a casual get-together. Then there's the $30 bottle, the one you bring out when good friends come from out of town or for a special dinner or just to treat yourself. There's nothing wrong with the $5 bottle. But it lacks the depth and complexity of its more expensive, more sophisticated counterpart.

The same is true of olive oils. The liter bottle of Colavita that sells for under $15 is a good extra virgin olive oil. I use it for sautéing and for marinades. It's less expensive because it's produced in large quantities, with olives bought on the market, and pressed in a modern and efficient factory.

But while I recommend it for everyday cooking, Colavita does not have the complexity of flavor or the character of, say, the $30 bottle of oil from the Tenuta di Valgiano in Tuscany. The latter is an estate oil — which means that all the olives used to make it are from the Valgiano estate. All are handpicked, and all are pressed within hours of being taken from the tree. As with a $30 bottle of wine, I use the estate oil for special occasions: on a simple (but delicious) pasta of olive oil, garlic, and Parmigiano-Reggiano; for wonderful salads; for ripe, just picked tomatoes. But unlike the $30 bottle of wine, which begins to oxidize as soon as you open it, this estate oil will grace your table a good twenty or thirty times before it's time to recycle the bottle.

Bottom line? While price isn't always a guarantee of quality (there are lousy oils sold for high prices), it is a good indicator. The fine estate-produced oils, with their wonderful, complex flavors, almost always cost more. But — big *but* — it's not an either/or decision. There's a place for both the $15 Colavita and the $30 Valgiano in the same cabinet. I usually have on hand no fewer than half a dozen oils in my pantry.

how long does olive oil keep?

As a broad rule of thumb, extra virgin olive oil can generally be stored for about a year. Because it is so low in free acidity, it is less likely to go bad than an inferior oil. Just keep it in a relatively cool, dark place. Heat and light are the enemies, so stay away from windowsills and stoves. There's no need to refrigerate good oil. (If you do, it will congeal, and you'll need to give it time to warm up so it will return to its original state.) Lower-quality oils with higher levels of free oleic acid tend to spoil more quickly.

Three footnotes: First, the shelf life of any oil starts not from when you buy it but from when it was pressed, so to estimate its shelf life, you need to know when an oil was actually made. Your supplier should know but frequently won't. Don't be deceived by the European Community "sell-by" dates you see on some bottles. They are based only on the bottling date (which is meaningless), not on the pressing. Second, oils pressed earlier in the autumn — that is, those with the more robust, green, peppery flavors and higher levels of polyphenols—generally hold their integrity more effectively than the gentler oils pressed later in the year. Finally, none of this information will be worth a thing if, somewhere along the distribution chain, the oil was improperly stored.

Don't have an anxiety attack. If you buy a bottle of oil and discover that within a month or so of purchase it's gone rancid, return it to the place you bought it for a replacement.

are greener olive oils fruitier?

Well, sometimes. Greener oils can be fruitier and fuller-flavored. But flavor—not color—is the way to determine which oil you want to buy. In fact, technical experts often pour oils into cobalt blue glasses for tasting so that their assessment won't be thrown off by the appearance of the oil. Although color is not directly linked to quality, some unscrupulous producers may add olive leaves to the fruit during the crushing to obtain a greener oil. The chlorophyll in the leaves adds visual luster but does nothing to boost flavor. (Worse, it may even help to mask defects in the flavor of the oil.)

what is "unfiltered" olive oil?

Most olive oils sent to America are filtered. The olive oil is run through a series of paper or cotton filters to clarify it. Unfiltered oils are left in their natural state—cloudier and sometimes nearly opaque from the natural particles of olive sediment.

Oil producers aren't in agreement about the benefits of filtering. Those who don't filter insist that their oil is more flavorful, that it retains some of the essential goodness which others remove for fear that consumers won't accept the cloudiness of an unfiltered product. Those who do filter, on the other hand, argue that the sediment does nothing for the oil and that producers who fail to filter are simply trying to sell something (the sediment) to the consumer that would otherwise be disposed of.

I lean toward unfiltered oils. I like the thicker mouth-feel, which reminds me of drinking coffee brewed in a French plunger pot.

how come my italian grandmother didn't use extra virgin olive oil?

Though it will come as a surprise to many (and certainly no offense is intended), most of the Italians who immigrated to North America didn't use very good olive oil when they got here. Most were poor, and even in Italy at the turn of the century, away from a farm or farm market, the best extra virgin olive oils were costly. Those Italians who did use the best extra virgin oils in their homeland couldn't find them here. The only place in this country in which olive trees are grown in quantity is California, where one hundred years ago most growers planted trees to produce table olives, not oil.

why does olive oil cost so much more than other oils?

Because it is harder to produce. Sunflower seeds, peanuts, canola, and the like can be processed in large mills, using continually turning presses that yield large quantities of oil at relatively low prices. Good olive oil, by comparison, is still made in much the same way it always has been—with all the costly, time-consuming traditions and limitations that nature imposes.

Olive trees take years to start producing fruit. Because the best oils come from handpicked olives that are pressed within a day of picking, mills must be located near the fields and production schedules are necessarily uneven. The whole year's supply has to be pressed over a period of a few weeks, and the equipment then sits unused for the other eleven months of the year. All of which adds up to relatively higher cost. Fortunately for us, the flavor of fine olive oil is as big as its price.

how do i know which oil to buy?

Have you used good olive oil before? If not, the answer is easy. Start with a good, affordable oil, like Colavita. The price tag won't knock your budget out of whack, and you'll get the flavor that only an extra virgin olive oil can provide. If you've already tried Colavita, you're ready to experiment with a better oil, at which point I'd ask you a series of other questions.

What do you want to do with the oil? I rarely recommend estate-bottled oils for frying, unless you're feeling flush. On the other hand, if you're looking for something interesting, say, for salads, then estate oils are perfect. Here's your chance to pour a rainbow of flavors onto your food, to anoint a bowl of just cooked pasta with a touch of a terrific Tuscan oil and make yourself a more than memorable meal.

What kind of flavors do you like? If you prefer a delicate oil, I'd recommend one from the Italian Riviera or from Catalonia. If you like oil that's really full-flavored, I might go with one from Tuscany, Baena in southern Spain, or Puglia in southern Italy. In between? Provençal oils tend to be quite smooth and buttery. There are also wonderful oils from other regions of Spain and from Greece. Taste and compare to see which ones you like.

How much do you want to spend? The wide spectrum of oils available means that there's probably an oil that's perfect for your price range. For under $20, you can get a fruity, delicious bottle of Unió oil, cold-pressed from handpicked Arbequina olives along the Siurana River valley in Catalonia. The full-flavored, much sought-after oils from Tuscany can cost more than $35. The hard-to-find oils of southern France are often priced at $40 or more.

I recommend stocking your kitchen with a selection of oils, each of which can make its own contribution to your cooking and eating enjoyment. And please taste before you buy. Everyone's palate is a little different. What I like, you may love, and I may adore an oil that you abhor. What's too fruity for one person is perfect for the next.

my first olive harvest

Even though I'd read about and tasted fine olive oils over the years, until ten years ago I'd never seen an olive being picked or pressed. That's when I made a pilgrimage to Italy, to get a firsthand taste of what great olive oil is all about. My only regret is that I waited as long as I did.

Probably the most surprising thing about the trip was the emotional intensity that accompanies the harvest. Olive oil in its homeland is no simple salad dressing. South of the Apennines, it's the single most precious component of Italian cooking—it permeates the economy, history, and culinary activity of the country in a way that is equaled only by wine. Great olive oil in Italy isn't the preserve of some small food elite; it's eaten and enjoyed by everyone, everywhere. Yet despite its popularity, it's rarely taken for granted. Italians treat olive oil with a reverence that Americans save for sports heroes and movie stars. Having watched this product being made, I can only say it deserves every ounce of respect it gets.

Visiting at harvest time left me with unforgettable sensory impressions: baskets of multicolored olives being brought into the *frantoio* (the mills where olives are pressed, pronounced frahn-TOH-yo), the powerful aroma hanging in the air as the olives are crushed, the green-gold oil pouring out of the separator (the final stage of the process) onto a slice of thick country bread.

As often as I'd heard about the process of making olive oil, I didn't get it until I saw it with my own eyes. I visited three different *frantoii* on that trip, each producing its own distinctive oil. Two—the Tenuta del Numerouno, on the west coast of Tuscany near Follonica, and De Juliis, in the Abruzzo (where Rustichella oil is pressed) on Italy's eastern coast—used traditional millstones. The third—the Laudemio oil produced on the estate of the Marchese Frescobaldi—had converted to the more modern sinolea method.

The flavor of the olive oil is affected not only by the producer's decision of when to harvest and press the olives but by geography. Italy's climate changes drastically as you move from north to south. Within each region, differences in altitude, proximity to the sea, and other factors affect harvest time. Then there is the matter of olive varieties: there are dozens of them, and each ripens on its own schedule. Finally there is the fact that even on a single tree not all the olives are ready at once. Workers may have to revisit a tree two or three times before it is completely cleaned of olives.

In the older fields, olive trees are often scattered haphazardly. Newer fields are more neatly planted; the trees are laid out in the same sort of orderly rows one would expect to see in a modern American apple orchard. In Tuscany most trees grow in the hills, where their twisted trunks and silvery leaves point to the sky at odd angles, so that they resemble old men struggling up an incline. Most trees today are pruned regularly to keep them at manageable picking height. In central Tuscany, where many of the trees were killed or damaged by the infamous frost of 1985, those I saw were still very young —thin, spindly things in comparison with the stout trunks of the older trees in other areas, some of which are hundreds and hundreds of years old and were being picked when Thomas Jefferson was in the White House.

the picking

Olives hang off trees in clusters, looking much like grapes or ripe dates. They vary in color and size, according to ripeness and variety. The darker the olive, the riper it is. Most of the olives I saw were being picked when they were still fairly green: firm, young, shiny, plump, bursting with color and energy. At that stage, the olive's oil content isn't as high as it will be when it's black and fully ripe, but the taste is more intense.

All the farms I visited harvest olives by traditional handpicking. The workers still go from tree to tree, making their way through the field as directed by the *fattore, the* "farm manager." The pickers—roughly half are men, half are women—use brightly colored plastic "combs" (not much bigger than the ice scraper I keep in my car) with four or five thick "fingers." Nets are spread under the trees to catch the olives that fall, preventing serious bruising of the fruit and keeping it free of dirt. They remove most of the stems and leaves before loading the olives into carts to go to the *frantoio*. An average-to-good picker harvests about 100 kilos (220 pounds) of olives a day. After pressing, that single day's work will yield only about 15 liters of olive oil. That's half an hour of work per bottle in the picking alone.

the washing

When the olives arrive at the *frantoio,* they are poured into a vat, where they are washed. The effect is kaleidoscopic: the olives arrive in dozens of colors, mostly shades of green, with a few browns, reds, purples and blacks. The olives must be clean to produce a well-made oil free of contaminants, so the fruit is first washed with cold water. Leaves float to the surface and are removed. Stones and dirt sink to the bottom. The olives are then run up a conveyor belt, which shakes off any remaining leaves. At every stage of the process, great pains are taken to avoid heat, which damages the quality of the oil.

the pressing

After washing, the olives are ready to be pressed. They are coarsely chopped and then dumped into a large stone "bowl"—if something fifteen feet across, three feet deep, and three feet off the ground can qualify as a bowl. In its center are the supporting actors of the pressing process—the millstones, or *pietre*. At Numerouno, the pressers use two *pietre;* in the Abruzzo, three. The Frescobaldi estate no longer uses stones but instead works with the sinolea technique using paper-thin stainless-steel blades. The old stones are in retirement, resting against the wall outside the *frantoio* with the dignity of ancient sculptures.

In my mind's eye, I had expected the stones to lay flat and crush the olives beneath their breadth. But they don't. The stones stand on edge in the bowl, towering over most everything

in the room. The ones at Numerouno looked to be about five feet high and a foot thick and were made of granite. The *pietre* spin round and round and round over the olives, turned at a surprisingly fast pace by a central axle attached to a motor below the bowl. In the process, they literally roll over the olives and crush them.

I have to admit that I was fascinated by the stones. I couldn't stop marveling at their size, wondering what would happen if one came loose from its moorings — the giant stone rolling recklessly up and over the edge of the bowl, careening its way through the *frantoio* toward the innocent American bystander, frozen in disbelief to his spot on the floor.

At Numerouno, I inquired as to how much it would cost to buy a new *pietre*. To me, it seemed like a straightforward question. But everyone just shrugged, raised his eyebrows, and shot me a look that said, Only an American would ask a question like that. Turned out that the press has been using the same stones for as long as anyone could remember. Signor Marengo, the farm manager at Numerouno, had been there thirty years, and the *pietre* were already in place when he started. After much discussion, the folks at the *frantoio* finally agreed that the current stones must be about forty years old and that new ones were likely to cost about $3,000 each.

Although I'd heard the process described many times, I had always assumed that the phrase "cold-stone-pressed olive oil" meant that the weight of the stones pressed the oil out of the olives, much as millstones grind grain into flour. Not true. The stones are actually three or four steps removed from any visible olive oil.

As the stones rotate, the olives gradually turn into a mash, or paste, made up of the just crushed skins, fruit, pits, water, and oil naturally found in the olive. The longer the stones go over the paste, the finer it gets. When it's deemed ready, this mash is then transferred to the *fiscoli,* the nylon or hemp mats on which it will be moved into the press. The *fiscoli* are about an inch thick and eighteen inches across, with a hole in the center. They start out new and white but quickly turn gray-green from the olive paste. A small machine pumps the olive paste from the bowl onto one mat at a time, spreading it evenly. The mat then slides onto a post on a nearby cart. Another mat is placed on top, then more paste, then another mat. The mats look like olive-paste Oreos, their creamy greenish gray filling sandwiched between the fiber disks. After four mats, a thin metal disk of the same diameter goes onto the cart. The process is repeated over and over until the cart is stacked to the top of its six-foot-high central pole.

The cart is then wheeled into a hydraulic press, a sort of vertical vice. From below, the press lifts the cart off the ground, slowly but relentlessly pushing it and its contents against the top of the frame. The fiber mats and the paste are squeezed, and the liquid between the mats escapes. As the press inches its way upward, more and more of the water and oil in the paste run down the sides of the mats. The stream of liquid is steady—never really pouring, but trickling down the sides like light rain on a window. A trough cut into the floor next to the press collects the liquid.

separation anxiety

The liquid at this stage of the process is not olive oil. Rather, it's a mixture of the natural water and oil contained in every olive. This liquid is pumped into a separator, which is the least imposing and most recent piece of equipment in the place. It looks like one of those old, round washing machines. The separator uses centrifugal force to spin off the water and pour a steady stream of olive oil from its mouth. This ancient food of the gods gushing from a completely unromantic piece of modern metal machinery seems like an anachronism. Nonetheless, there it is: beautiful, green-gold, wonderful extra virgin olive oil.

During the four or five hours that I spent at the De Juliis *frantoio* in the Abruzzo, the oil never stopped pouring out of the separator. One-hundred-liter drums—some plastic, some metal—were used to collect the oil. When one barrel was full, another immediately slid in to take its place. Every once in a while, an outsider would arrive, with his own barrel to be filled right from the separator; local families purchase one hundred liters at a time from the *frantoio,* the most economical way to buy good oil. That amount—consumed at the rate of a little more than two quarts a week—lasts an average family in the Abruzzo about a year.

rock around the clock

The *olio nuovo*—the new oil—that comes out of the separator is so bright that it looks as if it would glow in the dark. But from the moment the harvest starts in November until the time it ends in early December, the lights in the *frantoio* are never turned off. The crew works around the clock for weeks, bringing in the olives, making the mash, spreading it on the *fiscoli,* pressing, and separating.

When I watched, the crew was giddy, like students staying up all night to study for finals. Everyone's working, everyone's exhausted, everyone's having fun. And everyone is literally covered with olive oil. It's in the air, it's in people's hair, it's on their clothes.

dinner in the *frantoio*

In the Abruzzo, we ate dinner in the *frantoio.* While the stones turned, the presses pressed, the crew worked, and the separator separated, we sat at a table in the corner—watching, smelling, and eating a meal of bruschetta, then pasta, followed by an array of roasted meats, and finally a simple salad of romaine lettuce, all topped off with freshly pressed olive oil. Only a *frantoio* could create such an aroma. It was like being inside a gigantic bottle of olive oil.

The highlight of the meal was, of course, the oil. We slapped thick slices of bread on our plates, walked over to the separator, and slid them under the spout. In about two seconds, the green-gold oil covered the bread. Back to the table, to sprinkle on a bit of salt, and then we ate. "More?" the men on the crew asked me. Who could refuse?

At this stage, *olio nuovo* is very peppery, very

how to taste olive oil

You can taste the oil on its own or with bread. Either method works well, and at times I opt to do both. Professional tasters always taste straight — they don't want anything to encumber the flavor of the oil. Their routine goes something like this: They pour an ounce or so of oil into a glass, usually opaque, so as not to let the color of the oil influence their assessment. They cover it to capture the oil's aroma. Then, because the best flavor and aroma emerge when the oil is close to human body temperature, tasters cup the glass in the palm of their hand for a few minutes to warm the oil.

The tasters take off the lid and quickly push their nose inside. The scent of the oil is essential to evaluating its quality. Though I've occasionally come across the odd oil that has a huge aroma but a merely modest flavor, in general the perfume correlates pretty closely with the taste.

Smells safely filed away, it's time to try the oil. As the professionals do, put the glass to your lips and suck about a teaspoonful into your mouth. I say "suck," not "sip," because to taste properly, you must pull as much air into your mouth as oil. Essentially, you slurp, exactly as your mother probably instructed you not to do with your soup. Spread the oil around in your mouth, then put the tip of your tongue up to the roof and suck in some additional air. Aerating the oil helps you to taste its various flavor components. Take note of sweetness up front and bitterness toward the back. Don't judge too quickly. Many of the most prestigious oils have a pronounced pepperiness that won't appear until thirty to sixty seconds after you've put the oil in your mouth.

Warning: Don't taste like this on a first date; you'll sound like a glass of soda run dry when it's being sipped through a straw. On top of which, the professional technique calls for spitting out the oil after tasting, rather than swallowing. If you're not trying to be ultra-sophisticated, just swallow and enjoy. But either way, it's important to wait for the finish, the flavors that linger long after the actual oil is gone.

Alternatively, you can taste the oil with bread, which is how most Americans do it. Because few of us ever actually "drink" olive oil, it's probably more relevant to test the oil with food than on its own. Over the years I've come across a few oils that were unremarkable au naturel but great on a finished dish. The only caveat is to use the right bread, one that's not sour and not overly salty. The rest of the procedure is pretty much the same. It's best to warm the oil slightly in your hand or warm the bread a bit. Be sure to check the aroma. Notice the flavors in the various parts of your mouth and be sure to pay attention to the finish.

I'd recommend tasting three or four oils, one after another. If you've got an idea of what they're like before you actually taste, start with the mellowest and finish with the most flavorful. This kind of progressive tasting adds an all-important comparative context. Take notes that you can refer to later.

green, and very good. Opaque, thick, cloudy, it has a pleasant touch of bitterness that will gradually dissipate as the oil has a chance to sit and settle in storage.

exceptional olive oils

tuscany

For nearly six years, the world had to do without the olive oils of Tuscany. The killing frost of 1985 left Tuscan olive groves in ruins and Tuscan oil in very short supply. Since then, aficionados have lusted after its fantastically fruity flavor and pinch of pepperiness. Fifteen years after the frost, one Spanish producer, a well-respected businessman in his fifties, remembered it as if it had just happened. "In 1985 I did a trip by train near Florence," he told me, lowering his voice as he spoke. "All the trees were burned from the frost," he said shaking his head. He paused, then added, "I was crying."

The immediate impact on Tuscan oil was indeed significant. Impostors—oils produced elsewhere but sent out as "bottled in Tuscany"—flooded the market. The look was similar, but the flavor was lacking. Now Tuscan oils are again readily available. But still, impostors abound. I look for single-estate oils that say "produced and bottled in" and then list the name of a farm or town in Tuscany.

If you like olive oils with big, round, peppery, rustic flavors, you won't go wrong with any of them. Because every year's production has its unique flavor characteristics, you can't judge by brand name alone. As much as possible, taste before you buy. Or buy from someone whose taste you trust and who will guarantee the oils. Here are a few Tuscan oils that I've found to be of consistent high quality over the years.

CAPEZZANA The Capezzana estate near Florence has been making fine wines and extra virgin olive oil since the beginning of the ninth century. Nearly twelve hundred years later, Capezzana olive oil remains full-flavored, peppery, green, and delicious. Serve it over a Tuscan bean salad or a plate of freshly picked lettuces, drizzle it onto a bowl of piping hot bean soup, or pour it onto steamed new potatoes.

CASTELLO DI CACCHIANO If you like olive oils that make you stop and take notice, Castello di Cacchiano is for you. It's bottled in its natural state—never filtered. Clouded with tiny olive particles so that it's almost completely opaque, Cacchiano captures the rustic, regal flavor that is the trademark of traditional Tuscan olive oil. It's got a wonderful pepperiness that tickles the back of your throat.

Produced on the estate of the Baron Ricasoli Firidolfi in the traditional Chianti wine district, the bottle is marked with the same *gallo nero*, or black rooster, that denotes authentic Chianti Classico wines. When I first tasted this oil, I dipped in one chunk of bread after another until I'd cleaned the whole plate. This oil makes excellent bruschetta, and it's big and bold enough to hold its own on grilled steaks and chicken.

CASTELLO DELLA PANERETTA The Castello della Paneretta sits on a Tuscan hillside that's almost too typically Tuscan to believe, surrounded by fields of olive trees, vineyards, and cypress trees. Inside the property are the ruins of Cepparello castle, destroyed in 1260 in the Battle of Montaperti between the Guelphs and the Ghibellines. The oil is equally typical Tuscan: full-flavored, wildly fruity, very creamy, green, gorgeous, delicious.

LAUDEMIO The Laudemio Consorzio is a group of traditional oil producers from central Tuscany who banded together in 1990 to create their own, more restrictive production requirements. Each of the approximately thirty farms in the consortium has committed to working with very high standards of picking and pressing, assuring that all the olives used come from that farm, are picked by hand, and are pressed quickly after being removed from the tree. Because all the producers pack in the same faceted glass flask (though each has its own label), you might easily assume that there is only one Laudemio oil. In fact, each of the thirty producers has its own oil with an individual flavor and character.

Of all the Laudemio oils, Frescobaldi has had the greatest exposure in the U.S. market. (If you can find Laudemio oil from one of the organization's other producers, it's almost certainly worth trying as well.) The family has owned land in Chianti Ruffina, southwest of Florence, since the middle of the fifteenth century. The estate was among those hardest hit by the frost of 1985. But rather than lament its fate, the family set out to create a long-term program of modernization, replanting, and redevelopment. The Frescobaldis use a sinolea system for pressing, then decant and filter the oil, which has a clear, luminous green color, a fine aroma, and an exceptional flavor, with hints of freshly cooked artichokes. Like all good Tuscan oils, it's great on salads, bruschetta, fresh cheese — wherever you'll be able to taste its peppery, fruity flavor.

The oil is packed inside a box, protecting it from the debilitating influence of sunlight. If stored in direct light, it can discolor and turn rancid fairly quickly, so be careful when buying any that's been removed from the box.

PODERE DI PILLORE Alberto Passigli makes this oil in the Tuscan hill town of Fiesole. The farm is noteworthy for both its fine views of Florence and its excellent oil. Because Passigli is adamant about using only his own organically grown olives, quantities are limited. All the olives are handpicked, and the new oil is then naturally decanted for months in old-style terra cotta containers. Finally, it's packed into elegant, square green bottles, each hand-stamped with scarlet sealing wax. The oil has a big green flavor with suggestions of artichoke and green tomato. It has enough pepper power to be distinctively Tuscan, yet it's balanced enough to appeal to anyone who likes a well-made, full-flavored oil.

SAUVIGNOLA PAOLINA Located in the hills outside of Greve, the Fabbri family makes a very small quantity of a fine, unfiltered oil each year. It has a thick, creamy, buttery texture and a luscious mouth-filling flavor reminiscent of artichokes and almonds with a soft touch of pepper in the finish. It's packed in a tall, elegant black bottle.

TENUTA DEL NUMEROUNO The Numerouno estate is located on the western coast of Tuscany, just north of the town of Follonica. While the 1985 frost took a near deadly toll on central Tuscany, the moderating force of the sea kept coastal temperatures at more reasonable levels. Consequently, oil has been produced continuously at Numerouno, and the trees are much larger than those in central Tuscany. Seven different varieties of olives are grown on the estate, and many of the trees are hundreds of years old. The oil is unfiltered, which means that it has a thick, cloudy appearance from the tiny olive particles that remain suspended in it. It is gentler than the oils from central Tuscany, yet still quite flavorful.

aging gracefully

The flavor of fine olive oil will mellow over the course of a year in the bottle. Newly pressed oils generally have a pungency and pepperiness (or, as the Italians refer to it, *pizzica*) that you won't find in more mature offerings. Those who like their oil on the gentler side will want to find one whose flavors have had a chance to soften in the bottle. Neither way is better — it's strictly a matter of taste. But know that the flavor of an oil you buy in April will likely be fruitier than that of a bottle of the same oil purchased early the following autumn.

TENUTA DI VALGIANO The Valgiano estate, lying on Tuscany's west coast, about forty kilometers north of Pisa, has about three thousand olive trees. The area's clay soil contributes greatly to the exceptional character of the olives, which are handpicked, then transported in shallow, slat-sided crates to prevent any damaging heat from building up en route to the press. To enhance the freshness and flavor of the oil, the olives are pressed within thirty-six hours. If you like a full-flavored, fruity, spicy oil, try this one.

other regions in italy

COLONNA (MOLISE) Marina Colonna's oil from the Molise region in central Italy is full-flavored and delicious. Marina took over the family business a decade or so ago in order to bring this wonderful oil to the rest of the world. The oil is produced using only the handpicked olives grown on the family estate. All of the olives are pressed within a day of picking. Colonna oil is distinguished by its robust flavor; it treats your palate to flavors of green tomato and almond, and it has an enjoyable earthy pepperiness. The oil is carefully produced using the new sinolea method. Every bottle is hand-sealed on the estate with the family crest in red lacquer, adding a touch of class to an already top-notch product. I particularly like it for grilling chicken and making bruschetta.

Colonna also produces Granverde, a superb oil pressed from a blend of olives and fresh lemons (see page 24), and Arancio, an equally interesting oil of olives and Sicilian oranges.

olive oil 19

PETRAIA ORGANIC (PUGLIA) Petraia, the name of the oil, means "place of stones," a tribute to the farm's rocky soil. Interestingly, trees growing in stony soil tend to send their roots deeper in order to reach water and often produce more flavorful fruit. Petraia has an intense aroma that knocks you back with the smell of freshly cut grass and wild herbs. Its flavor is big, fruity, full. Its finish is significant—lots of the peppery pop that characterizes good Pugliese oils.

ROI OLIVE OIL (LIGURIA) The oils of the Italian Riviera in the region of Liguria are known for their elegant, almost flowery flavors. They're noticeably lighter than the earthier Tuscan oils. As a coastal region whose cooking relies heavily on fresh fish, Liguria produces oils that match well with delicately flavored seafood. Stronger oils from other regions will often overpower fish dishes. Liguria is the region that invented pesto. Long before it was in fashion, pesto was a practical way for Genoese sailors to consume vitamin C to fight scurvy on long voyages—and Ligurian oils also make the perfect base for blending with the sauce's traditional fresh basil, pine nuts, garlic, and cheese.

I prefer the oil of the Boeri family, produced in the town of Badalucco in the hills north of Genoa since the turn of the last century. Their oil is made exclusively from the local Taggiasca olives, grown at altitudes of 300 to 2,100 feet above sea level. It's buttery and sweet, with a subtle hint of almonds and almost no pepperiness. ROI's oil is excellent in any dish but especially so on salads and sautéed vegetables. Pour a bit over freshly cooked fish or shellfish. And, above and beyond all else, ROI's Ligurian oil is ideal for preparing an authentic Ligurian Pesto (see page 224).

LA SPINETA (PUGLIA) Food professionals typically put Pugliese oils in the same sort of position that the area occupies on a map of Italy—down at the heel. But when it's done well, Pugliese oil can be very, very good indeed, with a rustic olive flavor and a bold, spicy finish. Elia Pellegrino represents the fourth generation to manage this farm since the family first took over in 1890. Its La Spineta label is archetypal Pugliese oil made from the region's Coratina olives. It has plenty of pepperiness that is closer to "red" than to the more Tuscan "black" pepper.

provence

The bottom line for food lovers is that authentic French oil is frustratingly hard to find: Little is made. And most of that is consumed locally; a significant amount is still sold in unlabeled bottles at small market stands. In total, the whole of Provence now produces only about 2,000 tons (2 million liters) a year, less than 10 percent of the country's annual consumption. (By contrast,

Spain serves up about 300 times that total, nearly 600,000 tons.) For Provence, 4,000 to 5,000 bottles a year from a single farm is a very large production; in Italy, this amount is just enough to constitute a commercial operation. To convey further the small scale at which most Provençal producers are working, one of the regions most-respected artisan mills handles olives from about 500 to 600 different farms, yielding about 40,000 liters, an average of only 700 to 800 liters of oil per farm!

Because supplies of French olive oil are so short, many commercial packers sell North African oil bearing labels that accurately, if misleadingly, say "bottled in France." The following are some of the best of the authentic French oils that I know.

ALZIARI   The Alziari shop, in the old town of Nice, is filled with olives and olive oil and everything that goes with them. Over the decades, Alziari has become the center of oil culture on the Côte d'Azur, the place "where all the old olive people party after the harvest," according to Mort Rosenblum, a foreign correspondent for the Associated Press and the author of the excellent *Olives: The Life and Lore of a Noble Fruit.* The oil is typical Niçoise—very light and elegant. The tin in which it arrives is also exceptional—olives and olive leaves painted gold and green against a light blue flecked with silver. I like the design so much that I saved the very first tin I ever bought from the shop in the early 1980s. Alziari's oil is ideal for a salade Niçoise (see page 29) and a *pan bagnat,* the traditional beach sandwich of Nice which is essentially a salade Niçoise on a crusty roll. It's also excellent on what is known in Nice as *brissa* (what the Italians call bruschetta)—country bread

toasted, rubbed with garlic, doused with olive oil, christened with a pinch of sea salt, and eaten warm.

HUILE D'OLIVES DES TREILLES
I learned about Eric Martin's marvelous oil from Mort Rosenblum. It's delicious, very buttery, with a gentle but distinctive olive fruit flavor. As is common in Provence, the oil is left unfiltered and is quite cloudy. It's superb with any type of vegetable dish.

MAUSSANE-LES-ALPILLES   From the town of the same name comes a rich, golden nectar with a distinctive herbal character that no other oil can match. The Maussane oil is unequaled in its broad range of high and low flavor notes.

MOULIN DE BEDARRIDES
Situated in the western part of Provence, the Vallée des Baux produces some of the tastiest French oils. There are about half a dozen mills left making oil there. I've sampled most and enjoyed them all, but Moulin de Bedarrides is my favorite. Henri Bellon presses this oil in the town of Fontvieille (home of the writer Alphonse Daudet), in the shadow of the cliffs of Les Baux. Locally grown olives are brought to the mill, which has been in the Bellon family for five generations, and then cold-stone-pressed to produce this richly flavored, buttery-smooth oil.

spain

Olives have been in Spain since about the fourth century B.C., originally brought to Iberia by the Carthaginians. The Romans arrived at the beginning of the second century B.C. and proceeded to plant olives all over. Within a century, Spain had become the primary supplier of olive oil to the empire. Today Spain is the world's largest producer and exporter of olives and oil, working with a base of about 200 million trees!

Nearly every olive-growing region in Spain boasts its own varieties, each with a unique flavor that contributes to the character of the distinctive local cuisine. In Catalonia in northeastern Spain, the tiny, delicious Arbequina is the primary oil olive. Its nutty sweetness is responsible for the elegant, fruity flavor of Catalan oil. In the Baena district in Andalusia, the large, pointed Picual produces earthy, gutsy, full-flavored oil. The Hojiblanca olive (the name means "white leaf"), grown nearby in the southern districts around Córdoba, yields a sweeter, smoother oil. Cornicabra olives, grown primarily in Murcia and the area of Toledo, produce full-flavored oil with a lot of character.

L'ESTORNELL (CATALONIA) There are a number of different oils produced by the Vea family in western Catalonia, all in various versions of the L'Estornell label. I prefer their organic oil, made exclusively from handpicked, organically grown, cold-pressed Arbequina olives on an estate west of Barcelona. The oil has a pleasant fruit flavor, soft enough to use with fish, substantial enough so that it won't get lost on salads or in soups.

MARIANO'S (SIERRA DE GATA) One of my favorite Spanish oils is made in the Sierra de Gata in quantities so small that I'm hesitant to include it here. It's produced by Mariano Sanz Pech and his family from the organic Manzanilla Cacereña olives that grow on their farm in Extremadura in western Spain. The olives are picked carefully by hand quite early in the season and at very low temperatures, in order to increase the complexity of the flavor. The oil is excellent on salads, with grilled vegetables, on cooked beans (a Spanish favorite), or in soups.

NUÑEZ DE PRADO (ANDALUSIA) A rainbow of flavors makes this oil from Baena one of Spain's best. It has hints of freshly cut green apples and an intensely fruity, earthy flavor. The Nuñez de Prado family makes oil using the unique "Flower of the Oil" method—the olives are crushed as in Italy, but the resulting olive paste is never put into a hydraulic press. The only oil that makes it into the bottle is what drips naturally from the mash. Left in its natural unfiltered state, this oil captures the wild heart of the olive's flavor.

OLEI FLORIS (CATALONIA) With its sweet, lively flavor, Olei Floris is excellent on almost anything. The Ballbé family hand-gathers the fruit at the midpoint of ripeness, when the olives are turning from green to red, but before they're fully ripe. The olives are crushed within a day of being taken from the trees to ensure that their flavor is properly protected, yielding a superbly sweet, fresh, bright, and nicely balanced gentle oil that tastes of green apple.

california

Olive oil from California is hardly new. But for most of the last few centuries, the state's efforts were centered around growing olives for eating, not for oil. During the last decade, a whole new energy and enthusiasm for pressing great oil has emerged, an effort reminiscent of the early years that marked the respective revivals of American winemaking in the 1960s and cheesemaking in the 1980s. In fact I'd say that if you want to watch the future of olive oil unfold in the twenty-first century, keep a close eye on California. As with California wines, the improvement in quality has now started to come at a very quick pace. There are literally dozens and dozens of California oils on the market right now, and I encourage you to get out and taste regularly.

DAVERO Ridgely Evers and Colleen McGlynn have been working to deliver world-class oil at DaVero in the Dry Creek Valley in Sonoma since the early 1990s. Hand-harvested early in the autumn, it's got a wonderful big aroma that will hit you as soon as you open the bottle. It is made from a typically Tuscan blend of Leccino, Frantoio, Maurino, and Pendolino olives. Evers and McGlynn harvest the entire field at one time, looking for a mix of olives that is about a third dark and nearly ripe, a third quite green, and a third somewhere in between. All the varietals are harvested and pressed together. With each passing year, the DaVero oil has grown increasingly balanced and well rounded. The flavor is big, pungent, grassy, and full of fresh fennel and artichoke with a noticeably peppery finale. I've used it on potatoes, as a garnish for vegetable soups, and poured over freshly cooked pasta.

MCEVOY RANCH This oil is from Nan McEvoy's beautiful estate in the hills outside of Petaluma. McEvoy is home to one of fewer than ten olive presses in California, and it's one of the few producers to crush its own olives. The oil is very green and a bit earthy, with a touch of pepperiness. It's very nice on salads, meat, and poultry. Since most of the trees are under seven years old, they're just now approaching the time when the fruit will come into its own.

IL NOBILE Produced by Umberto and Sarah Chironi near St. Helena from a blend of Manzanilla and Mission olives, this oil is nicely balanced and quite flavorful. It's got the pepperiness that's characteristic of Tuscan oils but a California flavor all its own.

STORM OLIVE RANCH Bonnie Storm produces this oil on a 120-year-old cattle ranch in the Pope Valley of Napa Valley. She built on her family's history of olive growing by bringing back more than a thousand olive trees from Italy in 1994. The olives are all hand-harvested, and the oil is thick, cloudy, and unfiltered and has many of the characteristics of a good, pleasantly pungent Tuscan oil. It's also got some of that fresh-grass aroma that is so appealing in some oils from Sicily and the full flavor to stand up to grilled steaks and fish.

limonato: lemon olive oil from italy

The people of the Abruzzo and Molise regions, on the east coast of Italy, have been making this special combination of olives and lemons for centuries at the end of the harvest. Lemons were added to the olives for the final pressing of the year in order to freshen the equipment before setting it aside for the season, or perhaps to help preserve oil made from late-harvest olives. Because it's one of those things locals take for granted and never think worthy of mentioning to anyone else, the resulting lemon olive oil remained a local secret.

When it's done well, the oil is smooth, with a lemoniness that tickles your nose like the bubbles in a fine Champagne. You can do most anything with *limonato* you'd do with other oils, and then some. Pour it on freshly cooked pasta, and toss with chopped arugula, roasted peppers, toasted pine nuts, and some hot red pepper flakes. It's fantastic brushed on top of almost any broiled fish. If you want something interesting for a quick first course, a little *limonato* makes an incredible salad dressing, with a bit of grated Parmigiano-Reggiano and a splash of a delicate red wine vinegar.

I have even used limonato in desserts with great success, drizzling thin slices of toasted cinnamon raisin bread with it and topping the whole thing with a scoop of vanilla ice cream. Hardly traditional, but it made a big hit.

Beware the many commercially made "lemon oils" on the market, which are little more than lemon oil extract added to extra virgin olive oil. Their flavor pales next to authentic *limonato*. A few labels will assure you of their authenticity: Olio Agrumato in tall thin bottles under the brand Medi Terranea is excellent. Marina Colonna's Granverde (see page 19) is less widely available but equally good. In the United States, the folks at O in California are making a very good oil of olives and the unique California Meyer lemon. They also have a very nice Blood Orange Olive Oil. DaVero (see page 23) uses a blend of Meyer and Eureka lemons and its own estate-produced olive oil.

new zealand

MOUTERE GROVE Ed and Liz Scott have been working with Tuscan olive varieties on their fifty-acre farm at Moutere Grove since the mid-1990s. The soil is a unique clay loam, known for yielding full flavor to all the agricultural offerings of the region, at the top of the South Island of New Zealand. The olives are picked by hand and arrive the same day at the press, a continuous-process closed system. The oil is lightly filtered through cotton, then naturally decanted.

It has a big Tuscan spicy olive flavor with a generous peppery bite and lush accents of tropical fruit. The color is a vibrant green. The oil is great on salads, pastas, full-flavored fish, lamb, or beef.

everyday oils

While the carefully produced estate-bottled oils have an enormous complexity and high level of character, there are other less costly but still very good oils that are noteworthy for their versatility.

COLAVITA (MOLISE) The folks at Colavita in the central Italian region of Molise have put enormous energy into making a flavorful and affordable extra virgin olive oil, and they have played a major role in getting extra virgin olive oil into American kitchens. For that they deserve the thanks of everyone in this country who loves good olive oil. Whether you buy it in small half-liter bottles or go all the way up to the three-liter jugs, Colavita extra virgin olive oil gives you decent value and flavor. In recent years, Colavita oil seems to have gotten more pungent, showing more of the spiciness that's typical of oil from Puglia in the south of Italy. Of late, the bottles carry a seal certifying that the oil inside is 100 percent Italian.

MIGUEL Y VALENTINO (CATALONIA) This very affordable and very nice oil from Catalonia, Spain, is moderate on the flavor scale, with a touch of green apple, and it's good for everything from salads to soups to seafood.

UNIÓ (CATALONIA) Another very affordable and very accessible oil from Catalonia. Consistently of good quality and a good value.

fleur de france vinaigrette

This vinaigrette is easy to make. The subtly sweet Banyuls vinegar (see page 83) adds character to the dressing. Pour over a fresh green salad or just cooked potatoes.

- 2 tablespoons Banyuls or aged sherry vinegar
- 1 generous tablespoon Dijon mustard
- 6 tablespoons extra virgin olive oil, preferably Catalan or Provençal

In a medium bowl, whisk the vinegar into the mustard until fully blended. Slowly add the oil, whisking constantly, until velvety smooth. Whisk again just before serving.

makes about ½ cup

homemade mayonnaise

For some reason, most cookbooks seem to discourage you from making mayonnaise with a lot of olive oil. They recommend using part olive oil, part something else, to keep the flavor from being "too pronounced." To me, the olive oil taste is the only really good reason to go to all the trouble of preparing old-style mayonnaise from scratch. If you use an electric mixer or a food processor, mayonnaise is not hard to make. Serve with cooked potatoes, omelets, or salads of all sorts.

1 large egg
4 large egg yolks
1 tablespoon Dijon mustard
9 teaspoons fresh lemon juice
1¼ cups extra virgin olive oil, preferably a light Ligurian or Catalan
¼ teaspoon fine sea salt, plus more to taste
Freshly ground black pepper to taste

In a blender or mixer bowl, combine the egg, egg yolks, mustard, and 2 teaspoons of the lemon juice. Beat on high for 2 minutes, or until smooth.

Gradually drizzle in the oil, beating constantly, until the mixture is thick. (Depending on how thick and how rich you like your mayonnaise, you may or may not need the entire amount of oil.)

Blend in the remaining 7 teaspoons lemon juice, the salt, and the pepper. Check for seasoning and adjust to taste. The mayonnaise will keep for 3 to 4 days, covered, in the refrigerator. Serve cold.

makes about 2 cups

pinzimonio
fresh vegetables and olive oil

*P*inzimonio is a wonderful way to enjoy a great olive oil. To my taste, this Italian specialty is the best way to serve crudités. Just mix a bit of sea salt and your favorite extra virgin olive oil and serve as a dip for fresh vegetables, such as celery, fennel, radishes, and carrots.

> **An array of fresh vegetables**
> **Your favorite extra virgin olive oil (or better yet, try two)**
> **Coarse sea salt to taste**

Peel the vegetables, if necessary, and cut them into dipping sizes — sticks or wedges big enough to give your guests something to hold onto while they dip the vegetables into the olive oil. Arrange the cut vegetables around the perimeter of a large platter.

Pour the olive oil into one or two small bowls. Mix a bit of the salt into the olive oil, and place the bowls in the center of the vegetable platter. Then place a small bowl of additional salt nearby for those who like a lot. Dip the vegetables into the oil and enjoy.

salade niçoise

This salad is the centerpiece of a nice summer meal. All you need to go with it is bread to soak up any additional olive oil and something good to drink.

variation

If you prepare the salad in advance, you can spoon it onto a crusty hard roll to make *pan bagnat,* the traditional beach sandwich of Nice. The longer the salad sits on the bread, the more the bread soaks up the flavors of the oil and the tuna.

1	pound very small potatoes, preferably heirloom (halved or quartered if larger, to equal 2 cups)
4	ounces French green beans, trimmed
1	ounce mixed salad greens (2 cups, loosely packed)
1	(4-ounce) can Italian-style oil-packed tuna, drained
2	Roma tomatoes, cored and quartered
1	cucumber, peeled, quartered, and cut into ¼-inch-thick slices
4	large hard-boiled eggs, peeled and sliced
10	Niçoise olives
	Aged red wine vinegar to taste
	Extra virgin olive oil, preferably Provençal, to taste
	Coarse sea salt to taste
	Freshly ground black pepper to taste
4–8	anchovies (optional but highly recommended)

Steam the potatoes in their jackets until tender, about 15 to 20 minutes. Meanwhile, steam or parboil the green beans for 3 to 4 minutes, or until crisp-tender. Drain, rinse with ice-cold water, and drain again.

Arrange all the salad ingredients on a platter: start with the greens; top with the tuna, potatoes, tomatoes, cucumber, eggs, green beans, and olives.

Dress with vinegar, olive oil, salt and pepper. If you like, top with the anchovies. Then sit in the sun with a friend, eat, and enjoy.

serves 2 as a main course or 4 as a side dish

chopped wild greens salad

This salad was one of the culinary highlights of a recent trip to Crete. It showed me a whole new way to enjoy greens. The greens are "cooked" in the dressing, much as seafood is "cooked" in lime juice to make ceviche. On Crete it's common to find a dozen different greens— many of them gathered in the wild—in a bowl. An exceptional host may gather nearly twenty. You can use almost any moderately tender greens—dandelion, kale, chard, mustard, mallow, endive, or greens from beets. The more varied the greens, the more interesting the salad. Serve with crusty bread and white wine.

5	ounces greens, coarsely chopped (10 cups, loosely packed)
1–2	tablespoons full-flavored extra virgin olive oil, preferably Greek
2	teaspoons fresh lemon juice
¼	teaspoon coarse sea salt

variation

You can make a Cretan version of the typical Greek salad by adding olives and cubes of good feta cheese to each bowl.

In a large nonreactive bowl, toss the greens with the olive oil, lemon juice, and salt until well coated. Let stand, covered, for 2 hours. The greens should be fairly soft and wilted when they're ready. Check for seasoning and adjust to taste. Mix well, and serve.

serves 2

tuscan pecorino salad with pears

This salad is typical of autumn or winter in Tuscany. The sweetness of the pears is an ideal counterpoint to the richness of the cheese. The best cheese is true Pecorino di Pienza, but any Tuscan sheep's milk cheese will work well. It's important to use a good, full-flavored Tuscan olive oil. The spiciness of the pepper brings out the best in both the cheese and the oil.

2 ounces mesclun or other mixed salad greens (4 cups, loosely packed)

1 perfectly ripe pear, cored and thinly sliced

3 ounces aged Tuscan Pecorino cheese (without rind), coarsely grated (about 1 cup)

¼ cup walnuts, toasted and coarsely chopped

2 tablespoons full-flavored extra virgin olive oil, preferably Tuscan

4 teaspoons white wine vinegar

Freshly ground black pepper to taste

Arrange the greens in a large shallow salad bowl or distribute them evenly among individual bowls. Arrange the pear slices decoratively atop the greens. Sprinkle the grated Pecorino on top, then the walnuts. Dress with the olive oil and vinegar. Add a generous dose of pepper before serving.

serves 2 as a main course or 4 as a side dish

a note on toasting nuts

Toasting almonds, walnuts, and pine nuts is an easy and effective way to enhance their flavor and texture. Cook the nuts in a hot (not smoky), dry skillet over medium heat for 3 to 5 minutes, stirring occasionally, until they're lightly browned and their centers are slightly warm. Alternatively you can toast nuts in a 350°F oven by placing them on a baking sheet and cooking them, uncovered, stirring occasionally, for 10 to 15 minutes.

catalan lentil salad

I had this late-autumn salad in a restaurant in Barcelona. If you want to liven its look, you can surround it with colorful accompaniments such as roasted red peppers or grilled leeks.

- ½ pound dried brown lentils
- 8 cups water
- 1 medium carrot, quartered
- 1 medium red onion, peeled and halved
- 3 dried bay leaves
- 1 garlic clove, peeled and bruised with the side of a knife
- 1 teaspoon coarse sea salt, plus more to taste
- ¼ cup extra virgin olive oil, preferably Catalan
- 2–3 tablespoons apple cider vinegar
- 2 tablespoons coarsely chopped fresh Italian parsley or arugula
  Freshly ground black pepper to taste
- 6–10 ounces mixed salad greens (16–20 cups, loosely packed)
- 1 cup walnuts, toasted (see previous page) and coarsely chopped
- 3 ounces crumbled aged or fresh goat cheese (optional)

Rinse the lentils well under cold water. In a large pot, bring the 8 cups water to a boil over high heat. Add the lentils, carrot, onion, bay leaves, and garlic. Reduce heat to medium-high and simmer until the lentils are al dente, 14 to 18 minutes. Add 1 teaspoon salt just before the lentils are done.

Drain the lentils in a colander or strainer. Discard the bay leaves and garlic. Remove the carrot and onion and set aside to cool (you'll be adding them to the salad, so don't throw them out). Rinse the lentils well under cold water and drain well.

When the carrot and onion are cool, chop them into lentil-sized pieces. In a medium bowl, mix the lentils, carrot, onion, olive oil, vinegar, and parsley or arugula. Add salt and pepper to taste.

Arrange the salad greens in individual bowls and spoon the lentil mixture on top. Sprinkle the walnuts and goat cheese, if using, over the lentils and serve.

serves 4 to 6

oeufs brouillés

slowly scrambled eggs in the style of southern france

*O*eufs brouillés are essentially the French version of scrambled eggs. They're great any time you want an egg dish for breakfast or a light supper. The first time I had the dish, it was prepared by a friend of writer Mort Rosenblum in Provence. She stirred her eggs constantly in a double boiler, but if you're careful, you can cook them over very low direct heat. The key is to go slowly so the eggs don't seize up and get tough. It took Martine about ten minutes to cook six eggs, and they were still very soft. She used wild asparagus gathered from the nearby hills, but the dish can be replicated with almost any herb or green. Serve with a green salad or roasted potatoes and a basket of warm country bread.

variation

These scrambled eggs are great with 2 tablespoons of fresh goat cheese crumbled over the eggs just before they're removed from the heat. Garnish with a snip of fresh dill.

1 small bunch very thin asparagus (or wild asparagus, if you can get it), trimmed

6 large eggs

3 tablespoons whole milk

2 tablespoons extra virgin olive oil, preferably Provençal

Fine sea salt to taste

Freshly ground black pepper to taste

Steam the asparagus until tender, 7 to 10 minutes. Rinse with cold water until cool. Cut the spears into 1-inch lengths and set aside.

In a large bowl, gently beat the eggs. Add the milk and olive oil.

Add the egg mixture to a double boiler or skillet. (If you're using a double boiler, keep the water bath at a gentle boil; the upper pan should not touch the water. If you're using a skillet, be sure to use very low heat.) Stir frequently, but not constantly, gently moving just the slightly set bits of egg from the hottest spots in the pan to the cooler edges. Continue until the eggs are thickened. I like them as Martine made them, warm and very runny. But you certainly can cook them longer or shorter to your taste.

Serve immediately on warm plates with a pinch of salt and a twist of pepper.

serves 2 or 3

spanish fried egg "sandwiches"

Spanish-style eggs fried in a boldly flavored oil from the south of Spain make a good breakfast or lunch. Serve on toasted bread brushed with—what else?—additional olive oil. Enjoy these sandwiches for breakfast or wrap them and take them with you for a brown-bag lunch.

> 2 tablespoons fruity extra virgin olive oil, preferably Spanish
> 2 large eggs
> 2 slices crusty country bread
> Fine sea salt to taste
> Freshly ground black pepper to taste

In a medium skillet, heat 1 tablespoon of the olive oil over medium-high heat. Crack the eggs into the skillet. They will bubble around the edges, making them crisp. Break the yolks with a wooden spoon and spread them over the whites a little and cook until set, 3 to 4 minutes. Meanwhile, toast the bread and brush it with the remaining tablespoon of olive oil.

Place 1 egg on each slice of bread and sprinkle with salt and plenty of pepper. Serve hot.

serves 2

soup of dried favas, cauliflower, potatoes, and olive oil

first tasted this soup in Puglia in the south of Italy. It's an outstanding example of the impact of fine olive oil in cooking—the vegetables and favas act as perfect contrasts for the oil. The soup is garnished with additional olive oil, which adds flavor, and fried pasta, which adds texture. And it looks beautiful. The puree is cream-colored, dressed with a ribbon of green olive oil and sprinkled with golden brown fried pasta.

Be sure you're using split dried favas, not whole dried favas, or you'll be cooking them for hours.

- ¼ cup plus 1 tablespoon very fruity extra virgin olive oil, preferably Pugliese oil made from Coratina olives, plus more for garnish
- 1 large onion, coarsely chopped (1½ cups)
- 8 cups water
- ½ pound large split dried fava beans
- ½ pound potatoes, preferably Yukon Golds, peeled and diced (2 medium)
- ½ pound cauliflower florets, chopped (1½ cups)
  Coarse sea salt to taste
- 2 ounces small dried pasta pieces (Pugliese casarecci work well, but any small pasta shape or long pasta broken into 1-inch pieces will do)
  Freshly ground black pepper to taste

In a large heavy-bottomed stockpot, heat the ¼ cup olive oil over medium heat. Add the onion and sauté until soft and translucent, 7 to 9 minutes.

Add the water and fava beans and bring to a boil. Reduce the heat to medium and simmer until the favas are nearly tender, about 1 hour.

Add the potatoes and cook until they are nearly tender, about 12 minutes. Add the cauliflower and simmer until it is cooked through. Remove from the heat and let stand to cool for 10 minutes.

Pour the soup into a blender or food processor. (If necessary, you can process in batches.) Puree until smooth. Return the soup to the stockpot and reheat over medium heat. Add more water to bring to the desired consistency. Add salt to taste.

In a medium heavy skillet over medium heat, heat the remaining 1 tablespoon olive oil. When the oil is hot, add the pasta and stir well. The pasta will begin to brown quickly, so don't walk away. Fry, stirring, until the pasta is a consistent light brown. Remove from the skillet and drain on paper towels.

Ladle the soup into warm bowls. Dress with additional olive oil to taste, the fried pasta pieces, and a generous dose of pepper, and serve.

serves 4 to 6

jeannotte's provençal potatoes

This recipe is about as effortless a dish as you can find. The flavor is contingent on the quality of the potatoes and the oil. If you can find freshly dug potatoes, they'll be much more flavorful. I was inspired by the excellent potatoes grown by the food writer Mort Rosenblum's neighbor Jeannotte Romana in Provence.

2 pounds small potatoes, preferably Yukon Gold or another interesting variety
¼ cup extra virgin olive oil, preferably Provençal
Coarse sea salt to taste
Freshly ground black pepper to taste

Steam the potatoes in their jackets until very tender, 35 to 40 minutes, depending on size. With a knife, break the potatoes open into warm bowls, dress with the olive oil, salt, and pepper, and serve immediately.

serves 4 to 6

variation

To make a warm Provençal potato salad, prepare the potatoes as instructed, but place them on a bed of room-temperature arugula, mesclun, or other salad greens. The heat of the potatoes will wilt the greens nicely. Add a sprinkling of aged red wine vinegar and serve.

provençal mashed potatoes

This easy variation on mashed potatoes brings the flavor of Provençal olive oil to the fore. It's great with fish or with a plate of freshly cooked vegetables (dressed, of course, with more olive oil).

    2 pounds small potatoes, preferably Yukon Gold or another inter-
       esting variety
    ½ cup whole milk, warmed, plus more if desired
    ¼ cup extra virgin olive oil, preferably Provençal
    2 mashed anchovies (optional)
       Coarse sea salt to taste
       Freshly ground black pepper to taste

Steam the potatoes in their jackets until very tender, 35 to 40 minutes, depending on size. Pass the cooked potatoes through a food mill or ricer into a large bowl.

Stir in the ½ cup warm milk, olive oil, anchovies (if using), salt and pepper. Add more milk if desired, stir well, and serve hot.

serves 4 to 6

oven-roasted asparagus

Steamed green asparagus is perfectly fine, but it can be watery. Oven-roasting, on the other hand, concentrates asparagus's unique flavor. I like it slightly browned and much crisper than most people are used to. You can serve this asparagus as a side dish or cut the spears into smaller pieces and toss them onto everything from pastas and pizzas to sandwiches.

1½–2 pounds asparagus, trimmed
2–3 tablespoons extra virgin olive oil
½ teaspoon coarse sea salt

Preheat the oven to 450°F.

Place the asparagus in a single layer in a large roasting pan and toss lightly with the olive oil and salt. Roast the asparagus, turning occasionally, for about 20 minutes, or until light golden brown and tender in the middle. Serve.

serves 2 to 4 as a side dish

roasted carrots with rosemary and garlic

This dish goes well with lamb. The key is finding carrots with flavor. You can increase the recipe if you're having company.

    1½ pounds carrots (about 7 large), peeled and cut crosswise into
        3-inch lengths
    1   sprig fresh rosemary (about 4 inches)
    2   garlic cloves, peeled and bruised with the side of a knife
    3   tablespoons extra virgin olive oil
    ½   teaspoon coarse sea salt

Preheat the oven to 425°F.

Place the carrots in a 9-x-13-inch baking pan with the rosemary sprig and garlic cloves. Toss everything lightly with the olive oil and salt. Roast the carrots, stirring occasionally, for 1 hour, or until light golden brown, caramelized, and tender in the middle. Serve hot or at room temperature.

serves 2 to 4

penne with ricotta, black olives, and orange olive oil

I learned about this refreshing pasta preparation from Marina Colonna, who cooked it for me on her farm in the Molise region in central Italy. Make it in the summer because the preparation is minimal and the cooking time is quick. You can use any good-quality citrus olive oil (see page 24).

Coarse sea salt to taste
1 pound penne pasta
½ pound fresh ricotta cheese
24 Italian black olives, pitted and coarsely chopped
Orange or lemon olive oil to taste
Freshly ground black pepper to taste
Freshly grated Parmigiano-Reggiano cheese to taste

Bring a large pot of water to a boil. Add salt and the pasta and stir well. Cook until al dente.

Meanwhile, in a large bowl, mix the ricotta and olives. Add ¼ cup of the pasta cooking water, a generous dose of the citrus olive oil, salt, and plenty of pepper, and mix until thoroughly combined. Drain the pasta and toss it quickly with the sauce. Add a sprinkling of Parmigiano-Reggiano and serve.

serves 4

la fiorentina
florentine grilled steak

This steak is the classic dish of Florence: a big, thick T-bone, grilled rare, then seasoned with lemon, a bold green Tuscan olive oil, and sea salt. It's a good way to show off a great oil. Although it may seem counterintuitive to many American cooks, the oil goes on at the end, after the steak has been cooked. This recipe works best when the grill is very hot so that the outside of the meat chars while the inside remains rare. Start the meal with a green salad and serve the steak with roasted potatoes with rosemary and olive oil (see page 345).

1 10- to 12-ounce T-bone steak per person (1–2 inches thick)
   Coarse sea salt to taste
1 lemon
   Tuscan extra virgin olive oil to taste

Cook the steak on a very hot grill, flipping the steak once, 3 to 4 minutes total, or until a thermometer inserted into the thickest part reads 120° to 130°F, for rare. Transfer the steak to a warm platter. Sprinkle with sea salt, squeeze on lemon juice, then brush on plenty of olive oil. Serve hot.

serves 1 or more

minchilli meatballs

The recipe for these meatballs comes courtesy of the Rome-based food writer Elizabeth Minchilli. An American who's married to an Italian architect, she learned this dish from her mother-in-law. Without great oil, the meatballs aren't nearly so good. You can offer them on their own as an hors d'oeuvre, serve them hot over pasta, or use them to make a meatball sandwich.

6 ounces ground pork
5 ounces ground beef
5 ounces ground veal
½ cup minced onion
½ cup bread crumbs (see page 119)
⅓ cup freshly grated Parmigiano-Reggiano cheese
¼ cup finely chopped Italian parsley, rinsed and squeezed dry
2 garlic cloves, minced
¾ teaspoon coarse sea salt
1 teaspoon freshly ground black pepper
1 large egg
¼ cup plus 2 tablespoons full-flavored extra virgin olive oil
2–3 cups Homemade Tomato Sauce (page 144)

In a large bowl, gently combine the pork, beef, veal, onion, bread crumbs, cheese, parsley, garlic, salt, pepper, egg, and ¼ cup of the olive oil. Form the mixture into 30 meatballs about 1½ inches in diameter.

In a large heavy-bottomed skillet, heat the remaining 2 tablespoons olive oil over medium heat. Add the meatballs to the skillet, about 10 at a time, so as not to overcrowd it. Turn the meatballs with a spoon so that they brown evenly on all sides, 15 to 20 minutes. Remove from the skillet and repeat until all the meatballs have browned.

Add the tomato sauce to the skillet. Return the meatballs to the skillet and stir well. Bring to a boil, reduce the heat to low, cover, and simmer for 20 to 30 minutes, or until cooked through.

Serve the meatballs hot from the skillet or cool them and refrigerate for a few days. Reheat as needed or serve at room temperature.

serves 4 to 6

oLiVes

"The olive tree is surely the richest gift of heaven." ● Thomas Jefferson

Walk the markets of any medium-sized town anywhere along the Mediterranean coast and you're sure to see mounds of marvelous local olives glistening like precious stones in the summer sun. Jade green, onyx, amethyst—a wealth of colors, sizes, shapes, and flavors. This fruit helped make the Mediterranean diet famous.

The good news is that fine olives now proliferate on the American market as well, with new arrivals from Italy, Greece, France, Spain, North Africa, and California. Each one packs a bit of history, a hint of legend, a mod-

icum of myth, and a mouthful of flavor in every bite. The bad news is that it can be difficult to know what you're buying. So here you go: everything you need to know about buying olives, and then some.

An olive's quality and character start with the soil and climate of the region in which it was grown, the style and season of its picking, and the method used to cure it.

Native to the Mediterranean basin, olive trees require a range of temperatures to produce fruit. Hot summers and then cool winters that approach freezing are ideal; serious frosts cause serious damage to olive trees and their fruit. Generally you'll find fruit-bearing olive trees growing between the 30th and 45th parallels, an area that includes promi-

Those black olives in the can are an exception to the color rule; they're actually picked green and unripe early in the autumn. Cured in lye, they're then pumped with oxygen to make them black. Their newly adopted color is fixed in place with ferrous gluconate. Finally they're pasteurized and canned. All this processing makes for flat flavor and soft texture — olives that are about as unappealing as they get. In fact, they really don't taste like olives at all.

This process is the result of a botulism scare in the 1920s, when an outbreak due to improper bottling led to wide distrust of the fruit. Producers hoped that the pasteurization and safety mechanisms would offset the negative image. Many people who grew up eating these olives have fond memories of sticking them onto the ends of their fingers, which is probably their greatest, or maybe only, asset.

nent producers such as Spain, Portugal, Italy, Greece, southern France, Turkey, the Middle East, North Africa, California, and China. In the Southern Hemisphere, olives are grown in places like Peru, Mexico, Chile, Argentina, Australia, New Zealand, and South Africa.

why are some olives green, some black?

Contrary to what many consumers think, green and black olives do not come from two different trees. Instead, the color of an olive indicates the degree of ripeness at which it was picked.

As you would expect with a fruit, green olives are not ripe. In most cases, they are picked early in the autumn, in September or October. Green olives usually have a firm, almost crisp texture and a nutty flavor. Some of the best known include the Spanish Manzanilla, the French Picholine, the California Mission, and the Greek Naf-plion.

Black olives, on the other hand, have been allowed to remain on the branch until they're fully ripe. Usually they're gathered in November and December, though in some areas the picking can go on into January or beyond. (In the Southern Hemisphere, the harvests take place at the opposite times of the year.) As with other ripe fruit, these olives will be softer, sweeter, and richer than their green counterparts. What we often refer to as "black" really runs the gamut from light brown to beautiful shades of red and purple, all the way to deepest, darkest ebony. As a general rule, the darker the color, the riper the olive when it was picked. Better-known black olives include the Kalamata and Amfissa from Greece, the Niçoise from France, and the Ligurian from Italy.

handle with care

The quality of an olive depends very much on how any given grower chooses to harvest. The best are still picked completely by hand, ensuring that each olive is plucked at just the right stage of ripeness and that bruising is avoided. The benefits show up in a firm, even texture and sweet flavor. Careful handling during harvesting (and, for that matter, after) is critical.

From a planning and production standpoint, it would be optimal if all of an olive tree's fruit fully ripened on the same day. Unfortunately, nature has never worked that way. If you come across a jar in which each and every olive is identical in appearance, beware the use of artificial coloring agents. Traditionally cured olives, by contrast, will always show a healthy diversity of colors within any given batch, indicating slightly different stages of ripeness.

These days many commercial growers have neither the heart, the art, nor the patience for the slow speed of handpicking. Instead they opt to beat their trees with sticks or, alternatively, to shake them with modern machines that vibrate the entire plant until the fruit falls off. Either option is likely to leave olives bedecked with soft spots and bruises as well as unpleasantly bitter flavors.

the all-important curing process

Unlike most fruit we're used to, olives are inedible in their raw state. Their bitterness is due to the naturally high percentage of glucosides found in raw olives. To render the olive edible, you've got to cure it.

brine curing

Growers have brine-cured olives for millennia (up until the relatively recent industrial innovation of lye curing), and it's still the best way. In past centuries Greeks commonly had a big vat in their home to cure the family crop. They placed freshly gathered fruit in the vat, covered it with water and salt, and left it to cure. After about two months, the brine had killed any active enzymes in the fruit. In the spring—four to six months after harvest—solid salt was added to raise the salt levels in the brine further. By the end of the summer—roughly eight to ten months after harvest—the olives were ready to eat. The brine coaxed the glucosides, bitter despite their sweet-sounding name, out of the olives, while leaving the natural flavors intact. The master olive curers who still use this traditional technique need to manage their salt levels carefully, because olives will absorb it at different rates depending on weather patterns and variations in crop quality.

Cracking an olive allows the brine to penetrate more quickly and intensely into its flesh. Some olives are actually seasoned in brine as well. Greek Kalamatas, for example, are cured in brine that's been spiked with red wine vinegar, which contributes significantly to their distinctive flavor. Some producers start out with a sim-

handpicked

The best olives are always handpicked.

naturally cured

The curing can be done in either brine, salt, or the sun, never in lye.

fresh, not pasteurized

Pasteurized olives usually lack zip and complexity. But not everyone agrees. Hellas International (see Mail-Order Sources, page 446) imports some of the best Greek olives I've ever had. The people at Hellas say pasteurization allows them to keep salt levels to a minimum, enhancing the olive's natural flavor. In the case of their olives, it's hard to argue. The olives are uniformly excellent. But in general, steer clear of a pasteurized product.

varietals

A good olive will also have a good name. Avoid generic labels like "black-ripe" in favor of names like Arbequina, Manzanilla, Kalamata, or Nafplion.

ple salt-and-water brine, then later season their olives by giving them additional curing time with herbs, citrus, garlic, or spices.

lye curing

Used by nearly every large commercial olive producer in the world, lye curing is the most time- and cost-efficient method. It was invented in Spain in the 1920s. Raw olives are submerged in vats filled with a lye solution. The lye leaches out the bitter glucosides in six to fifteen hours. Unfortunately, it also produces far less tasty olives—the fast-acting lye takes with it much of the fruit's inherent flavor and leaves behind a slightly chemical aftertaste.

dry curing

In this method, freshly picked olives are rubbed with coarse salt and left to cure for a matter of weeks or months. The salt is later removed, though the olives may remain salty-tasting. Some producers coat the fruit with olive oil to keep them appropriately moist. Dry-cured olives have a deliciously concentrated flavor, with the wrinkled appearance and texture of prunes. Some olives, like the French Nyons, are dry-cured first, then aged in brine.

sun curing

In some spots, primarily in Greece, olives may be left on the tree until the time that they are dry, wrinkled, and ready to eat. Known in Greece as Throumbes, these olives are deep black, with a texture akin to raisins. They are meaty and intensely flavored. I like them a lot, but they're not for the faint of heart.

how's a buyer to know?

Dry-cured olives are easy to identify because of their wrinkled appearance. But beyond that it's almost impossible to tell from a label or from looks alone whether an olive has been cured in natural brine or in lye. While price never guarantees quality, naturally cured olives are likely to be more costly than their industrial, cured-in-lye cousins. The only way I know to tell one from the other is first to ask and then to taste.

The flavor of the brine-cured olive will be fuller, more complex. I don't discriminate against olives in jars—you can find both good and bad in bottles and in bulk in the deli case.

pit stops

Real olives have pits. Putting up with the inconvenience of the pits is a small price to pay for carefully picked and naturally cured olives.

To pit an olive mechanically, the producer has to add chemicals to the brine that firm up the olive enough so it can survive the stress of the pitting equipment. These chemicals impart off flavors, which is why so many prepitted olives are sold in marinades, where the garlic and spices can cover the poor quality. In the last few years, however, importers have been offering a few varieties of full-flavored, traditionally cured olives that have been pitted by hand. In some cases, the olives have been stuffed by hand with almonds or garlic.

olive varieties

There are literally hundreds of varieties of olives grown around the Mediterranean, in California, and in South America, each with unique characteristics.

greece

Olives are an essential element of Greek life, past and present; they play a prominent role in everything from ancient Greek myths to mod-

ern economics. In any Greek town today, you'll find mounds of olives of all sorts, piled high in barrels, baskets, and buckets. A "small" selection is usually half a dozen varieties. In the bustling market of central Athens, most olive stalls offer more than twenty types.

amfissa

These purple-black olives come from the area around Delphi, the legendary home of the Greek oracles. Picked very ripe, Amfissas are soft and sweet and almost melt in your mouth. They contrast nicely with sharp Greek cheeses and make an excellent, last-minute addition to a Mediterranean bean soup.

elitses

Tiny and dark black, these olives from Crete are very sweet and tender and the size of a large pine nut. They're very hard to get in the United States, so if you see them, grab them. On Crete, the locals eat them by the handful and spit out the pits like watermelon seeds.

hondroelia

The biggest olives I've ever eaten, in both flavor and size, Hondroelia are almost two inches long, so substantial you eat them with a knife and fork. The Greeks refer to them as "olives for heroes." They are grown in very small quantities in the state of Arcadia, in the eastern end of the Peloponnesian peninsula, in a single little town high up in the mountains. They're handpicked, then traditionally cured in a natural salt brine for an entire year to enhance their full flavor.

kalamatas

The best-known Greek olives, they come from the valley of Messenia on the western end of the Peloponnesian peninsula, near the town of Kalamata. They have a distinctive, pointed almond shape and a beautiful black-purple color. Kalamatas are cracked and then cured in a red wine vinegar brine that gives them an almost wine-like flavor.

The best Kalamatas are, without question, handpicked. There's a night-and-day difference between the silky-smooth, rich texture of the best handpicked product and the barrels full of inexpensive, slightly bitter, bruised Kalamatas that are commonly available in nearly every deli.

nafplion

Cracked green olives from the valley of Argos in the eastern half of the Peloponnesus. Nafplions have a nutty, slightly smoky flavor. A lemon-and-fresh-dill dressing is the perfect enhancement.

thasos

Also known as Throumbes, these shriveled, wrinkled olives come from the island of Thasos.

a brand to watch

The Vassilopoulos family has been in the business of curing and packing olives since 1948. In an industry rife with corner-cutters, their standards are exceptional. The company offers a cracked green olive marinated with hot peppers, lemon, and *throubi,* a sweet little herb that grows wild in Greece and adds zest to the already good olive flavor. The Hondroelia olives are outstanding, and the Kalamatas in extra virgin olive oil are some of the best I've ever had. The olives are sold in the United States under the brand name Morea from Hellas International.

After curing on the branch, they may be lightly coated with olive oil. Their intense flavor isn't for everyone, but I like them a lot. They have a nice meaty texture. Try them dressed with a little olive oil and oregano.

italy

cerignola

Naturally cured Cerignola olives from the area around Bari in the province of Puglia down in Italy's southeast corner make impressive additions to party trays or antipasto platters. Medium-ripe, they're light brown and the size of a walnut with the shell on. (Beware the mass-market, bright green Cerignolas that have been lye-cured and dyed with chlorophyll. They look impressive but have little flavor.)

gaeta

Purple-brown olives from central Italy, they're good in pasta dishes or on pizzas (nearby Naples is the home of the pizza).

taggiasca

These little black beauties are used both for oil and for eating. One of my favorites, they come from the Italian Riviera. Picked late in the season in the hills along the coast both east and west of Genoa, they're high in oil, with a delicate, sweet flavor. The Taggiasca (plural: Taggiasche) is a small olive, the size of the nail on your little finger. The variety was developed centuries ago by the Benedictine monks near the Ligurian town of Taggia. These olives are a bit bigger and maybe a little meatier than the neighboring French Niçoise, which grow a hundred miles to the west. The traditional cure is to soak the freshly picked olives for forty days in water, which is changed daily. From there, the olives are put into a brine solution of water and sea salt, scented with thyme, rosemary, and laurel bay leaves. I like to marinate them with a bit of orange peel, fennel, fresh garlic cloves, and olive oil (from Liguria, of course).

france

niçoise

The tiny black jewels of the olive world, real Niçoise olives have a unique, delicate flavor. They're essential to making authentic regional dishes like salade Niçoise with tuna, hard-cooked eggs, green beans, and tomatoes, or pissaladière, a Provençal onion, olive, and anchovy "pizza."

nyons

Real Nyons olives can be hard to get, and they're not inexpensive. But they're some of the best olives around. First dry-cured, then aged in brine, the olives of Nyons are plump and politely wrinkled, with large, smooth pits. They're particularly good dressed with Provençal olive oil and wild herbs like thyme and rosemary. But be sure you're getting the real thing—there are countless "French" olives being sold that are actually from North

Africa. Authentic Nyons from France are usually a bit duller in appearance than the North African impostors; the latter are shinier and slicker-looking. More important, the Nyons are deliciously, richly flavorful, whereas the North African olives have a flatness that reminds me a little of the (heaven forbid) California "black-ripe" olives out of the can.

picholine

Crisp, uncracked green olives from southern France, Picholines have a nice nutty flavor with anise undertones. Try them with fresh fennel and olive oil. They're also great for cooking in chicken or fish stews.

spain

arbequina

Small round brown olives from the province of Catalonia in northeastern Spain, Arbequinas are used extensively as both an oil olive and a table olive. The latter are harvested about a month before those used for oil are gathered. They have a unique nutty flavor and are excellent eaten out of hand.

farga aragon or empeltre

Lesser known in the United States, these sweet black olives are native to the region of Aragon in northern Spain. The name means "grafted" in Spanish, a reference to the standard procedure of grafting branches of older trees to start new ones. They are almond-shaped, succulently sweet, and, at their best, very ripe and very delicious.

gordal

These are more commonly known as "Queen" olives in the States, but I like the Spanish name. *Gorda* means "fat" in Spanish, an appropriate moniker for these large green olives. They have a firm, meaty texture and benefit from the addition of southern Spanish spices like cumin, garlic, thyme, and a splash of sherry vinegar.

manzanilla

Smaller, crisper, and nuttier than Gordal, these cracked brownish green olives are some of Spain's best. The name means "little apple," a reference to their round shape. Try them dressed with olive oil and a generous dose of chopped fresh garlic.

morocco

The olive markets of Morocco are an impressive sight, with mounds of multicolored olives dressed with an array of different spices. The most readily available in the United States are the dry-cured, black Moroccan olives, which have a meaty texture akin to dried prunes. They're excellent marinated with North African spices like cumin and hot chiles. Moroccans cook with them extensively and use them in chicken or lamb tagines (stews cooked in traditional clay pots).

south america

alfonso

Large, meaty, purple olives with a unique fruity flavor, Alfonsos are grown along the north and west coasts of South America. They are still unusual in the United States but are destined to become more readily available in years to come.

united states

Olives were brought to California by Spanish missionaries as they worked their way up the coast from Mexico. Although most American olives come from California, small quantities are grown in Arizona and Texas. The majority of California olives end up in cans, though some are traditionally cured. Most that I've tasted have been heavily seasoned with garlic and spices to make up for their so-so flavor.

mission

The most widely grown California olive, Missions were originally planted to be processed and canned, although some are picked early and pressed for oil. Fortunately, some are dry-cured for eating. They're shiny, wrinkled, and slightly bitter.

sevillano

Similar to the Spanish-style Gordal, Sevillano olives are large, brine-cured, green, and meaty.

a culinary caper

Capers are the cured buds of a wild bush, or, rather, a group of related shrubs, that grow all over the Mediterranean. Unlike so many other foods that are now available in cultivated form, nearly all the capers in the world today are still wild.

Caper bushes are very thorny, and they grow up and down dry hillsides, in rock crevices. Harvesting the buds in the height of summer's heat isn't easy. A typical plant produces only about ten pounds of buds in a good year. I've had fine capers from Spain, Italy, and Greece, and I'm sure there are equally interesting offerings to be had from pretty much every part of the Mediterranean.

Capers are graded by size, from tiny ones no bigger than peppercorns to veritable monsters that are akin to medium-sized grapes. The smallest, which are labeled as nonpareils, are generally what you see in slim two-ounce bottles. They're also the most expensive. I prefer larger capers, known in Spain as *gruesas,* meaning "thick." They have bigger and bolder flavors than nonpareils.

After picking, the caper buds must be cured in brine, then packed in vinegar (the most common in the United States) or in coarse salt. I prefer the latter. You have to soak them for a few minutes to remove the excess salt, but to my palate, the flavor of the caper comes through better than it does in the vinegar, which intrudes unnecessarily.

Capers are one of the most versatile ingredients around. They're good on almost anything, but they seem to have a particular affinity for seafood. They're well suited to any dish involving anchovies, tuna, or sardines, and they're a must if you're making vitello tonnato, the justifiably famous Italian veal in tuna sauce. They make a very nice garnish for salmon, both fresh and smoked. They also add life to salads of all sorts. Try them in salade Russe: potatoes, hard-boiled eggs, peppers, and olives in mayonnaise dressing. I like to add a few big capers to Greek salads with sheep's milk feta, roasted peppers, tomatoes, and cucumbers. If you're looking for something different, try pan-frying capers in a little olive oil until they're lightly browned before adding them to the salad.

Capers are the basis of what Italians refer to as salsa verde, which is made by tossing a couple spoonfuls of capers, some anchovies, garlic, and parsley in the blender along with a lot of olive oil and a generous dose of fresh lemon juice. If you like, you can add a bit of Dijon mustard. They're also very good in tomato sauces, especially if served over seafood. You can't make a good pasta puttanesca, the tomato sauce of anchovies, garlic, diced tomatoes, and olives, without capers.

In Murcia, Spain, capers are eaten in large quantities pretty much as they are, dressed with olive oil, salt, and lemon, and served with apéritifs.

seville olives

toasting spices for superior flavor

The flavor of dry spices, such as cumin, fennel seed, and even black peppercorns, will be better if you take a few minutes to toast them before using. Simply put the spices in a hot (not smoking), dry skillet over medium heat for 3 to 5 minutes, or until they smell fragrant. Stir regularly so you don't burn the spices.

It's worth making these olives for their aroma alone, which is as close as you'll get to the market of Seville in southern Spain without actually going there. The fat green olives are marinated in fruity Spanish olive oil, sherry vinegar, cumin, garlic, rosemary, fennel, and thyme.

- 1 pound Spanish Gordal, or Queen, olives (about 4 cups)
- ⅓ cup extra virgin olive oil, preferably Spanish from Baena
- ¼ cup aged sherry vinegar
- 2 dried bay leaves, lightly crushed
- 2 garlic cloves, peeled and bruised with the side of a knife
- 1 teaspoon cumin seeds, toasted and ground
- 1 teaspoon fennel seeds
- 1 teaspoon dried oregano
- 1 teaspoon dried thyme
- ½ teaspoon dried rosemary

Place the olives in a medium bowl.

In a small bowl, whisk together the remaining ingredients.

Pour the marinade over the olives and mix until they are thoroughly coated. Cover, refrigerate, and marinate for 2 days, stirring occasionally. The olives will keep for 3 to 4 weeks in the refrigerator. Bring them to room temperature before serving.

makes about 4 cups

marinated kalamata olives

When I first heard about combining citrus with olives, I thought the idea quite strange. But having tried it, I can tell you it's a delicious pairing. If you like, you can use lemon or tangerine instead of the orange. Serve these olives as an hors d'oeuvre with cubes of good feta cheese and some crusty bread.

- 1 pound Kalamata olives (about 4 cups)
- ¼ cup extra virgin olive oil, preferably Greek
- 4 teaspoons orange zest
- 2 garlic cloves, peeled and bruised with the side of a knife
- 1 teaspoon coriander seeds, toasted (see opposite page) and cracked
- 1 teaspoon fennel seeds, toasted

Place the olives in a medium bowl. Add the olive oil, orange zest, garlic, coriander, and fennel, and stir until well coated.

Cover, refrigerate, and marinate for 2 days, stirring occasionally. The olives will keep for 3 to 4 weeks in the refrigerator. Bring to room temperature before serving. makes about 4 cups

paprika and cumin marinated olives

**smoky paprika
from la vera**

The paprika in la Vera, or
Pimentón de la Vera, has a
uniquely rich flavor and
smokiness. It comes in both
hot and sweet versions and
brings something special to
any dish in which it's used.
Sprinkle it on potato salad,
scrambled eggs, roasted
pork, or baked chicken. It's
excellent cooked into rice
dishes, along with a bit of
sliced chorizo and some
chopped Piquillo peppers. Or
add it to mashed potatoes
seasoned with sea salt and
plenty of extra virgin olive oil.

I first tried this marinade in Portugal. It's tough to find Portuguese
olives in the States, so I use Farga Aragon (also known as Empeltre)
olives from Spain or even Niçoise olives. These olives are a mess to eat
—put out plenty of napkins—but they're delicious.

- 1 pound black olives (about 4 cups)
- ¼ cup extra virgin olive oil
- 2 teaspoons hot Pimentón de la Vera (Spanish smoked paprika)
- 2 garlic cloves, peeled and bruised with the side of a knife
- 2 dried bay leaves, lightly crushed
- 2 teaspoons cumin seeds, toasted (see page 54)

Place the olives in a medium bowl. Add the olive oil, Pimentón, garlic, and bay leaves.

Grind half the cumin seeds in a spice grinder or with a mortar and pestle. Add, along with the whole seeds, to the olives. Stir.

Cover, refrigerate, and marinate for 2 days, stirring occasionally. The olives will keep for 3 to 4 weeks in the refrigerator. Bring them to room temperature before serving.

makes about 4 cups

marinated manzanilla olives

first had these olives ages ago in a bar in central Spain. If you like eating garlic, they're for you. Serve with glasses of cold fino sherry.

1 pound green Manzanilla olives (about 4 cups)
1/4 cup full-flavored extra virgin olive oil
3 large thick strips lemon peel
3 garlic cloves, minced

Place the olives in a medium bowl. Add the olive oil, lemon peel, and garlic and stir until well coated.

Cover, refrigerate, and marinate for 2 days, stirring occasionally. The olives will keep for 3 to 4 weeks in the refrigerator. Bring them to room temperature before serving.

makes about 4 cups

caramelized fennel caponata with olives and capers

This dish is great for almost anything—serve it as a side, toss it with pasta, put it on pizzas, or offer it as an appetizer with crusty bread. It's a good base for vegetable sandwiches as well. The vinegar adds liveliness. You can prepare it a few days in advance.

6 tablespoons capers, preferably Sicilian capers packed in salt (2 ounces)

3 tablespoons extra virgin olive oil, plus more if needed

1 medium onion, halved, then cut into long, thin slices

1 medium fennel bulb, halved, then cut into long, thin slices

1½ pounds ripe tomatoes, peeled, seeded, and coarsely chopped

18 black Italian olives, pitted and coarsely chopped

¾ cup water

2 tablespoons aged red wine vinegar

Hot red pepper flakes, preferably Marash, to taste

1 tablespoon pine nuts, toasted (see page 31)

Coarse sea salt to taste

Freshly ground black pepper to taste

If you're using salted capers, soak them in a bit of warm water for 20 to 30 minutes, changing the water halfway through. Drain, rinse the capers, and dry them on a paper towel.

In a large heavy skillet, heat the olive oil over medium heat. Add the onion and fennel and cook, partially covered, until they are a rich chestnut brown and caramelized, 35 to 40 minutes. Add more olive oil if necessary and stir regularly to keep the vegetables from sticking.

Add the tomatoes, olives, capers, and water and simmer for 20 to 30 minutes, or until most of the liquid has evaporated. Stir in the vinegar and pepper flakes and simmer for 5 minutes more to blend the flavors. Add the pine nuts and salt and pepper to taste. Serve warm or cool, and store, covered, in the refrigerator. It will keep for about 5 days. Bring to room temperature before serving.   *makes about 3 to 4 cups*

nut oils

Nut oils are to nuts what olive oils are to olives: the essential expression of the flavor. The best nut oils are exceptionally, intensely, sensually, wonderfully perfumed. That said, they'll probably never be as popular as olive oil. Their shelf life is shorter, they're not inexpensive, and they aren't as versatile. Still, I believe strongly that a good nut oil can be one of the nicest and easiest additions to your cooking repertoire.

The most popular of these oils is walnut, followed in turn by hazelnut, almond, and then perhaps pistachio. (Although peanut oil is one of the largest-selling oils worldwide, the peanut is not a nut but rather an edible seed.)

walnut oil

Walnut oil has a long history dating back about twenty-five hundred years, to the days of ancient Greece. The Romans later planted walnut trees throughout their empire, both for oil and for eating, and to this day, walnuts are grown in most every country in Europe.

The oil today is used primarily in France, where it's been an important ingredient since at least the Middle Ages. In areas in which walnuts grow in abundance, like the Dordogne district in the west and Drôme and

Isère in the east, walnut oil plays much the same role as olive oil does in the Mediterranean. At one time there were dozens of mills in these regions, and the sight of farmers selling home-bottled walnut oil was as common as the ubiquitous maple syrup stands on roadsides in Vermont. Today only a handful of mills remain. Of these my favorite by far is the Huilerie Leblanc, located in the town of Iguerande in the district of Saône-et-Loire in central France.

The Leblanc mill, which sits in the center of the town of only about one thousand inhabitants, has been at it since 1878 and remains a family-run business, using essentially the same methods of production as it has for decades. But while most of the other owners in the area have long since closed their mills, Jean-Charles Leblanc, great-grandson of the founder, seems to be going strong.

The first time I tried Leblanc's walnut oil, it was as eye-opening as my initial experience with great Tuscan oil. The walnut oil I'd been accustomed to was pale, and its flavor was hardly compelling. By contrast, Leblanc's oil was far darker. Opening the bottle and pouring a bit into a bowl to taste, I was struck by the impressive perfume of toasted nuts and the bold, complex flavor.

The best nut oils always start out with top-notch nuts; lesser alternatives will never be able to offer up the intricate richness of their higher-quality counterparts. As with olives, the variety, the soil in which they're grown, and the care and handling of the freshly harvested nuts all contribute to the quality of the oil. The Leblancs buy from local farmers who bring in small batches—typically less than a hundred pounds each—of already shelled walnuts, hand-gathered on their own land.

The second significant contributor to quality is the production process. Traditionally the nuts are ground with granite stones. There are quicker methods, but they diminish the quality of the oil. Jean-Charles Leblanc told me, "When we use the old-style stone grinder, there are little pieces of the nut left in the paste," which is very important for the next step. As it toasts, the paste slowly turns the color of chocolate, and the praline aroma coming off the cauldron is exceptional. "The whole village smells of it," he said enthusiastically, "even when you're driving by in your car."

After the toasting is completed, the paste is spread on mats and slowly pressed to push out the oil. The yield for walnuts is a fraction of their original weight—from each fifty-pound or so batch, the Leblancs net about twelve liters of oil. (Other nuts are stingier still: fifty pounds of hulled hazelnuts will give about nine liters, and the same quantity of almonds produces a mere seven liters of oil.) The Leblancs decant the new oil to let some of the sediment settle out naturally but never filter it. Unlike olive oil, which is pressed once a year, nut oils must be pressed close to the time of consumption to preserve quality. The Leblancs buy freshly gathered nuts in the autumn, then store them for pressing as needed throughout the year.

what to look for— in a nutshell

Good nut oils are never inexpensive. Walnut is the most affordable, almond and pistachio the priciest. If you can, taste before you buy to check for quality. Well-made nut oils should never taste oily. Instead they ought to fill your mouth with a toasty, slightly sweet, sensually savory flavor. If the flavor is faint, you've found one of the lesser oils.

It's worth checking for freshness too, since even the best brands can go rancid sitting too long on store shelves.

BEST BRANDS The majority of the nut oils you'll see in American shops are pressed in France—primarily from the region of Périgord, in the southwest, and the area around Grenoble, in the east. No other brand rivals Leblanc, in my opinion.

In addition to the nut oil from Huilerie Leblanc, check out Loriva, the longtime leader in good-quality nut oils in the American market. Loriva does an excellent job of making affordable nut oils widely available. The company buys unfiltered walnut oil from a California producer and filters out impurities before bottling. The oil has a deep golden color, a delicate aroma, and a decidedly nutty flavor. The flavor is not quite as toasty as Leblanc's walnut oil, but it is less costly.

what to do with nut oils

Nut oils are at their best when they're poured straight from the bottle onto a dish that needs no further cooking. Don't try to use them for high-heat frying as you might olive oil. A few moments of gentle sautéing won't do much harm, but beyond that you're likely to lose most of the oil's delicate flavor.

walnut

Walnut oil is delicious in an updated version of a Waldorf salad: mixed lettuces or mesclun, topped with toasted walnuts, wedges of fresh apple, and crumbled fresh goat cheese. Dress the salad with a bit of walnut oil and a top-quality apple cider vinegar (see page 85).

Try it in a salade Comtoise, the traditional salad of the Franche-Comté mountains in eastern France. Line a large platter with fresh lettuce, then top with toasted walnuts, wedges of hard-boiled eggs and tomato, chunks of good-quality smoked ham, and well-aged Comté (see

---

storing nut oils

Nut oils are fairly fragile. After opening, store them well sealed in the refrigerator. Buying in small quantities (many makers now sell their oils in small half-pint or quarter-liter bottles) helps to hold freshness. Depending on the oil, nut oils last six weeks to six months at room temperature once opened, but there's really no reason to risk it. When cold, they congeal; bring them to room temperature before using.

page 244)—the mountain cheese of the region. (If you aren't able to obtain good Comté, substitute a well-aged Gruyère from across the border in Switzerland, see page 237.) Dress the salad with a vinaigrette of Dijon mustard, walnut oil, and a well-aged Champagne vinegar. The salad is hearty enough to serve as a summer main dish or as a substantial starter for a cold winter meal. I like to dress hot steamed potatoes with a walnut oil vinaigrette; add blanched green beans and toasted walnuts, and you've got a delicious potato salad.

Walnut oil is also used to good advantage in baking. Try it in walnut breads. Or better yet, brush the loaves with walnut oil when they emerge hot from the oven.

hazelnut

Hazelnut oil is probably the most elegant of the group and also the most popular among those who are tasting nut oils for the first time. Its deep, almost musky flavor is an excellent match for poultry or fowl—try it on a salad of cold roast duck meat. Jean-Charles Leblanc likes this oil on fish. Wild rice salads are wonderful dressed with a blend of hazelnut oil and sherry vinegar.

almond

The best almond oils will remind you of freshly roasted almonds. Trout amandine takes on a

pumpkin seed oil: green gold from the austrian alps

I've never tasted anything like this oil: deep forest green, darker and richer-looking than the greenest of olive oils. Despite its name it comes not from the big orange jack-o'-lantern pumpkins but from the small green-and-yellow-striped squash that are grown primarily in the Austrian region of Styria.

Pumpkin seed oil is delicious on salads, on steamed potatoes, and on grilled wild mushrooms. Dip a wedge of warm country bread in it and enjoy its amazing aroma and ethereal flavor. Its color makes it a beautiful accompaniment to almost any fish dish. To maximize the color contrast, pour a base of the oil onto a warm plate, then set the freshly cooked fish on top. (Warning: pumpkin seed oil will stain your clothes in a hurry. Enjoy with care.)

The best oils start with hand-sorted and hand-washed seeds, which are gently toasted and then delicately pressed to release their hidden cache. As with good olive oils, pumpkin seed oil should have a rich perfume and a full flavor and should never leave an oily or greasy feel on the palate.

whole new level of lusciousness when you brush a hot-from-the-sauté-pan trout with almond oil just before you bring the fish to the table.

pistachio

Pistachio oil has a beguiling emerald green color that's beautiful when you pour a little on the plate before placing a freshly cut slice of roasted lamb atop it. It's also great on salads and on fresh goat cheese.

And any of these nut oils are delicious drizzled over hot steamed or sautéed vegetables of almost any sort, especially green beans or asparagus.

sherry–nut oil vinaigrette

This delicious dressing for green salad topped with toasted hazelnuts is also excellent on potatoes, chicken salad, or even poached salmon.

2 tablespoons aged sherry vinegar (the older the better)
1 generous tablespoon Dijon mustard
6 tablespoons hazelnut oil or walnut oil

In a medium bowl, whisk the vinegar into the mustard until fully blended. Slowly add the oil, whisking constantly, until velvety smooth.

makes about ½ cup

oven-roasted beet, bacon, and spinach salad

Credit for this salad goes to Thad Gillies, who served as the chef at our delicatessen for many years. The salt has two functions. First, it keeps the beets from burning on the bottom of the dish, and second, it forms a seal on the bottom of the beets, allowing them to retain their natural moisture and flavor.

- 1 cup coarse sea salt, plus more to taste
- 1 pound medium beets, root ends trimmed
- 4 cups fairly tightly packed baby spinach leaves (6 ounces)
- 6 slices good-quality bacon, cooked, drained on paper towels, and crumbled
- ½ medium red onion, thinly sliced
- 5–6 large fresh basil leaves, torn
- 1 tablespoon aged sherry vinegar
- ¼ cup walnut oil
  Freshly ground black pepper to taste

Preheat the oven to 350°F.

Spread the 1 cup salt on the bottom of a 9-inch square baking dish. Place the beets cut side down on the salt. Bake for 1 to 1½ hours, or until the beets are fork-tender.

Discard the cooking salt or save it for another time. Cool the beets. Peel them and cut into ½-inch cubes.

In a large bowl, combine the beets, spinach, bacon, onion, and basil. Add the vinegar and toss. Add the walnut oil and gently toss again to mix the ingredients. Add salt and pepper to taste. Serve immediately in individual salad bowls.

serves 4 as a main course or 6 to 8 as an appetizer

balsamic vinegar and wine vinegars

Vinegar has been a kitchen staple for centuries—you'll find it called for in nearly every cookbook. Yet for all its honorable mentions, too often it's little more than a culinary footnote for food lovers. Wine is its first cousin: vinegar is the natural conclusion of the winemaking process. It's related to olive oil by marriage, forming one of the most frequently used and seemingly inseparable food combinations. But in either instance, vinegar —with a minor exception for balsamic— seems to take bottom billing. Despite its sour reputation, I've become increasingly intrigued by the variety and versatility of vinegar. I want the world to know that great vinegar is something special, worthy of active pursuit by any cook who cares about putting better-tasting food on the table.

a vinegary history

Wherever you go in the world, vinegar has long been a part of cooking and culture. You'll find it mentioned in the Bible almost as often as wine. Throughout the Mediterranean, fruits of all sorts were made into vinegar, including that made from dates seven thousand years ago in Babylonia. Ancient Greek cooks relied on sauces like *oxymel,* made from honey and vinegar. Spartan soldiers made a soup called *melas zomos,* or black broth, from pork, blood, salt, and vinegar. Centuries later, Roman soldiers blended vinegar and water into a refreshing cool drink, known as *posca,* reputed to be one of the sources of the empire's military success. In the kitchen, vinegar was mixed with spices and fermented fish to make *garum,* the all-purpose sauce of Roman cuisine. Roman hosts set an *acetabulum* — a bowl of vinegar — in the center of their dining tables and then dipped pieces of bread into it during meals. Medieval French cooks combined vinegar with spices and bread to make a *sauce caneline.* Their medical counterparts stirred vinegar with honey and sold it as a cure for coughs. In English kitchens of the era, vinegar was blended with ginger, fresh mint, parsley, saffron, garlic, sage, and other herbs and spices to serve with game.

how can you spot a good wine vinegar?

There are two questions to ask when you set out to check references on a vinegar's résumé.

1. was it made from great wine?

No amount of industrial alchemy can convert mediocre raw material into top-notch vinegar. Nevertheless, too many modern-day makers ignore this basic reality. I've learned that a few quick questions usually separate poseurs from purveyors of quality. "What kind of wine are you using?" I inquire of my potential vinegar suppliers. "Red wine," they answer confidently. Now, "red wine" is about as telling as "red fruit." What I want to know is the variety of wine. Cabernet, Bordeaux, Burgundy, Chianti? The better the wine, the better the vinegar. (Balsamic vinegar is an exception because it's made not from wine but from fresh grape juice.)

2. was the wine converted to vinegar naturally?

While the literal meaning of *vinaigre* is "sour wine," don't be fooled into thinking that professional vinegar making is a casual process. Crafting a great vinegar requires as much care as making fine wine or any other top-quality food. If you're looking for superior vinegar, its conversion must have happened naturally, using what is known in the vinegar world as the Orléans process. Wooden barrels are partially — but never fully — filled with wine, allowing the air remaining inside to interact with it. Holes are drilled in the sides or the top of the barrel to allow access to additional air. Bacteria, which occur naturally in the environment, convert the alcohol in the wine into water and acetic acid. After a time, most of the vinegar is drained off, leaving a bit to serve as a sour starter, more wine is added, and the process starts anew.

Unfortunately, most modern vinegar makers have long since abandoned the Orléans process and have turned instead to an industrial quick fix, known as a generator (or acetator). A generator forces the wine over bacteria-inoculated wood shavings, usually at warm temperatures

tasting the difference

Regardless of your experience level, if you're willing to taste-test, you'll be surprised by how much you notice among half a dozen different vinegars. You absolutely do not need to be a gourmand to tell the best from the bogus. A simple sampling quickly makes the point. All you need is ten minutes and four vinegars — two industrially made commercial options and two from craft-oriented traditional producers.

Before you taste, smell; the aroma will tell you much of what you want to know. Most everything you've heard about the bouquet of a fine wine also holds true for vinegar. It should smell good, with an aroma distinctly reminiscent of the fruit from which it is made. If the aroma beckons you further, follow your nose and taste.

Some experts recommend tasting vinegar by dipping sugar cubes into it and then sucking out the liquid; the sweetness is supposed to keep the taste buds open to the sourness. All I can taste, though, is the sugar. I prefer using a small piece of plain white bread. Alternatively, I like to taste vinegar straight, sipping from small spoons or out of wineglasses. In the case of Aceto Balsamico Tradizionale (page 69), convention dictates that you pour a drop on the back of your hand; your body heat warms the vinegar a bit, and nothing else gets in the way of the flavor.

Remember that most good vinegars are going to have a bit of an acid kick, so sip slowly; you're not doing shots. Just a drop or two is enough to get the flavor.

Well-made vinegar should taste alive, interesting, appealing. The acid should be noticeable, but it's not supposed to be dagger-sharp. The flavor ought to strike an enjoyable, lively, but manageable balance between the tingle of the acid and the fruit of the wine; it should be full-bodied, with a lingering complexity. Taste and compare: the flavor gap will be glaring. Take your time and let the tastes unfurl in your mouth. Wait and see how each vinegar finishes. Feel every sensation and notice every scent; the good, the great, the bad, and the ugly will quickly make themselves apparent. And, in the process, you'll pick out your personal preferences.

(90 degrees Fahrenheit), to convert it quickly into vinegar. This process requires about a week to make the conversion, as opposed to at least a month (and up to four or five months) for the traditional process.

Faster still—and even less desirable—is the "continuous" or "submerged-fermentation" process. Producers force-feed air into a sealed tank, converting the liquid in about a day. High temperatures and high-speed conversion leave little in the way of flavor.

balsamic: noble inheritance

Perhaps the most famous vinegar in the world is Aceto Balsamico Tradizionale, or authentic balsamic vinegar. This dark, rich, sweet-sour aristocrat of the vinegar world had been made in near obscurity since the eleventh century as a highly valued local specialty in the northern Italian town of Modena and its surrounding countryside. And then, bam! In the early 1980s, *balsamico* went mass-market and arrived in America. A little over a decade later, bottles of it were lined up on shelves at Kmart. But while the name remains the same, 99.9 percent of the stuff that's been shipped to the United States from Italy labeled "balsamic vinegar" is not the real thing. At least not according to Italian law, or according to the standards of legend and lore coming out of the town where it has been made for the past thousand years.

About forty minutes north of Bologna in the region of Emilia-Romagna, Modena is a pleasant little midsized town. Apart from *balsamico,* it's probably best known as the home of Pavarotti and Ferrari. It's also recognized as one of the most fashionable of Italian locations, a place where style and savoir-faire are evident in almost every aspect of daily life. This elegance carries over into the cuisine. Modena's tables feature superb stuffed pasta, lots of Parmigiano-Reggiano cheese, elegant Prosciutto di Parma, light, fluffy little squares of fried dough called *gnocco fritto,* and of course its now famous vinegar. Without question, Modena has the most courtly vinegar etiquette I've ever encountered; it's the only place I know where vinegar is the star of the show.

In Modena, vinegar is woven throughout the upper echelons of history, society, and cuisine. Tiny barrels of *balsamico* have been handed down from generation to generation or given as gifts to foreign dignitaries by local aristocrats. In centuries past, balsamic vinegar was used primarily as a drink or a *digestif;* it was kept in the family and passed from generation to generation as it aged. The vinegar was so valuable that it was locked in the attic, and only the head of the household had a key. When the family needed more vinegar, he would tramp up to the attic, taking a four-handled jug known as a *tragno* with him, and carefully fill it from the appropriate barrels. New vinegar was often started when babies were born and given as a life-gift for weddings held decades later. Burton Anderson, in his excellent book *Treasures of the Italian Table,* mentions that balsamics were being graded as early as the mid-sixteenth century, according to whether they were for cooking, for the table, or "for gentlemen." This last, and highest rating, is probably the best key to understanding the roots of this exceptional elixir.

Unlike almost every food in this book (fine chocolate is the other exception), balsamic vinegar has never ever been poor people's food. Rather, it was revered, crafted, and cared for primarily by and for nobility. Who else could have afforded to invest the necessary time and space in a vinegar that at best was sipped only on special occasions and was usually started with the idea that it would outlive the man who made it? With that in mind, it's interesting to note that the vinegar was almost always passed down not to the oldest son, but to the youngest daughter, who was

thought most likely to carry the vinegar the furthest into the family future for which it was made.

Up until about the early 1980s, you couldn't even buy balsamic vinegar in Modena. It was there: it just wasn't for sale. Vinegar was meant for the family, for gift giving, for inheriting, but certainly not for selling. Lynne Rossetto Kasper, who has been studying the foods of the area for many years, remembers coming to Modena in the 1980s and finding it almost impossible to locate a bottle for sale on the street. The good news for those of us who aren't descended from ducal families in Emilia-Romagna is that the drought has ended. The bad news is that in some cases the drive for sales has become so strong that the purity and character of the original product has been diluted by people willing to pawn off industrial impostors as the real thing.

how can a vinegar cost $50 an ounce?

You know those charts that show how $20 a month put aside for the next twenty years will be worth a ridiculously large sum by the time you retire? Same scenario when your assets are, shall we say, liquid. Stick a barrel of well-made vinegar in the attic, care for it, blend it on occasion with a touch of one of its acid ancestors, and let it develop over the course of three, four, five, or more decades. What went in as the acidic equivalent to a lump of coal comes out a vinegar diamond.

Evaporation alone accounts for a lot of the value. If you start with a hundred liters of new vinegar, after twenty-five years of aging, you're down to about 10 percent of the original volume —only ten liters or so will be left! Give it an additional forty to fifty years, and your yield might

LIQUID ASSETS

start — 100%

10 years — 65%

25 years — 10%

be little more than a single liter. As the vinegar ages, its aroma intensifies, and its texture gets denser by the day: twenty-five-year-old traditional Modenese vinegar is a third again as heavy as water. Add in all the work of carefully blending and shifting liquid from one barrel to the next, and it's actually impressive that good balsamic vinegar is not more expensive than it is.

Italians refer to the real balsamic vinegar as Tradizionale, or traditional, in contrast to the Industriale, or industrial, vinegar that's so prevalent on supermarket shelves. The two are oceans apart. Aceto Balsamico Tradizionale has an incredibly rich flavor, a deep, dark amber color, and an almost syrupy texture. Its flavor is intense, a perfectly calibrated burst of sweet and sour that starts as a tiny tingle at the tip of the tongue and slowly expands into a mouth-filling, smooth sweetness. The sourness is gentle and comforting, supportive but never intrusive. It hints of plums, black grapes, wild currants, vanilla, and a touch of oak. Industrial vinegar may be aged only a matter of hours, made from harsh wine vinegar sweetened with sugar and colored with caramel. To taste industrial after the real thing is like following well-aged cognac with a bottle of Coke.

How do you know when you've got the real thing? Well, for openers, real balsamic vinegar is always very expensive. You'll no more see real balsamic vinegar on supermarket shelves than you'll get genuine Gucci leather at a Brooklyn street market. Of course you might find expensive vinegar that is neither the real thing nor very good. So don't go by price alone.

Look at the label. It can't vouch for the flavor of what's inside the bottle, but it should give the prospective buyer some good background information. For openers, it ought to tell you where the vinegar was made and by whom. Like a great wine, balsamic vinegar is protected with the equivalent of a government-mandated "denomination of origin": the districts of Modena and Reggio Emilia are the only ones in which authentic Aceto Balsamico Tradizionale can be made. Check for the two-letter city code: "MO" stands for Modena, and "RE" for Reggio Emilia. Each group has its own bottle in which it requires its members to pack their vinegar, a sign of certification that consumers can trust. The bottle used by the Modenese is a thick, short glass sphere that sits proudly on a squared-off base. The Reggio bottle is taller and thinner.

A quick glance at the ingredient list is also telling. There's no need for extracts, sugars, preservatives, or colorings. The best vinegars will list nothing other than "grape must."

making balsamic vinegar

Like the real thing, the subject of balsamic vinegar is complex, intricate, and shrouded in intentional and unintentional mystery. Even for someone as stubborn as I am, it's not easy to penetrate the mysteries that emanate from Modena.

Unlike most vinegars on the market that are made from wine, Aceto Balsamico Tradizionale never lives any part of its life as a wine. Rather, it starts with the must—the fresh juice—of the

traditional balsamic vinegar from reggio-emilia

traditional balsamic vinegar from modena

local grapes, and hence it is not a "wine vinegar." Each maker uses his own blend of grapes, but Trebbiano is the most widely used variety, with Spergola, Trebbiano di Spagna, Occhio di Gatto, red Lambrusco, and/or Berzemino sometimes added into the mix.

Once the grapes are gathered, they're cleaned and carefully crushed. The freshly pressed juice is poured into open copper kettles (some producers now use stainless steel), then cooked down over wood fires until it is noticeably thicker than wine but still thinner than maple syrup. The cooking should be conducted the same day that the grapes are crushed in order to sterilize the liquid and avoid any unplanned fermentation. The vinegar maker takes care to cook the must slowly so that there is no caramelization or burning of the natural sugars in the grape juice; burned must will lead to bitter balsamic.

Depending on the flavor they're looking for, the makers will vary the cooking times. "We cook for twelve to twenty hours if we want a more acid product, and thirty-six to forty hours if we want a sweeter one," one producer told me. In the process the cooked must — known as *mosto cotto* — is reduced to between a half and a third of its original volume. Different producers shoot for different levels of reduction, all a part of their master plan. Although longer cooking would produce a denser vinegar, it is not desirable to thicken the must in this way. If the must is too thick, it won't successfully seal the barrels, the vinegar will leak, and the flavor will be overly sweet.

The reduced must is then shifted into large wooden barrels or steel tanks, where the next stage of production, the fermentation and acetification, begins. Some producers hold the must here to acidify and mature for two, three, or even four years. Others use it within a matter of months. At whatever point the vinegar maker is ready, the must is allowed to enter the *batteria,* the well-worn wooden barrels in which it will continue its transformation. A bit of old vinegar is blended with the new must, and the mixture is put into the largest barrel in a series to continue development.

roll out the barrels: aging the balsamic

Courtesy of a day's visit to the vinegar works, or *acetaia,* of the brothers Roberto and Giovanni Cavalli, I was able to see the aging process for myself. The Cavalli *acetaia* is in the calm, tiny town of Scandiano, about twenty minutes from Modena. A balsamic *acetaia* has to be a cooper's idea of heaven. Everywhere you turn, there are barrels — on the upper levels, on the main floor, even on the stairways. New barrels, old barrels, barrels built before the turn of the century, barrels that are six feet across and tiny ones no more than a foot high that look as if they were pulled out of a Lilliputian winery. Regardless of size and source, barrels are a very big deal in the world of *balsamico*. The Consorzio fra Produttori di Aceto Balsamico Tradizionale di Reggio Emilia — the body that certifies the authenticity of the genuine article for the district — starts its oversight with the wood in which the vinegar is aged. Years before the vinegar that goes inside will ever be sold or consumed, the consortium begins by first certifying the actual barrels. Each is inspected, then — if approved — branded with a special seal. From there the new barrels have to be seasoned: first submerged in boiling salted water, then drained, dried, and filled with strong standard wine vinegar. Twelve months later, that vinegar is discarded, and the barrel is again immersed in boiling salted water, drained, and filled with vinegar. Another twelve months down the road, the rawness of the new wood having finally been overcome, the barrel is ready.

Old *balsamico* barrels are treated with great reverence. To lose an aged barrel is a blow to a vinegar maker, like a small community losing a much-loved senior citizen. All those years of interchange with the vinegar give the wood a mellow richness. So when—after about a century of service—old barrels begin to break down, they are almost always rescued by newer, sturdier barrel casings.

At the Cavalli *acetaia,* there are barrels made of oak, cherry, mulberry, chestnut, and juniper. Other makers may also use ash and locust. Generally the bigger barrels are made of oak, the smallest of mulberry and juniper. The reliance on the now rare mulberry wood is a legacy of the region's previous role as a primary producer of silk. The trees that once provided food for fat white silkworms were used by coopers to contribute what became a standard component in the aging of better balsamics. These days, mulberry wood is in very short supply. Even harder to find is juniper, which has become the balsamic equivalent of old ivory. It's now illegal in Italy to cut down a juniper tree, so no new barrels are made from it. Hence the importance of saving older ones.

Buzzing around the opening of each cask are what the Modenese refer to merely as *mosche,* tiny vinegar flies that are found in every *acetaia.* The square five- to six-inch hole that's cut into each barrel to allow in needed oxygen is covered with a small screen and a piece of cloth, which combine to keep the flies out while allowing the precious vinegar access to the air it needs to acidify.

Although there are probably thousands of barrels up in their attic, the Cavallis seem to know each one intimately. Rarely reading the chalked labels, they walk around pointing here and there, like proud professors introducing me—in a mixture of English and Italian—to prized pupils: "This . . . gold label, fifty years old. This . . . very special gold label, one hundred years old, from aristocratic family. This red label . . . seventy years old." Throughout our tour, I can't help but admire the aroma, which is, without question, exceptional, redolent of wood, grapes, age, and attics.

One key to the aging of Aceto Balsamico Tradizionale is that the maturing rooms must never be artificially heated or cooled. Like the region's exceptional Parmigiano-Reggiano cheese and its exquisite Parma ham, part of the vinegar's character building comes from natural climatic swings. In the cool winter months, bacteriological activity in the balsamic is almost nonexistent. The vinegar rests, while moisture evaporates slowly. As the weather warms in spring, the acetobacters in the vinegar gradually pick up the pace. The activity approaches its height in July and August, the hottest months of the year in Modena. The process gradually slows down again through the autumn until the acetobacters reach near hibernation levels in midwinter. Attic spaces are optimal for this aging because they exaggerate these natural temperature swings.

It's important to understand that in the world of balsamic there is absolutely no such

thing as a vintage. While commercial balsamics almost always claim some specific number of years of aging on their label, you'll never see one on a bottle of Tradizionale. At best the makers will tell you about when the vinegar in question was started. In truth, no traditional balsamic vinegar ever really gets a fresh start; any time newly reduced grape must is added to a barrel, there's still a significant amount of the old vinegar inside. So even the youngest Tradizionale has a bit of ancient, aristocratic blood in its veins.

During the aging, the vinegars are gradually shifted through a *batteria* of different varieties of wooden barrels in the *acetaia*. Just as barrel aging develops the flavor and identity of a fine wine, so, too, each of these woods contributes its character to the flavor of the vinegar. Each vinegar maker uses his own formula, with the most recent one giving the most prominent flavor. The Cavallis start in the largest oak barrels, moving the vinegar to the next smallest, then again to the next smallest still. Eventually the vinegar reaches the smallest, often the rare mulberry or juniper. No barrel is ever fully emptied, merely topped up with liquid from the previous barrel. The first—and biggest—barrel in the *batteria* is filled in the autumn with the reduced

must, and the process begins anew. According to tradition, the topping up is always done—as is the bottling—when the moon is waning. The barrels are never filled all the way in order to permit oxygen flow, which is crucial to the process.

Whether it's for sale or for the family's salad dressing, the vinegar always exits from the smallest of the barrels, which is known as the *regina,* or queen. To ensure continuity, no more than 10 percent of what's inside these tiny barrels is ever drawn off in any given year.

There's some science, some skill, lots of experience, and a good bit of gut-level intuition involved in making traditional balsamic. Vinegar makers will taste, test, and blend, always trying to balance the desire for short-term sales with the need for long-term vinegar development. To sell everything off at once would send producers home with a lot more cash than they came in with. But in the world of balsamic, they'd basically be out of business.

When the makers determine that the time is right to sell off some of their wares, they blend balsamics of different origins to create their version of vinegar perfection. The removal of vinegar for bottling is almost always done in the winter months. Because the bacteria are the least active in the colder weather, the vinegar will be at its clearest then. The annual selection is the vinegar master's prerogative—a limited, expensive, and never-to-be-reproduced delicacy. At a minimum, the vinegar must be at least twelve years old, which potentially qualifies it for the first level of certification—"Red Label" in Reggio, or "Vecchio" in Modena. To carry the "Gold Label" or "Extra Vecchio," a vinegar must be at least twenty-five years old; for the midrange Reggio-grading of "Silver Label," a minimum of eighteen.

the official tasting

Once the vinegar has been blended and removed from the barrels, it's taken to the Consorzio Produttori Aceto Balsamico Tradizionale di Modena. There, a small sample of the vinegar is tasted, tested, and scored. Only the vinegars on which the panel bestows its seal of approval qualify as authentic Aceto Balsamico Tradizionale. In Reggio Emilia, where the Cavallis work, the highest grade is "Gold Label"; the next highest vinegars become "Silver Label," the rest "Red Label." In Modena, the vinegars are classed as Vecchio (old), which wear a white "cap," or Extra Vecchio (very old), which sport a gold one.

A team of five well-trained *maestri* (masters) assembles to judge the producers' submissions. The positions are unpaid, so not surprisingly most of the *maestri* are older men and women who've reached a stage of life in which they have the time to give. To qualify, they go through an extensive, decade-long training program. Even after they earn certification, they're required to sit in on nearly fifty formal tastings each year to keep their taste buds in shape.

Once they arrive, the *maestri* are seated at adjoining carrels, where they're presented with a series of dark vinegar samples in bulb-shaped glass vessels labeled only with a number. On the table each judge is armed with a candle, a ceramic spoon, a score sheet, and an extensive set of taste memories from having rated literally thousands of vinegars.

The judges begin by assessing the vinegar's visual qualities. They swirl each bottle, then hold it in front of the candle flame to illuminate the liquid inside, evaluating its density and viscosity by looking at its "legs," or the tracks that it makes on the inside of the glass when swirled. From there they move on to aroma, where they rate the vinegar for finesse, intensity, persistence, and—my personal favorite among the desired characteristics—*franchezza,* or frankness. Lastly, and also most important, comes flavor, accounting for nearly half of the total possible points. Here they mark for acidity, balance, and intensity. A great deal of emphasis is placed on harmony.

From a maximum of 400 points in Modena, Vecchio-quality vinegar (twelve-year minimum) must have at least 229 to receive the go-ahead for sale. An Extra Vecchio must have 255 points. In a perfect, acidically balanced universe, a *balsamico* could score up to 400 points before being sold. Apparently, though, it never happens. The really great vinegars show in the vicinity of 330 points. The most the judges in the room could remember giving a vinegar for sale was 336.

"It never gets more?" I inquired.

"If it did, it would never be sold," one judge explained with a sort of kindly condescension. "It would only be for the family." International acclaim aside, in the Modena area Aceto Balsamico Tradizionale is still much more about cachet than it is about commerce.

Roughly 40 percent of the entrants fall short of the minimum standards. These are returned to the *acetaia* with comments from the judges. Most makers return these "rejects" to the *batteria* so that the vinegar can develop further and return to the *consorzio* at a later date. A few producers sell off these shortfalls immediately,

As a special treat, the Cavallis gave me a chance to taste one of their oldest vinegars. "Would you like to taste some three-hundred-year-old vinegar?" Giovanni asked. "Sure," I said, trying to act at least reasonably casual about the whole thing.

Even the act of tasting real balsamic vinegar from the barrels is something special. Giovanni inserted a glass tube called an ampulla into the barrel and brought it back filled with syrupy brown-black vinegar. He had me hold out my hand, palm down, as if I were grasping a tennis racket, and then released a drop of the precious vinegar about where the bones of my thumb and forefinger come together. The vinegar formed a shiny, thick, dark droplet so dense that it sat on the back of my hand.

Slowly, carefully (I was terrified it might slide off onto the floor), I raised my hand to my mouth and plucked the drop of vinegar with the tip of my tongue. It was dense and thick with flavor, sweet yet pleasantly and mouth-tinglingly sour, with hints of the wood, vanilla, grapes, berries, of hundreds of years of history. It's hard to conceive of tasting something that was begun in the 1690s. *"Squisito,"* you might say if you were Italian. I just smiled and nodded my head.

labeling them *condimento,* an indication that the vinegar didn't pass Modenese muster. Sometimes, the maker isn't happy with the grade given, in which case he may take it back and return it to the barrels for additional aging.

If the vinegars do pass the point test and the maker is satisfied with the score, the *consorzio* will go ahead and bottle the vinegar. Aceto Balsamico Tradizionale is one of the only products I'm aware of in the world in which the producer surrenders the bottling of the product to the regulating agency. In either case, all the Tradizionale vinegars approved by the *consorzio* may be sold in one of the two regulation bottles, and each is sealed shut and stamped with a formal registration number.

down with the dating game

Despite our American fixation with dates and vintages, the key factor in assessing the quality of a traditional balsamic is never really the age but rather the flavor. Everyone who has anything to do with the traditionally made balsamic is adamant on this point. The challenge of the vinegar maker is to bring the flavors of the vinegar and the influence of the woods into balance.

Each tiny batch of Aceto Balsamico Tradizionale that's approved for bottling is unique. Each is good; each is also a bit different. Erika Barbieri of the Acetaia del Cristo, whose family was one of the founding members of the Consorzio Aceto Balsamico of Modena, told me: "Let's say we take two new barrels of the same capacity, made by the same person with the same working process, the same wood, and we fill them

with the same product, and we put them close together in the *acetaia.* One year later, we will get two different products with different volumes, flavor, and acidity." Why? Nobody knows. That's the magic.

That balsamic production remains limited would be an understatement. While all the recent hoopla has brought an increased interest from folks willing to take up the challenge, supplies are still very small. In 1991 only 17,600 of the regulation-sized 100-milliliter bottles of Aceto Balsamico Tradizionale were put on the market by vinegar makers in Modena and Reggio. Clearly the market is growing: in 1999 that number was more than 50,000.

what to do with a bottle of real balsamic vinegar

Getting your hands on real balsamic vinegar is like going morel hunting in Michigan's Upper Peninsula, like eating fresh white truffles in the south of France. It's not easy and it's not often, but it sure is good when you get it.

Aceto Balsamico Tradizionale is a terrific gift for anyone who loves exceptional eating, and "anyone" might well include oneself. So just what would you do with a vinegar so special? You sprinkle a few drops onto freshly cut greens for a special salad. You break off tiny wedges of Parmigiano-Reggiano and dip them in it after dinner. You wait until local strawberries appear at the farmers' market in June and bring a bunch of berries and your bottle of real balsamic to the park to celebrate whatever you can think of to celebrate. However you use it, remember that authentic balsamic prefers to be in the culinary spotlight; it's at its best when it's the featured player. If you like, do as the Modenese do,

and sometimes sip it as a *digestif* after dinner. They know what they're doing.

the best of the rest of the balsamics

To make balsamic-type vinegar that is affordable on an everyday basis, you have to compromise. And where each producer chooses to make that compromise determines the quality of his product. The rule of thumb with balsamic wannabes is as follows: the higher the percentage of grape must and the higher the quality of whatever is used to make up the rest of the bottle, the higher the quality of the finished product. Producers can also hasten the maturing process by keeping the vinegar in heated aging rooms. The artificially warm environment keeps bacteriological activity high year-round, stimulating the acetobacters in the vinegar to work at a much faster pace than they would under natural conditions.

The best of these affordable vinegars will still list only "grape must" as an ingredient on the label. Lesser alternatives will show "grape must and wine vinegar." The least desirable options include ingredients like sugar, caramel coloring, or other sweeteners.

balsamic condiment: the affordable alternative

I'm happy to say that a number of makers of traditional vinegars have come up with a way to get much of the flavor of balsamic to us in a way that's eminently affordable, while staying as true as possible to the taste of the real thing.

Since these vinegars are not authentic *balsamico,* they cannot be labeled as such by Italians who want to maintain its integrity. Instead their labels use alternatives such as *condimento* or *salsa* (sauce). The results can be delicious — certainly not as complex or intense as Tradizionale, but nevertheless full-flavored with much of the mellow smoothness and sweet-sour character that make balsamic such a hit.

In order to choose well, it helps to know the producer and the product. There are a half dozen or so very good vinegars that bear the *condimento* label. You can expect to pay between $15 and $50 per bottle.

The Cavallis make an excellent balsamic condiment. They blend equal parts Trebbiano grape must and aged wine vinegar and store it in wooden barrels for more than three years. It is affordable but very flavorful, excellent for salads, sauces, or drizzling over freshly roasted meats.

At Vecchia Dispensa in the little town of Castelvetro, southwest of Modena, Roberta Pelloni and Marino Tintori create a very delicious condiment from Trebbiano grapes. They use 100 percent must — no other vinegar is added. After it has aged for six years, they remove the vinegar from their *batteria,* offering some for sale as is and blending the rest with vinegar that would otherwise qualify as Tradizionale. The higher the percentage of Tradizionale they add, the better the flavor, the denser the liquid, the more costly the bottle. The amount of aged vinegar they add is anywhere from 8 to 20 percent (Vecchia Dispensa labels list these numbers).

Other good, affordable balsamic condiments include vinegar packed under the Giusti, Elsa, and Leonardi labels.

balsamic for beginners

Monari Federzoni, with the now familiar green and orange label, is the brand that took America by storm in the early eighties. At $5 or so a bottle, it's the most accessible balsamic, and it has found its way into millions of American homes. It's made with a small amount of grape must and filled out with unaged wine vinegar. The color comes from caramel, not from wood, as it would in a traditionally made balsamic. The whole thing is aged for only about as long as it takes the boat to get from Italy to the United States. While it's a far cry from the elegance and intensity of the real thing, it makes an acceptable everyday dressing for salads, and you can add it to tomato sauce or vegetable soup.

The Monari Federzoni bottles are not the end of the line. At the very bottom — the worst of the worst — are cheap vinegars sweetened with sugar and darkened with caramel coloring, yet labeled with the misused words "balsamic vinegar."

the extraordinary efforts of sherry vinegar makers

Why balsamic has become so popular while sherry vinegar remains in its culinary shadow is a mystery to me because most everything that's so appealing in balsamic is present in its Spanish counterpart. Maybe Italians just seem sexier. Granted, sherry vinegar isn't as sweet as balsamic, but to me that actually increases its appeal; sherry has a clarity and a lightness I don't find in balsamic's more syrupy sensations. With its enormous depth, subtle sweetness, and distinctive almond undertones, sherry vinegar deserves our attention.

Sherry vinegar is as old as sherry wine, and to this day nearly every sherry maker also makes vinegar. The commercial history of sherry vinegar in Spain began in 1933, when Francisco Páez Sánchez proudly put his label on bottles of "spoiled sherry" and put them out for sale. Until then, every producer had his private stock stashed somewhere in the cellar, each used it liberally in the kitchen, and most of the town's best cooks were well aware of which sherry houses were superior. But amazingly, like balsamic, it was never offered for sale.

Legend has it that each barrel of sherry chooses its own future. Those that declare their acid intentions by starting down the road to vinegar are removed to a separate building before they can influence other barrels into converting as well. In seeking out a first-rate sherry vinegar, try to find one made by a producer who still uses traditional barrel conversion methods

eight things to do with vinegar (besides washing windows)

Green Salads: Good oil with bad vinegar is like eating filet mignon with ketchup. Although everyone agrees that oil and vinegar are made for salad, there are no hard-and-fast rules about how to get them there. Italians simply sprinkle a few drops of each directly onto the lettuce. The French usually whip up a smooth emulsion with a bit of Dijon mustard, salt, and pepper.

Bread Salads: Using leftover bread in salads is quite common in the Mediterranean, and it's a great way to showcase the flavor of fine vinegar. Try a salad of cubed country bread, ripe tomatoes, aged sherry vinegar, olives, olive oil, and fresh basil.

Sauces and Soups: Vinegar gives lots of life to sauces. It's an essential ingredient in French classics like hollandaise and béarnaise. On a less traditional note, balsamic will give tomato sauce a little extra zip before you put it on pizza or pasta. Vinegar adds a sparkle to soup. A couple of spoonfuls of sherry vinegar contribute an interesting undercurrent to an already good gazpacho. Use a little raspberry vinegar to liven up summer fruit soups.

Marinades: The acidity of vinegar is an excellent balance for the richness of meat, game, or poultry. Add a bit of balsamic to a lamb marinade, aged sherry vinegar to a shrimp marinade, or Banyuls vinegar (see page 83) to chicken marinade.

Pickling: From peppers to peaches, cucumbers to carrots, the better the vinegar, the better the flavor of the pickles.

Drinks: Looking for a nonalcoholic alternative to wine coolers? Add a few drops of aged vinegar to cold soda water.

Fruit Salads: Most folks don't think of fruit and vinegar as natural companions. Good balsamic vinegar or sherry vinegar and fresh strawberries are such an incredible combination that once you try it you'll go back to it again and again.

Ice Cream: Aged balsamic is very good on vanilla ice cream.

and allows the vinegar the benefit of long aging.

The ultimate test is to pour a bit into a wineglass. Stick your nose in and savor the aroma. It should be clean, clear, and crystalline, with a hint of almonds that will show up even more markedly in its flavor. Now sip. A tingle crawls up and over your tongue. Smooth, light, with a trace of oak, it has a touch of sweetness, a suggestion of caramel, and perhaps a pinch of plum.

sherry, sherry baby

Authentic sherry and sherry vinegar are one-of-a-kind flavors that can't be duplicated anywhere else in the world. The best are made in Jerez de la Frontera in Andalusia, in southwest Spain.

The original vine varieties were planted by the Phoenicians when they founded Jerez three thousand years ago. The first attempts to regulate sherry production in the interest of quality and consistency date all the way back to 1483 and dealt with details of harvesting technique, barrel construction, and aging.

Today, sherry and sherry vinegar start out with the juice of the Palomino grape, one of the few wine grapes in the world that is also good for just plain eating. The area around Jerez has notoriously chalky soil; the heat "bakes" it to form a thick, clotted crust that helps hold onto the little bit of rain that falls. The warmth and dryness of the soil combine to make for an exceptionally flavorful fruit. The grapes are harvested each autumn. Some are left in the sun to raise their natural sugar content; bees and wasps feast on the fructose (the natural sugar in the fruit) as the grapes break down. It was at one time quite common to hire a watchman for the fields at harvest time to protect the valuable vines from intruders, prompting the Spanish saying, "Girls and vineyards take a lot of watching."

The fruit is then pressed and put into barrels, where it awaits the first of two natural fermentations. Up until the middle of the twentieth century, the pressing was still generally done by those whose work went by the now unused name of "treading." Four men would climb into a wooden *lagar,* or winepress, which was filled with grapes, and walk on them until the fruit was fully crushed. Typically the treaders worked from midnight to noon, the better to avoid the searing afternoon heat of Jerez. Today the crushing is done mechanically.

The new grape must is then left to ferment; the first fermentation takes about three to seven days and causes the liquid in the barrels to foam like a newly opened bottle of Champagne. The

raspberry vinegar

Finding well-made raspberry vinegar is harder than it ought to be. The best are made with nothing but fresh fruit and good-quality vinegar. I steer clear of those that are flavored with syrup or extract because they tend to be overly sweet. Good brands include Gegenbauer from Austria, Delouis from France, and Robert Rothschild Farm and B. R. Cohn in the United States.

One of the oldest ways to use raspberry vinegar is to sprinkle some over crushed, or shaved, ice and top it off with a spritz of soda water. You can use raspberry vinegar in vinaigrettes; it's especially nice blended with walnut or hazelnut oil, then drizzled over fresh spinach or chicken salad. It's also a great addition to fruit salads or a bowl of freshly cut cantaloupe.

second fermentation is slower and softer, taking about three months, at the end of which all the sherry's natural sugar has been converted to alcohol. Later, grape brandy is added to the wine to raise its alcohol content to about 16 or 17 percent. This additional alcohol puts sherry into the family of "fortified wines," which also includes Port, Marsala, Banyuls, and Madeira. The tradition is an old one, dating to the era of the Phoenicians, who boiled wines to ensure better keeping.

breezes and barrels: the solera system

One of the secrets of aging sherry and sherry vinegar is the *solera*—a pyramid-shaped pile of wide oak barrels, usually seven across the bottom, reaching up to three across the top. It is not unlike the multibarrel aging system used in Italy for balsamic vinegars. But while balsamics are aged in barrels of various woods, sherry vinegar is aged strictly in casks crafted from American white oak. No one is quite sure exactly when American oak first arrived in the area, but it likely dates to the sixteenth century, and its popularity with winemakers gradually grew until the nineteenth century, when it was generally acknowledged as the most desirable wood to use.

Vinegars of different vintages are slowly shifted down from the top barrels, which hold the newest vinegar, to the bottom dwellers, which hold the oldest. Each year, a bit of the older stock is left in the upper barrels to be blended with its younger, incoming relations. The term *solera* technically applies to the level of barrels closest to the floor, the ones containing the oldest wine or vinegar. (The name comes from *suelo,* Spanish for "floor.")

The taste and the nose of the *capataz,* or cellarmaster—not the year of the grapes' harvest—determine when a barrel of sherry or vinegar is ready to be sold. When a label reads "25 Years Old," it means that the bulk of what's inside the bottle hit the aging barrels twenty-five years ago, but there's a sampling of older vintages inside as well.

Like mosques facing Mecca, all the bodegas, or sherry houses, face the southeast, toward the sea. This positioning allows the makers to capture the westerly winds that are high in humidity and so important to proper sherry production. It also protects the sherry from the dry easterly winds coming out of the mountains. To enhance the humidity further, the bodega floors are made up of sand, limestone, and iron oxide. In the hot summer months, they're sprinkled with water to moisten the air. Large openings are left between the roof and the walls, allowing the breezes to blow through and around the barrels. The salty air influences the aging and the flavor of the wine or vinegar. Despite the circulating air, bodegas retain a cathedral-like, almost musty scent of age, wood, and wine.

sherry vinegar in the kitchen

Over the years I've discovered that a few drops of sherry vinegar can bring great depth to the flavor of dozens of foods, yet few folks will be able to identify it in the finished dish. One of my favorite summer salads is made with chunks of ripe tomatoes, tossed with comparably sized cubes of day-old country bread and some black olives. I add a good dose of freshly ground black pepper and dress it with a great, fruity extra virgin olive oil and aged sherry vinegar. Actually, almost any tomato dish is enhanced by sherry vinegar—add a little to icy cold gazpacho, hot tomato soup, or seafood and tomato stew.

Other savory sauces also benefit from the flavor of sherry vinegar. Sauté wild mushrooms and sprinkle them generously with it— eat them on their own or add a few to an omelet. Use a shot of sherry vinegar to marinate fresh shrimp before grilling. Enjoy boiled beets with a dash of sherry vinegar—add a little olive oil, salt, and pepper, and you have a great summer starter. Or you can simply toss a salad with a little sherry vinegar and some Spanish extra virgin olive oil.

sherry vinegar brands

Although nearly every sherry maker also offers vinegar, only a handful still work with traditional conversion methods. My personal preference is for the vinegar of Sánchez Romate and José Páez Lobato. Both offer bottles of very good vinegar at surprisingly reasonable prices.

Among the more specialized and extra-aged offerings, I've enjoyed all of the following.

SÁNCHEZ ROMATE'S V.O. SHERRY VINEGAR The firm was founded in 1781 by Don Juan Sánchez de la Torre, a well-known businessman and philanthropist. The Romate family joined later, by marriage. Sánchez Romate's wine and vinegar have long been held in high regard and have supplied the British House of Lords, the royal family of Spain, and the Vatican.

All the vinegars I've had from the firm are quite nice. For many years now my favorite has been Sánchez Romate's V. O. (as in "Very Old"), the base of which has over twenty years of aging; it's sensitively sweet, complex, and mouth-tingling, with distinctive hints of toasted almonds. Although I use it regularly, I've yet to tire of its terrific flavor.

The PX vinegar from Sánchez Romate is particularly special. In order to enhance its flavor, add richness, and soften the acidity of their vinegar, Jerez housewives used to add a small quantity of old Pedro Ximénez sherry. Today Sánchez Romate does the same thing at its bodega, and the results are superb.

JOSÉ PÁEZ LOBATO This firm was the first in Jerez to offer sherry vinegar for sale commercially. Francisco Páez Sánchez—father of the present owner—proudly put his label on in 1933, and the family has been producing top-quality vinegar ever since. It offers eight-year, twenty-year, and fifty-year-old vinegars, all naturally converted and all excellent.

Unlike other readily available sherry vinegars, this one is made from Manzanilla—the special sherry from the coastal town of Sanlúcar in southwest Spain. The producers don't say how old it is. "Undetermined but extreme age" is how they put it in print. No one can remember when it was made: "It's just been there as long as anyone can recall." It's as smooth as silk, savory, intensely fruity, with a touch of spice and the slight salt tang for which Manzanilla sherry is known.

an additional array of excellent vinegars

You'll know that vinegar has hit its stride when the salad course arrives at your restaurant table with a variety of well-aged vinegars carefully selected by the chef. Until then, it's up to food-loving folks like you and me to do the honors at home. Here are some to choose from.

message in a bottle: herb vinegars

Cooks have been using herb-flavored vinegars for centuries as an easy way to get a little extra flavor into a salad or a sauce. In the middle of the 1770s, the French firm of Maille in the town of Dijon (better known today for its mustard) offered more than a hundred varieties of flavored vinegar. Now, 230 years later, herb vinegars are ubiquitous; practically every specialty food shop in America stocks at least a couple. But buyers beware: all too often, they're nothing more than lousy vinegars filled with lovely-looking herb bouquets. One taste confirms the problem: nice herbs, nasty vinegar. Well-made herb vinegars start with top-quality vinegar. Worthwhile ones include Delouis, Fallot, and Martin Pouret.

france

banyuls

Banyuls is made in the town of the same name, in the foothills of the Pyrenees in southwestern France—Catalan country. Rarely seen outside its homeland, the vinegar is made from Banyuls, the famous fortified wine of the area. Production is small, only ten thousand bottles a year. The grapes grow on very old vines, which fight to survive in the region's rocky soil and steep hillsides. The wine itself starts with a year in oak barrels in stone cellars. It's then moved outside into even larger barrels to begin acetification, where it sits in the open air and sun for four years. In the fifth year, a good dose of old Banyuls vinegar is added to the wine to enhance the conversion. The vinegar is then returned to the cellars for a final six months of aging.

Banyuls has one of the smoothest, most feathery-light flavors I've ever tasted in a vinegar. It's subtly sweet, softly spicy, with a touch of almond, almost a whisper of dark chocolate, a hint of aged sherry. It's a perfect match with a buttery, delicious Provençal olive oil to dress a summer salad.

greece

morea

Morea has become one of my favorite sweet vinegars in recent years. It's often billed as a "Greek balsamic," which it isn't. What it is, on the other hand, is very good stuff in its own right. It's made in the Peloponnese region of Greece from sweet Korinthiaki and Moschofilero grapes. The fresh must is aged in oak barrels for a solid six months. I like it a lot on

Greek salads. It's also excellent sprinkled atop lightly floured and fried liver.

spain

cabernet and chardonnay (catalonia)

Josep Puig (pronounced "Poozh") crafts a Catalan Cabernet vinegar along the lines of traditional balsamic and sherry vinegars. It's made at a small vineyard in the village of El Vendrell, an hour's drive south of Barcelona. Puig starts with the unfermented grape juice, then blends it with some of the previous year's vinegar, leaving the mixture to convert naturally over six to seven months. The new vinegar is put into oak and chestnut barrels to continue aging. As with sherry vinegar, only a little is taken from each barrel every year, and the barrels are then refilled with new vinegar.

The Cabernet has a beautiful, gentle berry flavor that's perfect for salads, sprinkling on fresh fruit, or eating with bread. The Chardonnay dressing has a sweet, subtle, oak flavor that complements fish dishes. Puig sells his vinegar under the Forum label.

cava (catalonia)

Cava is Spain's superior sparkling wine, made in the Penedés, in the province of Catalonia. Just as sparkling wines produced outside a particular French district cannot go by the name "Champagne," so "Cava" refers only to the wine made in this region of Spain.

The bodega of Ezequiel Ferret Olivella, which sits smack in the middle of the small town of Guardiola de Font-Rubi, thirty-five miles south of Barcelona and about ten grape-intensive miles inland from the Mediterranean coast, has been making wine for four full generations and Cava since 1941. About fifteen years ago, Ferret decided that instead of discarding the sediment and the accompanying liquid that is a byproduct of the Cava-making process, he would save them, as a base for vinegar and age them in large oak kegs in the courtyard behind the house.

The unique mellowness and flavor owe a great debt to the nearly two thousand days that the vinegar spends in the wood. Topaz in color, it has a lightly sour, anise-like aroma and a smooth, clean, tingly flavor that hints of tarragon, peach, and, of course, the wooden barrels. It's great for salads of any sort. Whenever a recipe calls for "white wine vinegar," you can substitute Cava vinegar and count on getting a lot more flavor in your finished dish. The gentleness of the vinegar makes it an effective team player—it never dominates but instead brings out the best in other ingredients.

Note: In the United States, Ferret's vinegar is sold under the label Miguel y Valentino.

garnacha tinta

This vinegar is made from 100 percent Garnacha wine in the town of Sarroca de Lérida, in the western part of Catalonia. The Vea family uses the traditional Orléans process and ages its vinegar three years in oak barrels. Pink in color, it has a flavor that tastes of raspberries and a good rosé wine.

oils, olives, and vinegars

rioja

Rioja vinegar starts with northern Spain's premier red wine, which is at the lighter end of the world's red wine spectrum. It is quite versatile and won't overpower more delicate dishes. The GAR brand is a blend of Rioja wine and vinegar starter and is naturally converted over four to six weeks. The newly made vinegar is then moved into old oak barrels, where it spends a solid four years mellowing and intensifying. It has a full flavor with a suggestion of black raspberry.

united states

KIMBERLEY WINE VINEGARS (CALIFORNIA)

For over twenty years, Ruth and Larry Robinson have committed themselves to creating traditional vinegars, using top-quality California wines, the Orléans conversion method, and long barrel aging. The Chardonnay vinegar is golden, with an elegant, distinctively oak flavor. If you like Chardonnay, this vinegar offers a great way to dress your salad for dinner. It's also an excellent marinade for chicken.

The Cabernet Sauvignon vinegar is deep ruby red, with notes of black raspberries, ripe plums, and vanilla, and packs so much flavor that just a few drops are enough to dress a salad. Kimberley is one of the most flavorful red wine vinegars you'll find.

The Robinsons' Champagne vinegar is intentionally more delicate than their other vinegars, made from a Pinot Noir base.

apple cider vinegar

Considering that it was once a standard ingredient in kitchens across North America, it's amazing that it's almost impossible today to find traditionally made apple cider vinegar. After almost giving up, I happened upon a nice one made in the Montérégie region of Quebec by Pierre Gingras, a third-generation apple grower. Gingras starts by crushing only whole, handpicked apples (no windfalls are used, nor are scraps or scrapings from previous cider pressings) from his own orchards. The specifics of the blend are Gingras's secret. This new juice is allowed to convert to vinegar slowly and naturally, and then spends two years in eight-foot-high French oak barrels, where it mellows and matures. The vinegar is unfiltered and unpasteurized, and it really does deliver true apple flavor. I prefer Gingras's organic vinegar, which I find more flavorful than his regular version. It's excellent for slaws, salads, pickles, and preserved vegetables.

Gingras also makes an excellent "balsamic-type" cider vinegar. Aged for five years in a series of different woods, it's darker in color, sweeter, and more intensely flavorful than the typical cider vinegar.

gazpacho with sherry vinegar

When I first learned to make gazpacho in American restaurant kitchens in the late seventies, it was a cold, chunky vegetable soup seasoned with bottled Italian dressing. Unfortunately, this concoction is still what comes to mind for many Americans when they hear the word *gazpacho.* If you travel in Spain, though, you'll find that this version is about as representative of authentic Spanish cooking as Pizza Hut is of Italian cuisine.

In Spain, tomato gazpacho is generally a smooth blender-based recipe, more like an olive oil–infused version of V8 than something you'd get from a can of Campbell's Chunky Vegetable.

This soup is best when tomatoes are at the top of their flavor. The olive oil and sherry vinegar are key components. Feel free to adjust quantities up or down depending on your taste. I like to serve this gazpacho in chilled glasses so people can sip instead of spoon. It's a wonderfully refreshing way to start any summer meal. You can also serve it in bowls and offer the optional additional chopped vegetables or Salt and Pepper Croutons (page 344) for guests to spoon on top.

- 3 pounds ripe tomatoes, coarsely chopped (about 8 cups)
- 4 ½-inch-thick slices stale crusty white country bread, soaked in water for 1 minute and then squeezed dry
- 2 medium cucumbers, peeled, seeded, and chopped (about 2 cups)
- 1 small red bell pepper, seeded and chopped (about 1 cup)
- ⅓ cup packed fresh basil leaves
- 2 tablespoons finely chopped scallion greens
- 1 serrano chile pepper, seeded (optional)
- 1 garlic clove, halved
- 1½ teaspoons ground cumin, toasted (see page 54)
- 1½ teaspoons coarse sea salt, plus more to taste
  Freshly ground black pepper to taste
- 1 cup cold water
- 5 tablespoons aged sherry vinegar (the older the better), plus more if desired

3 tablespoons extra virgin olive oil, preferably a full-flavored
fruity one, plus more if desired

Additional chopped tomato, cucumber, bell pepper, and/or scallions for garnish (optional)

In a blender, puree all the ingredients, except the optional garnish, until smooth. The gazpacho should have the texture of thick tomato juice. Strain the soup through the fine disk of a food mill or a sieve to remove excess skins and seeds.

Although you can serve the gazpacho immediately, I prefer to chill it overnight so the flavors can blend properly. Check the seasoning and add additional oil, vinegar, or salt to taste. If you wish, serve with the additional chopped vegetables on the side. The gazpacho will last for a few days, so feel free to make extra. It's an excellent, healthful afternoon snack to have on hand for kids.   serves 4 to 6

risotto with parmigiano-reggiano and balsamico

Because of the cost of the Aceto Balsamico Tradizionale, I'd reserve this risotto for special occasions. But when you want something exceptional to treat yourself or your guests, this recipe is a great way to go. It calls for water rather than broth so as not to overwhelm the gentle flavors of the vinegar and cheese. The richness of the long-aged vinegar drizzled over the top is a fine sweet-and-sour foil to the delicacy of the rice. Because it's so rich, I suggest small servings.

- 4 ounces Parmigiano-Reggiano cheese (without rind)
- 1 tablespoon Aceto Balsamico Tradizionale, plus more for serving
- 6 cups water
- ½ teaspoon coarse sea salt, plus more to taste
  Parmigiano-Reggiano cheese rind (optional)
- 2 tablespoons butter or extra virgin olive oil, plus more for serving
- 1 small onion, finely chopped (about ¾ cup)
- 1 cup Italian short-grain rice, preferably Carnaroli
- ½ cup dry white wine, preferably Italian
  Freshly ground black pepper to taste

Using a small almond-shaped Parmesan knife or another small firm-bladed knife, break—don't cut—the Parmigiano-Reggiano into rough-textured ¼-inch pieces. Place the cheese pieces in a small bowl and drizzle with 1 tablespoon of the vinegar. Toss, cover, and set aside to marinate.

In a medium saucepan, bring the water to a boil and add ½ teaspoon salt. If you have some Parmigiano-Reggiano rind on hand, add a piece to the water. Reduce the heat to maintain a gentle simmer.

In a large saucepan, heat the butter or oil over medium-high heat. Add the onion and sauté until soft, 3 to 4 minutes (don't brown the onion or it will become bitter). Add the rice and stir well. Sauté for 2 minutes, or until the rice is hot and shiny.

Add the wine and stir until the rice has absorbed it. Add ½ cup of the hot salted water and stir until absorbed. Continue adding the water, ½ cup at a time, stirring and making sure it is absorbed before adding more.

The risotto is done when the rice is al dente, about 15 to 18 minutes from when it first went into the pan. Add a touch more butter or oil and a last ½ cup of water. Stir, then remove from the heat and let stand for 1 minute. Add salt to taste.

Serve in warm bowls topped with the vinegar-dressed Parmigiano, a generous grinding of pepper, and an additional drizzle of the *balsamico* if you're feeling generous.

serves 3 as a main course or 5 as an appetizer

sautéed sole with cava vinegar sauce

Cava vinegar makes an exceptional "Champagne sauce" for freshly cooked fish.

 3 tablespoons capers, preferably packed in salt (1 ounce)
 4 fresh sole fillets, 2–3 ounces each
    Coarse sea salt to taste
    Freshly ground black pepper to taste
 1 tablespoon extra virgin olive oil
 2 tablespoons Cava vinegar

If you're using salted capers, soak them in a bit of warm water for 20 to 30 minutes, changing the water halfway through. Drain the water, rinse the capers, and dry them on a paper towel.

Season the sole fillets with salt and pepper. Heat the olive oil in a heavy sauté pan over medium-high heat. Add the sole and cook for 1 minute, then turn and cook for 1 to 2 minutes more, until just done. Slide the fish out onto warm plates and leave the pan on the heat. Quickly add the vinegar and the capers to the hot pan. The vinegar will bubble furiously. Use a spatula to scrape down the sides of the pan and collect the bits and pieces of fish that are left behind. Pour the sauce over the fish and serve hot.

serves 2

balsamic onions

This recipe comes from Julie Stanley, who runs the radically good Food Dance Café in Kalamazoo. These onions are great on sandwiches or pasta or as a relish with meat or cheese. I use the ten-year-old vinegar from Vecchia Dispensa.

variation

If you have time and want a more intense flavor, roast the onions for an additional hour.

3   pounds Vidalia or other sweet onions (5–6 large)
3/4   cup well-aged balsamic condiment
1/4   cup full-flavored extra virgin olive oil
3/4   teaspoon coarse sea salt
1/4   cup dark raisins

Preheat the oven to 450°F.

Slice the onions in half from top to bottom. Peel and slice them into thin half-moons.

In a large bowl, toss the onions with the vinegar, olive oil, and salt.

Spread the mixture in a large baking dish and cover with foil. Roast for 1 hour or until golden brown and soft, stirring halfway through and scraping the bottom of the dish. Don't be afraid of the charred bits—the vinegar will caramelize nicely and add flavor to the onions.

Stir in the raisins before serving.

makes about 4 cups

strawberries with balsamico

Make this dessert whenever you find great strawberries in the market. Serve the strawberries as they are, or spoon them over ice cream, pound cake, or some of each.

> 2 quarts strawberries, hulled
>
> 5 tablespoons well-aged balsamic condiment, plus more for serving if you like
>
> Sugar (optional)

In a blender or food processor, puree ½ quart (1 pint) of the strawberries with the vinegar.

In a large bowl, toss the remaining strawberries with the strawberry puree. Add a little sugar if desired. Macerate in the refrigerator, covered, for at least 1 hour before serving. They will keep for several days.

If you like, drizzle on a little extra vinegar at the table.

serves 6 to 8

part 2.

grains and rices

bread

Back in the middle of the nineteenth century, the average Russian ate about 3 pounds of bread a day, or nearly 1,000 pounds per year! Today his great-great-great-great-great-grandson eats about a fourth as much. In France, per capita consumption can be close to 128 pounds per year; Germans put away nearly 155. The average American by comparison consumes only about 60 pounds per year. While I know that I'm not up to the nineteenth-century Russian standard, I can safely say that I seem to eat about twice what the average Frenchman consumes each day!

Personal extremism aside, I know for a fact that the sales of bread from better bakeries around the country are booming. And although I'm probably not exactly in the mainstream when it comes to bread consumption, I do know that I'm not alone in my persistent pursuit of a better loaf.

Neither bread eating nor baking played big parts in my childhood. My mother never made her own, and other than on Friday nights when we ate challah, most of what we were eating was Wonder bread or some store-brand all-white equivalent. On an occasional Sunday, we did have sliced rye, brought back from the local deli to accompany corned beef.

It's hard to remember any single formative event on my way to becoming a bread lover. It happened gradually. When Zingerman's opened in 1982, good bread was hard to buy in Ann Arbor. A few bakeries were already at it in selected cities: in Berkeley, California, Acme Bakery started up in 1983. But the choice for most Americans was presliced, plastic-wrapped bread or a few assorted ethnic offerings that had survived the push to cheap, industrialized supermarket versions.

Although these breads were better than sliced white, the truth is that most of them were more about image than flavor. I've had people bring me loaves of locally baked rye on which they lavish enormous amounts of praise. "This is the bread I grew up on," they say. "Wait till you taste it." My excitement rises, but I'm almost always disappointed. One taste and it's clear that the greatness of the bread is more in their memories than in their mouths.

the rise and fall of bread in western civilization

In the Bible, the word *bread* is used synonymously with "nourishment." The religious significance of breads like challah and matzo in Judaism and the communion wafer in Christianity are well known. Societal relationships were rooted in bread historically and etymologically: the word *companion* is derived from the Latin *companio,* meaning "one who shares bread," and the English word *lord* derives from the Old English *hlāford,* meaning "keeper of the bread."

The slang terms *dough* and *bread* for "money" say a lot about our twentieth-century priorities.

Up until about 4000 B.C., mankind was familiar only with what we now know as flat breads, products along the lines of tortillas or Chinese pancakes. Early strains of wild wheat needed to be toasted before they could be threshed; the heat blocked the gluten development essential to risen breads. The origins of raised bread date back to Egypt, where ancient agronomists developed a strain of wheat that could be threshed without heating, and six thousand years of bread-baking tradition got under way. The other key ingredient—yeast—likely came from brewers' vats, a practice that remains in use today.

The Romans were big bread bakers. They established a tradition, known as the *annona,* of giving free bread to the poor to help offset urban poverty, an idea we ought to bring back today. From Rome, bread baking spread across Europe. During the Middle Ages, it was a common practice to make bread dough at home and then bring it to the town baker to finish because homes at that time rarely had ovens. Among the most common and serious crimes of the era were short-weighting and adulterating.

Until the fifteenth century, when plates were first introduced, wealthy people ate off "trenchers" (from the French *tranchoirs,* meaning "slicers"), thick, flat slices of days-old bread. At the end of the meal, the trenchers were either eaten or saved and fed to the poor who were happy for the access to any food at all. This custom persisted in much of Europe into the seventeenth century.

The belief that white bread was superior to dark, that it was more pure, more refined, was a common theme in many cultures over the ages. The theory had already taken hold in Greece by the fifth century B.C., when darker, denser breads made from barley or rye were the breads of the poor. It took a lot more labor to grow wheat than other grains, so wheat breads were more costly; removing the bran and the germ to whiten the flour increased the work and the cost still further.

The white-versus-dark issue crosses cultures and chronology. In Ireland, white bread was revered and kept for company, and eventually came to be known as "priest's bread." "To know the color of one's bread" was the Irish way of referring to a person's proper social standing. Interestingly, up until the seventeenth century, there were even separate guilds for bakers of white breads and brown breads. By the nineteenth century, the color of bread became increasingly a sign of social status. Writing about nineteenth-century France in *The History of Bread*, Bernard Dupaigne comments: "White bread, with all its connotations of prestige and luxury, was for the leaders, for the bourgeoisie. Flour was washed and sifted to the limit, so that all its nutritional value and vitamins were lost. Black bread was like nature, with all its imperfections and torments." This prejudice against darker breads generally continued right up until the 1960s, when a growing consciousness about health finally seemed to turn the tide.

In North America, the most important native grain was corn. Ground into meal, it was made into a flat bread, which came to be known as "johnnycake" or "Indian bread." Later, European settlers brought wheat with them and planted large quantities of it wherever they settled. By the end of the eighteenth century, wheat had become the dominant grain of this continent. Both here and in England, home baking of bread continued to be common into the twentieth century.

wonderously soft: the story of bread

Karen Hess has written in the *Journal of Gastronomy* that "the standard American loaf . . . resembles in taste and feel nothing so much as damp hospital cotton." I've often wondered myself why bread in this country— descended as it is from the great European traditions—turned so . . . soft. There are probably several reasons: one factor was the eighteenth-century introduction of pan baking instead of hearth baking. Additionally, the predominance of soft wheat flours across the

American south contributed to the consumption of soft loaves. In the nineteenth century Americans developed a distinct distaste for "sourness" in their food. This preference led bakers to use baking soda, making bread softer still. In the 1870s, industrial milling techniques were introduced. Flour became whiter and whiter, and as bakers began adding sugar to get yeasts to react as they had in the past, the bread got even lighter. In fact, a consultant who works extensively with industrial bakeries once told me that people in the trade refer to their bread as—no lie—"edible napkins." As bland as it's been, it's no wonder that Americans today have often had a halfhearted attachment to bread.

getting your hands on better bread

Although there's still room for improvement, today it's almost easier to find great bread in the United States than in most of Europe. Even in France you have to be careful where you buy if you want to get something really good. In Italy and Spain, where there's so much great food, finding good bread can be downright difficult.

In the States, a number of exceptional bakeries have sprung up: Hi-Rise in Boston; Mrs. London's in upstate New York; Amy's Bread and Sullivan Street Bakery in New York City; Bread Line in Washington, D.C.; Metropolitan in Philadelphia; Grand Central in Seattle; the original La Brea in Los Angeles; and Acme, Semifreddi's, Bay Bread, and others in the San Francisco Bay area. And where good bakeries don't exist, mail order has helped to make better bread available to those who really want it. (See Mail-Order Sources, page 446.)

A lot of what is being marketed as artisan bread, however, is not. So what's a bread buyer to do? With a little practice and a willingness to compare one loaf with the next, you'll be well on your way to buying better bread. Here's what I look for.

check the crust

Never underestimate the importance of a good crust. It's the first clue to the quality of the loaf. On most industrial American breads, the crust has devolved to a thin, light brown layer without a hint of texture. Symbolic but hardly sufficient.

Instead, crust ought to offer meaningful contributions to both function and flavor. Like the rind on a well-made cheese, it prevents the inside of the loaf—"the crumb" in baker's lingo—from drying out. And although kids and many English people often prefer to pare it

off before eating, good crust actually adds enormously to the flavor of the bread. Why? Because as the bread bakes, the natural sugars in the dough caramelize, leaving the crust sweeter and nuttier, than the interior of the loaf. Aesthetically, crust also brings contrast in terms of both texture and appearance. Fortunately for inexperienced bread buyers, crust assessment is often the easiest place to start to suss out quality.

Check out the crust's color. Contrary to popular wisdom, lightly baked loaves are not better. In fact, when it comes to European country breads, I avoid light crusts if at all possible. To me, the best-tasting breads are almost always those that are significantly darker in color (see page 99). Don't be scared off by a chocolate brown, all-but-black crust. If the baker is good, brown doesn't mean "burned" but "beautiful." And I'll bet you dollars to doughnuts that it will taste better. The flavors of the crust and the crumb will be better balanced and the caramelization will have enhanced the natural sweetness of the flour.

After assessing the loaf from above, flip it over and look at its underside. If it's got a rough, uneven bottom (sort of like a topographical map marked with rustic rivers and valleys), it almost certainly was baked on a stone hearth, a likely sign of traditional baking at work. On the other hand, if the bottom and sides are completely smooth, you're probably looking at bread that's been baked in a pan. This isn't necessarily bad — squared-off sandwich loaves, by definition, are pan-baked breads. But in the case of country breads — which are traditionally baked on stone,

not in smooth-sided pans — this slickness is generally not a great indication. Other so-called country breads are baked on pans that have hundreds of tiny holes in them to encourage more even heat distribution under the bread. You can spot these loaves from the uniform pebbly bumps along the bottom of the bread. Not bad, but still not hearth-baked.

what's so great about hearth-baked bread?

The stone of the hearth holds the heat better than any other method of baking. "With hearth baking, you get what's called 'oven spring,'" Michael London, the mastermind behind Rock Hill Bakehouse and Mrs. London's in upstate New York, told me. "You just can't get that by baking on a tray in a convection oven because the air can't match the initial heat that you get from the stone." When you pop room-temperature dough into an ordinary oven, the heat will inevitably drop almost immediately. As a result, the texture of the loaves inside will suffer. While this drop is less extreme in commercial convection ovens, there is still a significant benefit to be gained by sticking to stone.

If you can get your hands on the loaf, you can continue your crust assessment before you buy. One touch tells you a lot, so give it a squeeze. A good hearth-baked bread should feel firm.

Squeeze a bit harder. An optimal crust will give you a nice crunch, or at the least a good bit of resistance. When the crust is correct, a good loaf of French country bread will respond with a catchy rendition of snap, crackle, and pop. Tiny crumbs fall to the floor. The aroma of the loaf is released into the air. Tiny particles of crust and flour dust fall into your palms. Different styles of bread will have different degrees of crustiness. (Soft breads like challah and brioche are exempt from these crusty criteria.) Baguettes may have a thin, crunchy crust, while that on a loaf of naturally leavened French country bread will be thicker and more pronounced. Of course, crust alone doesn't guarantee quality. Some breads have great crust but little flavor; others don't quite cut it in the crust category, but the crumb can still be quite tasty.

Crispness at the time of purchase may depend greatly on the weather. Crusty bread and high humidity aren't overly compatible. A well-made loaf from Florida is inevitably going to be softer a few hours out of the oven than the exact same loaf sitting on a shelf in Santa Fe.

dark shadows: my campaign for darker crusts

One of my longest-running challenges has been to persuade people that dark-crusted breads are better. From a selling standpoint, they usually spell doom. Americans have been led to believe over the years that darker crusts are undesirable, a sign of a bad baker pawning off overbaked loaves on an innocent consumer. Dozens of bakers around the country as well as countless Zingerman's staffers have told me that customers just won't buy darker loaves. But in truth, the consumer should demand that the baker be skilled enough to hit the peak of bread-baking perfection: that ideal balance between a dark, crisp, chewy crust and a soft interior crumb.

When you buy bread with a crust that's a nice deep black-brown, you're getting bread at its best. The greater the crunch, the bigger the contrast between the crust and the interior crumb. Whatever crust can do on its own, darker crust can do better. The darker it gets, the more the crust caramelizes, the sweeter and nuttier its flavor. Certainly one can overbake a loaf, producing a dark crust but an overly dry interior crumb. But I'm talking about *well-baked* breads.

Expert bakers concur. In Washington, D.C., Mark Furstenberg, who owns and runs the wonderful Bread Line restaurant and bakery, once published a piece entitled "Why We Burn Our Bread." In fact many bakers of traditional breads quickly confess their own preference for darker crusts. But when I ask why they don't bake their breads that way, most just shrug in frustration: "We just can't seem to get the customers to buy them." I guess I'm just too stubborn to give up that easily.

smell the bread

Our senses of smell and taste are inextricably linked.

This exercise in aromatics is a skill I learned from working with Michael London. I handed him a couple of loaves of a competitor's bread. He weighed each in his hand, quietly getting a feel for them, and then broke one open. He felt its texture, then lifted it up toward his mouth. I assumed he was going to taste it. But instead he pushed his nose into the bread, took a deep breath, exhaled, and repeated the process. And then, without ever tasting, he set the bread back down on the table.

"It's O.K.," I said. "You can eat it."

He looked at me calmly. "I don't need to eat it," he said. "I can tell from the smell. There's no flavor."

Try it yourself. Don't be shy—get your nose right in there and take a deep breath. There should be a rich, complex, pleasantly nose-tingling, mouthwatering aroma. Good bread smells of the grain—usually wheat or rye. In sourdough breads, look for a distinctive, though not overwhelming sourness.

All too often you'll find that the predominant aroma is yeast—a signal that what's inside is likely to be bitter, and often downright nasty. Yeast and bread are so linked in the minds of most Americans that it's hard for folks to conceive of the possible harm in it. How can bread not smell like commercial yeast? Simple. Many traditional breads—what the French refer to as *pain au levain*—are made without it, using nothing more than flour, salt, and water. Certainly, good bakers may opt to use modest amounts of commercial yeast to enhance their work. But the yeast should always be used gently, leaving the flavors and aromas of the grain itself to gather fame and fortune. The only trace of commercial yeast in a well-made bread should be in the ingredients list. If you find any hint of yeast in either the aroma or the actual flavor, the bread is in trouble. What does commercial yeast smell like? Buy a block and take a whiff. I can almost guarantee that you'll scrunch up your nose and shake your head the way a boxer does when the trainer gives him the smelling salts.

Note: I'm *not* referring to the aroma of warm loaves that have only recently been removed from the baker's oven. I'm talking about bread that's had a chance to rest and set up, bread that's a day or so out of the bakery before it gets anywhere near your nose.

check the ingredients

Generally, the simpler and shorter the ingredients list, the higher the likelihood that the bread in the bag will be good. Because there are so few ingredients in better breads, good bakers have to count on the quality and integrity of what they put in. The best country loaves are usually made with just flour, water, and salt.

Look, too, to see what's *not* on the list. Many traditional bread bakers eschew commercial

yeast. Similarly, my interest is piqued when I don't see sugars or shortening mentioned. The addition of these ingredients often means that shortcuts have been substituted for skill, shelf life given priority over flavor. (Challah, brioche, or focaccia, however, are meant to be sweetened with sugar or honey or enriched with eggs, butter, or olive oil.)

Bread that hits the tip of your tongue with a blast of sweetness but has little to back up that initial impact is more often than not loaded with sweetener. You can taste sugar, but you can't smell it. Sugar also acts to create faster fermentation, cutting down rise times and costs. Remember that the ingredients list may show sugars in other guises, such as honey, malt, or caramel.

Commercial bakers like shortening because it substitutes a mouth-filling texture for the truly full flavor of a well-made loaf. It also serves to enhance shelf life. Shortening may appear in the form of vegetable oil, palm oil, peanut oil, or margarine and usually leaves a greasy feel in the hand and mouth.

With the exception of traditional Tuscan bread—which is saltless by design—bread needs salt to taste good. "Unfortunately," Michael London laments, "a lot of bakers undersalt their bread. And if there isn't enough salt, the bread becomes insipid." And if the label says "salt," what sort is it? Sea salt or kosher salt makes a positive difference.

Remember, too, that the flavor and aroma of water matters and varies by location.

Where does the flour come from? Preferably, it will be "unbleached" and "unbromated." These two terms are what the linguist William Safire calls retronyms: "phrases with a modifier fixing a meaning to a noun that needed no modifier before." Up until the time of the Industrial Revolution, all wheat flour was unbleached and unbromated. But "progress" changed all that. Millers cleaned up flour's "unattractive" natural, dark cream color. Bromation, another industrial invention, made it possible for millers to pack and ship bags or bulk trucks within a day of milling rather than waiting the two to three weeks it takes for the flour to mature on its own. By adding bromate to the flour, industrial mills cut time (and hence cost) out of the process. The problem is that bromate has been found to be a potentially cancer-causing agent and has been banned in most countries of the Western world, though not, unfortunately, in the United States.

When breads call for other ingredients—nuts, raisins, olives, herbs—the better the quality, the more flavorful the finished bread. But even the best ingredients still need to be mixed, risen, and baked with great skill in order to be turned into exceptional bread. When you're buying fresh bread from unlabeled bakery shelves, you'll have to ask in order to get this sort of information. The bakery should be able to tell you what ingredients it's using.

note the time

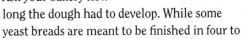

While you won't ever see it on an ingredients list, time is one of the most critical components in creating full flavor in bread. Ask your bakery how long the dough had to develop. While some yeast breads are meant to be finished in four to five hours, in general it's hard to get traditional breads to be as flavorful as they should be without giving them the blessing of time. Well-made breads can take up to twenty hours. The time factor is decidedly unglamorous. It's about letting the dough sit while the clock is ticking.

Most modern bakeries rely on heaping helpings of commercial yeast to eliminate this period of primary fermentation. The dough is mixed and then, almost immediately, shaped or put into pans for its final rise, a process also known as "proofing." Three hours after mixing, it's headed for the oven. The result is bread that may look fine but lacks flavor.

take a hole-istic approach

Bakers like to look at hole development the way stockbrokers fixate on financial ratios. Allowing for exceptions like brioche, challah, and rye,

three unscientific theories about bread

1. **Torn bread tastes better than sliced.** O.K., I have absolutely no scientific evidence to back up this claim. But to me, bread tastes better when it's broken or torn from the loaf than when it's been sliced off with a knife.

2. **Bigger loaves taste better.** Personally, I will always take a half of a three-pound loaf of bread over one that's a pound and a half. Having eaten literally thousands of artisan breads from hundreds of different bakeries over twenty years, time and time again I've found that breads baked into bigger loaves just plain taste better. Their texture is nicer. The flavor is fuller. The inside is moister. The crust is crustier.

3. **Character counts.** Loaves of great bread are a lot more like people than you might imagine. They have good days and bad days. They've got personalities, replete with strengths, weaknesses, and imperfections. Both have been known to behave rather inconsistently. Artisan breads are different every day.

Weather, humidity, subtle changes in flour, heat, oven spacing, the hands of the baker, all affect the finished loaf. The same baker working in the same kitchen with the same recipe and the same ingredients will get two different breads on two different days. That's not necessarily bad. It's character.

When I eat a loaf of bread, I look for the character traits I like. That loaf of Jewish rye that's especially cool and moist in the middle. The dark, burned bits on the bottom side of a crusty loaf of country bread. The crisp point on a French baguette. The patterns on the crust that form as the loaves bake on the stone hearth. These subtleties aren't there every day. But I watch for them. Character counts. Enjoy it.

what you want to see in an old-style artisan country loaf is nice, uneven, hole development. Like a spelunker, a skilled bread buyer is looking for plenty of big caverns, archways, and passageways through the loaf. The holes are a result of the carbon dioxide that the dough emits as it develops. High volumes of commercial yeast raise a dough much more quickly, but flavor—and, visually, the hole development— is sacrificed in the process. Poor hole development is a sign of trouble. Tiny holes are a sign that the bread in question is heavily yeasted or wasn't allowed an appropriate amount of time for its primary fermentation. When you eat it, you're not going to find much flavor.

taste for yourself

Looks can be deceiving. But good bread should taste as good as it looks, literally filling your mouth with fine flavor. It doesn't have to be strong or overpowering. As you bite it, the first thing you should notice is texture and sound, the crunch and crackle of the crust on your teeth. That should be followed closely by the first bit of flavor: a slight sense of subtle sweetness caused by the caramelization of the sugars in the crust. The crumb should be slightly soft but not overly so—you ought to get enough resistance to remember you're eating bread, not wet napkins. As you eat, notice the contrast in feel and flavor between the crust and the crumb. Keep chewing, letting the bread come into contact with all the various parts of your mouth. If it's a naturally leavened loaf, you should sense a slight, pleasant sourness at the back and sides of your tongue. The longer you chew, the more flavor you should find; give yourself time to notice the finish, the aftertaste. It ought to be pleasant, appealing, enjoyable enough that you want to go back for another bite. Slow down. Let each bite of bread linger.

At the end of the day, yours is the only taste that really matters. As Lionel Poilâne, the late master Parisian baker, told me, "I am always interested to hear the comments of my customers, who continue to surprise me even now by their very individual and totally unexpected conceptions of what is good bread." Each of us tastes, learns, likes or dislikes, and then tastes some more. As Poilâne put it, "One recognizes a good bread by a basket that empties itself very quickly."

should it be fresh? not necessarily!

"Is this fresh?" is the standard query. Although there's something warm and sensual about just baked bread, from a flavor standpoint there's a lot missing. A good country loaf isn't really "done" until hours, a day, or sometimes days after it's come out of the oven. It needs time to set up, to allow its flavors to develop, its crust to crisp, and its character to emerge. Many traditionally made, hearthbaked breads have even more flavor a day or so after you've bought them.

what's sourdough?

Over the years, I've noticed that there is a great deal of confusion over what is — and what is not — a sourdough bread. There is no official definition. But in the interest of clarity, here's a shot at it.

If you mention sourdough to most Americans, they'll immediately call up an image of a San Francisco–style sourdough: very tangy, acidic, noticeably sour, with a crisp, blistery crust. But there's a lot of sour starter used in breads that aren't San Francisco–style sourdough.

For example, nearly all well-made ryes and pumpernickels have some sour starter in them. Some have more, some less. Many French country breads are made with a sour. *Pain au levain,* the classic country bread of France, by definition is raised without the use of commercial yeast, meaning it, too, relies on the use of a sour starter. In all these cases, bacterial development in the dough contributes to the characteristic sour flavor.

Can a bread be too sour? Absolutely. Like anything else in life, sour starters are best when they're appropriate and when they're used in moderation. Not all breads are supposed to be made with sour starters. Most Italian breads, Parisian baguettes, and brioche aren't, so they should neither smell nor taste sour.

When the first artisan-minded bakeries got up and running in America in the late 1980s and early 1990s, there was an understandable race to escape from the blight of blandness that had enveloped the world of American baking. And not surprisingly, in many cases that wrought new problems. Inevitably some bakers went so far that their bread was excessively sour. The key is balance. A sour should enhance the flavor of the finished loaf but never dominate it.

the story of jewish rye

Does that perfect loaf of Jewish rye — the one everyone seems to remember from days gone by — really exist? Did it ever? I've gotten pretty skeptical. I've looked long and hard, in most every city in the country, and I've yet to find it. What really makes a great loaf of rye bread? And what makes it Jewish? The comedian Lenny Bruce once said, "B'nai B'rith is goyish; Hadassah, Jewish. Marine corps — heavy goyish, dangerous. . . . Pumpernickel is Jewish and, as you know, white bread is very goyish. . . . Chocolate is Jewish and fudge is goyish. Spam is goyish and rye bread is Jewish."

I wanted to know if rye bread had changed since my grandparents' time and, if so, why and how. I scanned book after book but found little to help me. I picked up the telephone and started calling everyone I knew who I thought might have some insight, especially older folks who might remember what the bread was like earlier in the century. Then I started calling people I didn't know. I went to Chicago and to New York. I even went back to the library and spent a couple of afternoons roaming the stacks. And slowly I pieced together the story.

Rye is the principal grain of the northern countries of Europe—Russia, the Baltics, Scandinavia, Poland, Britain, northern Germany—and is also grown in the United States and Canada. For Russians and Scandinavians, rye is the daily bread. In Germany, it's used to make the traditional *Schwarzbrot* and is also added to gingerbread. The French, who serve *pain de siegle* (rye bread) with oysters, first planted rye in North America in the seventeenth century. The new grain was milled and mixed with cornmeal to make what is still known in New England as "rye and Injun bread." In Boston, rye flour is used to make the sweet "Boston brown bread." And, of course, American Jewish bakeries have long blended rye and wheat flours and baked them into loaves of Jewish rye.

Rye is a relative newcomer among foods: people have been eating it for only about three thousand years. Originally it was nothing more than a weed, intruding into hard-to-maintain northern wheat fields. At some point, farmers must have given up fighting the rye and switched to growing it. Today it is the third most important cereal grain in the world, after wheat and rice.

Milled rye yields a brownish gray flour. Because it has none of the gluten you need to make a bread rise, it's usually mixed with other flours—barley, millet, buckwheat, or wheat—for bread-making purposes. The flavor of rye goes well with the traditional sour starters used to leaven bread before commercial yeast was available.

To most folks in America, rye bread is Jewish deli bread, but not to Russians, Poles, Ukrainians, Germans, and other ethnic groups who have been making and eating it for hundreds of years. It's likely that in various forms, they are the ones who taught the Jews how to make rye bread. Back in the late nineteenth and early twentieth centuries, when my great-grandparents came over from Russia (or various components of what was then the Russian Empire), most turn-of-the-century Russian Jews—whether in Russia itself or as new immigrants in America—lived with an overwhelming, constant, dragging poverty. The poor in Russia ate black bread, which was dark, of the earth, of poverty, of grinding out a living, surviving for tomorrow.

When your life depends on bread, it had better be good for you. On Friday nights—or on holidays—Russian Jews luxuriated in the sweet, soft, and rich braids of a freshly baked loaf of challah, made from wheat flour and enriched with eggs and honey. But the other six days of the week, it was rye—coarse, dark, and heavy but also nutritious. When times were tough, there was no challah at all.

I've yet to meet anyone who talks of eating "Jewish rye" back in the old country. Most everyone remembers "black bread," which is closer to today's Jewish pumpernickel but is also made with rye flour. A century or so ago, that rye flour would have been much, much darker in color and much more flavorful, with the germ and the bran left in, and the proportion of rye flour to wheat flour in the loaves must have been much higher, with just enough wheat added to get the rye to rise. But as Jack Wayne, a longtime

Zingerman's customer who grew up working in his father's Polish bakery in Lódź, pointed out to me, Polish Jewish rye is very different from Russian rye, for it contains more wheat and is lighter in color and texture. And it is, in fact, Polish—not Russian—bread that provided the basis for what we now know as Jewish rye.

In North America, Jewish rye became whiter than it probably was in the old country. Wheat flour was readily available and fairly inexpensive, and the rye flour used was more carefully milled and hence lighter in color and texture.

But if Jewish rye changed in America, it also did so because American Jewish culture changed as well. As Jews prospered, they continued to eat rye bread, but it got whiter. Most modern-day Jewish rye uses far less rye flour (and a much higher percentage of wheat) than it ever did; it's far lighter, much softer, and far less flavorful. (In fact, many consumers have come to confuse the flavor of the caraway seeds used to season these breads with the real flavor of the rye.)

And yet while the new immigrants gave up much of life as they knew it, food remained the strongest link they had to the past. Today, when American Jews want to hook up with their heritage, they eat chopped liver, gefilte fish, corned beef, and, of course, real rye bread. There may not be much rye flour left in it, but in our hearts, this bread is still Jewish.

a guide to good rye bread

Based on everything I've learned, here's what makes a good loaf of Jewish rye.

a good sour rye starter

The fact that a starter is "all-natural" isn't enough—it has to taste good too. All this became clear to me when I stuck my nose deep into the mixing bowl to catch a whiff of Michael London's rye sour. I expected it to be overpowering. Instead it smelled great.

rye flour

Most of what is sold in this country as "rye bread" has little more than a pinch of rye flour in it. A traditional Jewish rye bread needs a decent level of rye flour, about 20 percent rye, 80 percent wheat.

baked on the hearth

To get the right texture for the bottom crust, the bread should be baked on stone.

steam

Steam in the oven is essential for a good, chewy, amber crust that gives your jaws a solid workout. Steam allows the skin of the dough to expand as it starts baking, which keeps the crust from splitting.

time

Making real Jewish rye takes many hours. You start with a natural sour. The sour needs to be fed, allowed to build in flavor, is slowed by refrigeration, then fed again. Then the dough can be mixed and allowed to rise. Commercial yeast must be kept to a minimum. Excessive yeast saves time, but it doesn't allow for dough development and produces a rye that stales quickly and has less flavor.

no sugar, oil, or milk

Sugar and oil cover up a lack of flavor in the bread. Real Jewish rye is never made with milk.

The rules of kashrut would prohibit eating it with corned beef.

flavor

Rye bread should taste like rye with a touch of sour, though nowhere near as much as San Francisco sourdough or even German rye loaves. Rye has a deep flavor, a flavor of the earth, a flavor full of character that gradually fills your whole mouth. Good rye has guts. Steady, delicious, never wavering, it's rooted in the soil of northern Europe. Its sturdy texture and lightly sour flavor provide the perfect pairing for a thick schmear of cream cheese or sweet butter.

buying better baguettes

Only in a city setting—where getting more bread is only as hard as taking a walk down to the corner *boulangerie*—would anyone come up with a bread as ephemeral as the baguette. Baguettes are made, bought, and eaten in less time than it takes for the dough of a good country loaf to rise.

The baguette, which means "wand," is a Parisian invention, dating to the days following World War I. Around the turn of the century, most French breads were still country breads, baked in large rounds or, alternatively, in long, thick loaves. As consumers of the day demanded more and more crust on their loaves, bakers sought to respond by baking thinner and thinner breads, each with a higher ratio of external crust to interior crumb. The breads got thinner and thinner until eventually they became baguettes—long, thin loaves, with a crisp, crackling crust and a chewy white interior.

Finding baguettes is easy—they're everywhere. But even in Paris, good baguettes that taste of wheat, not of some frozen premixed dough, are hard to find.

Here's what to look for.

crusty crust

A good baguette should crackle when you break it.

diaphanous texture

The interior of better baguettes will be marked by a veritable lacework of nooks and appealing crumb-crannies. Very small, more regular air holes are usually a sign that an excessive amount of commercial yeast has been used in the dough.

sensuous smell

Better baguettes simply smell better. Break off the end and then stick your nose inside. You should get an outstanding aroma that hints of wheat and a whiff of fresh cream.

nix the microwave

Unless you're looking to make weapons for a stone-throwing contest, keep your bread away from the microwave. It gets nice and hot, all right, but wait about five minutes: like a rock, baby. All that's left to do at that point is chuck it or grind it up for bread crumbs.

full flavor

A good baguette should have an enjoyable, wheaty flavor with an undertone that's almost milky, the result of active bacteria that create lactic acid as the dough develops before baking.

care and handling of better bread

When you consider which bread to buy, remember that long, thin loaves with more surface area and less "middle" have a shorter shelf life and dry out more quickly. If you want a bread that will last a few days, don't buy a baguette.

consumer caveat: beware bread in plastic bags

Good bread keeps best when it is not stored in plastic. (Freezing is an exception.) Real bread needs to breathe. And sealed in plastic, bread breathes about as well as you or I would if we were shrink-wrapped. While the bread continues to exhale, it can't inhale. Moisture, which will turn even the crispiest crust soft, gets trapped in the bag, leaving the bread soggy. In the process, the plastic also creates an environment that makes bread prone to molding.

At my house, we simply leave the bread sitting on the counter, cut side down. This solution is so simple as to be downright radical. The bread does dry out a little. But just a little. Well-made breads (often those made without any, or with very little, commercial yeast) hold up much, much longer in this, their natural, state.

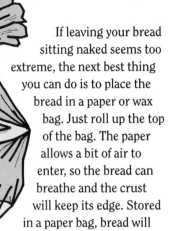

If leaving your bread sitting naked seems too extreme, the next best thing you can do is to place the bread in a paper or wax bag. Just roll up the top of the bag. The paper allows a bit of air to enter, so the bread can breathe and the crust will keep its edge. Stored in a paper bag, bread will not mold as quickly as it does in plastic. Breadboxes work well too.

The only thing worse than putting bread in plastic is putting it in plastic and then putting it in the refrigerator. The cold, moist environment of the fridge is bound to create even more moisture inside the plastic. If you want to keep a loaf of traditionally made country bread for more than three or four days, your best bet is to freeze it. In fact, the only time bread and plastic ought to meet is on their way into the freezer.

If it's a loaf you've ordered by mail or stored in the freezer, some time in the oven just before serving can add greatly to its aroma and texture. About 15 to 20 minutes at 350 degrees Fahrenheit works well.

recipe for a bruschetta party

Bruschetta is the Italian name for what is actually an all-Mediterranean blending of bread, olive oil, garlic, and salt. Go anywhere they make olive oil and you'll find some version of this dish. Each region alters the dish slightly, bestows its own name, and has its own twist on the order in which the ingredients are assembled. But everyone—and I mean everyone—eats it. When the new olive oil is being pressed each autumn, bruschetta is particularly big. Any food lover who's visited the Mediterranean in the fall will relate a romantic story of eating freshly pressed oil poured over thick slices of country bread. And for good reason—bruschetta is simply one of the best things I've ever eaten anywhere in the world. Keep the caviar—give me bruschetta.

If you're looking for a lively entertaining alternative, one that can feed thirty to forty people with a relatively modest amount of advance preparation, consider a bruschetta party. The idea is to set out an array of options for topping the bruschetta and let your guests go wild. Your role is to serve as the toastmaster—gather good ingredients, slice the bread, toast it, and leave the rest to your visitors.

bruschetta basics

Good country bread Get something with flavor and a nice crust. Bruschetta is a wonderful way to use up leftover bread, even week-old loaves of well-made bread. All sorts of white or wheat loaves of Mediterranean origin will work well. Cut the loaves by hand right before toasting (as opposed to having them machine-sliced at the shop) so that the slices have a more rustic feel.

Great extra virgin olive oil If you want to re-create the authentic flavors of a given part of the Mediterranean, find an oil that comes from that area. Or offer three to six different oils: a Tuscan oil, one from Provence, and one from Spain, Greece, or the Italian Riviera.

Sea salt I use sea salt because it doesn't taste of iodine. I prefer to use coarse crystals instead of the finely ground stuff; a pinch of crystals makes the salt a full-fledged ingredient rather than an innocuous addition.

Fresh garlic Aficionados can rub cut cloves onto the bread to their heart's content while others may opt to go without.

a good toasting technique

Choose a toaster that can handle a decent volume of bread, or alternatively you can manage the toasting from your broiler (be sure to keep a close watch on the bread so that you don't inadvertently transform it to charcoal). Best of all is an open fire.

When the bread has browned, remove it from the heat. If your guests want to use garlic, now's the time—quickly rub the cut side of the clove over the warm slice of toast. Otherwise, move right to the olive oil—guests can pour some straight onto the hot toasted bread. Sprinkle on a pinch of sea salt.

It's almost worth making bruschetta just for the aroma of the olive oil as it hits the bread. The rule is to use lots of oil. Don't drizzle—pour! And don't skip the salt—it's necessary to bring out the flavor of the oil.

variations on the bread-and-oil theme

Here are a few of my favorites.

Ligurian *pane e olio* In this case, the bread isn't toasted, just sliced and doused with a generous pour of Ligurian olive oil. Finish the dish by sprinkling on a bit of red wine vinegar and some coarse sea salt.

Ligurian *bistecca sanremasca* Rub toasted whole-wheat bread with a cut clove of garlic. Pour on some Ligurian olive oil. Cut a ripe tomato in half and rub it directly into the bread. Discard the tomato. Sprinkle on a little sea salt and serve while it's still warm.

Greek *papara* Dip untoasted slices of good crusty bread in lots of olive oil. Sprinkle with some sea salt and dried oregano. (Crush the oregano between your thumb and forefinger to release its full flavor.)

Murcian morning toast To make this specialty of the region of Murcia in southeastern Spain, toast a split baguette and then dress it with olive oil, a pinch of salt, and a generous sprinkling of sweet Murcian paprika.

Maltese *hobz biz-zejt* Rub slices of country bread vigorously with half a tomato, then dunk them face down into a plate of olive oil and smear them around to make sure they soak up plenty. Sprinkle with salt and pepper. Some Maltese add anchovies, shavings of good goat cheese, chopped olives, or fresh mint.

Sweet treat from Portugal Soak crusty white bread slices in olive oil, then sprinkle them with cinnamon and sugar. It may sound strange, but it's one of the most delicious desserts I've had.

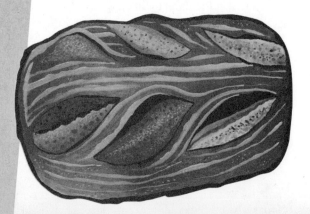

other fixin's

Anchovies Anchovies are stars, not also-rans, so find something special (and stay away from those nasty ones that cost $1.69 at the super-market). See page 112.

Arugula One of my favorite greens, it has a nice peppery flavor and lively green color.

Fennel Another of my favorites. Buy it fresh and keep the slices thin so they don't over-whelm the oil.

Mozzarella It must be freshly made.

Olive paste Also known as "olive jam" or "the caviar of the poor."

Parmigiano-Reggiano Cut into thin curls with a potato peeler just before serving.

Radicchio Braised in olive oil with a touch of garlic and sea salt.

Roasted red peppers I'm partial to the Piquillos from the Spanish Basque Country. They've got a superb, slightly peppery, smoky flavor that can't be beat.

Roasted tomatoes Halve the tomatoes and bake them in a 350°F oven for 1½ to 2 hours.

Tomato slices If you can't get your hands on ripe flavorful tomatoes, skip them and use roasted tomatoes instead.

Sardines I love to put these little fish atop a slice of toasted bruschetta.

party time

Set out all the accouterments on nice platters or in bowls. Toasting starts only when the guests arrive. You'll want to have a supply of warm bread available at all times. Provide a stack of warm plates for people to pick up their toast.

buying better anchovies

Why are most Americans so down on anchovies? Given the quality of the ones most of us have tasted, it's no wonder that there's so much antipathy. Ninety-seven percent of what we're served on pizzas and pseudo-Caesar salads is absolutely dreadful. As a result, the anchovy's image is so bad that many people — even some who work with food professionally — seem to take pleasure in deriding the little fish.

Though few Americans are aware of it, there are better anchovies out there. So this is it, folks — time to let go of your outdated pizza-parlor prejudices and get to know good anchovies. If your mental image is a thin, dark, little leathery strip of fish that comes packed in a tiny tin, think again.

How can you spot a superior anchovy?

look lively

Better fish look better: lively, rich, reddish, almost mahogany (not unlike a nicely cured piece of prosciutto), and free of the blemishes that can be caused by sloppy handling

or poor knife work as the fish are being processed. Inferior anchovies tend to look limp and lack the luster of superior specimens. If you're unfamiliar with brands, buy anchovies in glass jars so you can see what's inside.

buy fillets free from bones

If you want the convenience of fillets, buy those that have been properly and carefully cleaned. Bad anchovy fillets have an unpleasant crunchy texture because some producers cut costs by leaving in the bones. The best fillets have had the dozens of small bones removed with tweezers. The fillets are wiped clean with a cloth and then hand-packed in olive oil.

one sniff is worth a thousand words — and price tells the story

Like other good fish, well-processed anchovies smell softly, pleasantly seawater-fresh. As a test, I rounded up a bunch of different anchovies from the shelves of unsuspecting supermarkets. When I opened up some of those tins . . . oh my God! What a stink! You can't very well open a tin and take a whiff while you're standing in the store. But there is a pretty direct correlation between price and product quality in the anchovy world. Those $1.69 tins aren't going to get you top-grade fish. If you buy cheap, have a pair of nose plugs handy.

when buying oil-packed anchovies, look for extra virgin

Most oil-packed anchovies are pretty poor fish. Anchovies packed in sunflower or soybean oil aren't for me, thanks. I prefer those that are packed in extra virgin olive oil.

aficionado advisory: for the best anchovies, choose salt-packed

To the uninitiated, whole anchovies packed in salt don't look appealing . But eye appeal notwithstanding, anchovies in salt are the first choice for Mediterranean mavens because they retain more of their original flavor. Amazingly, well-cured salt-packed anchovies are often less salty than lousy anchovies that are sold in oil.

Granted, anchovies in salt are a bit more work, so if time is of the essence, you'll probably want to stick to fillets packed in olive oil. But if you're up for a little extra effort in the interest of increased flavor, give these babies a try. To use them, just rinse the fish in water to remove excess salt. Under gently running water, insert your thumb into the center, carefully remove the bone, and rinse away any excess bones or skin. Once you've cleaned and boned the anchovies, you're on your way to some very good eating.

pa amb tomaquet

catalan tomato toast

*P*a amb Tomaquet is a traditional Catalan treat that you can easily make at home. Nearly every olive oil–producing region has its own version of this dish. Catalan oil will give you the most authentic flavor, but any fine extra virgin olive oil will be delicious.

- 4 thick slices crusty white country bread
- 1 garlic clove, halved (optional)
- 1 ripe tomato
  Extra virgin olive oil, preferably Catalan
  Coarse sea salt

Toast the bread slices until lightly browned, or better yet, brown them outdoors on the grill. If you're using garlic, rub a cut side of the clove over the surface of the bread. Cut the tomato in half and rub it right into the bread—the bread should absorb much of the tomato's juice. Discard the tomato. (In their lust for this dish, Spaniards often dress both sides of the bread.) Pour on plenty of olive oil, add a pinch of sea salt, and serve hot.

serves 2

variations

Pa amb Tomaquet can be topped with anything from Serrano ham to roasted peppers. Although not particularly traditional, it's also great with a slice of Spanish cheese, such as Manchego or Idiazábal. In *Catalan Cuisine,* Colman Andrews mentions a Majorcan version that calls for slices of tomato instead of rubbing the tomato into the bread, adds a light sprinkling of red wine vinegar, and is topped with chopped olives and capers.

Up in the town of L'Escala, the anchovy capital of Catalonia, *Pa amb Tomaquet* will almost always be served with a couple of anchovies atop the toast.

bread and tomato salad

This salad is a very good way to feature fresh summer tomatoes when they're in season, while using up a bit of leftover bread in the process. The bread soaks up the liquid so it's important to use flavorful oil and vinegar. You can alter the ratio of oil and vinegar to taste.

1 garlic clove, peeled and bruised with the side of a knife

2 pounds ripe tomatoes (about 7 medium), cut into $3/4$-inch cubes

4–5 slices crusty white country bread, cut into $3/4$-inch cubes

2 Piquillo peppers (see page 277) or 1 jarred roasted red pepper, drained and coarsely chopped

8 large fresh basil leaves, torn

3 tablespoons blanched almonds, toasted (see page 31) and coarsely chopped

6 tablespoons full-flavored extra virgin olive oil

2 tablespoons Banyuls vinegar (see page 83) or aged sherry vinegar

$1/4$ teaspoon coarse sea salt, plus more for serving
Freshly ground black pepper to taste, plus more for serving

1 tablespoon pine nuts, toasted (see page 31)

Rub a large bowl with the bruised garlic and discard the clove or reserve it for another use.

In the bowl, toss the tomatoes, bread, peppers, basil, almonds, olive oil, and vinegar. Add the salt and pepper and toss again.

You can serve the salad right away, but I like it best after it's had 30 to 60 minutes for the oil and vinegar to soak into the bread.

Garnish with the pine nuts. Pass salt and pepper at the table so people can add them to taste.

serves 4 to 6

provençal pistou

I learned this recipe from Saul Wax, one of the most talented cooks we've ever worked with at Zingerman's. It's a great way to use up old bread, but I like it because it tastes so good. As with so many Mediterranean recipes, the flavor of the olive oil is essential—feel free to add more to taste.

3 tablespoons extra virgin olive oil, preferably Provençal or Ligurian, plus more if needed

2 medium onions, coarsely chopped (about 2 cups)

4 medium carrots, diced (about 2 cups)

3 garlic cloves, coarsely chopped

3–4 medium red potatoes (about 1 pound), peeled and cut into ½-inch cubes

Good-sized piece of Parmigiano-Reggiano cheese rind (optional)

13 cups water

½ pound fresh green beans, trimmed and cut into 1-inch lengths

1 cup cooked red kidney beans

3 ounces spaghetti, broken into 2- to 3-inch lengths

1 teaspoon freshly ground black pepper, plus more if needed

1 cup tomato paste

½ cup pesto (you can buy bottled pesto or use the recipe on page 224)

½ cup freshly grated Parmigiano-Reggiano cheese

1½ cups cubed baguette or other white loaf, crust cut off

Coarse sea salt

In a large stockpot, heat the 3 tablespoons olive oil over medium heat. Add the onions, carrots, and garlic and sauté, stirring occasionally, for 10 minutes, or until softened.

Add the potatoes, cheese rind (if using), and water. Bring to a boil, reduce the heat to medium-low, and simmer until the potatoes are tender, about 20 minutes.

Add the green beans, kidney beans, spaghetti, and pepper and cook for 10 more minutes.

Stir in the tomato paste and pesto until well combined.

Stir in the cheese a bit at a time until melted. Scrape the bottom of the pot occasionally to prevent the cheese from sticking. Add the bread pieces and simmer for 5 minutes more. The soup should be fairly thick with just a little broth. Check the seasonings and add additional salt, pepper, and olive oil to taste before serving. As with most soups, this one is even tastier the next day. *serves 6 to 8*

swiss peasant bread soup

This great, easy-to-prepare mountain dish can help get you through a dark winter's evening. It's peasant fare—stale bread, onions, and dried mushrooms gathered earlier in the year. To me, this soup is what "French onion soup" should be like, but here the cheese is a garnish, not a two-inch-thick topping as it so often is in restaurants.

(This recipe is best right off the stove rather than cooled and re-heated the next day, because the bread will break down and leave you with a texture akin to that of oatmeal.)

2½ cups boiling water
1 ounce dried porcini mushrooms (1 cup)
2 tablespoons butter
1 large sweet onion, such as Vidalia, Walla Walla, or Texas Sweet, coarsely chopped (about 1½ cups)
1 garlic clove, minced
1 sprig fresh thyme (about 4 inches)
6 cups chicken broth
½ loaf peasant bread (¾ pound), torn into 2-inch chunks
½ teaspoon coarse sea salt
1 teaspoon freshly ground black pepper
1½ cups freshly grated aged Gruyère cheese for serving

In a large heatproof bowl, pour the boiling water over the mushrooms. Soak, covered, for 20 minutes. Strain the mushrooms, reserving the liquid. Rinse and clean the mushrooms, discarding any tough stems. Set aside.

In a large stockpot, melt the butter over medium heat. Add the onion, garlic, and thyme and sauté until the onion is translucent, about 7 minutes.

Add the chicken broth and the reserved mushroom-soaking liquid. Bring to a boil, then reduce the heat to medium-low. Remove and discard the thyme sprig. Stir in the bread cubes and mushrooms.

Simmer for 10 minutes more, or until the bread is incorporated into the broth. Add the salt and pepper and serve immediately in warm bowls with a generous amount of Gruyère grated on top.

serves 4 to 6

bread crumbs, the poor person's parmesan

In Italy, the tradition of using bread crumbs in cooking probably dates back to ancient church law, which forbade the eating of all animal products—including cheese—on fast days. Unwilling to go without a topping on their pasta, Italians substituted bread crumbs for the more usual grated Parmesan. In the south, where poverty often prevailed, bread crumbs were a much more affordable alternative to cheese and were used for topping the daily pasta dishes at the table.

Toss bread crumbs with finished pasta dishes, mix into sauces, or sprinkle onto sautéed vegetables or casseroles.

½ loaf crusty white country bread (½–¾ pound)

Break the bread into chunks and leave them out overnight to dry or place them in a 200°F oven for about 10 minutes. If you're using the oven, be sure just to dry the bread, not toast it.

Grate the dried bread chunks on the largest holes of a box grater into a large bowl. You'll end up with various crumb sizes. Pour the crumbs into a colander with large holes and shake them into a large bowl. Finer crumbs for breading will fall through. Larger crumbs for soup and salad will stay in the colander.

Bread crumbs can be stored in a tightly closed container for weeks.

makes about 2 cups fine crumbs and
about 2 cups larger crumbs

the ultimate corned beef sandwich at home

Although we sell hundreds of these sandwiches every week at Zingerman's, you can make them at home as well. The corned beef has to be sliced just right to make it worthy of the name. Thin, but not too thin, and at just the right angle. Properly cut corned beef should have a thin layer of fat all along each edge. Take the fat away, and you lose a great deal of flavor.

- 1 pound very good, not too lean, corned beef, sliced
- 1 loaf really good Jewish rye bread, with or without seeds, purchased whole, not sliced
- Hot mustard to taste
- Pickles

Preheat the oven to 350°F.

Sprinkle the corned beef with a little water, then wrap it tightly in foil and place it in the oven. At the same time, put the whole loaf of rye, unwrapped, into the oven. After 15 to 20 minutes, remove the bread from the oven—the crust should be crunchy, but not overly hard or burned. Set the bread on the counter and let stand for 5 minutes.

As soon as the rye has cooled enough to handle, place it on a cutting board. Hold the loaf on its side in your noncutting hand, with its top crust facing away from you. Hold a bread knife at about a 45-degree angle across the corner of the bread and start slicing. The slices should be about the size of the palm of your hand. Cut 2 slices per person.

While the bread is still warm, spread each slice with mustard. Pile on the hot corned beef and set the second slice of bread on top of the sandwich. Cut the sandwiches in half diagonally and serve immediately on warm plates. Pass extra mustard and be sure to have plenty of pickles on hand.

makes 3 or 4 sandwiches

lex's roast chicken

My friend Lex Alexander turned me on to this recipe. It's a quick way to make a small Thanksgiving dinner without having to spend two days cooking. Slices of day-old bread are placed below the chicken in the roasting pan, so the bread soaks up all the juices of the meat. I use the free-range birds we buy at Zingerman's from Amish farmers in Indiana. Serve with a green vegetable and wild rice.

- 1 3- to 4-pound roasting chicken
- ¼ cup plus 2 tablespoons extra virgin olive oil, preferably a delicate Ligurian or Catalan oil
- 3 large onions (about 2 pounds), cut into half-moons
- 4 celery ribs, cut into ⅛-inch-thick slices (about 2 cups)
- 1 garlic clove, minced
- 2 teaspoons lemon zest
- ½ teaspoon dried thyme
- ½ teaspoon hot red pepper flakes, preferably Marash (see page 58)
- 2¼ teaspoons coarse sea salt
- 1½ teaspoons freshly ground black pepper
- ¼ cup chopped fresh Italian parsley, rinsed and squeezed dry
- ½ loaf day-old crusty white country bread, cut into ¾-inch-thick slices (if the bread is still fresh and soft, slice it and let it dry on the counter for a few hours before using)
- ¼ cup fresh lemon juice

To butterfly the chicken, place the chicken breast-side-down and remove the backbone by cutting along the length of it on each side. Turn the chicken over and press on it with the back of your hand to flatten it.

Preheat the oven to 375°F.

In a large skillet, heat ¼ cup of the olive oil over medium heat. Add the onions and celery and sauté for 10 minutes, stirring occasionally. Add the garlic, lemon zest, thyme, pepper flakes, 1¾ teaspoons of the salt, and ½ teaspoon of the black pepper. Sauté until the onions and celery are soft and translucent, 5 to 7 minutes more. Remove from the heat, stir in the parsley, and set aside.

Lightly oil a roasting pan. Arrange the bread slices to cover the entire bottom of the baking dish. (If the bread is too big to fit in the dish easily, cut the slices into smaller pieces.) Layer the onion-celery mixture over the bread in the roasting pan.

Place the chicken skin side up on top of the onion-celery mixture. Rub the chicken inside and outside with the remaining 2 tablespoons olive oil, the remaining 1 teaspoon black pepper, and the remaining ½ teaspoon salt. Pour the lemon juice over the chicken.

Roast for 1 hour 30 minutes, or until a meat thermometer inserted into the thigh registers 160° to 165°F. (Start checking the chicken for doneness at about 1 hour 15 minutes to avoid overcooking.) The skin should be golden brown and the bread should have absorbed all of the chicken's juices.

Remove the pan from the oven and let stand for 10 minutes. Transfer the chicken to a cutting board and cut into quarters. Spoon some of the bread and onion mixture onto each plate, place a chicken quarter on top, and serve.

serves 4

pasta

"Nothing else, not opera or Renaissance art or Roman ruins or even pizza, so exemplifies Italy as pasta." ● **Burton Anderson,** *Treasures of the Italian Table*

Americans often approach pasta as little more than a convenient way to convey large quantities of sauce from plate to palate. But for serious Italian eaters, the point is the pasta as much as it is the sauce. Although few Americans know it, good pasta actually tastes good.

Perhaps the reason most of us don't think much about its flavor is that our culture has relatively little experience with this food. At the beginning of the twentieth century, American pasta consumption was so small that, per capita, it barely registered at all. By 1930 it was up to nearly four pounds per person per year. In the early 1980s, the amount had risen to more than eleven pounds a year. Today the average American consumes about twenty pounds each year, but we still have a long way to go to keep up with our Italian counterparts—we eat barely a third of what they do.

Italians divide pasta into two categories. One is *pasta fresca,* or "fresh pasta." Usually made at home or in the kitchens of quality-oriented restaurants, fresh pasta is made with flour and eggs. Many dishes rely on its softer texture and richer flavor. My focus is on what Italians call *pasta secca,* or "dried pasta": how to buy it, how to cook it, and best of all how to eat and enjoy it.

Back in the 1980s, when fresh pasta was all

the rage in America, most folks falsely assumed that fresh and dried pastas were simply two different versions of the same thing. They are not. They serve two different purposes in Italian cooking, and you can rarely substitute one for the other.

pastas past: a tangled but tasty history

Though their prominence in North America is relatively recent, noodles are hardly a new form of nutrition. The ancient Hebrews ate them. The Chinese have been serving noodles since as early as the first century A.D.; by the tenth century, noodle shops were popular in much of the country. Nearly everyone knows the tale of Marco Polo, who supposedly brought pasta back to Italy from China at the end of the thirteenth century. The story has been largely discredited; in various forms, noodles seem to have shown up in Italy long before Mr. Polo's trip. It's likely that both Indians and Middle Easterners were also eating noodles extensively by the twelfth or thirteenth century. The inventory of a Genoese merchant made in 1279 shows stocks of macaroni. By the start of the fifteenth century, dried pasta, usually then referred to as "vermicelli," was commercially produced in Italy.

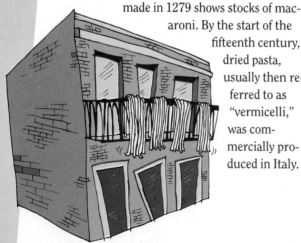

To grasp why Italians put so much emphasis on the flavor and texture of the pasta they put on their plates, it's important to understand that in Italy the serving ratio of sauce to pasta is far lower than in most of North America. Italians generally offer smaller servings, lightly tossed with a sauce or simply served with a dollop atop the noodles. By Italian standards, the sauce should accent, never overwhelm; no upstanding Italian chef would ever drown a pasta dish in sauce. With this guideline in mind, it only makes sense that the pasta itself has to have a flavor and character of its own.

Pasta's enormous popularity in Italy dates to the early eighteenth century, when new machines made even wider commercial production possible. Naples became the main source of pasta in the modern era. The all-important hard durum wheat was well suited to the soil, and daily cycles of hot mountain winds alternating with milder sea air created an ideal climate for drying the pasta. By the end of the century, the number of pasta-making shops in the town had grown nearly fivefold.

Dried pasta was at that time eaten primarily by the Italian upper class. Much like coffee or chocolate, dried pasta was a manufactured item, which meant that it had to be paid for in cash and was hence too costly for everyday eating. For the most part, noodles were eaten for dessert.

British travelers brought pasta back home from Naples, and from there it made its way to North America. Thomas Jefferson is said to have shipped Neapolitan pasta back to Virginia in 1789. A year earlier a Frenchman opened a pasta factory in Philadelphia. Although there were hardly any Italians in the United States at the beginning of the nineteenth century, by 1910 there were nearly 4 million. As their population grew, pasta making in America boomed. Italian-Americans still generally opted for the imported product because it was made from the harder, tastier durum wheat. Much American-made pasta started with inferior softer wheat, often deceptively colored yellow to give it the look of semolina.

choosing great dried pasta

The basic process for producing dried pasta is fairly simple. Flour and water are mixed into a dough, the dough is extruded through metal dies to create a multitude of shapes and sizes, and the freshly pressed pasta is then dried to preserve it. Finally the pasta is packed and shipped for sale. But while the basic recipe is consistent, there are drastic differences in quality from one noodle to the next. How can you tell which ones are at the top of the market and which are only at entry level? There are three key indicators.

1. better pasta tastes better

I'm not talking about the finished dish, just the noodles, au naturel, in the nude. A good pasta should be able to stand out with only a little olive oil or butter, and maybe a light sprinkling of freshly grated Parmigiano-Reggiano.

2. the importance of texture

Texture is another piece of the pasta puzzle; the integrity of the noodle after it's been cooked is critical. Poor-quality pastas can literally fall apart in the pot; turn your back and they turn soft and mushy in a matter of minutes. Well-made macaroni, on the other hand, is supposed to have texture; when you take a bite, you should know you're eating something significant.

The difference is evident as soon as you open the box or bag and lay your hands on the raw pasta inside the package. Grab a fistful of commercial spaghetti. It's shiny, slick, and as straight as a set of plastic pick-up sticks. Or feel a bit of mass-produced elbow macaroni. It's lightweight, brittle. The stuff seems ready to shatter at the touch.

Now heft a handful of top-grade pasta made by an artisan producer. It's solid. Heavier. More substantial. Its surface is rough, like a set of sun-washed and wind-worn seashells gathered on the beach.

3. better pasta smells better

Aroma is the third essential element in distinguishing excellent pasta from run-of-the-mill. And when you drop a handful of top-notch noodles into boiling water, they release an enticing whiff of wheat. No, it's not overpowering, but it's definitely there. In fact, if you go into a small pasta plant, the first thing you're likely to notice is the smell of the grain. It's a lot like the scent of a good bakery. The air is warm and humid, perfumed with the aroma of milled wheat.

making a better pasta

So how does a producer go about making a better grade of pasta?

the grain

All the best Italian dried pastas start with *semola di grano duro* (durum semolina), the coarsest grade of milled endosperm from hard wheat (*Triticum durum*). In fact, since 1967 Italian law has actually required it. (Up until recently, you couldn't sell soft wheat pasta in Italy, but European Union codes have forced the Italians to open their market to imports from other EU countries.) Unlike flour that is very finely milled to a powder, semolina is granular, almost like sugar or finely ground cornmeal. Durum semolina makes superior pasta primarily because of its high gluten content—when properly developed in the dough by the maker, these glutens trap the starch inside the pasta and keep it from flowing out into the cooking water. Additionally, the glutens help to ensure the firmness that is such an essential element in great pasta. Because of its harder nature, durum semolina requires longer kneading, adding time and cost but contributing mightily to the flavor and texture of the finished pasta. It also gives the glowing golden appearance that is typical of Italian pasta, as opposed to the whiter look of a low-end product.

Unfortunately, only Italy imposes such a requirement for the use of semolina. In other countries it's perfectly permissible for a pasta maker to start with soft wheat (*Triticum vulgarum*), which is far less costly but produces an inferior product. You can usually spot soft wheat pastas as soon as you drop them into boiling water; the pasta breaks down and clouds the cooking liquid.

Buying the best pasta isn't just a function of finding a label that lists "semolina" among its ingredients. Just as coffee roasters work with an array of green beans, the best pasta makers are masters at buying and blending durum semolina from various sources. Each producer has his own suppliers, his own mix; long before the grain ever gets into the pasta machines, the pasta maker adjusts his recipe annually to take into account alterations in crop yields and flavor. The variety of the wheat is important; as with other agricultural products, older varieties of wheat are often the most flavorful, but they also have lower yields and higher risk of disease, which keep more cost-conscious producers at arm's length. Some pasta makers prefer wheat from the various regions of

Italy; others won't buy anything but Canadian durum.

The point is merely that the best dried pasta should taste of the grain; if you already know a noodle with flavor and character, it's likely that the maker has managed to buy grain from better sources.

the water

Although few people think about it, the flavor of the water with which the grain is mixed is a matter of great concern to quality-oriented pasta makers. Since the water in any given area has its own chemical and mineral makeup, it will alter the flavor of any item it's blended with, as it would in brewing coffee or tea. The same grain mixed in California instead of Campania is likely to yield a different flavor in the finished pasta.

the mixing

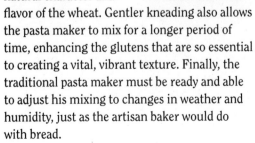

As with bread dough, excessive heat during mixing is the enemy of the quality-conscious producer. Slow, gentle, low-temperature mixing helps to preserve the natural character and flavor of the wheat. Gentler kneading also allows the pasta maker to mix for a longer period of time, enhancing the glutens that are so essential to creating a vital, vibrant texture. Finally, the traditional pasta maker must be ready and able to adjust his mixing to changes in weather and humidity, just as the artisan baker would do with bread.

the extrusion

Once the dough has been mixed, it's then extruded through variously shaped dies. The early versions were developed at the end of the nineteenth century, allowing pasta makers to expand their offerings significantly. (Before that, noodles had to be hand-cut.) The dies are not unlike the cover plate on an old-fashioned meat grinder, but with a differently shaped die for each of the dozens of types of pasta being produced. Strands of spaghetti or other long pastas are pushed through small holes, then cut at the appropriate length by rotating blades. Short tubular pastas like penne start out by winding their way around a rod suspended from the top of the die, then exit through a smaller hole at the bottom. This narrowing forces the dough to come back to form the hollow tubes and twists we're all accustomed to. Notches in the holes can force the exiting dough to curve or curl, conjuring shapes like "elbow" macaroni.

Most modern commercial operations now extrude pasta dough through smooth Teflon-coated dies. The Teflon lasts a long time and allows for more rapid (and hence cost-reducing) extrusion, but it yields a pasta so slick that it seems to shine. When you dress it, your sauce is certain to run right off, leaving a bunch of nearly naked noodles lying atop an unappealing pool of liquid.

The best dried pastas are those that are extruded through old-style dies made of bronze, what Italians refer to as *trafile di bronze*. An essential component of artisan pasta making, the bronze dies are themselves an artisan product. Although the first phases of their production are now done by machine, the dies must be

checked, adjusted, and finished by hand in order to produce near-perfect pasta. Bronze is a soft metal, meaning the life of the dies is shorter, the extrusion is slower, and replacement costs are higher compared with commercial equipment. But the beauty of these old-fashioned forms is that they produce pasta with a coarser, more porous surface—the seemingly sea-washed roughness you feel when you hold it in your hand. Yet aesthetics is not the only issue. The little pits in the pasta embrace the sauce with open arms.

Take note, too, that the speed of extrusion can also affect quality. In pasta making, as on the highway, speed kills; in this case, it can cause unwanted heat, and hence damage to both texture and flavor. Those who take the extrusion process at a more leisurely pace protect the natural glutens in the dough, which in turn ensures that the pasta's all-important texture is preserved during cooking.

the drying

The drying takes the moisture content of the fresh dough down to less than half of its original 25 percent, giving packaged pasta its long shelf life and arguably making it one of mankind's ul-

timate convenience foods. Up until the beginning of the twentieth century, all Italian pasta was dried in the sun, often for up to a week, to reach the desired level of desiccation. Pasta makers, it was said, had to be as good at reading the weather as are fishermen or farmers. Sadly, in these days of air pollution and depleted ozone layers, sun-drying noodles is no longer an option, but fortunately for food lovers, pasta-drying machines were invented around 1900.

Faster-moving, more cost-conscious factories use high heat to dry the pasta in a mere matter of hours. The problem with this speed-dried stuff is that the excessive heat essentially bakes the pasta; the finished noodles are often brittle and easily broken, and many of the subtleties of the grain may be lost.

Smaller, artisan *pastaii* work at much lower temperatures than their industrial counterparts, taking as long as twenty-four, thirty-six, forty-eight, even fifty-plus hours to dry their pasta. This type of drying takes place in very warm (but never hot), humid environments in which moisture can be reduced slowly, without damaging the texture of the finished product. This slow, gentle drying preserves the noodle's natural moisture, wrapping it inside its rough exterior surface.

While the production of artisan dried pasta may seem straightforward in theory, it is difficult to do well. Machines may do the actual extrusion, but the human element remains essential. Each pasta maker has a "recipe" for drying, and each seems certain that his technique is the best. Watching the pasta production at Martelli, an artisan pasta producer in Tuscany, I noticed that every so often Dino Martelli would grab a piece and pop it—raw—into his mouth.

"Are you checking the pasta?" I inquired uncertainly.

"Absolutely!" he answered adamantly, as if I should have known that. "We check the pasta by taste and by feel all the time." Like cheesemaking or bread baking, traditional pasta production remains a craft, not a science.

a visit to the mecca of *maccheroni*, martelli pasta

While I have enormous respect and appreciation for all of the traditional pasta makers I list in this guide, the truth is that if I had only one pasta to put in my pot for life, I'd unhesitatingly opt for Martelli.

To find the Martellis and see their pasta making in person, you have to travel to the classic hill town of Lari in eastern Tuscany, about fifteen miles inland from the city of Pisa. The Martellis live and make their marvelous *maccheroni* at 3 Via San Martino, which has been a pasta factory since the 1870s. The Martellis took over in 1926, when the father and uncle of Dino and Mario Martelli bought the place, after working there for years as hourly employees.

The Martellis long ago outgrew the space, but, driven by their commitment to the town and to tradition, they figured out a way to make it function effectively. The actual pasta making and initial drying take place on the main floor. The mixing of the dough begins on a small landing, halfway up a narrow stairway, in a steel hopper into which golden semolina is fed. Head the rest of the way up the stairs, turn left, pass through a glass doorway, and you run into a wall of seemingly solid humidity. If you're wearing glasses, they'll fog up immediately. You're now

in a cramped hallway, lined on either side with ancient-looking, wood-framed, glass doors. Behind each door are tin-lined drying rooms, each filled with racks of moist pieces of still fresh pasta. Go back down the stairs, then head outside and straight across the street into the Martelli annex, where the pasta is hand-packed into its bright, sunny yellow bags with the original hand-lettered spaghetti loops spelling out the family moniker.

Every bag of pasta reads: *prodotti dalla famiglia Martelli*—"products of the Martelli family." And that's exactly what they are. All the employees are Martellis: the two brothers, their respective wives, and their six collective children.

The selection of Martelli pasta shapes and sizes is small. The family makes only the same four simple pasta shapes that their father and uncle started out with seventy-five years ago: thick spaghetti, thinner spaghettini, ridged *maccheroni,* and penne.

The Martellis' story is a textbook case illustrating commitment to pasta quality. They use the hardest durum wheat flour; they call all the way to Canada to find the firmness they're looking for. The grain is brought intact to a local spot for milling in order to protect its fragile flavor. Mixing and extrusion are executed slowly and at low temperatures. Drying is slow, also at low temperatures —the process takes place over fifty hours, at about 65 degrees Fahrenheit. In deference to the tricky nature of the drying, someone from the family goes upstairs to the drying rooms every five or six hours. "We have to check it even on Sundays and holidays. We really have to be weathermen," said Dino Martelli. "We have to watch the weather and adjust the drying according to its changes."

Although machines are part of the process, Martelli remains essentially a hand-crafted pasta. While the modern world pushes toward increased efficiency, the Martellis steadfastly maintain their ties to tradition. Quality—of pasta and of life—definitely takes precedence over expansion or growth. "What we make in one year, Barilla [Italy's biggest and best-known pasta producer] makes in one hour," the Martellis told me more than once, always with a smile. "With industrial machinery," Chiara Martelli, a member of the up-and-coming third generation, said, "one person alone can make ten thousand pounds of pasta in an hour. Here, with the whole family working together, we make two thousand pounds in a day."

Instead of worrying about competitors, the Martellis focus on maintaining the integrity of their own product. On my most recent visit, we were watching the extrusion of quill-shaped penne, talking about how the machines cut it. When one "tube" became dislodged, the pasta started running too long. Valentina, another of the Martelli daughters, pointed

out that they looked like . . . well, actually, she couldn't recall the name. "Dino," she yelled over to her father, her voice rising, "what's the name of those long tubes of pasta?" "Ziti?" he answered. "*Sì*, ziti," she said. Small town, small *pastificio*, small world. Only a Martelli family member—one who's eaten the same four Martelli shapes for most of her life—would have a hard time remembering ziti, one of the most common pasta cuts in Italy. There are no ziti in Lari.

mangia martelli

The whole Martelli enterprise could easily be written off by skeptics as an overly romantic relic of days gone by. Perhaps the best endorsement for Martelli came from its competitors. Granted, there are only a handful of small, artisan pasta makers still around. But when I asked those I've met, "Which pasta would you serve your family if you couldn't serve your own?" they all gave the same answer: "Martelli."

To me—I'm both a traditionalist and an optimist—Martelli is a big part of the future of food, at least the one I'm working toward. A future that's respectful of tradition, but also open to new ideas and innovations. One in which people are committed both to hard work and to enjoying the little things in life, where serious attention is paid to the details that contribute to better quality and more flavor in our food. A bowlful of Martelli spaghetti on the table is my idea of value, a small price to pay for such enjoyable eating. You can keep the Rolls-Royce and the million-dollar condo. For me, eating Martelli is the good life.

other good brands of dried pasta

CAVALIERI Down in the town of Lecce, in the region of Puglia, the heel of the Italian boot, Benedetto Cavalieri continues to craft exceptional pasta as his family has done since early in the twentieth century. The Cavalieris use primarily old varieties of low-yielding, full-flavored hard durum wheat grown in the surrounding hills. On the package, Cavalieri appropriately shares credit for the quality of his pasta with "the farmer and the miller." Without great wheat, the pasta maker is helpless, and Cavalieri uses a different blend of grains and a different dough for each cut of pasta that he makes.

The mixing is done in a six-foot square hopper mounted on a metal platform. A boundlessly energetic man whose enthusiasm remains undimmed even after thirty years of pasta making, Cavalieri insists on using room-temperature water, to protect the character of the wheat. As at the Martelli pasta factory, the mixing proceeds at a fairly leisurely pace, and the extrusion is done through old-fashioned bronze dies.

The short shapes of newly made pasta are placed into eight-foot-high wooden drying cabinets built in the 1930s. The family has a different dryer for each shape and size. The antique equipment lends a cultured, well-crafted air to the operation. But the effect is practical as well as pretty: good ventilation and very slow drying are essential, and the wood allows that.

Cavalieri takes his time with the drying: thirty-six hours for the short cuts, and just under two very deliberate days for the longer shapes. The drying is done at about 100 degrees Fahrenheit, roughly half the temperature employed by speed-oriented industrial pasta makers. The key, Cavalieri explains, gesturing with his hands, is "not to shock the pasta," to protect the integrity of its nutrition, texture, and flavor.

I love the label as much as I do the product. A bold blue background with white lettering, it's the same one that was first designed for the family in 1918. As with Martelli, when you drop this pasta into boiling water, you'll be struck by the wheaty aroma that rises from the pot.

LATINI Latini is a very good brand of artisan pasta from the Marche region along Italy's east coast. It's not my top choice, but it's the favorite of many in the food world, including the Italian cooking expert Faith Willinger. Carlo and Carla Latini grow much of their own wheat and stick to slow, gentle kneading, extruding through bronze dies, and slow drying. The Latini farm has been in Carlo's family for four generations (since 1888), and he's passionate about growing the best possible durum wheat for pasta. Last I knew, Latini was growing nearly a hundred different types of wheat.

Of particular note is the Latini Senatore Cappelli spaghetti, made from an antique variety of wheat that Carlo has helped to revive. It's a low-yielding, high-flavor varietal that has a fine fragrance when it hits the pot. The Latinis' long-term goal is to match each pasta shape to a variety of wheat. I'm also particularly fond of the Latini fusilli.

RUSTICHELLA Rustichella, from Abruzzo, uses only bronze dies and allows nearly two days for drying. The essence of the craft comes through in the pasta—the flavor and texture are superb. Of the dozens of unusual shapes and sizes, I've come to love the fettuccine, which is by far the best I've ever had. Rustichella linguine is a close second, but you won't go wrong with any of its pastas. Its egg pasta is especially good.

different cuts for different cooks: a guide to pasta shapes

I once asked a pasta maker which cuts he would recommend for soup. His immediate answer: "Which kind of soup?" A recent survey of Italian pastas counted something like five hundred cuts. Italians take their shape selection pretty seriously. Here's a quick guide to matching cuts with appropriate sauces:

- Generally, long, thick styles like spaghetti are associated with strong-flavored sauces: olive oil and garlic, tomato, cheese. Long, hollow noodles like bucatini or pici might be paired with spicy sauces. Long, thin pastas like linguine or even angel hair would marry well with more delicate sauces, often those made with seafood.

- Short, hollow shapes like penne or macaroni are meant for meat or vegetable sauces; solid bits and pieces of the sauce will collect inside the tubes, integrating pasta and sauce. Very short pastas are a good match for sauces with dried peas, lentils, or beans. Flat pastas like farfalle (bow ties) are a good match for cream or cheese-based sauces.

- Tiny, short shapes are ideal for soup. The general guideline: the lighter the soup, the smaller the pasta. For broth, go with shapes like anellini, stellini, acini, or orzo. Chunkier thick soups need bigger shapes, such as tubetti, ditalini, or maybe even macaroni. For all soups, add the pasta at the end so it won't overcook.

Acini di pepe "Peppercorn" pasta, well suited for broth.

Anellini Tiny pasta rings for soup.

Cannelloni Rectangles of pasta wrapped around assorted fillings and then baked.

Capellini Very thin angel hair. Lidia Bastianich, the superb chef-owner of Felidia in New York, gave me this tip: "Take them out when they're still almost stiff, drain them, add a bit of oil, toss, and then finish them for a minute in the sauce. Otherwise they turn into mush."

Casarecci A typical pasta of Puglia. The name, meaning "home style," refers to two-inch-long thin twists.

Conchiglie Pasta shells, well suited to sauces made with meat and/or cut vegetables.

Corzetti A specialty of Liguria, these pasta shapes look like stamped coins from ancient times.

Ditalini Little thimbles, good for vegetable soups.

Farfalle Butterflies, or bow ties, very nice with cream sauces.

Fedelini Another long, thin shape. The name is from *fedele,* meaning "faithful," or *filo,* meaning "thread" or "wire."

Fettuccine A *fettuccia* is a tape or a ribbon. Narrower than the northern tagliatelle.

Fregola A unique Sardinian pasta made from a dough of coarsely ground semolina that is rubbed into small round balls (about the size of Israeli couscous). It's lightly toasted, so it has an interesting nutty flavor. In Sardinia, it's used in soups and stews (often with clams), as well as baked with tomato sauce.

Fusilli Although the name is common, the cut seems to be different in every area of Italy. Some are long, curly corkscrews; others are

half-inch-long pig-tail twists. Good for cream sauces.

Lasagne Broad, flat rectangles.

Lasagnotte Wide ribbons that are typical of Puglia. The Pugliese break them into two- to three-inch pieces for cooking, then serve them with a strong sauce, like rabbit sauce, or a vegetable sauce of onions, carrots, tomatoes, and fresh ricotta.

Linguine Flat spaghetti. The name means "little tongues." A classic with clam sauce.

Lumache "Snails," good for sauces with moderately sized pieces of meat or vegetables. The snail shape collects the sauce.

Maccheroni About two-inch-long hollow pastas. In the United States the name "macaroni" has come to mean all pasta. In seventeenth-century London, the term "macaroni" was used to refer to the avant-garde, who regularly indulged in pasta as well as other imported luxury foods. Over time, the term came into use as slang for anything of exaggerated elegance, like the feather in Yankee Doodle's cap.

Malloreddus Half-inch-long ridged Sardinian pastas that look a bit like small worms. Also known on the island as "gnocchi," though they are nothing like actual gnocchi.

Orecchiette "Little ears," the most typical of all Pugliese pastas.

Orecchiette Maritate "Married" orecchiette. A Pugliese blend of casarecci (long and thin) and orecchiette (round), which consummate their "marriage" in the pot when you cook them together.

Orzo "Barley seeds," used for soups or pasta salads.

egg pasta

For delicate dishes, dried pastas made with egg, not water, are generally used. And as with all pasta, making a good one is a craft, not a science, and relies on the skill of the pasta maker, the selection of flours, and the care exercised in the drying.

I like egg pastas with simple sauces. Butter and cheese sauce is my favorite. Or butter and cheese with toasted nuts (see page 250). Browned butter and fried sage leaves with some freshly grated Parmigiano-Reggiano make a great sauce, as do fresh ricotta and a good dose of a delicate olive oil. So too does a simple sauce of saffron, sautéed onion, a small amount of chicken broth, and maybe some little bits of leftover lamb or chicken.

al dente

America's leading artisan egg pasta, Al Dente, has been made in the Ann Arbor area by Monique and Dennis Deschaine for over twenty years. Monique learned her technique from none other than Marcella Hazan, as good a teacher as one could ask for. Following Hazan's recommendations, Monique swears by a blend of semolina and extra-fancy durum flour that she mixes with fresh eggs. She prefers that her pasta not be exceptionally eggy, so it's less intense than comparable Italian offerings. She insists on "sheeting," or rolling out the pasta (the alternative is extrusion, or pressing out the dough, which works well for dried pasta but toughens the texture of tender egg noodles). Sheeting the dough makes the finished fettuccine as close to homemade as possible. As a result, Al Dente noodles are very light and delicate and cook up in a mere two to three minutes. Al Dente makes many fine flavored noodles — wild mushroom and spicy sesame are my favorites — but I'm still partial to the original recipe for the egg fettuccine. The spinach noodles are also noteworthy, made exclusively with fresh spinach.

maccheroncini di campofilone

If you like a lot of egg in your egg pasta, this is the way to go. A third-generation, family-owned producer of pasta since the 1930s, Maccheroncini di Campofilone is probably Italy's premier packaged egg pasta. The women of the town of Campofilone in the Marche region have long been known for their pasta-making skills. They too use only fresh eggs, but they're at the other end of the egg spectrum from Al Dente — the Campofilone pasta is very rich in eggs, very golden, almost orange in color.

Paglia e Fieno "Straw and hay," used to denote green (spinach) and yellow (egg) noodles mixed together. Good with cream or tomato sauces.

Pappardelle Broad egg noodles that are big with game meats, like hare or wild boar.

Penne Macaroni cut like quills, or pens. Good with meat, cream, and vegetable sauces.

Pezzoccheri Buckwheat pasta from the Valtellina in the north of Lombardy. Traditionally a winter dish, served with cabbage, potatoes, and garlic, all mixed together and baked with cheese.

Quadrucci Tiny pasta squares, used primarily for soups.

Sagne Long Pugliese pasta, shaped like ribbons wrapped around a rod or candle.

Spaghetti The most famous pasta. The name comes from *spago,* meaning "string" or "cord"; spaghetti means "little strings." Good with tomato and olive oil–based sauces.

Spaghettini Thin spaghetti.

Spaghettoni Very thick spaghetti that is made into two-foot-long strands that are usually broken up before cooking. Typically served in Puglia with olive oil and fresh garlic.

Stellini "Little stars," used in broth.

Tagliatelle The name is from *tagliare,* meaning "to cut." The Bolognese serve it with prosciutto and other meat sauces.

Trofie Small twists of pasta, a bit like two-inch pieces of twine folded in half, then gently (never tightly) twisted. The preferred Ligurian pasta for pesto.

Vermicelli Literally "little worms," they are essentially like spaghetti or spaghettini.

Ziti Neapolitan macaroni. *Ziti* means "groom," and this pasta is typically served in Naples as a first course at weddings.

simple steps to proper pasta cooking

Proper cooking technique is as imperative as proper purchasing of the raw materials. To cook the best dried pastas:

1. Bring lots of cold water to a boil. The emphasis is on lots. You want to have plenty of room for the pasta to move around in the pot, reducing the risk of sticking, and plenty of water for the dried noodles to absorb. Using enough water also ensures that the pasta won't cool off your cooking liquid. Start with at least a gallon, even for only a small portion of pasta. For a pound of dried pasta, give yourself a good 6 to 7 quarts of water.

2. When the water has come to a rapid boil, add a tablespoon or two of sea salt, which unlocks the flavor of the grain.

3. Add the pasta to the rapidly boiling salted water. When I was a kid, we always broke up long cuts of pasta into more manageable lengths, but Italians almost never do (though

two bonus tips
on cooking pasta,
from a pro

Faith Willinger, a woman who's done as much as anyone to advance the cause of great Italian food, shared these tips with me.

1. Add a touch of the pasta cooking water to your sauce. The pasta water is filled with the natural starch from the pasta and will help to bind and thicken the sauce naturally.

2. Finish your pasta in the sauce. Instead of waiting until the pasta is al dente, remove it from the cooking liquid a minute or two early. Toss the slightly underdone pasta with the simmering sauce, then cook for another minute or two, stirring regularly to avoid sticking. Since the pasta is still absorbing moisture, it will pull in the sauce (and hence its flavors). The result is a much better integration of pasta and sauce.

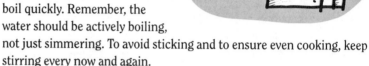

there are regional exceptions to this rule). Simply add the pasta as is, then stir well to make sure the strands don't stick to one another or to the bottom of the pot.

4. If you've got a good amount of water and a high source of heat, your cooking water should come back to the boil quickly. Remember, the water should be actively boiling, not just simmering. To avoid sticking and to ensure even cooking, keep stirring every now and again.

5. Test the pasta. The better the quality of the pasta, the more reason not to overcook it. Properly cooked pasta is done when it is al dente, tender on the outside, slightly firm on the inside. Generally, better-quality pastas are a bit more forgiving to the careless cook. Inferior products can go from raw to ridiculously overcooked in just a couple of minutes. My experience is that the top pastas are best when they're nicely firm (not raw, mind you) in the middle. Take note that in general, Italians prefer their pasta far firmer than we do in the United States.

Pastas made from harder wheat will take longer to cook than soft-wheat pastas. Similarly, those that were dried slowly will usually require more cooking time than those dried quickly and at higher heat. Don't adhere blindly to cooking times on packages. Depending on the quantity of water, the particular batch of pasta, and the strength of the heat source, actual cooking times will vary. So keep taking out a piece or two of pasta and tasting to check for doneness.

6. As soon as the pasta is done, get it out of the cooking water as quickly as possible. Don't dally. Most American cooks drain through a colander. Make sure your sink and drain are free of unwanted debris, and if your drain is slow, be ready to lift the colander out of the sink quickly. Alternatively, Italians use pasta tongs, which help keep long pastas from tangling. Pasta pots that come with colander inserts offer the best of both worlds, allowing you to remove the pasta all at once while avoiding tangling.

If you're serving the pasta hot, never, never rinse it with water. Instead, moving as quickly as possible, transfer the pasta to prewarmed plates or bowls, and dress with sauce. Serve ASAP—the sooner you get the plates to the table, the better.

Note: Remember that portions in Italy—where pasta is often followed by a main course of meat or fish—are smaller than those we've become accustomed to in the States. An Italian serving starts with about two ounces of dried pasta; an American main course would call for three to four ounces.

pugliese orecchiette and broccoli rabe

O recchiette is the prestigious pasta of Puglia, the heel of the Italian boot. The name means "little ears," and the indentations in the pasta catch the sauce. The rim of the orecchiette, a bit thicker than the depressed center, stays firm when you cook it, creating an interesting textural contrast as you eat.

The traditional Pugliese way to eat orecchiette is with broccoli rabe, also known as rapini, in a simple sauce seasoned with hot peppers and anchovies. It has become one of my favorite meals.

2 tablespoons extra virgin olive oil, plus more to taste

1 small onion, finely chopped (about ½ cup)

2 garlic cloves, minced

1 serrano chile pepper, chopped, or hot red pepper flakes, preferably Marash (see page 58), to taste, plus more for serving

3 anchovy fillets

Coarse sea salt to taste

1 pound orecchiette

1 small bunch broccoli rabe or dandelion greens (4 ounces without tough stems), coarsely chopped

Freshly grated Pecorino Romano cheese

Freshly ground black pepper to taste

Fresh ricotta cheese, for serving

Bring a large pot of water to a boil. Meanwhile, in another large skillet, heat the olive oil over medium-high heat. Add the onion and garlic and sauté until soft, 3 to 4 minutes. Add the serrano pepper or pepper flakes and sauté, stirring for 2 to 3 minutes.

Add ¼ cup of hot water from the other pot and the anchovy fillets to the onion mixture. (They'll melt into the sauce, so there's no need to chop them.)

When the water in the first pot boils, add 1 to 2 tablespoons salt and the orecchiette, stir well, and cook until the pasta is almost al dente.

Meanwhile, add the broccoli rabe or dandelion greens to the onion mixture. Stir, add a pinch of salt and another ¼ cup of the pasta cooking water, cover, reduce the heat, and simmer until the pasta is done. Add more of the pasta cooking water, if necessary, to keep the greens "saucy."

Drain the pasta and add it to the greens. Stir and simmer for 2 minutes, or until well combined. Add a little more olive oil, some grated Pecorino Romano cheese, and black pepper. Serve in warm bowls with a dollop of ricotta cheese and additional hot pepper flakes on the side.

serves 4

pasta with anchovies and capers

This dish makes a great dinner if you like anchovies. The addition of dried currants adds a subtle sweetness. Because good spaghetti takes about 13 minutes to cook, you can probably finish the sauce while the pasta is cooking. Italians generally don't use cheese on pasta dishes that include fish, but if you're not holding an Italian passport, you can toss a little grated Parmigiano on top. Either way, it's excellent.

1	tablespoon capers, preferably packed in salt
1–2	tablespoons coarse sea salt to taste
½	pound spaghetti
1	tablespoon full-flavored extra virgin olive oil, plus more to taste
1	small onion, coarsely chopped (about ¾ cup)
2	garlic cloves, finely chopped
10	anchovy fillets
1	tablespoon dried currants
1	cup coarsely chopped dandelion greens, arugula, or Swiss chard
1	2-inch square of Parmigiano-Reggiano cheese rind (optional)
1	tablespoon pine nuts, toasted (see page 31)
½	teaspoon hot red pepper flakes, preferably Marash (see page 58)
	Freshly ground black pepper to taste
	Freshly grated Parmigiano-Reggiano cheese (optional)

If you're using salted capers, soak them in a bit of warm water for 20 to 30 minutes, changing the water halfway through. Drain the water, rinse the capers, and dry them on a paper towel.

Bring a large pot of water to a boil. Add the salt and the pasta; stir well. Cook until almost al dente.

Meanwhile, in a large skillet, heat the olive oil over medium heat. Add the onion and garlic and sauté until soft, about 3 to 4 minutes. Add 2 of the anchovy fillets and stir well. Add the currants and stir again. Add 3 tablespoons of the pasta cooking water, the greens, capers, and Parmigiano-Reggiano rind (if using) and stir well. Cook until the greens are slightly wilted. Add more pasta water if needed to keep the sauce properly soused.

Drain the pasta, add it to the pot with the sauce, and stir well.

Add the remaining 8 anchovies, the pine nuts, red pepper flakes, and a little more olive oil. Stir until the anchovies are heated through, being careful not to overcook and melt them.

Fish out the rind and serve in warm bowls with a generous grinding of black pepper on top and a little grated Parmigiano, if you like.

serves 2 as a main course or 4 as a side dish

linguine with arugula, olive oil, and hot peppers

This is the kind of fast food I like to eat. You can make the entire recipe, start to finish, in 15 minutes and have time to make a salad while it's cooking. Use more or less olive oil, as you wish. The more— and better—the oil, the better the pasta will taste.

Coarse sea salt to taste

1 pound top-quality linguine

¼ cup full-flavored extra virgin olive oil, plus more for serving

4 garlic cloves, peeled and halved

1 small onion, coarsely chopped (about ¾ cup)

Hot red pepper flakes, preferably Marash (see page 58), to taste, plus more for serving

1 pound fresh young arugula leaves, any large stems removed (if the leaves are large, tear them in half)

1 tablespoon pine nuts, lightly toasted (see page 31)

1 cup freshly grated Pecorino Romano cheese, plus more for serving

Freshly ground black pepper to taste

Bring a large pot of water to a boil. Add 1 to 2 tablespoons salt and the pasta, stir well, and cook until the pasta is almost al dente.

Meanwhile, make the sauce. In another large pot, heat the oil over medium heat. Add the garlic and sauté for 1 to 2 minutes, until softened. Add the onion and sauté for 3 to 4 minutes, or until soft. Add the pepper flakes and sauté for 1 to 2 minutes more. Discard the garlic.

Drain the pasta when it is almost al dente. Add the arugula leaves and pine nuts to the onion mixture and toss quickly so that the arugula wilts slightly. Add the drained pasta to the arugula mixture, add the grated cheese, and toss well.

Serve in warm bowls, finished with an additional ribbon of olive oil on top. Pass extra pepper flakes, grated Pecorino Romano, and salt and pepper at the table.

serves 4

fettuccine with fresh tuna, lemon, capers, and olives

Rolando Beramendi of Manicaretti Imports inspired this recipe. It's as comforting as tuna-noodle casserole and incredibly delicious. Sautéing the lemon slices with the skin on contributes to both the flavor and the texture of the dish. If you like, add an extra blessing of olive oil or *limonato* (lemon olive oil—see page 24) at the table.

- 2 tablespoons capers, preferably packed in salt
  Coarse sea salt
- 1 pound top-quality fettuccine, preferably Rustichella brand, or other pasta
- ½ cup extra virgin olive oil
- 2 garlic cloves, finely chopped
- 24 black olives (not canned), pitted and coarsely chopped
- 1 lemon, quartered and thinly sliced (if you can find a Meyer lemon, use it)
- 2 anchovy fillets (optional)
- 1 pound fresh tuna, cut into 1-inch cubes
- 3 tablespoons coarsely chopped Italian parsley, rinsed and squeezed dry
  Freshly ground black pepper to taste

If you're using salted capers, soak them in a bit of warm water for 20 to 30 minutes, changing the water halfway through. Drain the water, rinse the capers, and dry them on a paper towel.

Bring a large pot of water to a boil. Add salt and the pasta, stir well, and cook until the pasta is al dente.

Meanwhile, make the sauce. In a large skillet, heat the olive oil over medium-high heat. Add the garlic and sauté for 2 to 3 minutes, or until softened. Add the olives, lemon, capers, and anchovy fillets (if using), and sauté for 1 to 2 minutes. Add the tuna and sauté for 2 to 3 minutes more, until the fish is rare to medium-rare in the center; do not overcook.

When the pasta is al dente, drain and add it to the sauce. Add the parsley and salt and pepper to taste. Serve in warm bowls. serves 4

homemade tomato sauce

Although bottled tomato sauces abound on store shelves, it's pretty easy to make one from scratch. The key is the quality of the tomatoes and the olive oil. If tomatoes are in season, fresh is the way to go. During the off-season, I use canned, preferably the San Marzano variety.

(This sauce is versatile. You can use it on pasta or to cook Minchilli Meatballs on page 43.)

For times when you're in a hurry or don't feel like cooking, there are some good bottled tomato sauces on the market. My favorites among the Italian imports include Il Mongetto, Rustichella, and Torre Saracena. Rao's and Dave's Gourmet are two American brands that I've found to be consistently good.

variations

- Add ¼ cup chopped fresh basil at the very end of cooking.

- Fry 6 to 8 fresh sage leaves in olive oil until golden brown. Gently crumble the sage over the pasta just before serving.

- Add 6 ounces fresh goat cheese to the sauce.

- Add additional olive oil at will—the more, the better, to my taste.

- Add 2 ounces of good-quality balsamic vinegar.

> ¼ cup extra virgin olive oil
>
> 1 large onion, coarsely chopped (about 2 cups)
>
> 1 large carrot or 2 small carrots, coarsely chopped (about ¾ cup)
>
> 3 garlic cloves, finely chopped
>
> 5 large tomatoes, coarsely chopped (about 4 cups), or two 28-ounce cans whole tomatoes, drained, coarsely chopped
>
> 2 tablespoons tomato paste
>
> Coarse sea salt to taste
>
> Freshly ground black pepper to taste

In a large heavy skillet, heat the olive oil over medium-high heat. Sauté the onion and carrot for 2 to 3 minutes, reduce the heat to medium, cover and sweat the vegetables over medium heat for about 25 minutes, or until soft and golden. Add the garlic, stir well, cover, and sweat for 5 minutes more, until softened. Add the tomatoes and tomato paste. Bring to a boil, reduce the heat to medium-low, and simmer uncovered for about 10 minutes to blend the flavors.

Push the cooked sauce through a food mill or blend in a food processor and push through a sturdy small-holed strainer into a large bowl. Add salt and pepper to taste.

The sauce can be cooled and stored in the refrigerator for up to 1 week, or frozen for up to 3 months.

makes 3 to 4 cups, enough to serve 6 to 8

polenta

"In a slower world, ignorant of frenzy, polenta keeps time like a clock — it is a unique, golden dish, a refuge." ● Giovanni Arpino

In North America, polenta is little more than an asterisk to Italian cooking. Most Americans are familiar with it only from its relatively recent appearance in fried form on restaurant menus, and few feel particularly strongly one way or another about it. But for many Italians, polenta carries an emotional charge. For some, it is the height of good eating. Others associate it more with deep poverty and privation because it was for centuries the staple food of the poor.

Although corn arrived in Europe only after Columbus's first visit to the Western Hemisphere, the tradition of making porridges from flours of chickpea, chestnut, millet, and barley was established in early Roman times. Corn came to Italy in the beginning of the sixteenth century. Like the potato in Ireland, the new arrival was seen as a long-needed, low-cost way to feed the poor. In a surprisingly short time, polenta became the daily fare of common folk across much of the north, and it remained the mainstay of their diet through the early years of the twentieth century.

the best little polenta mill in italy

To see the pride that Italians take in polenta, you could do as I did a few years ago and visit the Marino mill in Piedmont, the area of Italy that starts in the north at the Alps and descends southward to the Riviera. Like the rest of northern Italy, the region has a three-hundred-year-old tradition of growing, drying, grinding, and cooking cornmeal. And the Marinos are carrying that tradition forward with enormous enthusiasm.

I can't say with certainty that the Marino family makes the best polenta in Italy—there are a handful of other small mills scattered around the country that may make similarly superb products. But I can tell you that the Marinos' cornmeal is so far superior to that of the commercial brands that it seems almost another product altogether. Despite its higher price, restaurateurs and locals alike line up to buy it, quite simply, they say, because it tastes so much better than any other polenta around.

The mill sits in the tiny town of Cossano Belbo, high in the Piedmont hills. It's near the truffle town of Alba, not far from coastal Liguria, the land of the Italian Riviera, and about an hour's drive down from Turin. On a cool, sunny autumn afternoon, I walked through the yard beside the mill with the men of the Marino family, hearing their history and that of polenta in their native Piedmont. I was hoping to hear a romantic story. Perhaps polenta making had been in the family for hundreds of years? Or maybe the Marinos were the first Italians to grind corn after Columbus's return voyage from America? But as it turns out, the Marinos are actually relatively new to polenta. A mere three generations—the youngest of which is only in his early teens—have worked the mill.

Felice Marino, the father and polenta patriarch, was born in 1922, and he's still active in the work of the mill. He grew up in a family of farmers, but he seemed fated to end up a miller. As a boy he worked as a day laborer, carrying grain to what is now the family mill. Later his sister married a miller. The older he got, the more he was drawn to milling. In 1955, at the age of thirty-three, Felice followed his heart, left the family farm, and bought out the ready-to-retire miller who'd employed him as a youth. At that time, he told me, there were nine other mills in the valley. Today his is the only one left.

As we walked, Felice's sons, Ferdinando and Flavio, enthusiastically explained the milling, answering questions, sharing stories, demonstrating the workings of each piece of equipment. That they have a passion for their work was obvious.

Like almost every other old millhouse I've ever visited, the Marinos' operation has a complex, almost comedic, spaghetti-like setup of old wooden gears, pipes, augers, wires, and widgets of various shapes and sizes. On the wall behind the stones is an assemblage of weathered wooden tools. The back half of the fifteen-foot-square space is taken up by a raised wooden platform on which sit two pairs of powerful granite millstones. The set on the left is for grinding wheat, the one on the right for cutting corn. Unlike those used to press olives, which stand on edge, the stones used for milling grain lie horizontally, one atop the other. Each is about ten inches thick and roughly four feet across. The stones spin steadily if slowly by modern standards, at about 150 revolutions per minute, compared with the 600 or so of the more commercial mills. Today the mill is powered by electricity, but it was water-powered up until the 1950s. Hanging above the spinning stones is a wooden spout that flows out from a hopper holding the dried corn. As the spout vibrates, corn kernels drop into the vortex of the moving millstones. A steady stream of new yellow polenta pours from another spout below the stones. A hand-carved, well-worn wooden "basket" catches the milled grain as it tumbles out.

born to mill

The milling system the Marinos use is known as *palmenti.* The bottom stone stays still while the top one spins. Put your palms together parallel to the floor, then rotate the top hand slowly and you'll get the idea. The bottom stone has a pattern of deeper grooves radiating from its center at off-angles, interwoven, in turn, with a tapestry of similar, but narrower slots. The two stones never touch but are close enough to cut—not grind—the dried kernels as they catch in the grooves. The thinner grooves then grind the

polenta as finely as needed. The centermost ring of the stones is known as the *cuore,* or "heart." The narrower grooves guide the newly ground corn toward the outer edge of the stones, where it falls into the wooden frame and then out the spout into baskets below. At the same time, the deeper canals etched into the stone allow outside air to pass between the wheels, protecting the grain from overheating.

feelin' groovy

To ensure effective operation, the stones must be removed from their housing a couple of times a month (after fifteen to twenty tons of corn have been milled) so that their channels can be checked, then recut as needed. American millers call this procedure "dressing the stones." After extricating the wheels, the brothers run a board with natural red pigment over them to mark the spots where the surface has been ground down. They then set to work with an old wood-handled hammer and a chisel to get the grooves back into shape. The hammering is hardly heavy-handed; it takes skill and a delicate touch. Different hammers are used to chisel out different groove depths. Most of the red pigment must be removed before the stones are again ready for use.

The Marinos proudly—and repeatedly—pointed to a stack of four extra sets of stones sitting off to the side of the yard. Since the stones can last decades, such a stockpile signals a miller's commitment to the future.

meal in the mill: polenta four ways

The highlight of my visit was sitting at the table with three generations of Marinos to eat their freshly ground polenta. Their family dynamic was similar to that of every big family dinner I can remember from my own childhood. The women kept mostly to the kitchen, cooking, conversing, and stirring, emerging occasionally to offer up another course and check the group's progress on the last. Meanwhile, the Marino men and the guests sat at the table, where almost everyone seemed to talk at the same time. The food, on the other hand, bore no resemblance to what I grew up on.

While we finished up the cold antipasti, the polenta dishes started to appear. First came *polenta fritta,* made by cutting cooked, cooled polenta into thin rectangles, coating them with additional, uncooked polenta, and then, finally, frying them in olive oil until they were the color and texture of crisp French fries. The polenta pieces were truly golden, both inside and out, a shade so vibrant I'd come to expect it only in advertising. "When you fry our polenta," said Flavio proudly, "it gets more yellow."

Lightly crisp and slightly chewy on the outside from the coating of raw cornmeal, the slices were tender and soft on the inside. The polenta pieces tasted so sweet I asked if there was sugar in the mix. "No!" came the quick reply. "Just the polenta."

The second course came out of the kitchen on a large white oval platter, fresh from the oven: circles of cornmeal cut, again, from sheets of cooked, then cooled polenta quickly pan-fried in olive oil, then topped with a creamy sauce of salt cod and spices.

Next came a big, beautiful white bowl of just cooked coarse polenta. It was incredibly sweet, with an intense corn flavor and the texture of thick, homemade mashed potatoes. Amazed at how good it was, I asked one of the Mrs. Marinos what was in it. "Polenta," she said matter-of-factly. I sat quietly for a minute before she realized I was looking for a little more information. "The polenta," she repeated, " . . . with water, and salt." I was stunned by just how good something so simple could taste. Accompanying the polenta was something I didn't expect to find in landlocked Piedmont: a tomato sauce, laced with tuna, coarsely chopped hard-cooked eggs, garlic, and lots of olive oil.

Moments later, another big white bowl arrived, this one filled with steaming hot, finely ground polenta. Texturally, it was slightly softer and a bit moister than the coarse. The sauce was similar to the previous one, but with anchovies instead of tuna and a higher dose of hot pepper and chopped garlic.

In every case the fullness of the corn flavor in the polenta was astounding.

keys to incomparable polenta

There are enormous differences in the quality of artisan polenta, made from top-quality corn in small stone mills, and the emasculated, industrial cornmeals that sit on supermarket shelves. The flavor of the Marino polenta—and that of any traditional polenta—is attributable to four factors.

1. the quality of the corn

Corn is to polenta what milk is to a cheesemaker. Milling merely unlocks the flavor; even the most skillful stone work can't make mediocre, mass-market maize taste any better than it is.

With the quality of the cornmeal in mind, the Marinos grind only full-flavored old varieties, primarily one known as Otto File. The ear has only eight rows of very large—huge compared with what we're used to seeing in the United States—well-rounded kernels. They're a deep gold, much darker and more intensely colored than anything I've seen on the home market, other than the multicolored "Indian corn" hung for decoration at Thanksgiving.

Although it's more difficult to grow, Otto File is far more flavorful than standard commercial corn. It's also more expensive to grow than more common seed varieties. Yields are low and each stalk offers up only a single ear. It must be planted earlier than more modern varieties in order to avoid cross-pollination. And it must also be left longer on the stalks in order to enhance its natural sweetness; the Marinos don't harvest it until late September or early October.

2. proper drying

The Marinos prefer to dry the corn in the sun, although if it's raining heavily at harvest time, they will resort to a mechanical dryer. The key is to dry the corn slowly to protect its natural flavor. Industrial operators speed the process by using high-heat dryers, but by doing so they damage flavor.

3. the milling

Without question, the vision and skill of the miller make a huge difference in the quality and flavor of cornmeal. Today 99 percent of it is industrially milled, produced first for price, then consistency, but certainly not flavor. The key for the polenta lover is to find a mill that's trying to grind great-tasting meal. There aren't that many left, but they are out there.

One thing that makes the Marinos' polenta so good is that they leave in the germ. Since it holds over three quarters of the kernel's natural oil, it really does enhance flavor. Unfortunately, it also cuts shelf life; germ-retaining polenta is a surprisingly perishable product. For that reason, industrial mills remove it.

4. freshness and storage

Freshness and proper storage are huge contributors to the quality of any good ground cornmeal you buy. On this subject, the Marinos are tenaciously adamant that their polenta must be kept cool in storage to maintain its flavor. "Fifty to sixty degrees Fahrenheit," they say with the seriousness of a doctor dispensing medical advice to the mother of a sick child.

And if it gets warmer? "Catastrophe!" fires back Ferdinando Marino. "It gets bitter. And it gets bugs."

Properly refrigerated or frozen, the polenta can keep for six months. But the point is to eat it when it's freshest and most flavorful.

Unfortunately, as far as I know there's no way to tell from a polenta label whether or not the germ has been removed. If you're buying meal that's freshly ground at the mill, it's likely still going to have the germ intact and be of very high quality. But packaged polenta sitting for weeks on end on warm shop shelves instead of in a cooler or freezer is almost assured to be of lesser quality.

OTHER GOOD POLENTA BRANDS Aside from the Marino polenta, two other top-quality Italian brands available in the United States are Moretti and Nicoli. Another very good artisan polenta from Piedmont is that of the Mulino Sobrino. In North America, South Carolina's Anson Mills makes a very good organic polenta.

cooking polenta

Getting a consensus on polenta preparation from Italians would be akin to getting southerners to agree on the optimal way to make barbecue. Suffice it to say that debating polenta technique is not for the faint of heart.

The traditional technique is to add a thin but steady stream of dry polenta to boiling water, stirring continuously at the outset to avoid lumping, then to cook and stir for an hour or more until it's done. At best the process can be tricky, at worst you wind up with an annoyingly large number of unpleasant little lumps. In her book *In Nonna's Kitchen,* the Italian cooking expert Carol Field suggests mixing the meal with cool water. I'm with Carol.

proper proportions

Ultimately, the proportion of water to polenta is partially a function of how you like your finished dish. The thicker you want it, the less water you should use. At two to one, you'll get a very firm polenta, sort of the texture of dry mashed potatoes. It's best for meat sauces and for any recipe in which you want to cool the polenta and slice it for later frying. Less dense but still fairly firm would be a ratio of roughly four parts to one, which is the one I use most often. This ratio might be more appropriate when you're melting cheese into the polenta, for tomato sauces, and also for use in *pasticciata,* in which the polenta is layered with sauce and cheese—like lasagna—and then baked. A looser polenta could result from a six-to-one ratio and would often be served with seafood. At eight to one, the polenta will be very soft, fairly liquid, and it would make a good, soft breakfast porridge.

cooking time

The one thing almost everyone seems to agree on about polenta is that longer cooking is better. For proper polenta, the cooking time can't be brief; it's at least thirty minutes, but really more like an hour or two. Undercooked polenta can taste raw or bitter, with an unpleasant, somewhat gritty texture. A few extra minutes on the heat will never hurt; I like to put the polenta on plenty early and let it simmer for hours to get the best texture and flavor possible.

choice of pot

Old-time Italians would do the cooking in a *paiolo,* a copper pot used specially for polenta. The copper conducts the heat well. Many cooks prefer cast iron; when you cook the polenta slowly, it develops a bottom crust. The crust is considered a special treat by many Italians, in the same way that Spaniards seek out the special

cutting the cornmeal: knives, spoons, and strings

Italians have all sorts of superstitions about how to handle polenta during the cooking and cutting (if the polenta is very firm and will be sliced rather than spooned up to serve). The standard wisdom is never to use metal. Stirring should be done with a wooden spoon. Slicing cooked and cooled polenta should be done with a string, never with a knife. "But never, ever use a black string," one Venetian warned me.

"Why not?" I wondered.

He paused, looked me straight in the eye, and said with gravity, "It will bring you very bad luck."

crisp grains of rice (called the *socarrat* —see page 84) that stick to the bottom of the pan in a traditional paella.

stirring

It doesn't take a Ph.D. to figure out that the amount of stirring required to make a proper polenta has probably prevented it from attaining a popularity equal to that of pasta. Even I have to admit that 60—not to mention 90 to 120—minutes of steady stirring is hard to come by in our hurried American society.

But you can also stir only occasionally, which works just fine. Italians address the issue by not stirring with any force at the bottom of the pot and allowing a crust to form, which protects the rest of the polenta, as a rind would a traditional cheese. Other people handle the stirring issue by keeping the polenta pot on the stove only long enough for the mixture to thicken. They then shift it to the oven for the final forty or fifty minutes of cooking.

I will warn you away from stirring with a whisk—the polenta gets caught in the whip, leading to lumps. And whatever sort of spoon you use, make sure it has a long handle, to avoid being splattered and burned by bubbling bits of hot cornmeal.

Lastly, if you're cooking your polenta on the stove and don't plan to stir often, put a cover over the pot to prevent the formation of an undesirable skin on top.

serving

You can serve pretty much anything you like with a bowl of hot, freshly cooked polenta: heavier sauces in colder months, lighter fare in the

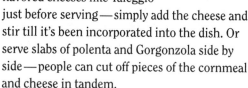

spring. Light tomato sauces are terrific in late summer and early autumn when the tomatoes are at their best. Wild mushrooms go well with polenta too. In winter, it's delicious with meat sauces or slices of salami. Any time of the year, a bowl of polenta is excellent with almost any fresh soft cheese crumbled on top. You can stir in full-flavored cheeses like Taleggio just before serving—simply add the cheese and stir till it's been incorporated into the dish. Or serve slabs of polenta and Gorgonzola side by side—people can cut off pieces of the cornmeal and cheese in tandem.

Although it's certainly not what Italians would have put out a hundred years ago to impress guests, today—when time may be the most precious gift of all—a big pot of great polenta can be something really special. And think how impressed your guests will be that you cared enough to stir for so long.

basic polenta

H ere is the basic recipe for polenta. Once you've cooked it, you can eat it a thousand different ways, with everything from butter, salt, and pepper to complex sauces, such as Piedmontese Spicy Anchovy and Tomato Sauce (page 155). The longer you cook the polenta, the better it's likely to be.

     8 cups water
 1½ teaspoons coarse sea salt
     2 cups uncooked polenta

In a large heavy pot, heat the water over medium-high heat. Add the salt and stir well. Just before the water begins to boil, slowly add the polenta, stirring almost constantly with a wooden spoon, to form a thick, smooth porridge. Bring to a boil, then reduce the heat to low. Simmer, stirring frequently for at least 30 minutes, adding more water if needed. When the polenta is ready, it should be thick and smooth, with no trace of grittiness. The longer you cook it, the better it will be. Taste it to check for salt and doneness.

Serve the polenta in warm bowls.   serves 4

polenta fritta
fried polenta

This great little appetizer is the sort of thing that few Americans ever think of making but are likely to love. These rectangles of cooked polenta have an additional jacket of raw polenta that gets crispy and golden as it cooks. If you're having a casual dinner, you can let your guests eat them with their fingers right in the kitchen as soon as they've cooled enough to handle.

Basic Polenta (page 154), cooled in the refrigerator in a
9-x-13-inch pan until firm, preferably overnight
½ cup uncooked polenta for dredging
3–4 tablespoons extra virgin olive oil
Coarse sea salt to taste

Slice the cold polenta into 20 squares. Dredge the squares in the uncooked polenta until evenly coated.

In a large heavy skillet, heat 1 tablespoon of the olive oil over medium heat. When the oil is hot (don't let it smoke), place several polenta squares in the skillet, but don't overcrowd it. Fry until golden brown, 4 to 5 minutes per side. Remove from the skillet and drain on paper towels. Add more oil to the skillet if needed, then repeat with the remaining polenta rectangles. Serve hot, sprinkled with salt to taste.

serves 4

piedmontese spicy anchovy and tomato sauce

The Marinos serve this traditional sauce over polenta, and it's excellent on pasta as well. You can adjust the levels of garlic, hot pepper, and olive oil to your preference.

- 2 tablespoons extra virgin olive oil, preferably Ligurian, plus more for serving (optional)
- 1 small onion, finely chopped (about ¾ cup)
- 1½ teaspoons hot red pepper flakes, preferably Marash (see page 58), plus more if needed
- 2 ounces anchovies (about 18 fillets)
- 3 garlic cloves, minced
- 2 large tomatoes
- 2 teaspoons tomato paste
- 2 tablespoons finely chopped Italian parsley, rinsed and squeezed dry

In a medium saucepan, heat the 2 tablespoons olive oil over medium-high heat. Add the onion and sauté until soft, 3 to 4 minutes. Reduce the heat to low and add the red pepper flakes, anchovies, and garlic and stir well. Sauté for 2 to 3 minutes, or until the anchovies melt into the oil.

Meanwhile, cut the tomatoes into quarters. Squeeze them through a food mill or a small-holed colander into a bowl. Add the juice and pulp and tomato paste to the saucepan and simmer over medium heat until thick, 10 to 15 minutes.

Taste for seasoning and add more hot pepper if desired. Stir in the parsley and remove from the heat. Stir in some additional olive oil, if you'd like, before serving.   makes about 2 cups, enough to serve 4

polenta with taleggio cheese

This polenta is great for a party, especially if you cook it over an open wood fire in the autumn. I had this comforting dish in a summer cabin in the mountains of the Valsassina region in northern Italy.

8 cups water

½ teaspoon coarse sea salt, plus more to taste

2 cups uncooked polenta

6 ounces Taleggio cheese

½ cup freshly grated Parmigiano-Reggiano cheese

Freshly ground black pepper to taste

Butter at room temperature for serving

Remove the rind from the Taleggio and cut the cheese into small pieces.

In a large heavy pot, heat the water over medium-high heat. Add the salt and stir well. Just before the water begins to boil, slowly add the polenta, stirring almost constantly with a wooden spoon, to form a thick, smooth porridge. Bring to a boil, then reduce the heat to low. Simmer, stirring frequently, for at least 30 minutes. When the polenta is ready, it should be thick and smooth, with no trace of grittiness. The longer you cook it, the better it will be. Melt in the cheeses when the polenta is ready. Add additional salt and pepper to taste. Serve with a generous pat of butter on top of each bowl.

serves 4

breakfast polenta

The idea for this recipe came from Evan Kleiman, who's written a number of excellent cookbooks, including *Cucina Fresca, Cucina Rustica,* and *Cucina del Mare.* You can sample Evan's cooking at Angeli Caffe, her restaurant on Melrose Avenue in Los Angeles, or make this breakfast yourself on a cold winter weekend morning.

6 cups whole milk

1 teaspoon coarse sea salt, plus more if needed

1 cup finely ground uncooked polenta

½ cup golden raisins

Butter at room temperature for serving

In a large saucepan, heat the milk to just below a boil. Stir in the salt. Slowly add the polenta, stirring constantly. (A polenta made with milk tends to splatter a bit more than one made with water, so you may want to use a splatter screen.) Simmer, stirring constantly with a wooden spoon, until the polenta has thickened. Reduce the heat slightly, cover, and cook for at least 30 minutes, stirring frequently until the polenta is thick and smooth, with no trace of grittiness.

Remove the polenta from the heat and stir in the raisins. Add more salt if needed.

Serve with a bit of butter atop each bowl.

serves 4 to 6

italian rices

"They bring you at dusk a preparation which seems to you to be made of grains of gold, and you are delighted already by nothing more than the sight of those grains of rice, each one distinct, each one gilded."

● Edouard de Pomiane

I don't think you can say you've experienced great Italian food until you've had the chance to taste a great risotto. The rice dish of northern Italy, risotto does for short-grain rice what pasta does for wheat—takes the natural goodness of the grain to new heights by making it the vehicle for all sorts of ingredients. The result is a dish with a rare combination of grandeur and down-to-earth goodness that few others can match.

Imagine a bowl filled with a mound of steaming, softly gilded, richly creamy, savory rice, each grain still distinct, yet each clinging to its neighbor. The hot risotto is graced with a sprinkling of freshly grated Parmigiano-Reggiano and a generous twist of coarsely ground black pepper. When you put a forkful on your tongue, you'll experience the contrast between the overall creaminess of the dish and the al dente firmness that remains in the heart of each grain.

This creaminess is the distinguishing feature of Italian rice. It has a higher starch content than most rices and the ability to absorb large quantities of liquid without getting mushy. Though there are other dishes you can make from Italian rice, risotto stands supreme, and a good risotto can be made only from Italian rice.

the story of
italian rice

Although the claim that the Chinese gave Italians pasta is now almost universally rejected, no one seems to dispute that the other major starch dish of Italy—rice—was brought to the boot from Asia, where it was cultivated as far back as 5000 B.C. Traveling gradually westward, rice arrived in Europe in time to be a small footnote in Greek and Roman history. The Arabs introduced it to the Spanish, who in turn brought it to the island of Sicily, which they then ruled. Surprisingly, all three of these great cooking cultures rarely used their newly acquired product as food. Instead, rice was reserved mostly for medicine and was sold in apothecaries.

Only in the middle of the fifteenth century did rice growing in Italy rise to significant levels. From Sicily, it worked its way north—the first part of the sixteenth century saw the introduction of intensive rice farming in the Po River valley. In an era when plagues were plentiful and wars all too common, the population was often short of food, and rice showed itself to be a fairly reliable crop. More often than not, it was used in conjunction with other grains to make bread or a polenta-like porridge.

Risotto did not become an everyday option in Italy until the twentieth century. Even then it was primarily eaten on Sundays or holidays; only recently has it become a dish made on a more regular basis. Today's top rice varieties for risotto were introduced at the end of the Second World War, when Italians began to have more money for food. Most rice in Italy is now grown in Lombardy and Piedmont, with small quantities found in other parts of the country.

Italian rice is a mere afterthought to international rice-growing statistics: 90 percent is grown in Asia. Nevertheless, its unique cooking characteristics make it noteworthy. You don't need to be an agronomist to tell that Italian rice is different from Uncle Ben's. Pour a little into the palm of your hand: the grains are pleasantly plump, oval, and off-white, far fatter than the thin long-grain rice that most of us grew up on. If you look closely, you'll see that the biggest part of each grain is nearly transparent, almost opalescent. Inside each, you can see a spot of white, what Italians refer to as *la perla* ("the pearl"), a core of less-developed starch at the center of the grain.

The secret of Italian rice lies in two kinds of starches, which together give it its unique cooking properties. The first, a translucent exterior layer of a soft starch known as "amylopectin," dissolves easily in liquid as the rice cooks. The amylopectin surrounds a second, sturdier starch, known as "amylose," which makes up the pearl. While amylopectin breaks down quickly to create the trademark creaminess, amylose stays firm, leaving each grain with the desired al dente texture. The combination of the two allows the rice to absorb a lot of liquid while still retaining its textural integrity. No other rice can pull off this seemingly contradictory feat.

how to buy the right italian rice

For starters you should know that the name of the rice you want is not *risotto*, as many people think. *Risotto* refers to the dish itself. Using authentic Italian rice in your risotto is guaranteed to elevate its quality well beyond anything you'd get from any other variety. If you're already buying Italian rice, is it worth going out of your way to find a better brand? If you make a lot of risotto and you're dedicated to making the best you can, then it most definitely is.

choose the right variety

Buying "Italian rice," however, is akin to picking up a block of cheese simply labeled "Cheddar"—there's a huge variation in quality from one source to the next. There are something like fifty varieties of rice raised in Italy today, each with unique cooking characteristics. For risotto making, the most desirable varieties are those with the highest levels of amylopectin starch, and those in which each grain retains its individual identity during cooking. The higher the amount of transparent outer core on each grain in comparison to the opaque inner "pearl," the higher the level of amylopectin in the rice. In other words, the more transparent the grain, the better the risotto.

arborio

Arborio is the premier name in risotto making, the variety that was first introduced to Americans. To this day, it remains the most popular Italian rice in the United States. Unfortunately, its good name also makes Arborio the most likely candidate for adulteration or misrepresentation in commercially packaged rice. Despite its reputation, Arborio accounts for less than 10 percent of rice grown in Italy.

Introduced right after World War II, it received its name from the village of Arborio, about half a dozen miles from the renowned rice capital of Vercelli in Piedmont, in northwest Italy. Compared with American long-grain varieties, it is a short, squat grain with a high percentage of starch; Arborio is able to absorb a good deal of broth and will yield a fine risotto—provided you have the real thing.

carnaroli

This rice is the one that draws raves from the experts—almost all the well-known food people I've talked to in Italy tell me they cook their risotto with Carnaroli. Developed in northern Italy in the 1940s, Carnaroli can absorb more liquid than other varieties while still keeping its structure intact. Carnaroli's cost is high because it's difficult to grow and has small yields. It accounts for just over 1 percent of Italian rice production. I'll throw my hat in with the Carnaroli crowd — given a choice, this is the variety of Italian rice I use for risotto.

vialone nano

Originally grown in the area around Venice in the late 1930s, Vialone Nano is smaller in size and rounder in shape than the other varieties I've mentioned. (*Nano* means "dwarf" in English.) Again, it's not the easiest rice variety to grow — it accounts for only about 3 percent of production. In the Veneto, Italians eat a great deal of rice cooked in *minestra* — a dish that is brothier than a risotto, thicker than a soup — for which Vialone Nano is ideal. Additionally they eat it in the classic *risi e bisi* — rice and peas — which is also brothier than a risotto, though thicker than a *minestra*.

beware impostors: look for the stork

Perhaps the most challenging problem for an American consumer trying to buy good Italian rice is that there is a great deal of intentional mislabeling and misrepresentation on the Italian market. The government grading system in Italy plays right into this problem: the categories merely measure the size of the grain in question. The smallest rice, which comes closest to replicating the old regional varieties of Piedmont, is known as *comune,* or *originario.* Then — listed from shortest grain to longest — come *semifinos, finos,* and, finally, *superfinos.* Superfine rice is generally — but not universally —

acknowledged to be the best for making risotto. It is definitely the biggest — nearly a quarter inch in length. Under Italian law, any *superfino* rice can be retailed with the name of any other *superfino* rice, meaning that lesser varieties can legally be labeled as the more desirable ones, such as Arborio or Carnaroli.

Misrepresenting Italian varieties is, unfortunately, only the tip of the "riceberg." Asian-type rices — which have two to three times the per-acre yield of Italian rices and far lower per-pound costs — are often repackaged as authentic Italian. Italian factories buy this rice and blend it with Italian rice, then sell it off in Italy or export it back to the United States.

So what's an innocent risotto lover to do? You can start by looking for the seal of the rice growers' consortium. Established in 1997 by seventeen small Italian companies, it has the less than catchy name of Consorzio di Tutela e Valorizzazione delle Varietà Tipiche di Riso Italiano e delle Sue Tradizioni (Association for the Protection and Development of the Typical Varieties of Italian Rice and Its Tradition) and guarantees the authenticity of the type of rice inside each bag. It also sets high standards for environmental and agronomic activity in the fields. You can spot the Consorzio rice from its seal that shows a stork—a common sight in the rice regions—standing in the fields.

A few of the companies in the Consorzio grow, process, pack, and sell rice under their own labels, including Tenuta Castello, La Lodigiana, Greppia, and Principato di Lucedio. I recommend all of their rices. Another excellent rice from a full-cycle producer is Acquerello, whose owners assured me they would soon join the Consorzio. Additionally there are five rice processors in the Consorzio that buy raw rice from other growers in the group and finish it. This group includes excellent rice from Riseria Ferron in Verona, Riseria di Lenta in Vercelli, and Riseria La Gallinella in Pavia.

other considerations

It's imperative that the rice be consistent in size and in cooking properties. Higher percentages of broken grains lead to inconsistent cooking because smaller pieces will be well done before bigger grains are ready. Italian law allows a maximum of 5 percent broken grains per bag, but quality-conscious producers set more stringent standards for themselves.

Although most of us imagine rice to be about as shelf-stable a product as you can get, the truth is it's subject to all the same sort of factors that affect the quality of any agricultural product. The character of the rice changes each year. And within the same farm, it varies from one field to the other. If you find that a particular brand of rice cooks up a bit differently from what you're used to, it may well be a new crop coming onto the market.

The best Italian rices are aged longer in the husk before being released for sale. The longer the rice ages, the more its moisture evaporates. The drier the rice, the more broth it will absorb in the making of a risotto without going soft on you. And the more broth it absorbs, the more flavorful the risotto. All of the top-level growers do at least some aging; three months seems to be the minimum.

a visit to a venerable rice grower

The Principato di Lucedio is one of only a handful of small rice growers left in Italy, one of the remaining independents that has chosen the challenging path of marketing its rice on its own, under its own label.

The Lucedio is owned by the Contessa Rosetta Clara Cavalli d'Olivola Salvadori di Weisenhoff, whose family dates its first connections to the lands of the Lucedio nearly a thousand years ago. The story of the Lucedio offers some insight into what better Italian rice is all about and also into the history of rice growing in the region.

Up until a decade or so ago, the Salvadoris sold their rice off in bulk to one of the big growers who blended it with rice of significantly lower quality. In the 1980s, the family decided to pack its own product, in the process committing itself to the finer points of good rice growing.

Unlike the big packers, the Salvadoris use only rice grown on their own land. They use no chemicals, sprays, or pesticides on the rice, although they don't have organic certification because they are unable to verify the sources of all their water.

The estate lies in the northeast corner of Piedmont near Vercelli, the home of the Piedmont rice exchange, an hour's drive from Turin. The land in this part of the world is flat: you can see for miles. This terrain is essential to keep the rice fields properly flooded. When you're there, it's hard to remember that the area sits less than a hundred miles from the Alps, but cold blasts of mountain air can arrive at almost any time during the year to wreak havoc on the region and its growers.

Although the Lucedio is small by modern commercial rice growing standards, it seems enormous and impressive to visitors. In the center of a square formed by the various buildings, there's a huge courtyard that was the heart of what was once a medieval town. In 1123 an ancestor of the current contessa donated the estate to Cistercian monks from Burgundy who taught rice-growing techniques to the local peasants. The Lucedio became a village in its own right, with a population in the hundreds. Today the Lucedio estate is run by a comparatively small staff of six, four of whom live on its land.

Looking out through the wrought-iron bars on the Lucedio's windows, you can see flat rice fields crisscrossed by irrigation canals and roads. The seasonal cycles of planting and harvesting have changed little over the centuries. In the later winter months, the fields are dug up, the earth turned over. The fields must be leveled to avoid unwanted

runoff after they are flooded. In early spring young shoots are transplanted from seedbeds. The most prestigious types of rice are sown earlier; lesser varieties have shorter seasons and go in later. The fields are then flooded with water, which originates in the mountains and moves through the plains in a series of ancient underground rivers and man-made canals. The water drowns weeds and acts as a blanket to protect the crops from weather extremes.

The rice shoots sprout through the water's surface like loose hairs.

Later they expand into a lush green field. In summer, the fields go from green to gold as the grain ripens on its stalks. In the fall, the fields are drained, and the rice is harvested, dried, and threshed.

For most of the past century, hardly any agricultural machines were being used in the area; the rice planting and harvesting was almost all still done by hand. This changed drastically in the 1960s, when tractors were taken into the fields. Four decades later, there is almost no handwork left. Leveling is now done with the help of lasers; planting and harvesting with combines; drying with machine heat instead of that of the sun. Quicker harvesting capabilities also allow growers to save their crops more often than not when bad weather threatens in the fall.

The final processing of the rice is spread out across the rest of the year and allows the kernels to age, ensuring more complete drying and superior cooking properties. This final milling removes the outer brown bran layer, leaving the rice with a delicate flavor and a pale pearly white appearance.

making risotto

Like pasta, risotto can be made from start to finish in less than thirty minutes. And like pasta, the dish is well suited to all sorts of occasions, from fancy dinners to impromptu meals that take advantage of tasty tidbits in the refrigerator. It's great comfort food: a hot, creamy bowl is just the thing to get you through a cold winter night.

Making great risotto requires attention to both process and content. To help you get at the glories, I offer my rules for risotto making.

rule #1. use short-grain italian rice

The rice, not any other more impressive-sounding ingredient, is the star of a serious risotto. It's got to be short-grain Italian.

rule #2. buy—or make—better broth

There's no way around it: the better the broth, the better the flavor of the finished risotto. In a pinch, canned broth will do. (I like the organic broth from Pacific Foods of Oregon.) Italians are known for their reliance on packaged bouillon cubes, but they impart the unpleasant aftertaste that is so often associated with processed foods. In all, you'll need roughly four to six times as much broth by volume as uncooked rice.

rule #3. use the right pot

To make a good risotto, start with a wide, heavy pot. You want the rice to have room to roam while the risotto is cooking. Nonstick pots help, though you'll still have to do a lot of stirring.

Heat a little olive oil and/or butter in the pot. I usually opt for oil, but many cooks believe that butter makes better risotto; others like using a bit of each. When the oil/butter is hot, sauté a little chopped onion until it's soft and golden. Add the rice. Stir to coat the rice with the fat and sauté it for a couple of minutes. Look into the pot and you'll see a mélange of soft golden onion pieces and hard white rice grains. In a couple of minutes, the rice should be hot and glistening.

rule #4. wine with rice is twice as nice

Italians say, "Rice is born in water, and dies in wine." Most recipes, after instructing you to sauté the rice, will tell you to add half a glass of white wine before adding the broth. The wine adds depth to the finished dish. But I've certainly made perfectly delicious risotto without wine, so I'll leave the call to you. As always, the better the wine, the better the risotto.

rule #5. add the broth slowly (and keep it hot)

Now begin adding the broth. You want the broth to be hotter than the rice, so that when you add it to the pot, it doesn't cool down the rice. Be sure to bring it to a slow boil. Cool broth makes for mushy risotto. Add the broth slowly—let's say a ½-cup ladleful at a time—enough so that the rice stays wet, surrounded by small rivulets of boiling broth, but never so much that it runs the risk of drowning. When the rice has absorbed all the liquid from the last ladle, add another ladleful.

rule #6. keep the rice pot hot

This piece of advice may seem like a given, but I've seen many people ruin risotto by letting the flame get so low that the rice doesn't cook properly. How hot is hot enough? When you add the first bit of liquid, it should seemingly go up in

smoke. You want to hear a swoosh and see a puff of steam rise from the pan. No puff? Then the pan isn't hot enough. However, if the rice is sticking almost instantly to the bottom no matter how much you stir, the pan is too hot, so quickly reduce the heat.

rule #7. stir, stir, stir

There's a fair amount of stirring involved in making a good risotto, but you don't have to stir every single second that the pot is on the stove. Stir enough so that the rice doesn't stick to the bottom of the pan and the liquid and rice stay evenly distributed. I stir with a wooden spoon.

rule #8. keep it simple

I've yet to find anything reasonable that couldn't be added to a good risotto: vegetables of any sort, most any cheese, olives, meat, fish, chicken, cream, herbs, nuts, seafood, or saffron. Additional risotto ingredients seem to work well in pairs, threesomes at best. More than four fogs the flavor of the finished dish.

As a general rule, you can add the flavorful, but somewhat invisible, ingredients early on. Chopped fennel, celery, shallots, or carrots might go in the initial sautéing with the onion and garlic. Add other ingredients to (or blanch them in) the broth as it heats—mushrooms or asparagus, for example. On the other hand, ingredients that you want to present intact when

the risotto comes to the table are best added at the end, so that they aren't broken to bits by the stirring or overcooked in the pot; salmon, chicken, and arugula come to mind.

Cheese should also be added at the very end of the cooking process, so that it doesn't overcook.

There's something about the sweet, subtle nuttiness of Parmigiano-Reggiano that makes it the ideal end to risotto preparation. Standard Italian cooking wisdom dictates that Parmesan not be added to risotto made with fish or shellfish. Usually I add it anyway.

rule #9. taste-test for doneness

Depending on the variety and age of the Italian rice you use and the level of heat, the risotto will be ready in fifteen to twenty minutes. The only way to know for sure is to start tasting a grain or

italian rice without the stirring

If a lack of either time or patience stops you from making risotto, but you still want to enjoy the rich flavors of Italian rice, check out *riso in bianco.* While it lacks the creamy richness of risotto, it also requires much less cooking.

Riso in bianco calls for preparing Italian rice as you would pasta. You cook the rice in boiling salted water or broth until it's al dente, then drain it. Be careful not to let the rice overcook or it will turn into mush. Top the hot rice with almost anything you like. A simple sauce of lightly browned butter and freshly grated Parmigiano would be a good start. But you can top *riso in bianco* with most anything from a simple tomato sauce to a touch of earthy truffle oil.

two at about the fifteen-minute mark. Just before the rice is done, add any final ingredients: cheese, fish, whatever. And, of course, give it a good stir.

When the risotto seems done and ready to remove from the stove, add one last ladleful of broth to give the risotto something to "sip on" as it sits in the bowl for a minute or two before you eat, leaving it with a fine creamy texture and keeping it from getting too dry.

You may also want to add a spoonful of butter at the last minute. This step is known in Italian as the *mantecatura*. As the butter melts, it coats each grain of rice, yielding a richer, creamier risotto.

two exceptional brands

FERRON The Ferron family has owned and run this seventeenth-century water-powered mill in the Isola della Scala near Verona since 1921. The family also runs its own rice restaurant on the Pila Vecia; if you travel to Verona, be sure to check it out. The Ferrons grow all the varieties, but their specialty is the Veneto's Vialone Nano.

PRINCIPATO DI LUCEDIO See page 162.

risotto with fontina cheese and porcini mushrooms

I cook risotto almost every week. This one is a favorite. The subtle flavor of Fontina is at its best with the earthy tones of wild mushrooms. For an extra touch of elegance, drizzle a bit of truffle oil on top of each bowlful before you serve it.

2½ cups boiling water
1 ounce dried porcini mushrooms (1 cup)
4 cups chicken broth
2 tablespoons butter or delicate extra virgin olive oil, preferably Ligurian, plus more to taste
1 small onion, finely chopped (about ¾ cup)
1 cup Italian short-grain rice, preferably Carnaroli
½ cup dry white wine, preferably Italian
4 ounces Fontina Val d'Aosta cheese (without rind), cut into ¼-inch cubes
2 tablespoons finely chopped fresh Italian parsley, rinsed and squeezed dry (optional)
   Additional butter for blending in at the end (optional)
   Coarse sea salt to taste
¼ cup freshly grated Parmigiano-Reggiano cheese
   Freshly ground black pepper to taste

In a large heatproof bowl, pour the boiling water over the dried mushrooms. Soak, covered, for 20 minutes. Strain the mushrooms, reserving the liquid. Rinse the mushrooms and discard any tough stems. Coarsely chop the mushrooms and set aside.

Pour the strained mushroom liquid into a large saucepan along with the chicken broth. Bring to a boil. Reduce the heat to maintain a medium simmer.

In another large saucepan, heat the butter or oil over medium-high heat. Add the onion and sauté until soft, 3 to 4 minutes (don't brown or the onion will become bitter).

Add the rice and stir well. Sauté for 2 minutes, or until the rice is hot and shiny. Add the wine and stir until it has been absorbed by the rice.

Add ½ cup of the broth and stir until absorbed. Repeat, adding broth ½ cup at a time, until the rice is almost al dente in the center, about 15 minutes.

Add the mushrooms and Fontina and stir until the cheese is melted, 1 to 2 minutes. Add the parsley, if using, and stir well again. The risotto is done when the rice is al dente, about 18 minutes from when it first went into the pan.

Add a touch more butter or oil if you like and a final ½ cup broth. Stir and remove from the heat. Let stand for 1 minute. Add salt to taste. (If you've used up all the broth, you can use hot water.)

Serve in warm bowls topped with grated Parmigiano cheese and a generous grinding of pepper.

serves 2 as a main course or 4 as an appetizer

champagne and parmigiano-reggiano risotto

I learned this recipe from Laura di Collobiano, the woman who has helped to revive the Tenuta di Valgiano estate in the western part of Tuscany. She told me she makes it whenever she has leftover Champagne. If the Champagne is too fresh, the heat of the alcohol will dominate the dish. It's important to open the Champagne the night before and let it become flat.

4 cups chicken broth
2½ cups flat Champagne
   Parmigiano-Reggiano cheese rind (optional)
2 tablespoons butter, plus more to taste
1 small onion, finely chopped (about ¾ cup)
1 cup Italian short-grain rice, preferably Carnaroli
4 ounces Parmigiano-Reggiano cheese (without rind), broken into ¼-inch pieces, plus ¼ cup freshly grated cheese for serving
2 tablespoons finely chopped fresh Italian parsley, rinsed and squeezed dry
   Coarse sea salt to taste
   Freshly ground black pepper to taste

In a medium saucepan, combine the chicken broth with 2 cups of the Champagne. If you have a Parmigiano rind on hand, add a piece to the pan. Bring to a boil, reduce heat to medium-high and simmer for 10 minutes. Reduce the heat to maintain a medium simmer.

In a large saucepan, melt the butter over medium-high heat. Add the onion and sauté until soft, 3 to 4 minutes (don't brown, or the onion will become bitter).

Add the rice and stir well. Sauté for 2 minutes, or until the rice is hot and shiny. Add the remaining ½ cup Champagne and stir until it has been absorbed by the rice. Add ½ cup of the broth mixture and stir until absorbed. Repeat, adding the broth mixture ½ cup at a time, until the rice is al dente, about 18 minutes from when it first went into the pan.

Add a touch more butter and the last ½ cup of the broth mixture. (If you've used up all the broth, you can use hot water at this stage.) Stir and remove from the heat.

Add the Parmigiano pieces and parsley and stir well. The cheese should still be in chunks—don't let it melt into the dish. Let stand for 1 minute. Add salt to taste. Serve in warm bowls. Top with the grated Parmigiano and a generous dose of pepper.

serves 2 as a main course or 4 as an appetizer

risotto with scallops and fennel

Italians would likely eschew the cheese in this elegant seafood risotto, but I'll let you decide for yourself. (In a pinch you can substitute a delicate extra virgin olive oil and 1 teaspoon fresh lemon juice for the lemon olive oil.)

- 1/4 lemon
- 6 cups Saffron Chicken Broth (page 357)
- 1 tablespoon extra virgin olive oil
- 1 small fennel bulb, cut into 1-inch pieces (about 1 cup)
- 3 tablespoons butter, plus more to taste
- 1/2 pound fresh sea scallops
- 1 small onion, finely chopped (about 3/4 cup)
- 1 cup Italian short-grain rice, preferably Vialone Nano
- 1/2 cup dry white wine, preferably Italian
- 2 tablespoons torn fresh basil leaves
- Coarse sea salt to taste
- Freshly ground black pepper to taste
- 2 tablespoons lemon olive oil (see page 24)
- 1/4 cup freshly grated Parmigiano-Reggiano cheese (optional)

Cut the lemon—rind and all—into 1/8-inch-thick slices. Cut each slice into quarters. Set aside.

Bring the broth to a boil in a medium saucepan. Reduce the heat to maintain a medium simmer.

Meanwhile, in a small skillet, heat the olive oil over medium heat. Add the fennel and sauté, stirring occasionally, until soft and golden, about 20 minutes. Set aside.

In a large saucepan, melt the 3 tablespoons butter over medium-high heat. Quickly sear the scallops, about 1 minute per side. They should still be raw in the center so that they won't overcook when you add them to the risotto later. Remove the scallops from the pan, cut them into quarters, cover loosely, and set aside.

Add the onion and lemon pieces to the pan and sauté until soft, 3 to 4 minutes. Add the rice and stir well. Sauté for 2 minutes, or until the rice is hot and shiny. Add the wine and stir until it has been absorbed by the rice. Add ½ cup of the broth and stir until absorbed. Repeat, adding broth ½ cup at a time, until the rice is almost al dente in the center, about 15 minutes. Reserve ½ cup of the broth.

Add the scallops and fennel to the risotto and mix well. Cook until the scallops are heated through, but don't overcook or they'll become rubbery. The risotto is done when the rice is al dente, about 18 minutes from when it first went into the pan. Add a touch more butter and the remaining ½ cup broth. (If you've used up all the broth, you can use hot water.) Stir and remove from the heat. Add the basil and salt and pepper.

Serve in warm bowls with the lemon olive oil drizzled over the top. Add a sprinkling of Parmigiano, if using, and give each bowl another generous grinding of pepper.

serves 2 as a main course or 4 as an appetizer

risotto in salto
what to do with leftover risotto

Saltare means "to jump," and these little rice pancakes will jump from the pan to the plate and please the palate. Anyone who likes potato pancakes is likely to love these. Sometimes I cook extra risotto for dinner just so I can make this dish the next day. You can use any leftover risotto, but if it contains chunky ingredients, cut them into ¼-inch pieces. If your risotto was made without much cheese, use two eggs instead of one to help hold the patties together. You can easily double this recipe or vary the ingredient quantities, depending on how much leftover risotto you have.

variation

You can serve the patties as a part of a warm salad, atop a bed of mixed salad greens. •

1   cup leftover risotto, at room temperature

1   large egg, lightly beaten

¼   cup fine bread crumbs (preferably homemade — see page 119)

2   tablespoons extra virgin olive oil

In a medium bowl, mix the risotto and egg until well blended. The egg should bind the rice so that it clings together. Form the mixture into ½-inch-thick patties, about 4 inches wide. Dredge the patties in the bread crumbs until well coated.

In a large heavy-bottomed skillet, heat the olive oil over medium heat. Fry the patties, a few at a time, for 2 to 3 minutes on each side, or until golden brown. Don't crowd the skillet. Serve immediately on warmed plates.

serves 2

spanish rices

Paella now has much the same standing that risotto had a decade ago. Almost anyone who's interested in food and cooking has heard of it. While it appears quite often on American menus, however, it's almost impossible to find a good one in a restaurant. Like risotto, paella is a lot easier to make than most people think. And as with risotto, once you learn how to do it well, paella can provide you with a lifetime of eating pleasure. But if you're going to make the dish properly, you've got to get the right rice, and the right rice for paella is not Italian, Asian, or American but Spanish.

why spanish rice is special

A quick glance at a handful of Spanish rice will tell you you're dealing with grain that's different from what most of us are used to. Instead of being long and thin, Spanish rice is short and squat, almost ivory in color. The Spaniards refer to it as *redondo,* or "round." Like its cousins from Italy, Spanish rice can absorb a good amount of liquid and still retain its internal structure—an al dente texture that's at the other end of the rice spectrum from the soft grains we've come to expect. This ability to soak up other flavors is essential for proper paella. Spanish recipes rarely cook the rice in water but rather in some sort of broth with other ingredients. The more liquid the grains can absorb without losing their integrity, the better-tasting the finished dish.

Although it does look quite a bit like the short-grain Arborio rice of Italy, Spanish rice is not interchangeable with Italian. Risotto requires a high starch content in order to induce the creaminess that's so desirable. This creaminess is in fact the opposite of the texture of a good paella, in which you want each and every grain to be distinct, delicately adhering to its associates, but easily separating at the merest nudge of your fork.

the story of spanish rice

Rice arrived in eastern Spain in roughly the eighth century in the hands of the Moors, and it's remained a significant factor in the area's agriculture ever since. In our own era, rice growing may seem like a pretty innocuous vocation, but back in Medieval times it was controversial. The water in the rice fields was thought to contribute to malaria and other diseases; in 1448 rice growing was banned under penalty of death. Malaria, a common, often fatal, malady, earned Valencia the name "land of rice, land of tears."

To coax rice to grow along the coast, fresh water had to be channeled down from the mountains and routed toward the rice fields. The Moors set up an irrigation system centuries ago, and much of it is still intact today. To ensure water rights and appropriate distribution, Valencia created a group of authorities, known to this day as the Judges of the Waters, who meet every Thursday at the Gothic gate of the cathedral in the center of town to hear any disputes relating to water use in the area. There are no written rules. They simply listen to each case, then decide what they believe would be best for the community.

The rice-growing cycle in Spain is similar to that in Italy. Starting in February or March, the fields are prepared by plowing, then leveling, and, finally, flooding. Seedlings are set in the soil in April and early May, then allowed to grow in shallow water. The planting is typically done in east-west rows to make sure each riceling gets its fair share of sunlight. The water protects the young plants by maintaining a consistent temperature in the fields, drowning out un-

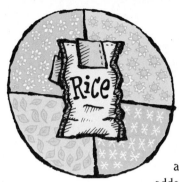

wanted weeds and fighting off the fickle winds. As the new shoots begin to poke above the surface, up to six inches of additional water is added. As the months pass and the plants prosper, the paddies grow ever greener. According to an old Spanish saying, the deeper the green, the better the rice.

Each year, at the end of July, a mass is held in honor of Saint Abdon and Saint Senen, the patron saints of rice growing. Statues of the two are taken out to bless the crop and protect it against rain, hail, or other blights. A month or two later, the fields are drained for the ensuing harvest, which takes place between mid-September and early October. Traditionally, newly harvested rice was left in the sun to dry; today most is machine-dried for speed and consistency.

Even though rice is a summer crop, the grower's work doesn't end at the harvest. In the off-season, banks must be mended and ditches cleaned to prepare for next spring's planting. And then the whole cycle begins anew.

which spanish rice is best?

To get good Spanish rice, you'll want to take into account two major overlapping factors: first, the geographic source of the rice; second, the varietal. Spanish cooks judge the quality of the rice by looking at three key characteristics.

1. The actual flavor of the grain.

2. The rice's ability to cook to an al dente texture without turning mushy.

3. The amount of broth the rice can absorb during cooking.

the big three rice regions of spain

Valencia, the Ebro, and Calasparra are the three major growing regions. All produce good rice, but the latter two are generally recognized to be the sources of the most exceptional offerings.

valencia: the largest region

In addition to being the home of the original paella and the source for some of the world's best oranges, the Valencia region accounts for the majority of the rice grown in Spain. The area is home to the Albufera — a series of lakes, canals, and lagoons—about half an hour's drive in traffic from today's city center. Historically the region was rural, filled with rice fields; today it's a protected nature zone, a little piece of the past surrounded by the city of Valencia and its suburbs.

Valencian rice makes a perfectly good paella, and it's far preferable to any non-Spanish short-grain rice.

ebro: excellence amid beauty

The Ebro Delta lies at the southern end of Catalonia in northeast Spain. The area is unique, and not just for its rice. For openers, the land is almost entirely treeless and amazingly flat, a strange concept in a part of the country that's only a few miles from the mountains. The Ebro is also a bird sanctuary, and all sorts of elegant, odd-looking birds rise out of the rice fields: flamingos, herons, wild ducks, and nearly three hundred other species. Rice came relatively late to the Ebro, but by the second half of the nineteenth century it was already a major local crop. The best Ebro rice is very, very good.

calasparra: source of a superior grain

I like the rice from the Calasparra region best of all. Located in the mountains of Murcia in southeastern Spain, along the Mundo and Segura River valleys, the area has been recognized for the quality of its rice

for centuries. Calasparra accounts for only about twenty-five hundred tons of rice a year, less than 1 percent of Spanish production. Seventy-five percent of it is eaten inside Spain, where rice connoisseurs know the name and quality of the grain. In 1986 Calasparra received the Denomination of Origin protection from the Spanish government, guaranteeing that the name can be used only for rice grown within the defined geographic region. It remains the only DO rice in the European Community. Look for the official seal on the package, which shows a drawing of an old map of Murcia, marking the town of Calasparra. Each bag is numbered, an indication of authenticity.

About sixteen hundred feet above sea level, Calasparra is as romantic a setting as you'll see for rice growing. Set into small mountain valleys, the fields are uneven segments divided by earthen berms, on which some farmers cultivate narrow vegetable gardens. Deep green forests grow in the background. Just above the fields, the river waters flow into the valley and are then channeled through and around the fields. The water moves slowly but steadily at all times, unlike the standing water of the rice fields in the lowlands of Valencia. Likewise, Calasparra's cooler summer weather and cold river water make for a longer growing season and slower ripening of the rice plants. The result is a harder grain with a capacity to absorb more liquid, while retaining the all-important firm texture.

Since 1982, most of Calasparra's rice has been grown organically, benefiting from a two-year planting cycle. The rice seed is sown by hand in early

May. By the end of the month, the green shoots of the plants break through the water and point skyward. The paddies are weeded by hand throughout the summer: backbreaking work made even more difficult because of the hot summer sun of Murcia. At the end of September, the paddies are drained, and the soil firms up enough to allow mechanical harvesters to gather the grain in October, a good thirty days later than the rice harvest at lower altitudes in Valencia.

José Ruiz Egea, head of the rice cooperative in Calasparra, told me, "What makes this special is the quality. The rice here takes twenty minutes to cook. Other rice takes ten minutes. Once you try this, you don't go back to the other." Calasparra rice can absorb up to twice as much broth as standard Spanish rice, meaning that a ratio of roughly four to six parts liquid to one part rice might be appropriate.

spanish rice varietals

Of the two major short-grain Spanish varietals, Balilla and Bomba, Balilla is the most commonly available. It accounts for about 90 percent of Spanish rice production. If you're looking at labels and you see "Rice from Spain" or "Valencia Rice," it's likely you've got Balilla. As a rule of thumb, Balilla will absorb twice its volume in liquid and goes from raw to ready in about fifteen minutes of cooking.

Balilla rice from Calasparra, sold with the Denomination of Origin seal on it, can cost two to three times as much as the same variety grown elsewhere in Spain. If you want something special, it's a very sound investment.

My own favorite is the Bomba varietal. It's harder to find than Balilla, but I think it scores higher on flavor, texture, and absorption capacity. It can soak up very large quantities of liquid—two to three times the level you'd use for standard Spanish rice. At the same time, it's a high-integrity grain. Even though it absorbs all that liquid, it's still firmer and more distinct than Balilla.

Bomba has been almost unknown outside of Spain until the last few years. Although all three regions grow Bomba, most producers have switched to Balilla because Bomba is so hard to grow. Even under ideal conditions, Bomba yields are far lower and the plants grow tall, making them much more susceptible to wind and weather-related damage. But I'm sure Bomba's struggle to survive each summer adds to its inherently high flavor. Those who still choose to grow this varietal usually dedicate only a small section of their land to it, reserving the rest for sturdier, better-yielding varieties.

At the Cooperativa del Campo Virgen de la Esperanza, I asked José Ruiz Egea about Bomba. He was clearly puzzled at my interest in a rice that's little known even in Spain. Then I asked him what rice he ate at home. He raised his eyebrows, and said with a shrug, "Bomba." Point taken: Bomba is better.

BOMBA BRANDS Valencia-grown Bomba rice is produced under the label Arcesa. Better still is Bomba from the Ebro; the Montsia brand is quite tasty. Best of all is Bomba from Calasparra. The Calasparra Bomba from the Cooperativa del Campo Virgen de la Esperanza holds its texture best. Some is sold here under the Flor label.

paella party!

Word has it that every Valenciano has three paella recipes in his head—one from his spouse, one from his mother, and one of his own—and pretty much every native I've ever asked has had at least that many.

To this day, paella remains a popular outdoor dish, though it's now generally reserved for Sundays or holidays (it's considered too time-consuming for a busy family during the week). There are many Spaniards who swear it tastes better cooked over a wood fire, and many Valencian restaurants still make the dish outdoors. Its affinity for open-air preparation makes paella an effective option for American cooks. While our stovetops are often a bit too small to accommodate a paella pan of any size,

we can easily move out to the patio and do the deed on the grill.

In Spain, paella is not the fancy seafood dish it is in this country. Instead, it's meant to highlight whatever is best at the market and can be easily adapted to the particular idiosyncrasies and finances of the cook. It doesn't have to have seafood in it at all, nor does it require meat. Like a jazz piece, it has a basic structure but leaves lots of room for creative improvisation. Before you get going, you'll need three things: a real paella pan, authentic saffron, and an understanding of the proper technique for paella making.

the right pan

The first key to paella is a paella pan, a round steel vessel with short, shallow sides, maybe an inch or so high and sloping outward at about a thirty-degree angle to its flat bottom. Two simple wire handles are positioned at opposite sides of the pan, making it look somewhat like a medieval cymbal. The shape is essential for good paella—the pan's shallowness and sloped sides allow the rice to cook without steaming and

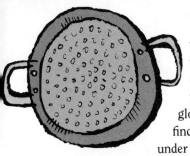

turning mushy. Try to cook paella in a deep-sided skillet and you'll end up with gloppy rice. You can find a good paella pan for under $20, a small investment in good eating.

Paella restaurants in Spain hang dozens of pans of widely varying sizes from their racks; chefs must be able to cook the right size paella for the party that has ordered it. The pan isn't just a cooking implement; it's also the serving dish. Paella is never transferred to individual platters before being brought to the table. To protect the table's surface (or the tablecloth), people use wood trivets, metal rings, or, my favorite, empty egg cartons.

Paella pans are available in iron, stainless steel, and other cheaper metals (see Mail-Order Sources, page 446). The older iron pans conduct the heat most effectively. If you buy a new iron paella pan, season it before you use it. Pour about a cup of red wine vinegar and ¼ cup of salt into the pan. Set it on the stove and simmer over medium heat for about twenty minutes. Pour off the remaining liquid. Wipe the pan dry with a clean cloth and then rub it with olive oil to avoid rusting. Repeat this last step after every washing.

Roughly speaking, here's a guide to pan size and the number of servings:

For 2–3 servings, a 12-inch (30-cm) pan: use 1 cup dry rice

For 4–6 servings, a 13½-inch (34-cm) pan: use 1½ cups dry rice

For 6–8 servings, a 16-inch (40-cm) pan: use 3 cups dry rice

real saffron

The second key to an authentic paella is the saffron. You can toast it in a dry pan or in the oven for a minute or so, then crumble it onto the rice as it is sautéing. I like to soak the saffron threads in a bit of very hot water or broth for at least a few hours and up to a full day ahead of time. When you're ready to heat up your broth, add the saffron threads and soaking liquid and simmer together for a few minutes.

the right technique

The third essential element is proper cooking procedure. You must sauté the dry rice in olive oil so it begins to pick up the flavors of the other sautéed ingredients and so its starches can begin to break down. A few minutes later, add boiling broth to the pan. If the broth isn't boiling, the rice will cool and turn mushy. Stir well to mix and then put your spoon away. The rice cooks and the steam rises, then escapes from the shallow pan. The bottom layer of rice starts to stick to the bottom of the pan, forming the *socarrat,* the crisp, golden crust of rice that Spaniards fight over.

spanish rice
with a crumb crust

Spaniards do far more with rice than just make paella. Spanish rice is a great base for salads, and it can be added to soups and stews. Cooks in Spain make a range of dishes like this one, typical of the region of Murcia, which includes the Calasparra growing district. Although the procedure may seem unfamiliar at first, it's actually very easy.

The paprika is an essential ingredient. It's the core spice in Murcia kitchens. Typically, Murcia paprika is made from the Nyora pepper, the same one that's used in Catalan Romesco sauces and other dishes. The paprika is exceptionally aromatic and sweet. The best peppers are sundried, which protects their flavor and aroma. I recommend the Odalisca paprika made by a fourth-generation producer, one of the oldest in Murcia.

This dish is a good example of how Serrano ham can be used as an accent; a little bit adds a lot of flavor. You can make the dish for vegetarians by leaving out the ham and using vegetable stock instead of chicken stock.

RICE

6 cups chicken broth

1/2 teaspoon saffron threads, soaked in 1/4 cup hot water for at least several hours and up to a day

3 tablespoons full-flavored extra virgin olive oil, preferably Spanish

1 small onion, diced (about 1/2 cup)

2 garlic cloves, minced

1 1/2 cups Spanish short-grain rice, preferably Calasparra

3/4 teaspoon coarse sea salt

1 15-ounce can chickpeas, rinsed and drained

1 1/2 teaspoons sweet Spanish paprika, preferably from Murcia (see note above)

Freshly ground black pepper to taste

2 ounces Serrano ham or other aged Spanish ham, coarsely chopped

6 large eggs, beaten

2 tablespoons warm water

¼ teaspoon fine sea salt

¾ cup coarse bread crumbs (see page 119)

Preheat the oven to 350°F.

For the rice: Bring the broth to a boil in a large heavy-bottomed stockpot. Add the saffron threads and soaking water. Reduce the heat to maintain a medium simmer.

In a 13½-inch paella pan, heat the olive oil over medium heat. Add the onion and sauté until soft, 3 to 4 minutes. Add the garlic and sauté for 2 to 3 minutes more. Add the rice and salt and stir to coat with the oil. Sauté for about 5 minutes, or until the rice is slightly golden and transparent. Stir in the chickpeas, paprika, and pepper. Add 5 cups of the simmering broth in a steady stream and stir well. Add the ham and stir well again. Keep the mixture at a steady simmer, moving the pan around occasionally so the rice cooks evenly. Continue cooking until the rice is nearly al dente, about 15 minutes, adding more broth if needed.

Meanwhile, for the crust: In a medium bowl, whisk together the eggs, water, and salt and set aside.

When the rice is nearly done, remove it from the heat. Gently pour the egg mixture evenly over the top. Sprinkle with the bread crumbs.

Bake for 20 minutes, or until the top is golden brown. Serve hot.

serves 4 to 6

zingerman's patio paella

socarrat

If you're lucky, when you start serving, you'll find a layer of golden brown crispy rice stuck to the bottom of the pan. Don't worry; you didn't burn it. This is the *socarrat*, the most prized part of the paella. The *socarrat* is the best reason I can give you not to succumb to the temptation to stick your paella in the oven to finish cooking; oven-cooked paellas won't end up with one.

Paella isn't a dish that you can easily whip up at home after a long day of work. It's a dish for an occasion. Having some friends over for a weekend get-together? Looking for a new twist on a holiday dinner? Having a big group over to watch a game? Better yet, invent your own occasion to give you an excuse to make—and of course eat—paella.

The traditional—and certainly the most romantic—way to cook paella is outdoors over an open wood fire. Valencianos have elaborate arguments about which type of wood is best—some say clippings from grape vines, others argue for wood from orange trees. If you want to try a slightly easier technique, the Weber kettle grill on your patio makes a great paella-cooking tool. It's got the right round shape, and you can adjust the grill's height as you cook to keep the paella from burning. But you can also cook paella indoors on your stove. For all but the smallest paella pans, set the pan over two burners and turn it frequently as the paella cooks to distribute the heat evenly.

Be sure to use Spanish—not Mexican—chorizo. The Spanish version is a cured, ready-to-eat, coarsely cut pork sausage that's scented with paprika and garlic. A small amount sautéed in your paella pan in hot olive oil early in the cooking process adds a wealth of flavor to the finished paella. You'll need a 13½-inch seasoned paella pan (see page 181). Note that the shrimp are cooked in the shell so they release their full flavor to the dish.

6–8	cups chicken or fish broth
½	teaspoon Spanish saffron threads, soaked in ¼ cup boiling water for at least several hours and up to a day
2	tablespoons extra virgin olive oil, preferably Catalan
12	raw medium shrimp in the shell, preferably fresh Coarse sea salt to taste
6	chicken thighs, preferably free-range
4–5	ounces Spanish (*not* Mexican) chorizo, cut into ¼-inch-thick slices
1½	cups Spanish short-grain rice
6	raw clams, scrubbed

6 raw mussels, scrubbed and debearded

4 Piquillo peppers (see page 277) or 2 jarred roasted red peppers, drained and coarsely chopped

¼ cup fresh or frozen (thawed) peas (optional)

8 sprigs fresh curly parsley for garnish

1 lemon, cut into wedges

In a large saucepan, bring the broth, saffron threads, and the saffron soaking water to a boil. Reduce the heat to maintain a medium simmer.

Set a well-seasoned paella pan over medium-high heat. When the pan is hot, add the olive oil. (If the pan is properly hot, the oil will heat up very quickly. Don't let it start to smoke.) Add the shrimp to the pan. Sprinkle with a little salt and sauté until the shells have turned pink and the shrimp are almost cooked through. Don't overcook. Remove and set aside. (Don't skimp on the salt—it's the "secret" key to the paella treasure chest. Keep tasting and checking the salt level as you go and add more as needed.)

Add the chicken thighs to the pan and cook until browned well on all sides, 6 to 8 minutes. Add the chorizo and stir well. Sauté for 4 to 5 minutes, until lightly browned.

Add the rice. The level of rice should not be higher than the handle rivets. If you pack the pan, the grains will steam and the texture will be ruined. Stir the rice to coat it with the oil. Add a bit more sea salt to taste. Sauté the rice for 4 to 5 minutes, or until it starts to become transparent, maybe even very slightly golden.

Now add the broth. Start with 5 cups. Exactly how much broth you'll end up using is hard to say—it depends on the exact size of your pan, the intensity of the heat, and the type and age of the rice (older rice is drier and hence has a lower moisture content). It's a lot easier to add extra broth if your rice isn't quite done than it is to try to spoon excess broth off the top. Always keep more broth on hand than you'll need, but always start out by putting a bit less broth in the pan than you expect to use.

Once you've added the broth, give the rice a good stir. After everything is evenly distributed, set the spoon aside. Keep the heat high enough so the liquid stays at a medium boil throughout the cooking.

After 10 to 12 minutes, use a fork to fish out a grain or two of rice from the pan every few minutes to check for doneness and salt. Avoid overcooking.

When the rice is about half done, start to arrange the clams and mussels seam side down in a ring around the edge of the pan. After 2 to 3 minutes, place the shrimp and the red peppers in the center. Sprinkle the peas (if using) and sprigs of parsley across the top. If the broth has all been absorbed before the rice is ready, add a bit more to the pan to allow the rice to keep cooking.

Standard Spanish rice should take 16 to 18 minutes to cook. Better grades, such as Calasparra or Bomba, may take 25. The rice should be al dente—cooked but still firm in the middle. How firm is up to you. Remember that the rice will continue to cook in the pan, even off the heat, before you dig in.

When the rice is al dente, remove the pan from the heat. Discard any unopened clams or mussels. Set the paella on a trivet in the middle of the table, where everyone can appreciate its incredible color and aroma. Let the paella rest for a few minutes before you serve it. When you start eating, the paella should be between hot and room temperature. Serve with the lemon wedges and insist (politely but firmly) that guests squeeze them over the paella before they eat.

serves 4

REALLY WILD wiLd rice

As a longtime fan of wild rice, I'm more than a bit frustrated that our native North American grain has somehow remained stuck in relative culinary obscurity, while risotto, pasta, and polenta have taken off. Except in the state of Minnesota, where it's maintained a meaningful presence, wild rice has mostly been relegated to holiday meals like Thanksgiving and Christmas, to the menus of historical American dinner retrospectives or of restaurants that want to exhibit their interest in the exotic, or to commercially conceived "wild-rice-blend rice mixes." Which is a shame, because the more I eat it, the more I'm convinced that wild rice should again be an essential element in the modern North American diet.

the straight story

If you check statistics, you'll see that there are something like 20 million pounds of "wild rice" being grown in North America today. But the data are deceptive. Despite the name, the truth of the matter is that *most of the wild rice sold in America isn't actually wild.* On the contrary, about 85 percent of the stuff consumers spy on store shelves is now grown in cultivated, man-managed, machine-harvested fields that are about as wild as suburban subdivisions.

When I talk about wild rice, I mean the genuine article, *really wild* wild rice. The cultivated product, on the other hand, can go by its industry moniker, "paddy rice."

At its best, real wild rice has a light, nutty, delicately earthy, and very delicious flavor that is so far superior to that of paddy rice that the two barely deserve to be considered in the same category. The problem with paddy rice is that it just doesn't taste very good. Despite my attempt to find a spot for it in my pantry, I've discovered that its flavor can be almost unpleasant, out of balance, like badly mixed music.

When you do eat real wild rice, you're about as close to the taste of centuries past as you're going to get. Because wild rice reseeds itself naturally year after year, the only necessary human role is the gathering of the ripe grain in the autumn. Other comparable foods (such as wheat, oats, rice, barley, or corn) have evolved over the years through human intervention and breeding or even genetic modification. But the true wild rice we get today—apart from annual variations in flavor—is essentially the same food North Americans ate two or three hundred years ago.

a short history of wild rice

The vast majority of wild rice history is un-recorded. But the oral traditions of Native Americans make clear that for many millennia wild rice was the single most valuable food of the tribes of the Upper Midwest and central Canada. Essentially, wild rice was to those regions what corn was to the American Southwest or what rice is to Asia: a much revered and economically important food that was a part of both everyday eating and nearly every spiritually significant event.

Nutritionally, wild rice was the staple that kept people fed much of the year. In summer it was cooked into soups and stews with fish and game; in winter it was often the only food available.

Early English and French explorers quickly realized its value. For a century or more, wild rice was one of the only

canada

u.s.a.

readily available nonperishable staple foods for European settlers in the Midwest. For many, laying in a good supply of wild rice—through regular trading with native tribes—was the only way to ensure food for the winter. Like every other oddity of the Americas, wild rice was shipped back to Europe for royalty and other people rich enough to afford it. In the nineteenth century, British botanists tried—unsuccessfully—to grow it in England. (I often bring it as a gift to food-loving friends in London.)

Wild rice plays a particularly important role in the traditions of the Ojibway tribe, also know as the Chippewa. In centuries past, the Ojibway moved steadily westward from what is now upstate New York toward the Upper Great Lakes, where the rice beds were most abundant. In his memoir, *The Rez Road Follies,* the Ojibway writer Jim Northrup explains, "Wild rice, *manoomin* in our language, is the annual gift from the Creator." This belief leads to a good deal of discord among Native activists about state regulations that restrict the harvesting and handling of their rice.

To this day, Northrup writes, "it appears at every celebration or sorrowful gathering." Treaties with other tribes or with Europeans were usually negotiated with the rice in mind. On each lake where rice was gathered, a rice chief was chosen from the tribe's upper echelon, selected for his expertise in all aspects of wild rice harvesting and curing. Although he carried little legal authority, he was held in such high esteem that people nevertheless did what he directed. The rice chief's job was to balance the nutritional needs of the tribe with the growing requirements of the rice. As world leaders today know, such equilibrium is not always easy to maintain.

state of the grain

Despite the name, wild rice isn't rice at all. It's actually an aquatic grass, more biologically akin to wheat than rice. To grow, it needs clear fresh water, two and a half to three feet deep. The water must move at a steady but moderate clip; the rice won't grow in stagnant settings, nor can it survive in swiftly moving currents. The rice "fields" can be enormous and also stunningly beautiful. According to Thomas Vennum's *Wild Rice and the Ojibway People,* Catherine Traill, writing in 1836, reported that "when the rice is in flower, it has a beautiful appearance with its broad grassy leaves and light waving spikes, garnished with pale yellow-green blossoms, delicately shaded with reddish purple, from beneath which fall three elegant straw-colored anthers, which move with every breath of air or slightest motion of the waters."

Wild rice reseeds itself each autumn when unharvested seeds slip back into the water. The seeds have a specific gravity greater than water and hence sink almost straight to the bottom, where they may lie dormant for up to a decade, protecting the plant's future against poor crop years. Consequently, the rice spreads very slowly and almost always in a downstream direction. Seed growth starts when the weather warms in the spring. The first green shoots slice through the water's surface in June and continue to grow until the stalks reach heights of three to eight feet above lake levels.

The plant is sensitive to shifts in its environment. If water levels are low, it won't grow well. Conversely, high water causes problems because sunlight can't penetrate to the seedlings below the surface. And at any point in the season, storms can wreak havoc. People, though, are probably the biggest problem: dams, pollution, and powerboats have all become serious threats to the plant's survival.

The harvesting of true wild rice is traditionally the province of Native Americans. The harvest takes place sometime between mid-August and mid-September, depending on the latitude of the lake in which the rice is grown. In Minnesota, where the bulk of traditional wild ricing is done, the harvest is timed and managed much like fishing or hunting seasons. At each lake and river where rice grows, you'll find thin cardboard signs stating whether the area is open for ricing; at the bottom of each is the inevitably illegible signature of an officer of the state's Department of Natural Resources. The more southerly the lake, the earlier the harvest, so Canadian rice generally comes in last. Also, the rice on the smaller bodies of water is usually ready first, that on larger lakes last.

the coming of cultivation

The domestication of wild rice began in the 1960s. In 1968, paddy rice production in Minnesota was negligible; by 1971 it surpassed the harvest of real wild rice. Paddy rice came later to California: before 1977 there was no crop to speak of there; by 1982 it had increased to twice the volume of genuine wild rice being gathered in Minnesota.

From the beginning, paddy rice was bred to yield smaller, supposedly quicker-cooking grains. It's machine-planted in the autumn; in the spring, the fields are flooded so that the plants can start growing. Water levels are then mechanically maintained. In August, the fields are drained, allowing them to dry so that they can be harvested with combines. Unlike real wild rice, most paddy rice is grown using conventional agricultural techniques, meaning it relies on commercial insecticides to control pests. Because the seeds of paddy rice all ripen at the same time, it's far easier to harvest than the wild plant. And it's certainly ideal for big packers who need the consistency that can be obtained only from a cultivated product.

One unintended benefit of the advent of paddy rice is that it smoothed out the supply cycles. Over a four-year period, real wild rice generally produces one small crop, two so-so harvests, and one bad one. Having paddy rice available in large quantities has taken some of the stress off the supply of the real wild product. In fact, Uncle Ben's — influenced by a bad crop year in 1965 — was instrumental in supporting the development of paddy rice in an effort to get

a consistent supply of grain for its blends. The growing stockpiles of paddy rice in the 1970s and 1980s allowed real wild rice a respite from the overharvesting earlier in the twentieth century.

still wild after all these years: the harvest

Dating to the 1930s, Minnesota state law requires that real wild rice be harvested using traditional techniques, which are pretty much unchanged from two to three hundred years ago. Two people head out onto the lake or river in a canoe. One of them is called the poler—he stands at the rear of the canoe and uses a long forked stick to push the boat slowly through the rice beds. Canoe paddles are of little use once you get into the rice beds because the plants grow so closely together that there's not enough open water in which to use them. Experienced ricers pick their poles with the same sort of mystical machinations that chefs use to select the perfect knives.

While the poler pushes, the other ricer squats or kneels in the belly of the canoe and uses a pair of three-foot-long wooden sticks, known as "knockers," to gather the grains. The knockers are typically made from very light wood, such as cedar, to reduce the strain on the harvesters, who may well be out for an entire day. To gather the rice, the ricer uses one of the knockers to pull an armful of stalks over the edge of the boat. He then taps the second knocker lightly once or twice over the top of the stalks to dislodge the ripe grains —roughly four inches long in their outer husk—which then fall into the canoe. Raw rice—mixed with bugs, stalks, and other lake plants—gradually fills the boat as the day wears on. Unripe grains remain on the stalk. Ricers may return to the same spot for a couple of days or even a week straight, continuing to gather newly ripened grains each time.

I don't want to romanticize traditional harvesting. Like most agricultural activities, hand-harvesting true wild rice is very hard to do. In a day, an experienced pair of ricers might bring in between two and three hundred pounds of raw rice. Having riced only once, I can assure you that whatever price you and I pay for wild rice, we've got the easy end of the deal. Although we think of northern Minnesota as one of the coldest spots in the country, in late August it may also be one of the hottest, and certainly one of the most humid. When there's no wind, the moisture in the air weighs heavily. High winds can kick up, in which case the poler has to push the canoe into the wind and up against the rice stalks to keep them from bending too low. The husks of the rice grains are so sharp that they get caught in clothes, hair, and just about anything else. "They stick in you like spears," one ricer told me with a wince.

Amazingly, ricers actually wait eagerly each year for the lakes to open up so they can get going. And they rice almost every day. Many reservations on which wild rice grows have a standing policy—the agricultural equivalent of "family leave"—allowing any of their employees to take time off to go ricing during the harvest season. Others adjust work and travel schedules accordingly. Still, says Dennis Harper, who's been ricing for more than forty years, "There's no good time to work during the season. Any time you spend at work is time you can't spend out on the lakes ricing."

the four parts of production: curing, parching, jigging, and winnowing

After harvesting, the fresh rice first has to be cured and then parched to preserve it. In general, the lower the residual moisture content, the better the rice. The curing, or initial air drying, must take place within three or four days to avoid the risk of mildew and mold. Curing can run from twenty-four to seventy-two hours, depending on who's doing it. Many people now skip the curing, instead watering the rice to keep it "alive" while it's waiting to be parched.

Parching does for raw wild rice what roasting does for green coffee. During the parching, the rice is stirred or tumbled over high heat, loosening its hull and reducing its moisture content from its natural level of 40 percent to 10 percent or less. Since the sixteenth century and beyond, many native North Americans parched in European iron or brass pots, which were known as "treaty pots" because they were almost always included in treaty-based trades. Ojibway families pass them down from generation to generation, and a lot of people still have them on hand today. The pots were used in the autumn for parching wild rice, then set aside until spring when they were brought out for boiling maple sap into syrup and sugar.

Today most parching is done in rotating oil drums. But a small amount of true wild rice is still cured the old-fashioned way, by hand-parching. Using short wooden paddles, two people push the rice back and forth across a heavy heated pot for twenty to sixty minutes. Hand-parching results in lighter-colored rice because most of the grain's outer covering is loosened in the process. Ultimately, this process will decrease weight and, hence, increase price. It also reduces cooking time. Perhaps most important to those interested in flavor, the open wood fires impart a wonderful, subtle smokiness to the rice.

Even after parching, the grain's long barbed husks are still intact. To remove them, the rice is cooled, then threshed, or hulled. Traditional

threshing involved sinking a two-foot-wide, round wooden "bucket" of parched rice into a shallow hole in the ground. Wearing clean moccasins, men would "tread" the rice to loosen the hulls, much as medieval grape crushers would mash the fruit by foot for winemaking. This technique was known as "jigging," "running," or "dancing."

Alternatively the rice could be hulled by hammering it with long wooden pestles. Once the hulls were loosened, the rice was then poured onto blankets, letting the loose chaff blow away in the wind as the grains fell. The finished product was set aside and stored—often underground—for future use.

These days the work is usually done with some combination of traditional hand techniques and (more often than not) improvised modern equipment. Revolving propane-fired drums are used to dry and thresh the rice; vibrating separators may be used to sort out foreign objects and remove the hulls.

Finally, the rice has to be winnowed, or fanned, to separate the husks from the seed. The traditional technique was to work with birch bark baskets, pouring the rice out so that the husks could be blown away by the wind. Today the winnowing is done by machine.

By the time the entire production process has been completed, the rice will lose roughly half of its original weight.

the label

The key question for consumers is "If you aren't an expert, how can you tell the difference between paddy rice and real wild wild rice?" Unfortunately, it's not as easy as I'd like it to be. Even if you argue that there's room for both the wild and the paddy-grown rice, what's troubling is the way the paddy product is marketed. All along the highways of northern Minnesota, you can find stands or shops selling "wild rice" that isn't wild. I saw some once at a gas station: WILD RICE, the sign said, $1.99/POUND. With no marketing, no transport, and no middlemen, the real thing would be at least $3 to $4 a pound at cost. So rest assured that the product was certainly paddy rice.

Minnesota state law requires that paddy-grown rice be labeled as such or say "cultivated." Unfortunately, Minnesota law is of limited value in the other forty-nine states. Mislabeling is rampant. Too often labels are subtly deceptive; boxes of paddy rice are often labeled only as "wild rice." And even when they say "paddy-grown," or "cultivated," the words are written in small letters and have little meaning to most consumers. At times I've seen paddy rice and wild rice sold for the same price side by side. Ironically the paddy packaging is usually nicer.

the look

To a casual observer, paddy rice and the real McCoy can look a lot alike, though the paddy product is consistently smaller and darker in color. The best really wild wild rice is dull gray to almost blond in color. The paddy product by contrast is almost always extremely and uniformly dark. My experience has been that the rougher and more varied the color of the grains in the bag, the more likely it is you've latched onto something really special.

the origin

Regardless of political boundaries, the actual geographical source of the rice will be one of the biggest factors in its flavor. Each body of water yields rice with its own distinctive character. And rice from the same water source will vary from year to year, just as you'd expect with any other annual crop of naturally grown product. Old hands claim they can often tell you the source and vintage of blind rice samples.

California is the largest producer of "wild rice" in the world, but none of it is the real thing. If you see "California" on the label, you know you're buying paddy rice.

Really wild wild rice comes from Minnesota, Wisconsin, and (in smaller quantities) Michigan. The Canadian crop is also the genuine article, grown in Ontario, Manitoba, or Saskatchewan.

Canadian genuine wild rice tends to be very large; the grains can be more than an inch in length. Canadians use airboats to harvest because they increase yield and cut the cost of labor. The airboats make only one pass through the fields and strip down every stalk in their path, regardless of ripeness. Minnesota traditionalists claim that as a result Canadian rice contains a high percentage of unripe grains. The traditional canoe harvesting, on the other hand, means that one can make multiple passes through the rice beds and gather only ripe grains. To my taste, the most flavorful wild rice is hand-harvested in Minnesota. It is also the most expensive.

the cooking time

When you'll probably best be able to tell paddy product from true wild rice is in cooking it. To taste the difference between the two side by side, I bought a couple of boxes of a nationally known brand of (nicely labeled) paddy rice. Because I'd always been told that it was raised to be quicker to prepare, I was shocked to see that the package called for an hour of simmering. Following the instructions, I cooked the ¼ cup rice in 2¾ cups of boiling water. To my surprise, after a solid sixty minutes of simmering, the rice was still very hard, crunchy, and nowhere near ready

to eat. Pretty soon I had to start adding additional water. By the time the rice was ready, I'd doubled the amount of liquid called for on the box, and the rice had been boiling for over an hour and a half! Ironically, this inconsistency is exactly the kind that paddy rice is supposed to avoid.

In light of my experience, I had to laugh at Jim Northrup's recipe for paddy rice in *The Rez Road Follies*. "First," he says, "find a baseball-sized rock. Add that to the water/paddy rice mixture that is boiling. Cook until the rock is soft; that means your rice is almost done."

With real wild rice, the lighter the color of the rice, the less cooking time it will take. The larger, blacker-grained Canadian crop cooks in about forty-five minutes to an hour. Wild rice is done when it's al dente — tender but still somewhat firm — and the grains have burst wide open. If they've merely begun to puff, they're not done yet. Some can be ready in as little as fifteen or twenty minutes. None of the really wild wild rice I've sampled has needed more than sixty minutes.

final thoughts

Although I expect to pay more for more flavorful, traditionally made food, I don't expect less flavorful, commercially produced products to cost as much as the real thing. But this backward equation seems to apply to wild rice. Paddy rice in supermarkets often sells for about $8 per pound, only a bit less than you pay for the most accessible versions of the really wild article.

Although I'd like to be able to say that there is a place for both paddy and really wild wild rice, in good conscience I can't. The real thing wins on all counts: flavor, history, cost/value, and cultural and ecological soundness.

WILD RICE BRANDS Mahnomen rice from Minnesota is excellent. (*Mahnomen* is the Ojibway name for wild rice, meaning literally "good berry.") A certified organic product, it's available directly from the source and is also sold under the Zingerman's label. And while most wild rice these days is machine-dried, this rice is hand-parched over open fires. The hand-parching imparts a light, slightly smoky flavor. Don't rinse this rice, or you'll lose the smokiness.

Other brands of integrity include Singing Pines and Grey Owl Foods. Because these (and other suppliers) stock both really wild wild rice and cultivated paddy rice, be sure to specify that you're interested in the former.

basic *really wild* wild rice

The ratio of liquid to rice will vary from rice to rice. Generally, the ratio is five parts liquid to one part rice. If you don't see package directions to the contrary, I'd start at four to one and see how it goes. You can use water or broth of almost any sort. Bring it to a boil, reduce the heat, and simmer until the grains burst open (a bit like popcorn) and the rice is tender but firm. If there's any liquid left in the pan when the rice is done, just pour it off and give the "dry" rice a minute or two over low heat to cook out the excess moisture. Serve as a side dish or in salads and soups.

> 5 cups water or broth (chicken, vegetable, or fish)
> 1 cup real wild rice
> ³/₄ teaspoon coarse sea salt

In a large saucepan, bring the broth to a boil over high heat. Add the wild rice and salt and stir well. Reduce the heat slightly and simmer, stirring occasionally, until the rice is tender but firm and the grains have burst open, 20 to 60 minutes, depending on the rice you're using. Drain off any excess liquid, add salt to taste, and serve. *serves 4*

wild rice with maple sugar and butter

Other than Native Americans who grew up on it, few people think of wild rice as morning fare. But this breakfast dish is delicious and easy to make. Almost everyone I've served it to loves it. When you serve real wild rice and maple sugar together, you've got two of North America's greatest culinary contributions in one wonderful bowl.

I like this dish best with authentic, hand-harvested wild rice from Minnesota. The cooking time for that rice will likely be less than 25 minutes. Canadian wild rice may take up to 45 minutes. In any case, it's important to check the rice for doneness as you cook.

Granular maple sugar is available from stores that specialize in maple syrup or from specialty food shops.

    5 cups water
    1 cup real wild rice, preferably from Minnesota
    3/4 teaspoon coarse sea salt
    4 tablespoons butter, at room temperature
    4 teaspoons maple sugar, or more to taste (see note above)

In a large saucepan, bring the water to a boil over high heat. Add the wild rice and salt and stir well. Reduce the heat slightly and simmer, stirring occasionally, until the rice is al dente, 18 to 45 minutes, depending on the type of rice. If there's excess water in the pot, simply drain it off.

Transfer the rice immediately to warm bowls. Top each with 1 tablespoon of the butter. Sprinkle 1 teaspoon (or more, if you like) of maple sugar onto each as well. Serve hot.

serves 4

fried wild rice

This dish is great for Sunday brunch with eggs. Note that this cooking technique will work only with the hand-harvested wild rice that's light in color like the Mahnomen (see page 195).

    3 cups water
    1 cup real wild rice
    3 strips smoked bacon
    ¼ cup thinly sliced scallion greens
       Coarse sea salt to taste
       Freshly ground black pepper to taste
    ¼ cup chicken broth

Soak the wild rice in the water for 4 to 6 hours. Drain.

In a medium skillet, fry the bacon over medium-high heat. Turn off the heat and remove the bacon, keeping 1 tablespoon of the fat in the skillet. Coarsely chop the bacon and set it aside.

In the skillet, heat the bacon fat over medium heat. Add the scallion greens and sauté until soft, 2 to 3 minutes. Add the wild rice and sauté for 10 minutes over medium-high heat, until the rice is lightly browned. Add salt and pepper to taste.

Add the chicken broth, 1 tablespoon at a time, until the moisture content is to your liking, waiting until the rice absorbs it before adding more. Depending on your taste and the texture of the rice, you may not need all of the broth. The rice should be dry.

Add the chopped bacon to the rice and stir well. Check the salt and pepper, adding more to taste. Serve hot.

serves 4

wild rice pancakes

These unorthodox pancakes are good at any time of the day. They're an excellent hors d'oeuvre, dabbed with sour cream and a sprinkling of minced scallion greens. You can enhance the palette of the dish by cooking with different-colored bell peppers.

4 tablespoons butter or bacon fat

2 small bell peppers, finely chopped (about 1³/₄ cups)

¹/₄ cup thinly sliced scallion greens

2 cups cooked real wild rice, at room temperature (see page 196; use about ³/₄ cup raw)

6 tablespoons all-purpose flour

4 large eggs

1 cup whole milk

¹/₄ teaspoon coarse sea salt

Freshly ground black pepper to taste

Sour cream or butter for serving

In a large heavy skillet, heat 1 tablespoon of the butter or bacon fat over medium-high heat. Add the bell peppers and scallion greens and sauté until lightly browned, about 5 to 7 minutes. Remove from the skillet and let cool in a large bowl.

Stir the cooked wild rice, flour, eggs, milk, salt, and pepper into the bell pepper mixture. Let stand for 10 minutes.

In the skillet, heat the remaining 3 tablespoons butter or bacon fat over medium heat. Drop in tablespoonfuls of the batter to form pancakes. Fry in batches until golden brown, about 3 minutes per side. If you're serving them all at once, keep the cooked pancakes warm in the oven while you finish cooking the rest of the batter. Serve with sour cream or butter.

makes about 30 silver dollar–sized pancakes, enough to serve 4

wild rice soup

Wild rice is excellent in soups. Unlike white rice—which adds mostly texture—genuine wild rice has a full flavor that makes a meaningful contribution to the taste of the finished soup.

- 2 tablespoons butter
- 2 cups chopped leeks, white and some of the pale green parts (about 2 large leeks)
- 1 celery rib, chopped (about ³⁄₄ cup)
- 1 tablespoon finely chopped Italian parsley, rinsed and squeezed dry, plus more for garnish
- 1 garlic clove, minced
- 5 cups chicken broth, plus more if needed
- 3 medium potatoes, cubed (about 3 cups)
- 1 medium parsnip, sliced into chunks (about 1 cup)
- 1½ cups cooked real wild rice (see page 196; use ½ cup raw)
  Coarse sea salt to taste
  Freshly ground black pepper to taste

In a large stockpot, melt the butter over medium-high heat (be careful not to burn it). Add the leeks and sauté until wilted, about 7 minutes. Add the celery, 1 tablespoon parsley, and garlic and sauté for 2 minutes more. Add the chicken broth and stir well. Bring to a boil, reduce to a simmer, then add the potatoes and parsnip. Simmer for 20 minutes, or until the potatoes are very tender.

Remove the mixture from the heat, cool slightly, and puree in a blender or food processor until smooth.

At this point the soup is nearly ready to serve, but it's best if cooled overnight and reheated the following day. When you're ready to serve, return the puree to the pot, stir in the cooked wild rice, and heat through. Add more broth if needed to thin, as well as salt and pepper to taste. Garnish with chopped parsley.

serves 4 to 6

part 3.

cheeses

a guide to buying cheeses

"Buying cheese is an art."

● Pierre Androuët, *Guide du Fromage*

Given the choice of one food to take with them into an isolated existence, most folks would probably choose chocolate. Me, I'd go with cheese. That and a loaf of good country bread. I could live—and actually have lived—on nothing else for days at a time. Assuming it's well made and properly matured, I can't think of any sort of cheese I wouldn't eat with pleasure. Fresh, creamy, delicate goat cheeses. Classic blues like Roquefort, Gorgonzola, or Stilton, or newer ones like Great Hill or Harbourne. Choice Cheddars from Somerset, England, or Vermont. Marvelous well-aged mountain

cheeses from the Alps. Sharp sheep's milk cheeses from southern Italy and central Spain. Creamy Camemberts, pungent Pont l'Evêques, both from Normandy in northern France. And best of all, two-year-old slivers of what might be the most wonderful cheese in the world, Parmigiano-Reggiano.

Fortunately, in the final two decades of the twentieth century, we've seen an enormous improvement in the range of offerings available in the United States. Today you can probably find an artisan dairy in almost every state and most of Canada, where cheesemakers are actively crafting a range of new cheeses: fresh and aged, blues and Cheddars, Bries and Camemberts. At the same time, well-deserved attention is again being given to some long-standing American originals, like Dry Jack,

Maytag Blue, and Teleme. Imports, once limited to bad Brie (once commonly sold in this country in flip-top cans) and the ever present Jarlsberg (the "famous" Norwegian "Swiss"), are now available in greater variety and are of better quality.

understanding cheese: an overview

seasonal factors

One of the most important things to understand about traditional cheese is that it once was a very seasonal product. As with peaches, pears, or plums, there were seasons when certain cheeses were at their best, other times at their worst, still others, unavailable altogether. In the natural cycle, cheesemaking is tied to the birth and weaning of babies. Most cows, goats, and sheep start the cycle in the autumn, making milk for their young. Only after the young have been weaned and left to feed for themselves can the mothers be milked on through the spring, summer, and, often, early autumn. This milk is used for cheese, butter, and cream as well as quick liquid consumption. When autumn ends, breeding is again allowed to begin, and until the next spring season starts, no additional milk is available. To this day, Roquefort is made only seven months a year, though adjustments in storage techniques permit a consistent supply to the market.

In recent times, the vast majority of cheese producers in Europe and North America organize their herds to give birth in sequential groups, allowing for year-round milk.

That said, seasonal production is on the way back in some areas, contributing to better-tasting cheese. In Wisconsin, Pleasant Ridge Reserve, an aged, firm-textured cheese, is produced only when the cows are eating in open pasturage, from June through October. Shelburne Farms in Vermont lets the animals go dry in winter. Cheese is made when the cows are out on fresh pasture, and the entire herd gives birth in its natural season. (This natural cycle has an extra benefit: it allows the cheesemaker to take some time off!)

topography

To understand a cheese, you have to take note of the topography of the area in which it originated. Dairymen in places with plenty of rich pasturage usually raise cows. Think of England, Holland, Switzerland, northern France, northern Italy, most of the United States, and Canada —all have lots of open space with nice green grasses, expansive meadows, lush mountain pastures—the sort of places a cow would want to hang out. Consequently, the traditional cheeses of those areas are, more often than not, made from cow's milk.

On the other hand, in drier, rockier regions, you're far more likely to find herds of sheep or goats that are able to climb the terrain and can fend for themselves when food is in short supply. Think of Provence, southern Italy, most of Spain, and much of Greece, where you'll find mostly goat's and sheep's milk cheeses.

climate

People in warmer climates have traditionally made fresher cheeses. Why? Because hot weather meant that cheese was difficult to keep for long periods of time. And, historically, those who lived in temperate climates had less need for long-lasting cheeses. Because winters were milder, many fruits and vegetables had longer seasons, and food was more readily available all year round. When the farmers did make firmer cheeses for maturing, they tended to be drier and saltier and hence better suited to survive the hot temperatures.

In colder climates, on the other hand, people have tended to make harder, longer-lasting cheeses. These cheeses were made in large, often enormous, forms: in Switzerland, two-hundred-pound wheels of Swiss, or in England, the original sixty-pound Cheddar. They had good keeping qualities, an important consideration since cheese was often one of the only — if not the only — form of protein available during the arduous winters.

America is an exception to both climatic and topographical influences. Our cheesemaking patterns are tied more to the locations in which particular European ethnic groups chose to settle. Hence, in Wisconsin we see lots of Swiss- and German-type cheeses; in California, many French and Spanish cheeses.

the role of starter cultures

Starters are the big unspoken "secret" of the cheese world. It's not that anyone in the industry hides their use, but few consumers seem to know they exist and cheesemakers rarely discuss them in depth except with other cheesemakers. Nonetheless, their selection and management can have a huge impact on the flavor of the finished cheese.

A starter does for cheese what a sour does for bread: it introduces consciously chosen strains of bacteria into the mix in order to enhance certain flavor characteristics. Back in the preindustrial era, cheesemakers relied — for better and for worse — on the natural bacterial behavior in the milk to make cheese. Rennet was added to

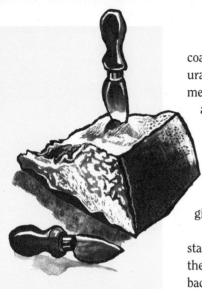

coagulate the milk into curd. But beyond that, cheesemakers used natural bacteria to create the flavor of the cheese. In some cases, this meant making one's own starter by holding back some of the day's whey and letting the bacteria ripen overnight, then using that to "start" the next day's cheese. Even so, the process was rarely very closely controlled, meaning the quality of the cheese varied widely. Some days it worked, others it didn't, and no one understood exactly why. A handful of traditional cheeses today are still made with starters cultured on site by the cheesemakers. Parmigiano-Reggiano, for one, requires that the starters be made in this way.

The need for stronger and more consistent strains of commercial starter cultures grew significantly as pasteurization came into use in the twentieth century. Because the pasteurization process kills off all bacteria in the milk—both the desirable and undesirable ones—it's important for cheesemakers to reintroduce enough bacteria for the needed flavor development in the milk. Hence the trend toward adding prepared starter cultures. Today, the cheesemakers generally purchase starter cultures from labs in powdered form. Because these bacterial cultures help build flavor, the selection and handling of the starters have become meaningful components in crafting a cheese. Cheesemakers often guard the customized combinations of their starter strains jealously.

ten questions to guide you to great-tasting cheese

When it comes to buying cheese, flavor always comes first for me. I want cheese that's so savory and so delicious that I can't help shaking my head with amazement. Shopping for this sort of full-flavored, traditionally made cheese can be challenging. It's not a standardized commodity, so you can't just pick up the phone and order something great by product number the way you might a computer part. Because each wheel is different, you can't buy by name alone. In addition, the way a retailer handles the cheese greatly affects the flavor, quality, and integrity of what you take home.

Probably the most important part of the process is finding a cheese seller who can become familiar with your tastes. Once you've built up a shared sense of what you like and don't like, you can settle into an enjoyable shopping and eating routine.

1. who made the cheese?

The best cheese sellers always get to know the people who made the cheese, and they should be able to share what they've learned. What's the producer's name? Has cheesemaking been in the family for generations, or is it a new venture? Is the production large or small? Seasonal or year-round?

Traditional cheesemaking is not a science. It's a craft. The milk, the animals, the atmosphere, the aging, the feed, the flowers in the fields, all come together to form something akin to a dairy-based symphony. The cheesemaker is the conductor whose efforts effectively orchestrate all these seemingly wild, yet nevertheless wonderful, elements of nature.

2. in what region was it made?

Cows don't carry passports; when it comes to cheese, region is really much more relevant than country, which is, after all, a political creation.

There's an old saying in Spain: "You cannot deceive the land." If you were to airlift an entire herd of cows from Normandy to North Dakota to make "authentic Camembert," you'd end up with a different cheese—not necessarily a bad one but not the same. Because of the impact of the grazing herd's diet, there is no way to replicate the flavor of a particular cheese when you relocate its production. Even within a given region, you'll find variations as you move from

one farm or field to the next. The French have a single word that defines this principle: *terroir*. Every food-savvy Frenchman uses the term in the context of any agricultural product—wine, fruit, vegetables, olive oil, cheese.

Take the cheese called "Fontina," which is made in Sweden, Denmark, the United States, and all over Italy. None of these cheeses can hold a culinary candle to the flavor of the real thing—Fontina Val d'Aosta—which comes from a single valley in the northwest corner of Italy. The difference between the original and these faux Fontinas is the difference between freshly squeezed orange juice and canned frozen concentrate.

3. what were the animals eating?

Typically, the most flavorful cheeses are those made when the animals feed in the pastures. More specifically, the most interesting flavors are likely to be found when the herds are:

- grazing on open-grass pasturage. The more varied and interesting the animals' diet, the more flavorful the cheese.

- grazing on the first grasses of each spring.
- eating slow-growing grass in the autumn.
- feeding at high altitudes. In mountain regions, dairy herds head higher in the summer. They graze in unplowed, unplanted meadows, where the flora is far more diverse and makes for much more interesting eating than that in plowed, lowland pastures.

Conversely, milk that comes from cows feeding on silage is likely to be less interesting. Silage, a modern-day creation that allows farmers to feed animals conveniently in winter, is used when there is nothing freshly available in the fields. If you've ever driven through rural regions of the American Midwest in early autumn, you may have noticed large bales wrapped in black trash bags sitting in the fields. This is silage. Freshly cut hay is allowed to ferment inside the plastic, essentially making the bovine version of sauerkraut. Because of its deleterious effect on flavor, many of the best traditional cheese regions of the world—those that produce real Swiss and Parmigiano-Reggiano, to name two—ban the feeding of silage to dairy herds.

4. which animals were milked?

I don't mean you have to know the animals by name (though most small dairy farmers *are* on a first-name basis with their herds). But you should know the type of animal being milked. Or, better yet, the breed.

Different animals give different milks, which, in turn, yield

very different cheeses. There's a big difference in flavor from cow's to goat's to sheep's milk cheeses. In the area around Naples, water buffalo are the traditional milk providers, giving the characteristic flavor to authentic *mozzarella di bufala.* Each type of milk has its own particular chemistry, its own enzymes, and its own production peculiarities. Because the enzymes and acids in each are different, so, too, the flavor of the finished cheese will vary from type to type. Consequently, people who expect goat's milk cheese to taste pretty much the same as that made from cow's milk are in for something of a shock.

The milk output of each type of animal is also very different, directly affecting the cost of the cheeses made from the respective milks. In general, cows have the highest yields, goats are a distant second, and sheep are the stingiest of all, though their milk provides the highest return of solid cheese per liquid gallon. (This connection to cost is made irrelevant wherever government interferes with market forces, usually in the form of significant subsidies. For example, Pecorino Romano generally goes for less than half the cost of other sheep's milk cheeses.)

Then there's the largely ignored issue of breed. Once upon a time, dozens of different breeds of cattle (or goats or sheep) were being milked; often a given breed was found primarily only in a particular region. For example, the flavor of traditional Double Gloucester cheese is said to have depended on the milk of the Gloucester cattle. Today the old breeds have been largely lost; most are nearly endangered species, having been replaced by Holsteins, the big black and white cows you see on the side of the road when you drive through rural areas in North America. While they have very high yields, their milk has never been known to have a particularly great flavor. Harder-to-find Jerseys and Guernseys, on the other hand, make richer milk, but the fat content is too high for optimal cheesemaking. Other old breeds like Shorthorns, Ayrshire, and Brown Swiss are often considered to produce the best milk for cheese. So why wouldn't everyone want their milk? While the flavor is superior, yields are lower, and costs are higher.

5. what was the quality of the milk?

Cheese can never be better than the raw material from which it is made, and the quality of the milk as it arrives at the dairy plays a huge part in the flavor of the finished cheese.

Milk quality is very much a function of sanitation. The cleaner the animals and the more care the farmer takes in herd management and milking, the better the finished milk. How the milk was handled after it left the animal also af-

a cream cheese worthy of the name

Most Americans know only one kind of cream cheese: the foil-wrapped, mass-produced block available in every supermarket. In taste and texture, this cream cheese is to the handmade kind what packaged American singles are to farmhouse cheeses.

Happily, traditional cream cheese, lost from the American culinary landscape for most of the twentieth century, is making a small comeback. A few artisans are turning to the slower, but far more flavorful methods that were used until the 1920s, when commercial manufacturers, in the interests of efficiency, began to add vegetable gum to firm their product and extend its shelf life.

To make hand-crafted cream cheese, the cheesemakers gently pasteurize newly arrived milk, adding cream (hence the name "cream cheese"). They pour the mixture into a cheese vat, adding vegetarian rennet and active cultures to begin the flavor development and set up the curd. After a few hours, they cut the newly formed, soft-textured curd with stainless-steel knives, then ladle it by hand into cloth bags, where it hangs to drain off the excess moisture. Six to seven hours later, they mix in some sea salt.

Handmade cream cheese is wonderfully smooth in texture, with a fresh, milky flavor and none of the pasty mouth-feel of the gum-laden supermarket sort.

Traditional cream cheese is available from Zingerman's Creamery. In California, Sierra Nevada makes a good cream cheese as well.

fects the cheese. In general, the less turbulence or stress to which the milk is subjected, the more its natural flavors and delicate fat globules are protected. Unfortunately, most milk used in commercial dairies is a blend from different farms, each of varying quality, which is then shipped to the factory in large tanker trucks. Loading and unloading is done with mechanical pumps, causing unwanted turbulence and further lowering the caliber of the finished cheese.

In quality-conscious Switzerland, milk for that country's traditional cheeses must by law be delivered to the dairies in old-style metal milk cans, meaning the milk has never been pumped at high pressure. Ironically, in Michigan (and some other states), the use of milk cans has actually been made illegal because—unlike tanker trucks—they don't come with built-in refrigeration.

How does a cheese buyer have any clue as to the condition of the milk? One challenging (though often very rewarding) choice for the committed cheese hound is to take a field trip to the farm. Ultimately, the best way to judge the quality of the milk is to taste the cheese. The more you get to know good cheese, the more you'll also be able to taste undesirable off flavors. And more often than not, these flavors are the result of less-than-stellar milk quality.

6. is the milk raw or pasteurized?

Pioneered by Louis Pasteur in the Franche-Comté region of eastern France in the second half of the nineteenth century, pasteurization heats milk to high temperatures, in the process killing off the bacteria in the milk. Although pasteurization has brought consistency and

safety to the world of mass-market cheese, it's also made it possible to produce passable cheese from very mediocre or even poor milk.

The problem with pasteurization is that it kills *all* bacteria in the milk, both undesirable and desirable. Unfortunately for the cheesemaker, desirable bacteria contribute much of the flavor to the finished cheese. Without them, the cheesemaker is fighting an uphill battle, trying to obtain an exceptionally full-flavored cheese from less than full-flavored raw material. It can be done, but pasteurization removes much of the complexity and character that make great cheese great. By using top-quality milk in its natural raw state, a cheesemaker has ready access to the full range of natural bacteria that can help to create an exceptionally flavorful, traditional cheese.

So why would anyone advocate milk pasteurization for cheese? American law prohibits the sale of raw-milk cheeses that have not been aged at least sixty days. Some scientists say that raw-milk cheeses that aren't aged for this two-month period can be a health risk. *But this claim has never even come close to being proven.* In fact, the vast majority of incidents of cheese-borne illness have come from cheeses made from pasteurized—often improperly pasteurized—milk! Forced pasteurization would probably create more consistency but also eliminate some of the highest-quality, most interesting cheeses from the field.

7. how old is the cheese?

Without question, age plays a significant factor in flavor. If you're considering buying a piece of cheese, a good shopkeeper should be able to tell you about how old it is.

Some cheeses—mozzarella, ricotta, fresh goat cheese, and handmade cream cheese—are meant to be eaten as fresh as possible. Fresh cheeses taste mostly of the milk; they are delicate, subtly sweet, creamy on the tongue.

On the other hand, many cheeses are at

their best only after long maturing. The difference in flavor from immature to ripe and ready can be significant. Try a taste from two wheels of Swiss Gruyère, one at three months, another at thirteen. The young cheese will likely be fine, much more supple in texture and gently fruity. The more mature cheese will be far firmer, packing a big flavor punch. The younger version will make a good sandwich. The older version will be the one connoisseurs line up for, to eat after dinner, savored in small slices with fine wine or fresh fruit.

8. how was it aged?

Aging well—as many of us know from personal experience—is an art, not a science. And that's as true for cheese as for people. In France, the art of aging cheese is known as *affinage.* In Britain it's called "maturing." By moderating temperature and humidity, through the careful turning, washing, and rubbing of rinds, an *affineur* (or maturer) will bring an already good cheese to new heights of flavor greatness.

Affinage does for cheeses what great coaching does for athletes. An *affineur* goes to cheesemakers and tastes a range of their still young cheeses. He selects and purchases those he believes will mature most effectively, then brings them back to his aging cellars. There he sets to work maturing the cheeses. And then—when he decides the cheese is ready—he sells it, at times directly to consumers but more often to cheese shops or restaurants. Two wheels of cheese from the same farm, made on the same day but aged by two different *affineurs,* will result in two different cheeses.

Although *affinage* has been practiced in Europe for centuries, it's been almost unheard of in North America up until the last ten or twelve years. Recently, however, some select retailers of traditional cheeses have begun to practice the art of *affinage* in North America, including Zingerman's; Formaggio Kitchen in Cambridge, Massachusetts; Dean and DeLuca in Napa, California; and Fairway Market in New York. Some restaurants, including the Baricelli Inn in Cleveland and Artisanal and Picholine in New York, have undertaken similar aging activities.

In many cases, extra aging can bring out more flavor and complexity. But older cheese isn't always better. Each cheese has an optimal point of flavor and maturity. A Stilton at two months will be immature, at four or more, may be perfect, but at six months it may be overripe. The *affineur*'s assignment is to find that perfect point.

The temperature at which a cheese is matured can significantly alter the speed at which it ages, which is one reason why you can't judge a cheese by age alone. A hurried *affineur* may choose to age it at warmer-than-optimal temperatures, and the resulting flavors may be out of balance.

aging gracefully

In the world of cheese, a cave (pronounce it with a short *a* as in the original French) is the aging room in which the cheese is matured. The cave's natural humidity and relatively constant temperature (it is protected from extreme changes) are ideal for aging. Commercially built caves are modern-day re-creations of the conditions that a shepherd would have found inside a natural cave. With a little help from humidity-control gauges and ventilation systems, modern caves may even provide a more consistent environment.

Caves are almost always quite damp. The walls and floor are made from stone to hold the humidity, and the floor is washed down regularly with fresh water to add more moisture to the air. Humidity levels range from 80 to nearly 98 percent. All of which helps keep the aging cheese from drying out too quickly, and encourages flavor development.

The temperature in the caves varies from cheese type to cheese type, but is usually about 50 to 60 degrees Fahrenheit, warm enough to allow the cheese to mature properly, cool enough to prevent spoilage or excessive sweating (and therefore loss of precious butterfat).

Aging in traditional caves is almost always done on wooden shelves because, despite the modern world's predilection for supposedly ultrasanitary plastic, cheese ages more effectively on wood: the wood breathes better, allows for more even maturation, and provides a safer, more sanitary environment.

cheese care

Here are a few tips that can help you handle your cheese more effectively once you get it home.

get it cut to order

I'm a big advocate of buying cheese that is cut to order instead of the stuff that's been precut and sealed in plastic for days, weeks, or even months before you buy it. Prepackaging isn't always evil, but I can assure you that the cheese isn't improving while it's sitting in its airtight protector.

wrap it in paper, not plastic

The best way to go is to keep it wrapped in proper cheese paper. Commonly used in France but still hard to find in the States, the paper has one shiny and lightly waxed side while the other side has a matte finish. The shiny side protects the cheese, allowing it to breathe without drying out. Wax paper is a good, readily available option. Other suitable substitutes include: double-layered parch-ment paper; medium-weight cotton tea towels; and brown paper grocery bags, cut and then folded around the cheese. Note: don't wrap different cheeses together, as they're likely to pick up aromas from one another.

store it carefully

One of the best ways to protect the texture and integrity of a cheese is to avoid frequent temperature changes. If you're going to eat the cheese within a day or so and you're in a cool environment, you may be able to leave it right on the counter. If you're in a warmer space or if you're going to keep the cheese longer, it's probably best to store it in the refrigerator. In every case, wrap the cheese properly.

eat it at room temperature

If you want to serve your cheese at its fullest flavor, put it out on the counter well before you're ready to eat.

9. what kind of rind does the cheese have?

A rind protects the paste (the technical term for the inside of a cheese) in the same way that a crust protects the interior crumb of a loaf of hearth-baked bread. A quick look at a cheese's rind will tell you a lot about what you're likely to find inside. The best cheeses are almost always those that have been allowed to develop natural rinds, with the exception of fresh cheeses, which have no rind at all. Traditional cheesemakers work hard to put proper rinds on their cheeses. Salt, brine, or cheesecloth are the most common tools of the rind builders.

Many hard cheeses are traditionally matured in cloth "bandages," which allow the cheese to breathe as it matures. As the cheese loses moisture, its flavor is slowly concentrated. Unfortunately, most commercial cheeses are now aged in sealed plastic for practical purposes. The plastic prohibits mold growth and reduces moisture loss and, hence, cost. But aging in plastic also minimizes flavor development and traps moisture in the cheese, which can wreak havoc with texture.

10. may we have a taste?

Any good cheese seller will gladly give you a sample of his wares before you make your purchasing decision. Ultimately, the only opinion that really counts is yours. And even if you've diligently asked every one of the previous nine questions, the deal still isn't worth sealing unless you like the taste of a cheese. So don't be shy. Ask to try it before you hand over your hard-earned cash.

the cheese course

There are few things nicer than the European custom of the cheese course. Both in formal restaurants and in casual home settings, it's the norm to bring out the cheese near the end of the meal, after the main course is finished. Typically, dessert follows.

Choose cheeses whose flavors are compatible with the main course you've just served. When you've made a pungent garlic and saffron-scented bouillabaisse for dinner, for instance, you'll want to find cheese that won't get lost in the aftermath, such as a nicely aged sheep's milk cheese or perhaps a bit of beautiful blue Roquefort. On the other hand, if you're serving up a delicate fresh trout, look for cheeses with softer, less assertive flavors, such as a nicely aged Comté or a mild fresh goat cheese.

The only cheeses that don't work well after dinner are smoked or spiced; their flavors tend to be too intrusive when you're trying to make your way gently from savory to sweet.

For a casual dinner, a single, simple, superb cheese will do just fine. If you're entertaining, I'd recommend that you pick between one and five cheeses to serve after the main course. More than that, and you start to overwhelm your guests' palates.

Look for cheeses that offer diversity in shape, color, and size, as well as flavor. A standard recipe for a good five-cheese board would be an aged Cheddar, a semisoft cheese like Pont l'Evêque, a well-aged mountain Gruyère or Comté, a pungent goat cheese, and a blue cheese like Stilton or Roquefort. Eat them in that order—mildest to strongest, so the flavors of the stronger cheeses don't overwhelm the subtleties of their milder comrades.

Bread and crackers are fine accompaniments. If you want to meld the cheese and dessert courses, fresh fruit can be great too— a handful of grapes, a couple of ripe figs, a tree-ripened peach. Toasted nuts, such as walnuts, hazelnuts, or almonds, are also nice.

Follow the regional styles of the main dish. More often than not, the cheeses of the region will be well suited to the local cooking. After a few hundred years together, one will have adapted to the other to create a mutually rewarding culinary relationship.

If you're serving food from a cuisine that doesn't include much cheese, such as Asian, it's a good idea to skip the cheese course.

Buy small quantities, and buy the best. A few slivers of a great cheese will satisfy in a way that a mediocre offering never will. Eat it slowly.

Don't rush to judgment. Let the flavors settle on your tongue. This soft melt-in-the-mouth cheese moment is what makes eating cheese toward the end of the meal such a potent pleasure.

a few cheese board ideas

English Farmhouse Cheddar, Farmhouse Cheshire, Farmhouse Lancashire, Stilton. Be sure to seek out true farmhouse versions of other British cheeses. Their factory counterparts are usually severely lacking in flavor. Stilton is the lone exception; it hasn't been made on the farm for decades.

French Camembert, Comté, Pont l'Evêque, Roquefort, Selles-sur-Cher (or another nicely aged goat cheese).

Italian Fontina Val d'Aosta, Gorgonzola, Parmigiano-Reggiano, Taleggio.

Goat Cheeses Four goat cheeses with contrasting flavors, shapes, and sizes.

Mountain Cheeses Aged Comté, Fontina Val d'Aosta, well-aged Gruyère, and Reblochon.

A Bevy of Blues Gorgonzola, Point Reyes Blue from California, Roquefort, Stilton.

parmigiano-reggiano cheese

Everyone knows the name *Parmesan,* and even the term *Parmigiano* is used liberally. What many folks don't realize is that (a) Parmigiano-Reggiano cheese is a very specific member of a large family of grating cheeses made in Italy, and (b) although hundreds of creameries bear the seal and stamp of the Consorzio del Formaggio Parmigiano-Reggiano, there is a good deal of variation among the many dairies that produce this king of Italian cheeses.

Founded in 1934, the Consorzio is a self-governing association of about six hundred dairies in the provinces of Parma, Modena, Reggio Emilia, and parts of Mantova and Bologna. Each creamery is a member, so in essence the Consorzio works for the cheese-makers. That said, it's the Consorzio—not individual producers—that puts in place high standards of operation and runs ongoing tests to make sure those standards are met. You can see the Consorzio's certification mark on every wheel of Parmigiano-Reggiano. A dozen or so inspectors ensure that any wheel that wears its round seal has earned it.

The most impressive thing about the work of the Consorzio is that its standards have kept production of Parmigiano small, yet still economically viable. The average Parmigiano-Reggiano dairy makes a grand total of eight or nine wheels of cheese each morning, roughly the same level as the smallest of American cheesemaking farms.

Time is short, and it's a lot easier to let someone else's fingers do the grating. But you'll
never get wonderful cheese if
you buy grated Parmigiano. For
openers, it's exposed to air at a
rate that will quickly diminish
both aroma and flavor. (Think
of the difference between buying ground coffee and grinding
fresh beans right before brewing.) In addition, when stores
grate, some of the natural mold
spores on the rind will inevitably make their way into
the cheese. Buy Parmigiano in
chunks and take the two minutes to grate your own right
before you use it.

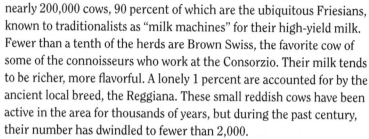

cows and curds

Approximately 7,000 farms sell milk to the 600
Parmigiano dairies, drawing daily on the output of
nearly 200,000 cows, 90 percent of which are the ubiquitous Friesians,
known to traditionalists as "milk machines" for their high-yield milk.
Fewer than a tenth of the herds are Brown Swiss, the favorite cow of
some of the connoisseurs who work at the Consorzio. Their milk tends
to be richer, more flavorful. A lonely 1 percent are accounted for by the
ancient local breed, the Reggiana. These small reddish cows have been
active in the area for thousands of years, but during the past century,
their number has dwindled to fewer than 2,000.

Although Emilia-Romagna is one of Italy's prime dairy regions, you
can drive all the way across it and see scarcely a single cow. The cows
are no longer grazed outdoors because the land is so valuable that it's
reserved for cash crops. Instead the farmers bring freshly cut grass and
hay into the barns. The Consorzio allows no silage or other fermented
feed. The most flavorful Parmigiano is very often made at higher altitudes, though it's difficult for consumers to know which cheeses are
made in the mountains. Generally, cows in these mountainous parts
have more interesting eating opportunities. There — in season — they
graze on wildflowers, herbs, and grasses
from unplowed meadows.

Fresh milk is delivered twice a day to the
dairies directly from local farms, arriving in
almost identical condition to the way it left
the cows. (There are a handful of farms that
use only their own milk.) No pasteurization
or other processing is allowed, so milk
quality must be high. The milk is often
transported in shiny cans, which are carried and poured into vats by hand (the
Consorzio prohibits pumping). The
Consorzio checks the milk every fifteen days to verify cleanliness and
quality control.

a visit to a parmigiano dairy

Not long ago, I visited a Parmigiano dairy, under the guidance of the Consorzio's Giovanni Morini, who has been involved with Parmigiano most of his adult life. About five foot ten with soft gray eyes, he reminds me of Jason Robards. He wears a black felt hat, an odd match with his long white inspector's coat.

As we walk through the dairy, the first things to catch my eye are the copper cheesemaking kettles. The kettles are one of the requirements imposed by the Consorzio on all authorized makers of Parmigiano-Reggiano. Consorzio representatives have told me that the copper is used for its thermal properties and has no impact on the taste of the cheese. But many Swiss cheesemakers, who also use copper kettles, are adamant that the copper leaves trace elements in the cheese that contribute to its final flavor.

Some dairies have only one or two kettles, others as many as fourteen. Consorzio regulations stipulate that there be no more than seven kettles for a single *casaro* (cheesemaker) to oversee, so a fourteen-kettle dairy always has two certified cheesemakers on-site. A master cheesemaker must have ten to fourteen years of active apprenticeship—the same sort of training time the United States requires of brain surgeons—before the Consorzio will turn him loose on the liquid milk. (To the best of my knowledge, all the *casari* are men. Cheesemaking is one of the few fields that has yet to admit women to its inner circles.)

The kettles are roughly five feet in diameter at the top, and each holds about 1,100 liters of milk. All told, it takes about 8.5 liters (about 9 quarts) of milk to make a pound of Parmigiano-Reggiano. The lower third of each parabola-shaped kettle sits below floor level. In the old days, wood fires heated the kettles. Today gas-generated steam does the job.

Production of Parmigiano-Reggiano takes place today pretty much as it has for centuries. The evening milk is skimmed of cream, then blended with new morning milk the next day. The mixture is warmed gently, and liquid starter culture and rennet are added. The Consorzio requires that the starter be the old-fashioned type, made on-site in each dairy using some of the previous day's whey, which has been allowed to ferment overnight. Regulations also require use of natural animal rennet from calves.

Eight to twelve minutes later, the liquid milk has been converted to a seamless, cream-colored curd. It looks a lot like a giant cup of custard. Gently the cheesemaker begins to break it, starting the process that separates the curds from the whey.

The kettle is stirred mechanically, while being heated to allow further separation of curd and whey and to enhance the development of acidity.

When the proper acidity level is reached, the stirring ceases. The curd settles to the bottom of the vat, where it knits into a single solid mass.

The decision to move to the next stage belongs to the *casaro*. In part he bases it on temperature and acidity levels. But it's also an art. The cheesemaker feels the curd, squeezes it, tests its resilience in the palm of his hand, and may or may not move it to the following phase. Said Giovanni Morini, "The fingers of the *casaro* are critical. Bad timing can be fatal."

The *casaro* then takes a pair of two-foot-long sticks and ties each to opposite corners of a large square piece of cheesecloth. He dips the cloth into the whey to moisten it, then slides it underneath the solid curd. At this point the cheese looks something like a big round of fresh white mozzarella. The cheesemaker pulls the curd, still dripping copious quantities of whey, up out of the vat, and suspends it to allow it to drain. When it has attained the appropriate level of firmness, the *casaro* cuts the curd in half with a long knife. The newly separated cheeses are resubmerged in the whey, tied into their own individual cheesecloths, and removed to straight-sided forms lined with more cheesecloth, where they continue to drain for most of the day. The cloth is changed every one to one and a half hours. Bad management at this stage can cause a highly acidic layer to form on the outside of the cheese.

In the evening the cloth is removed, and white plastic sheets that have the words "Parmigiano-Reggiano" stenciled in pin dots up and down their sides are slid between the forms and the still impressionable cheeses. This step was added in the mid-1960s, part of the Consorzio's never-ending effort to differentiate Parmigiano-Reggiano from its many imitators. Plastic stamps mark the cheese with the month and year of manufacture and the dairy's number.

After a few days of restful draining, the young *parmigiani* are moved down to the cellar and placed in baths of brine. They float, bobbing like a flock of orderly rubber ducks, and are rolled regularly to ensure even salt distribution.

The salt in the liquid naturally pulls moisture out of the young cheeses and also enters the curd, the only salt that is added. The wheels spend twenty-four to twenty-eight days in the brine, after which they are removed to storage rooms. The salt continues to make its way into the heart of the cheese; all told, it takes a good six to eight months before it completes its crystalline journey to the center of the wheel.

aging the cheese

In the maturing rooms, the wheels of Parmigiano are stacked on pine shelves, which fill the room from the floor to the thirty-foot-high ceiling. The cheeses spend anywhere from twelve to forty-eight months in these rooms, most making their way out in eighteen to twenty-four months. Temperatures are left to the swings of nature,

One of the magical things about biting into a piece of really well aged Parmigiano-Reggiano is the feel of those tiny sharp crystals crunching on your tongue. Many folks mistakenly think these are salt crystals, but they aren't. During the aging process, the proteins in the cheese break down into smaller nutritional units (peptones, peptides, and free amino acids, in case you were wondering). Some of them — particularly tyrosine — are naturally converted into a crystalline structure. Their presence is one of the signs of a well-made cheese and long aging.

and seasonal changes are an important part of the cheese's ultimate flavor. Throughout, the cheeses are brushed regularly to prevent molding and turned frequently to ensure even moisture distribution. During the aging, they will reduce in weight by about 20 percent.

checking the cheese

Inspectors check all the cheeses at the end of twelve months. Using a small metal hammer, they tap the top and sides of each wheel, much as pediatricians check children's reflexes by tapping their knees. They listen, shift a few inches to the right, then quickly hammer again, until they have tapped their way around the entire form. A well-made wheel will have a consistent, solid sound to it. If a cheese has physical faults or gaps, the blows will sound hollow or uneven. In that case, the pin dots embedded in its sides are scraped off. These cheeses are salable as common grating cheese, but never with the name Parmigiano-Reggiano and never for export.

Now and again, the inspector will probe a cheese with a thin metal auger to slide out a tiny sample of the interior paste. Any fault is immediately noticeable to the trained nose. If the cheeses pass inspection, they are stamped on their side with the Consorzio's certification.

To this day, when folks in Parma go into a store to buy a couple of pounds of Parmigiano, they simply ask for a kilo of cheese. No need to say which one—everyone knows. The name may vary from town to town. In Parma, it's "Parmigiano," but farther south in Reggio, people ask for "Reggiano."

head-to-tail flavor

The key to good Parmigiano, locals insist, is the flavor, not the number of months a cheese has been matured. But to get some insight into what a given wheel will taste like, locate the stamp on the side of each wheel that tells you the month and year of its "birth."

To be ready for optimal eating, Parmigiano must be aged through two summers. Summer is when the cheese sweats, concentrating its flavor and expelling unneeded moisture. It's also when the natural bacterial activity in the cheese is at its highest, meaning that the summer months make a disproportionately high contribution to the flavor of the finished cheese. With this in mind, Italians divide the Parmigiano calendar into three parts:

1. January through April is known as the "head." Cheeses made during these months get two full summers of aging and so are ready in just eighteen to twenty months.

2. Cheeses made in the months of May through August are said to come from the "body" of the year. Because these wheels don't get started in the aging rooms until midsummer, they often need more than eighteen months to mature properly.

3. The "tail" is September to December. By definition, cheeses made in this part of the year almost always need nearly two years of maturing time.

grand opening

A good cheesemonger never cuts a wheel of Parmigiano. Instead he opens it slowly, like the secret door to a treasure cave. First, he carefully wipes the wheel with a dry cloth. A special set of Parmigiano cutting knives are brought to the table. Using a hook-shaped blade, the cheesemonger scores the outer rind of the cheese all the way around the wheel. Then he pushes a six-inch-long pointed blade into the top and inserts an almond-shaped knife into each side of the wheel. The knives taper toward their points so that the part near the handle slowly coaxes the cheese open. After allowing the cheese to rest for a few minutes, he removes the knives, turns the wheel over, and re-peats the process. Again, after a suitable wait, the cheese is ready: a simple twist of one of the handles opens the wheel right up.

The newly split surfaces of the cheese are uneven, never smooth. It's best to use this same method when breaking Parmesan into smaller pieces at home: straight-sided cubes sim-ply don't taste as good as small, rough chunks.

The opening of a cheese is a memorable event. As the rind of the cheese is scored, the aroma beckons. And when the wheel is actually opened, the scent is amazing. It's sweet and subtle. It smells of cream, sometimes of lightly toasted nuts. At times there is a distinct smell of fruit, per-haps pineapple. It's impossible not to want to taste on the spot.

buying primo parmigiano-reggiano

Although the Parmigiano-Reggiano pin dots tell you that the cheese was made according to Consorzio specifications, they don't tell you whether what you're buying is great or just good. Here are a few other tips for the taste-conscious consumer.

buy pieces cut from whole wheels

Generally, shops that sell a relatively small volume are caught in a bind. They want to keep their cheese fresh, so they buy in quarter wheels. In my experience, however, the cheese that comes from these precut and vacuum-packed pieces is generally not the best. Even less desirable are the precut one-pound wedges that are packed in Italy and shipped overseas in plastic casings.

soup bones for vegetarians: reggiano rinds

Rinds from Parmigiano-Reggiano are the absolute best thing you'll ever add to soup stock, sauce, or broth. (See Provençal Pistou, page 116.) The rind on a wheel of Parmigiano is merely dried cheese: no wax, no coloring, no additives. So when you throw it into your stock, it's essentially like adding a bit of cheese. The rind adds enormous flavor and richness to whatever you're cooking. When the stock is done, simply fish it out, and then with a sharp knife (carefully) cut off any cheese that's softened up enough to take off. Chop the cheese and add it to whatever you're cooking. If you like, you can even cool off the rest of the rind, wrap in foil, and save it to use in a second batch of soup.

look for the special seal

Each dairy has the option of asking (and paying for) the Consorzio inspectors to return and recheck what it feels are its best cheeses for certification as "Extra Quality" (or, alternatively, "Export Quality"). The seal shows that the cheese is completely free of physical defects that might damage aroma or flavor. These cheeses do cost more, but they have no internal or external faults and are likely to contain more flavorful cheese. This seal won't guarantee incredible cheese every time because there are still significant differences in flavor from one wheel to the next, but it will get you close more often than not.

check the month and year of making

This date is stamped into the side of all wheels of Parmigiano so any shop that buys whole wheels should be able to tell you. It's in Italian: for instance, GEN is Gennaio, or January; MAG is Maggio, or May; GIU is Giugno, or June; LUG is

One of my favorite meals is just cooked spaghetti tossed with lots of Parmigiano-Reggiano, a really flavorful olive oil, some freshly ground black pepper, and maybe a few toasted pine nuts on top. You might even add a little fried chopped garlic.

Of course, Parmigiano-Reggiano isn't just for putting on pasta. It's excellent grated onto a green salad. You can also cut slivers of it with a vegetable peeler and use them as garnish on salads of all sorts. A little olive oil and Parmigiano add immeasurably to any vegetable soup.

To me, though, the best way to enjoy this cheese is simply to eat it as is. Its rich, sweet, nutty flavor is the perfect way to segue from the main course into the dessert. Better still, if you're not in the mood for dessert, Parmigiano is a great way to end the meal. Dip small pieces into aged balsamic vinegar, or drizzle chunks of the cheese with chestnut honey and small pieces of toasted walnuts or pine nuts (see page 225).

Luglio, or July. Remember, you want cheese that's been aged through two summers. If it's a spring or winter cheese, it should be aged at least eighteen months. If it's an autumn cheese, it should be more than two years old.

Summer cheese has the most eye appeal. Since the cows are eating feed brought in from the more floral summer pastures, Parmigiano made in June and July will almost always be more golden. The summer cheeses also tend to be the most piquant. They're particularly good for making pesto because they can hold their own when blended with basil, garlic, and olive oil.

Spring cheese can be good too. The new season's grass is coming up in the fields, creating great complexity in the flavor. Spring milk has less butterfat, though, and hence the cheese is drier in texture. Consequently, spring cheeses can be more difficult to cut, and they don't have the luscious, creamy mouth-feel associated with autumn cheese.

Autumn cheese is generally credited with being the most desirable. It's usually more balanced in flavor with a higher butterfat level, so it tastes very rich and full. Autumn cheese is usually the most enjoyable for sitting down and eating as is.

Before 1984, official Parmigiano-Reggiano practice dictated that the cheese be made only between April 1 and November 11. Cheeses made in winter are not the most prized wheels. But they too can be excellent, whiter due to the cow's winter diet, with deliciously delicate flavors.

Cheeses that have been aged for three or even four years are more intense than younger cheeses, which are soft and gentle. By local standards, the best Parmigiano-Reggiano is sweet, mellow, and mild. As locals see it, Parmigiano should always complement, never overwhelm. Most turn up their noses at stronger cheeses, shipping them to the south of Italy, where the preference is for Parmigiano with more piquancy.

get a taste

Taste is the key. Almost every piece of Parmigiano starts out tasting good. But the best don't stop there. They seem to have a fourth dimension, building until they fill every inch of your mouth with rich, complex, buttery, nutty, pleasantly sweet Parmigiano flavor. There's a liveliness in these cheeses that's lacking in lesser versions. They're crackly, crunchy, and creamy all at the same time.

salsa di noci
ligurian walnut sauce

*S*alsa di Noci is typically served on stuffed pasta. It's great on toast too—I think of it as a savory Italian version of a peanut butter sandwich. You can vary the proportions of the nuts to your taste. And you can toast or not toast them. Toasting will deepen the flavor and darken the color. Untoasted, you'll get a more delicate sauce. Either way it's excellent.

- 1 garlic clove, peeled and halved
- 5 ounces walnut halves ($1\frac{1}{4}$ cups)
- 2 ounces hazelnuts ($\frac{1}{2}$ cup)
- 1 ounce pine nuts (2 tablespoons), preferably Mediterranean
- 2–3 tablespoons delicate extra virgin olive oil, preferably Ligurian
- 2 ounces Parmigiano-Reggiano cheese (without rind), freshly grated (1 cup)
- Coarse sea salt to taste

Food processor method: Finely chop the garlic in a food processor. Add the nuts and pulse until coarsely chopped. With the motor running, add the olive oil a little at a time to help process the nuts into a moderately smooth paste with the texture of chunky natural peanut butter. Add the Parmigiano and process to blend. Add salt to taste.

Mortar and pestle method: Slowly work the garlic and a few pinches of salt into a paste with a mortar and pestle. Working slowly, add a few of the nuts, crushing them into a paste each time before adding more. Add a little oil as you're adding the nuts to moisten the mixture. Add more nuts and oil until the paste has the texture of chunky natural peanut butter. Add the Parmigiano and blend well. Add salt to taste.

The sauce will keep, covered, in the refrigerator for 2 weeks, but be sure to bring it back to room temperature before you use it.

makes about 2 cups, enough to serve 4 to 6

ligurian pesto

While there are thousands of ways to make pesto, this recipe is—from my experience—the closest you'll get to the real thing. It's made with a mortar and pestle, not in a food processor. (You'll need a mortar with a diameter of at least 8 inches.) This pesto should look more like guacamole than most bottled pesto sauces, which are usually blade-chopped bits of basil suspended in so-so olive oil. The garlic is a key flavor contributor, but it won't overwhelm everything else.

      2 cups loosely packed fresh basil leaves
         Pinch coarse sea salt
      1 garlic clove, peeled and halved, center sprout removed
    ¼ cup pine nuts, or more to taste, preferably Mediterranean
    ¼ cup freshly grated Parmigiano-Reggiano cheese, or more to
         taste
    2–3 tablespoons extra virgin olive oil, preferably Ligurian

Wash the basil and pat it dry (or if you're prepared to be authentically Ligurian, wipe each leaf with a clean, slightly damp kitchen towel). Be sure the basil is dry so that you don't add unwanted water to the pesto.

If the leaves are large, tear them into smaller pieces—don't slice them with a knife, which will cause them to blacken.

Start by putting a pinch of sea salt and a few basil leaves in the mortar. With a pestle, slowly crush the basil gently but firmly against the sides of the mortar. The leaves should gradually disintegrate as you move the pestle around in a circular motion.

Continue this process, adding a few basil leaves at a time, until you've used them all. Add the garlic and mash it into the basil mixture. Add the pine nuts and mash them into a paste.

Add the Parmigiano-Reggiano and stir to combine. Add the olive oil slowly, stirring to make an almost opaque sauce with a creamy consistency.

The sauce can be kept, covered, in the refrigerator for 2 weeks. Be sure to bring it back to room temperature and give it a good stir before using.

makes ½ to ¾ cup, enough to serve 4 to 6

parmigiano-reggiano with honey and walnuts

If you're at all like me in preferring cheese to sweets, here's something to serve after dinner that combines the cheese course and dessert into a single delicious and luxurious interlude. You can vary the honey if you like, but the cheese should be the best Parmigiano you can put your hands on.

3   ounces Parmigiano-Reggiano cheese
1   tablespoon chestnut honey or other full-flavored honey
2   tablespoons walnut halves, toasted (see page 31)

Break the Parmigiano-Reggiano into bite-sized pieces. Don't cut it into cubes with a knife. Part of the enjoyment of eating it this way is the rough texture and the odd shapes and sizes you'll get by breaking it with a Parmesan knife (see "Grand Opening," page 220). Arrange the cheese pieces on a serving dish. Drizzle the honey over the top, sprinkle on the walnut halves, and serve.   serves 4 to 8

cheddar cheese

Despite the increased interest in more exotic fare, Cheddar remains far and away the most popular cheese in North America and probably the world. Unfortunately, the vast majority of what's out there provides consumers with a mere shadow of how great a great Cheddar can be.

days of cheddars past

As long on history as it is on flavor, Cheddar dates back to the sixteenth century. The town of Cheddar is in Somerset County in the southwest of England. Its original notoriety came not from the cheese that bears its name, but from the geological attraction of the nearby Cheddar Gorge, a deep fissure in the Mendip Hills. Eighteenth-century tourists, seeking escape from the increasingly grim urban life of London, were drawn to the natural wonders of the area. Much as they would today, many took home wedges of the local cheese as a savory souvenir, which they called by the name of the nearby gorge. Before long all of the Somerset dairy farms—both in the village and throughout the county—adopted the name Cheddar for their cheeses.

England

somerset

The seeds of Cheddar's international success started with the global growth of the British Empire. Like cheesemaking versions of Johnny Appleseed, British colonists planted the seeds of Cheddar production in every temperate climate they conquered. Look at a map from the era of the empire and you'll see the signs of their success. Cheddar is made across the United States, Canada, Scotland, Ireland, New Zealand, and Australia. (The heat of the equatorial colonies in Africa and the West Indies has kept spots like Kenya, Jamaica, and Barbados off the list.) Why Cheddar? Its long keeping qualities have made it adaptable where other cheeses couldn't cut it. Additionally, Cheddar fits large-scale factory production more easily than other British cheese staples.

Cheddar came to North America in the seventeenth century, arriving with the Pilgrims, spreading through New England and then westward across the continent. In 1790 the first American-made cheeses were exported back to Britain (where good Cheddar was—and still is—in short supply). Over the years, American exports increased. For many years the Cheddar

sent back from the Western Hemisphere was known in the United Kingdom simply as "American cheese." This term was abandoned only in the early part of the twentieth century when American cheese came to mean the processed fare we all know today.

In the nineteenth century, significant scientific and industrial changes improved cheese consistency and quality, but also signaled the rapid decline of traditional Cheddar making. The first cheese factory in the world—built specifically to make Cheddar—was opened by Jesse Williams in Rome, New York, in 1851. Up until that point, all cheese—Cheddar included—had been made on farms. Within fifteen years, New York had more than four hundred cheese factories. Today nearly all the world's Cheddar is made in commercial factories, and there are fewer than four to five dozen Cheddar farms left.

You don't have to be a cheese connoisseur to tell the difference between a fairly flavorless factory Cheddar and a more traditional one. Still, with so many offerings available, which are the best? And why would cheeses that bear the same name be so different depending on where they were made?

how traditional cheddar is made

In large factories, Cheddar is manufactured in enormous quantities in closed vats with minimal human intervention. But in a few small dairies in the United States, Canada, and Britain

(among others countries), Cheddar is still produced primarily by hand, using techniques that rely on the skill and craft of the cheesemaker. Although each maker will inevitably have his own variations on the Cheddar theme, in abbreviated form the basic method of production is the same:

starting the cheesemaking

Traditional Cheddar is made from cow's milk. The milk is slowly warmed, then rennet and starter cultures are added. The starter encourages bacterial activity, which in turn enhances the natural flavor of the milk. The rennet gets the cheesemaking process in motion, slowly causing the milk to "set up" into curd in the vat.

The new curd is as fragile as a soufflé freshly taken from the oven and must be handled with great care. A sudden bump into the side of the vat at this formative stage can cause

the curd to crack, releasing the liquid whey too soon. In order to tell when the curd is ready for cutting, the Cheddar maker simply sticks his finger into the solid, placid mass to make a tiny slit. A soft but clean break means the curd is ready to cut.

Rectangular metal frames, each with half a dozen thin blades, are inserted into the vat. The initial cuts turn the curd loose from the whey, leaving a slowly swirling mass that must be continuously, though gently, stirred. If the stirring stops, the solids will settle to the bottom of the vat and firm up too quickly. Stir too hard and the still fragile curd will be damaged. During this time, the curd is heated. When the right level of acidity is reached, the stirring stops and the curd is allowed to set up. The curd then settles to the bottom of the vat, and the liquid whey is drained off. The cubes of curd are raked into long rows on either side of the vat, where they rest for a short time, allowing the natural knitting process to continue and acidity levels to rise.

cheddaring

Although most of us know Cheddar as a cheese, cheddar also refers to the method by which this traditional cheese is made, and today it is the process—more than the flavor and texture—that is the defining characteristic of Cheddar. Developed in England in the middle of the nineteenth century, cheddaring requires that the reformed curd be cut into five- or six-inch-wide blocks, which are then stacked one on top of the other, two high, and allowed to rest while their natural weight forces the whey to trickle out. Stacking the blocks also helps the curd retain warmth, which in turn encourages the acidity development that is critical to the final flavor of a good cheese. After ten minutes or so, the blocks are rotated and restacked, first three high, then four high, and so on, up to seven feet. The higher the stacks get, the more the weight of those on top compresses the blocks at the bottom. At the end of the process, the blocks have drastically flattened, and the curd is far firmer and drier than it was when the cheddaring started. At this stage, the curd is described —both casually and professionally—as having the textural quality of "cooked chicken breast." All told, the process may take two to three hours.

Finally, the curd blocks are fed through a metal-toothed mill, which chops them into cubes a couple of inches wide. Salt is added and stirred in to ensure even distribution. The shredded curd is scooped into "forms," each lined with light plastic or cheesecloth. The forms are mechanically pressed and expel additional whey for another day, and are then sent to the aging rooms to begin a stay of months or, better yet, years on the shelves before being shipped off to stores for sale.

english versus american cheddar

Although English and American Cheddars began as essentially one cheese, they have become quite different. Other than on a cheese board, where I'm pretty open to variation, I'd almost never substitute one for the other.

The first distinction between the two starts in the soil. The pasturage of southern Vermont is significantly unlike that of Somerset in southwest Eng-

land. For that reason, the milk and, in turn, the cheeses will taste noticeably different. The techniques used for aging the cheese in the two countries are also dissimilar.

cloth aging versus plastic aging

Although nearly all the world's Cheddars, including most American ones, are aged in plastic, a handful of remaining English farms still age their Cheddars the traditional way, in cloth. Aging in cloth means that moisture evaporates more quickly, resulting in a closer-textured, drier, more intensely flavored cheese. When you open the wheel, you'll see that a half inch or so of the outer edge of the cheese will be markedly darker and drier. The flavor of this border zone is noticeably earthier, tasting more of the stone of the aging room than does the sheltered light golden interior of the cheese.

Because it "protects" the cheese from mold growth and minimizes moisture loss, plastic also tends to inhibit flavor development and al-

ways results in a moister, more malleable texture. In contrast to the cloth-wrapped English Cheddar, an American block that's aged in plastic will have a uniform texture and flavor throughout.

While American cheesemakers usually age their Cheddars at less than 40 degrees Fahrenheit, English cheesemakers mature their Cheddars in rooms that are about 25 percent warmer, in the range of 50 degrees Fahrenheit. The combination of the cloth wrapping and the warmer environment promotes the development of mold on the outside of the cloth. This mold gives the cheese the mustiness that the English love. By contrast, American Cheddars aged in plastic are cleaner-tasting but also less complex in flavor. Because it loses moisture much more rapidly than a plastic-wrapped Cheddar, an English Farmhouse Cheddar of eighteen months may well have twice the flavor intensity of an American Cheddar of the same age.

As a result of the differences in aging techniques, English and American cheesemakers have completely different expectations about the texture of a well-made Cheddar too. The English like theirs drier and flakier: pull off a piece and bend it back and it should softly break, or flake, like a tender piece of piecrust. Americans, on the other hand, believe that better Cheddar should be pliable, softer, wetter, and capable of a good bit of bending before it breaks.

With both English and American Cheddars, I look for buttery, rich, smooth, mouth-filling flavor. Well-made Cheddar of every origin avoids the bitter flavor pitfalls of most industrial versions. Great farm Cheddar should taste good at first, then better, then great. A minute or two after you've swallowed—if you stop long enough to take notice—you'll discover a whole range of complex follow-up flavors. That said, there is an ocean of difference between what Americans and British like in the flavor of their Cheddar.

great english farmhouse cheddars

Because it's so different from what most of us are used to, English Farmhouse Cheddar won't win over every palate. To me, it's clearly one of the world's great cheeses. On looks alone, it's something special—golden yellow, the color of summer butter made fresh on the farm. It's deliciously close-textured—"dry" by American standards. The best of it is notably nutty and often has a flavor that I can describe only as "eggy." It has a distinct earthiness, a touch of wild mushroom that tugs on the back of your tongue after you've swallowed.

Sadly, there are only about thirty Cheddar farms still at it in England. And of those, only two—Keen's and Montgomery's—are still making true farmhouse cheese from the raw milk of their own herds. Both do traditional cloth wrapping of their cheeses. And both work extensively with Neal's Yard Dairy, the respected London cheese shop and *affineur*. The folks at Neal's Yard taste and select the best cheeses from the farms' production (a bit less than half of what the two make in total), and then mature the cheeses even further. The best of the best of this traditional English Farmhouse Cheddar is sold under the Neal's Yard brand with the farms' names listed on the label. I look for those that are aged at least twelve months.

KEEN'S FARM George and Stephen Keen are the latest generation of their family to oversee cheesemaking at Moorhayes Farm in Somerset County in the southwest of England. Their land lies near the village of Wincanton, about halfway between London and Land's End, the "right foot" of England (if you turn the map of Great Britain on its side), which looks as if it's about to boot Ireland over toward North America. The farmhouse is picturesque, one of those rambling, two-story stone buildings with orange-tiled roofs that are so much a part of the English countryside. Dorothy Keen, who learned cheesemaking from her aunt, has slowly passed her sixty-some years of accumulated knowledge on to her sons, who, I hope, are passing it on again to the next generation. At its best, the Keens' cheese has a golden color; a close, nearly flaky texture; and a nutty, penetrating, memorable flavor.

MONTGOMERY'S The Montgomery family has been working the land of Manor Farm in Somerset for over a hundred years. Their Cheddar has consistently been one of the best in Britain, and probably in the world, for many years. The Montgomerys use only the raw milk of the farm's herd of Friesian Holsteins. Over the last few years, the Montgomerys' cheese has been as good as I've ever tasted it: impressively complex and surprisingly sweet, with hints of fruit, nuts, and a gentle, long finish without a trace of bitterness.

traditional american cheddars

We have over three hundred years of Cheddar-making history behind us in this country. As in England, only a handful of traditional makers are left, but in the last few years, there has been a slow, steady move to return to traditional techniques. Generally American cheesemakers shoot for "sharpness" —a bit more up-front intensity built around the basic Cheddar's buttery, full flavor. These Cheddars are my favorites.

GRAFTON VILLAGE The folks at Grafton Village have long been dedicated to creating traditional full-flavored cheese. All the Cheddars are handmade and have been for decades. The cheese is made exclusively from the raw milk of Jersey cows, an old breed whose milk is particularly rich and produces notably more flavorful cheese. The cheeses are aged from four months to four years. Grafton makes some of the best American Cheddar you'll have anywhere. It's buttery with a creamy texture and a finish that makes you want to keep eating more, but without any unpleasant bite or bitterness that marks so many aged Cheddars.

SHELBURNE FARMS For nearly two decades, Shelburne Farms in Vermont has been hand-crafting some of the most flavorful Cheddar in the United States. Its cheese is made from the fresh, raw, unpasteurized milk gathered from the farm's herd of Brown Swiss cows, making it a rare American Farmhouse Cheddar. At its best, the cheese is exceptionally full flavored— creamy on the tongue, rich, buttery, and nutty without any of the harshness or bitterness that marks most commercial Cheddars.

OTHER GOOD CHEDDARS Other worthy American Cheddars include those of Vella Cheese

in Sonoma, California; Widmer's from Theresa, Wisconsin; and Carr Valley Cheese from La Valle, Wisconsin.

FISCALINI FARMSTEAD: A CLOTH-WRAPPED AMERICAN This well-made newcomer from the West Coast is made by Jorge "Mariano" Gonzalez, who was the cheesemaker at Shelburne Farms (see page 231) for many years. Fiscalini Farm dates back to the 1920s, when John Fiscalini's grandfather Mateo moved to the town of Modesto. The family can track its roots back to 1705, when it was already involved in dairying and cheesemaking in Switzerland. Today the Fiscalinis have about 530 acres and a herd of about 1,400 Holsteins. Theirs is a true farmhouse cheese—they use only the raw milk of the farm's own herd. The flavor is somewhere between the English Farmhouse Cheddars and the Vermont Cheddars: nutty, a little earthy, very clean, with no bitterness or off flavors and a long finish that has just a touch of sweetness.

cheddar dream sandwich

Scott Fletcher has been the cheesemaker for more than thirty years at Grafton Village. This is his favorite sandwich, good for breakfast, lunch, or dinner.

- 1–2 tablespoons butter (enough to coat the skillet)
-    2 large eggs
-    2 tablespoons whole milk or heavy cream
-      Pinch fine sea salt
-    4 slices challah, ½ inch thick
- 1½ cups grated Cheddar cheese, preferably Grafton Village
-   ¼ cup maple syrup

Preheat a large skillet over medium-high heat for 2 to 3 minutes, but do not let it smoke. Add enough butter to coat the skillet.

In a shallow dish, beat together the eggs, milk or cream, and salt. Dip a side of 2 of the bread slices into the batter and place them batter side down in the skillet.

Top each with half of the cheese. Dip one side of the remaining 2 slices in the batter and place them atop each sandwich, batter side up.

When the bottom slices are golden brown, 3 to 4 minutes, carefully flip the sandwiches with a spatula. Cook until the second side of each sandwich is golden brown, 2 to 3 minutes. Transfer to a warm plate and top each sandwich with a generous drizzle of maple syrup.   serves 2

macaroni and cheese

Although I grew up on Kraft macaroni and cheese, this stuff is about 18,000 times better. It's amazing what happens when you use artisanally made macaroni and marvelously good farmhouse Cheddar instead of industrial noodles and cheese. I use an American farmhouse Cheddar that's at least a year old. The older the cheese, the better the dish.

Coarse sea salt
1 pound macaroni, preferably Martelli
2 tablespoons butter
1 medium onion, coarsely chopped (about 1 cup)
1 garlic clove, peeled and bruised with the side of a knife
1 sprig fresh thyme (about 4 inches)
1 sprig fresh rosemary (about 4 inches)
$\frac{1}{4}$ cup dry white wine
2 tablespoons all-purpose flour
$3\frac{1}{2}$ cups whole milk
2 tablespoons Dijon mustard
Freshly ground black pepper to taste
12 ounces farmhouse white American Cheddar cheese, grated ($4\frac{1}{2}$ cups)

Preheat the oven to 400°F.

Bring a large pot of water to a boil. Add 1 to 2 tablespoons salt and the pasta and stir well. Cook for about 10 minutes (if using Martelli), or until the pasta is 2 to 3 minutes from being al dente. You'll want it underdone so that it doesn't get mushy in the oven. Drain it and set it aside.

Meanwhile, melt the butter in a heavy-bottomed pot over medium-high heat. Add the onion, garlic, thyme, and rosemary and sauté until the onion is soft, about 5 minutes. Add the wine and reduce the mixture until it thickens, 3 to 4 minutes.

Remove the garlic, thyme, and rosemary from the pot. Add the flour, stirring constantly. Cook for a minute or so more while you continue to stir.

Slowly add the milk, a little at a time, stirring constantly to avoid lumping. When the flour and milk have been completely combined, stir in the mustard and some salt and pepper. Keep the mixture at a gentle simmer (not at a high boil) until it thickens, 2 to 3 minutes. Reduce the heat to medium. Working a handful at a time, stir in 3 cups of the cheese. When the cheese has melted into the sauce, remove the pan from the heat. Taste and adjust the seasonings if necessary.

Stir the pasta into the cheese sauce. Pour the macaroni and cheese into a 9-x-13-inch baking dish and top with the remaining 1½ cups grated cheese.

Bake uncovered for 25 minutes, or until the cheese is golden. Serve hot.

serves 4 to 6

mountain cheeses

Opposites attract, so I suppose my fascination with mountain cheeses comes in part from growing up in one of the biggest and flattest of the world's cities, laced with flat gray expressways and even flatter black factory parking lots. You've got to go a long way from Chicago to get to a mountain. The mountains for me are something special: fragrant pastures, bells on cows, milk in dented metal cans carried on horse-drawn carts.

Mountain cheeses were created out of a common struggle to deal with the difficulty of life at high altitudes. Huge snowfalls often isolated entire communities for months at a time, so the cheeses had to be held for long periods. The high elevations generally have abundant sources of pure water and pastures filled with many different species of wildflowers and herbs. These pastures serve as food for cattle, which give milk that is consistently more flavorful than that of their lowland counterparts.

I've seen mountain cheesemaking in Switzerland, Italy, eastern and western France, and Greece. The similar heritage of these cheeses is evident in their flavors and semifirm to firm textures as well as in the comparable methods of their production and aging. Although they have many things in common, each cheese has developed its own personality, distinctive flavor, and character, and of course its own name.

switzerland

a guide to gruyère

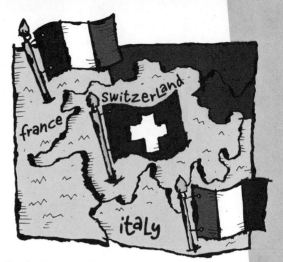

The term *Gruyère* is used to describe a specific cheese from Switzerland and also to refer to the group of mountain cheeses as a whole. In the first meaning, Gruyère is the cheese of eastern Switzerland. Produced throughout the region of Fribourg, it's made into eighty-pound wheels that are roughly three feet or so across and about four inches thick. The cheese itself is close-textured with pea-sized holes. Flavorwise, Gruyère is much fruitier than Emmentaler (see page 241) with a wonderful nose that reminds me of German Gewürztraminer.

Although it's fairly easy to get Gruyère in America, there's an enormous quality gap between what's readily available and what's really good. Nearly all the Gruyère sold in the States is, to my taste, too young and too boring. The same goes for Swiss Emmentaler, Appenzeller, French Comté, and Beaufort.

But there are some superb wheels of Gruyère out there—you just have to keep tasting until you find one that blows you away with the full fruitiness of its incredible flavor. So how do we find good Gruyère or, for that matter, any well-made mountain cheeses?

look for those that are produced from raw milk by tradition-minded cheesemakers

Gruyère made by small, artisan cheesemakers using raw milk is far likelier to be tasty than that made in moderately large factories. While the recipe is basically the same, the attention to detail and the quality and complexity of the milk make a meaningful difference in the flavor of the finished cheese.

find alpage cheeses

If you can, find alpage cheeses, mountain cheeses that have been made in the warmer summer months, when the animals are taken higher up the unplowed mountain pastures to graze. (The English name for this herd movement is the less-than-sexy "transhumance.") The pastures in the alpage are filled with dozens, if not hundreds, of varieties of grasses, flowers, and herbs—and when the herds graze on them, the flavor of their milk is guaranteed to be more interesting.

choose cheeses that are particularly well aged

Look for wheels that have been aged twelve, eighteen or, if possible, a solid twenty-four months. In Swiss Gruyère, a secondary fermentation kicks in at about twelve months, providing an additional flavor level that is missing in young cheeses. (One expert told me this point in the process is "the moment of the truth for Gruyère.") Because this stage is tricky—a make-or-break time—most cheeses are sold off before they get to be more than ten months of age. One sign that you've got something special is that the best-matured mountain cheeses will offer you those same small crunchy crystals that you'll find in well-aged wheels of Parmigiano-Reggiano and other long-aged cheeses. Although they're not that easy to find in North America, these well-aged cheeses are available here. If you ask often enough, the Swiss will admit the really mature cheeses exist. Vote your preference with your pocketbook: buy older cheese.

check the look of the cheese

The best aged Gruyère should have a creamy texture; it should stick ever so slightly to the knife when you cut it. Additionally, the best wheels will usually have small holes, or "eyes," the size of green peas. In days past, these holes were much more common, but today cheesemakers have opted for higher consistency at the expense of complexity. Changes in cheesemaking procedures have also eliminated most of the eyes. In Swiss Gruyère, avoid wheels that have horizontal cracks, usually a sign that the secondary fermentation has not worked well. As with most traditional cow's milk cheeses, Gruyère made in the summer months will be more golden in color, while that from the winter will be whiter.

buy from a cheese seller whose taste you trust

In the end, a trustworthy purveyor is your most likely assurance of obtaining great Gruyère. Since the name of the cheese remains the same, you must rely on his taste. That and tasting for yourself are the keys. If you doubt your ability to tell the difference, you have only to pick up a package of plastic-sealed Swiss Gruyère in the supermarket and compare it with a piece from a well-aged wheel that bears the same name. The mature Gruyère will have a far more enticing aroma, a firmer texture, an infinitely fuller flavor, an enjoyably balanced, nutty, sweet taste with a long, pleasant finish.

l'etivaz: the secret cheese of switzerland

One of my favorite mountain cheeses is L'Etivaz. Although you won't find it in supermarkets, L'Etivaz has become increasingly available in the United States in recent years.

L'Etivaz is time travel for your taste buds, the closest you'll get to true Gruyère, the way it would have tasted a hundred years or so ago. It's a product that owes its existence to the near fanatical passion of the people who make it: rebels with a cause, committed to maintaining their heritage in the face of growing pressures to industrialize. But above and beyond all else, what makes L'Etivaz more than just a good story is its flavor.

One sliver will tell you that a well-aged wheel of L'Etivaz is something special: exceptionally buttery, with a hint of spice; surprisingly sweet,

yet not at all salty or bitter; somewhat less fruity than a comparably aged Gruyère. Smooth and sensual, it fills your mouth with flavor and finishes with a tiny wisp of woodsmoke, the mark of the open fires over which it is made.

How could such an amazing cheese remain almost unheard of among a constellation of other stellar, internationally renowned Swiss cheeses? First and foremost, it's because L'Etivaz is not a part of the ultraefficient operations of the Switzerland Cheese Association. The Swiss do such a sensational job of getting the word out about their big-name cheeses—Gruyère, Appenzeller, Emmentaler—that the few that aren't officially affiliated are pretty much unknown outside their home villages.

Although Switzerland stands well above every other nation in setting strict codes to protect the quality and consistency of its traditional cheeses, the families of L'Etivaz felt strongly that the government code was too loose, lenient to the point that it was destroying the authenticity and quality of the mountain cheese they had grown up with. For years they'd sold their cheeses to a nearby cooperative, which lumped them in with everyone else's less traditional, less flavorful fare. So in sort of a dairy version of *The Mouse That Roared,* the folks who make L'Etivaz left the rest of their cheesemaking peers behind, to do things their own way.

a league of their own

In 1932, while most of the cheese world was choosing industrialization, seventy-six families who farmed the land around the town of L'Etivaz in southwestern Switzerland withdrew from the government-managed Gruyère program to create their own cheese. In doing so, they turned away from significant government subsidies awarded to officially approved cheese-

makers in Switzerland. The L'Etivaz makers set up an exceptionally strict code of production, oriented toward preserving tradition and authenticity.

- L'Etivaz cheese must be crafted completely by hand—no mechanization of any sort is allowed.

- The cheesemaking may take place only when the herds are up in the alpage, the mountain pastures surrounding the village, between 3,500 and 6,500 feet above sea level.

- The cheese can be made only in a demarcated region around the town of L'Etivaz.

- Each family can make cheese only from the milk of its own herd—no buying of milk is allowed.

- L'Etivaz (in this case, like all Swiss Gruyère) must be "cooked" in copper kettles.

- No chemicals can be used at any point in the process, from field to finished cheese. L'Etivaz is an organic cheese.

- Milk must be heated only over open wood fires.

- L'Etivaz may be made from May 10 through October 10. (In actual practice, though, the season is often shorter because many of the mountain pastures are too cold for the grazing cows in the first and last months.)

all in the families

L'Etivaz is a limited edition in every sense of the word. There's no way to add additional cheesemakers to the group because all of the alpage pasturage in the approved zone around the town is already being used. Among them, the L'Etivaz families own approximately 2,800 cows, primarily Simmenthal and Tachete Rouge breeds. In total, the families craft about 14,000 cheeses a year, or about 200 each.

The L'Etivaz rule dictating that each family may make cheese only from the milk of its own herd means that each has total control over the quality of its cheese: it raises the animals, manages the herd, protects its pasturage, and cooks and cuts its own curd. Since each family has only a certain amount of milk each day, some wheels are inevitably larger, others smaller, unlike government-regulated Gruyères, which are about eighty pounds apiece. All have a brushed, light brown natural rind on the outside, marked with the L'Etivaz seal of authenticity.

Although the production of L'Etivaz is rustic, it's by no means sloppy. Each maker keeps a careful logbook in which he records each day's yield of milk, the weather, and any other details of note. The cheesemaking room I visited was spotless, and all the utensils were diligently sanitized in boiling water. The process starts with milk from the previous evening, which is partially skimmed and then left to stand in a cool room overnight. The mountains never get very hot so refrigeration is unnecessary. The next day, the cheesemaker mixes in morning milk, carefully arranges wood for a fire, and then lights it up.

Once the heat is sufficient to start, the cheesemaker swings the milk-filled kettle over the fire, and adds rennet and starter cultures to begin the separation of curd and whey. The curd is allowed to set up slowly until it's about the texture of tofu. Then the cheesemaker cuts it, using a steel wire "harp," to make the pieces

the size of small pebbles. The curd continues to "cook" at 135 degrees Fahrenheit, until most of the whey has been expelled, enhancing the smooth, close texture of the finished cheese. The curds are gathered together in cheesecloth, left to drip for a short while, then lowered into a wooden cheese mold. Hand-operated cheese presses are used to expel the remaining whey.

The cheeses are brined, then aged in the L'Etivaz cooperative's caves, anywhere from six months on up to two years and beyond. Each cheese is marked so that everyone knows who made it. A family may choose to keep up to 10 percent of its cheese each year for personal use, and the cooperative sells the rest.

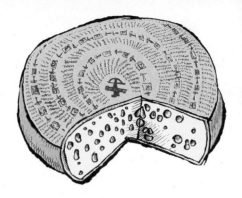

emmentaler: king of the swiss cheeses

Despite the number of so-called Swiss cheeses available in the world, I'm guessing that at most 10 percent of the world's cheese eaters have actually had the chance to try the real thing. When it's authentic and well aged, Emmentaler is one of the most versatile, best-tasting cheeses anywhere.

Emmentaler has probably been made since the thirteenth century. Although it's often referred to rather generically as "Swiss cheese," Emmentaler originated in a particular part of the country, the valley of Emme (*tal* means "valley"), which lies in the foothills of the Alps in the Bernese Oberland of north-central Switzerland.

Emmentaler is a large cheese in almost every sense of the word, from production volume to the size of the finished wheel. Each one is about as big as a truck tire, roughly three feet across, a foot thick and about two hundred pounds.

By Swiss law, Emmentaler must be made with raw milk that is less than a day out of the cow. It can be made only in copper kettles from partially skimmed milk. New cheeses spend two days floating in a brine bath. From there the wheels proceed to a warm fermenting cellar, where they spend six to eight weeks. It's during this warm stage that Emmentaler's famous holes are formed. Natural bacteria, which originate with the cheese's starter cultures, are enhanced by the relatively warm aging temperatures and give off carbon dioxide. This gas is, in turn, trapped in the paste of the new cheese in the form of round holes. (Newer production techniques often preempt the six-week stint in the warm cellar with three weeks in cooler storage cellars. From there the wheels go into a warmer room for a few weeks, then eventually back to cold again.)

When you cut through the thick natural crust of an Emmentaler wheel, you'll find a pale white to cream-colored interior with eyes the size of plump walnuts. You can usually tell what time of year the cheese was made merely by looking at it—wheels made in the winter months are quite white, while summer stuff is more of a straw yellow. If the cheese was well made, the eyes should be nicely rounded, never bent, twisted, or misshapen.

A good piece of Emmentaler is never strong

or bitter. Even after a year of aging, it won't bite. Instead it should have a gentle, mouth-filling flavor with a touch of nutty sweetness that makes it one of the most versatile of cheeses: ideal for everything from sandwiches and salads to soups, fondue, and after-dinner eating.

buying the best

A well-handled wheel of Emmentaler should have a dry rind, never soggy or sticky. A wet rind is usually a sign of suboptimal aging: the cheese might have been matured in too moist an environment or may have been sealed up in plastic Cryovac.

When you cut into a top-notch wheel, the eyes will weep, a byproduct of the natural fermentation that has taken place during the aging. By contrast, wheels that are matured at very low temperatures in the interest of consistency and cost reduction will almost never cry when you cut them.

But ultimately it's the flavor that counts. In general, I prefer older cheeses. Most of the Emmentaler available in the United States is on the young side, three to four months tops. You can find some, however, that has been aged for ten, twelve, and even eighteen months; those cheeses are far more interesting.

sbrinz: switzerland's secret "parmesan"

While the Italians prize Parmesan, the Swiss savor Sbrinz, a richly buttery, elegant grating cheese. The Swiss are sure that Sbrinz predates Parmigiano; they contend that Sbrinz was made in Switzerland for centuries and that Italian traders picked it up and brought it back to Parma. I'm sure Italian cheese enthusiasts will quickly "correct" that version by reversing the historical flow. Nevertheless, the two cheeses are clearly related.

Sbrinz is softer, more buttery, richer than Reggiano. Where Parmigiano-Reggiano is made from partly skimmed milk, Sbrinz starts with whole milk. Additionally, Sbrinz makers cut the curd much smaller, which yields a finer-textured, creamier cheese. The really old cheeses—aged for over two years—have wonderfully warm flavors.

Sbrinz is the perfect Swiss kiss to top off a homemade vegetable soup or a bowl of spaghetti with fresh herbs and olive oil.

appenzeller

This Swiss classic is from the area of Appenzell in northeast Switzerland near the frontiers of Germany and Austria. Appenzeller is an ancient cheese, with origins likely dating to the sixth century. A thousand years ago, it was already one of the most popular cheeses in the Alps. The name means, literally, "Alpine cell," referring to the high mountain valleys where the cattle are taken in the summer. During its aging, Appenzeller is washed with a brine of white wine or cider and spiced with pepper and herbs, which accentuates its natural piquancy and makes it special among the family of Swiss cheeses. Appenzeller has small eyes and a dense paste; the best have a full flavor, with a bit more nose—and even more fruit—than Gruyères. Of those made by the larger dairies, I prefer extra-aged Appenzeller wrapped in black foil. The more common cheese in silver foil is much mellower. And even better than the black-foil cheeses are handmade wheels from a few of the Appenzell area's quality-conscious dairies. The only real way to know you're on to one of the handmade cheeses is to watch for one that is not wrapped in foil and to ask your cheesemonger.

italy

taleggio

Taleggio (pronounced Ta-LEDGE-yo) is one of Italy's best-known soft cheeses. It comes originally from the Valle Taleggio in the Valsassina in northern Italy. The name is from local dialect, "TAY-vech," which in turn is from *tagliare,* meaning "to cut," a reference to the valley's narrow bottom. Taleggio is *the* cheese of the Valsassina. Depending on where and when you get it, it can be anything from boring to beautiful. According to local taste, Taleggio should be quite plump and its paste extremely creamy. It should not, however, be as runny as a Brie, which it often is in the United States.

The Denomination of Origin for Taleggio requires that the cheese be made of pasteurized cow's milk in its typical eight-inch-square forms and aged for a minimum of forty days. The rinds are first rubbed with dry salt, then, after a week, washed with brine. This washing is repeated every five to seven days for about six weeks. When the cheese is new, it's actually quite crumbly, but as it ages, it gets softer and smoother, first near the rind, and then gradually into its interior. The brine, along with the high humidity in the maturing rooms, develops the natural pinkish red crust that contributes so much to both the look and flavor of real Taleggio. Locals call this rind *la crosta rossa* and almost always eat it, but outside the area few folks seem to do so.

Taleggio is delicious on sandwiches. It's also great melted into polenta or over potatoes.

france

comté

Comté (pronounced Cone-TAY) has been made in the Jura Mountains for centuries, long before there was a country called France. It's the cheese of the Franche-Comté, the district of France that butts up against the Swiss border. In France, the cheese's formal name is Gruyère de Comté.

Comté was the first of France's cheeses to be recognized and rewarded with an AOC—*appellation d'origine contrôlée*—to guarantee its authenticity. No small achievement in a country that takes its food and itself as seriously as France does.

Made into large, flat seventy-five-pound wheels, Comté has a rough dimpled brownish rind and a smooth, firm white to yellow interior. The best Comté has a wonderful nutty, buttery flavor.

By law, the milk must come from the traditional local breed of Montbeliards. Beautiful russet and white cows, they have been the main milk producers in the Franche-Comté for centuries. In the Comté, farmers treat cows with the care and concern that we normally associate with Hindus. Cars stop as the bovines parade across country roads, strutting like the local gentry that they are, cowbells ringing off leather collars. Strict codes dictate what the cows are allowed to eat (no silage) and where they can eat it.

Every facet of the milk handling is monitored. No pumping of the milk is allowed, in order to protect the delicate fat globules so crucial to good cheesemaking. The milk must be fresh (from the morning the cheese is made and the previous evening) and unpasteurized. Bacteria counts must be very, very low.

Since the middle of the thirteenth century, Comté has been made not on farms but in *fruitières,* small village dairies that pop up throughout the region. The *fruitières* make cheese with the milk brought to them each day by a group of farms from the surrounding countryside. In turn, the *fruitère* passes its young cheeses on to an *affineur,* who matures them until the time they are sold, anytime after three months.

The wheels are aged on shelves, which by law must be made from local pine. To reach the mountain peak of majestic flavor, Comté has to be aged for at least ten to twelve months. Only then is it really ready to be savored. Best of all are the wheels that have been matured for over eighteen months.

Comté is a great eating cheese, a cheese for all seasons, from simple snacking to elegant entertaining. Its versatility makes it a pleasure at almost any meal and at most every time of day. It's excellent in sandwiches, salads, omelets, and fondues.

beaufort

Known in France as the "prince of Gruyères," Beaufort (pronounced BO-for) is surprisingly obscure internationally, especially by comparison to the fame of mountain cheeses like Emmentaler and Swiss Gruyère, but it can be one of the most delicious cheeses you'll ever try. It's native to the Haute-Savoie, the section of eastern France that's tucked up under the western end of Lac Leman. Beaufort is made into large, concave-sided eighty-pound wheels. Unlike many mountain cheeses, Beaufort is made from full-fat milk, primarily the ultrarich milk from herds of the old local breeds of Tarine or Abondance cows, and is creamier than its cousins. It shouldn't have any of the piquancy of Gruyère or Appenzeller. Nor does it have any holes; aging in cooler cellars prevents the development of the carbon dioxide that creates the eyes in other Swiss-type cheeses.

Beaufort has a long mountain tradition. Cistercian monks at the Abbey of Tamié are believed to have been instrumental in clearing the mountain meadows in the Savoie as far back as the twelfth century. For hundreds of years, the pasturage was owned by the monasteries but available to the peasantry to use cooperatively. The parishes built chalets and stables to make the cheesemaking operation viable; in return, the peasants supported the monasteries. Up until the 1950s, only summer Beaufort from the alpage was available. Today it's made year-round, but I still seek out the summer alpage cheeses, preferably after they've been aged for a year to develop their flavor.

reblochon

Unlike most mountain cheeses, Reblochon (pronounced Reb-law-SHONE) is made in small (about a pound), semisoft disks, veritable mice on the backs of elephantine

eighty-pound wheels of Beaufort. Tradition has it that back in the thirteenth century, taxes were paid according to the amount of milk one's cows gave. Since shorting the taxman is nothing new, farmers recorded the milk for a small batch, then went back to finish off the process with a second, secret, batch. This second milking was richer in butterfat and got credit for the cheese's special flavor. The name *Reblochon* could then come from *blossi,* meaning "milking" in Savoie dialect, hence re-*blossi,* or "to re-milk." Alternatively, in dialect *rablassa* means "stealing." Either makes sense.

Atypically for the area, Reblochon was traditionally made by women, not men. Up until the seventeenth century, it was produced only in the alpage. As demand grew and taxes were finally reduced or eliminated, production became a year-round activity.

Reblochon has a straw-colored paste and a pink rind. The rind should be smooth and

moist but not sticky. The flavor hints of the fir boards the cheese is aged on for about two months before being ready to eat. Real Reblochon is always packed between two thin wood disks to protect it in its travels. The best Reblochon is still made on small farms from raw milk, where the curd is hand-ladled into molds to drain. You can spot it from its green labels, which should say "Haute-Savoie." Aged for barely sixty days, it's often unavailable in the United States. It has a mushroomy, woodsy flavor and a full, pungent aroma.

morbier

Morbier (pronounced Mor-bee-AY) is from the same family of medium-sized, semifirm, fruity, full-flavored mountain cheeses that includes Fontina Val d'Aosta and Vacherin Fribourgeois. Named for the small town in which it got its start, Morbier was originally made from leftover Comté curd. The best Morbier is still traditional, raw-milk cheese, made in the Franche-Comté. Unfortunately the raw-milk cheese now accounts for less than 30 percent of production. Morbier is now made in factories on the other (western) end of France, completely removed from its native *terroir* and culture. When you can find the real thing, you'll have a mellow, gently fruity flavor and a semisoft, not quite creamy but definitely not firm, texture.

A line of light, blue-black ash runs horizontally across the cheese. Legend has it that the cheese was originally made in two stages. In the early nineteenth century during the summer months, the cheesemakers were always short of the milk needed to craft a full cheese. The ash was used to coat and protect the first part of the cheese until the second section was made and laid on top the next morning. These days the ash serves no practical purpose other than signaling that the cheese in hand is actually Morbier.

Morbier is ideal after dinner or for snacking, excellent with fresh fruit or buttered bread.

spain

Spain makes some of the world's finest mountain cheeses. They rarely leave the Iberian Peninsula, so when you get the chance to try them, don't miss out. A Frenchman I know who's been working with traditional cheeses for over twenty years told me, "The cheeses of France are famous, but the cheeses of Spain have flavor." Taste for yourself, and you'll find a phenomenal amount of personality in every bite.

idiazábal

This treat of a cheese is from the Basque country, made from the raw milk of the regional breed of Latxa sheep. Protected by a Denomination of Origin, Idiazábal is smoked over beech wood, a practice that began fortuitously. Centuries ago, shepherds used to set new cheeses on shelves in their huts, where the smoke from these wood-burning fires would leave its flavor mark on the cheeses. The best Idiazábal to my taste are those with over six months of maturing. Go for one that's got a good firm texture and a fine full flavor. Idiazábal has a chestnut-colored rind and an ivory paste with a few scattered holes. Its firm texture makes it eminently sliceable for sandwiches or for preparty snacking.

zamorano

One of the secrets of Spanish cheesemaking, Zamorano is the most pleasant cheese surprise I've had in ages. Made from sheep's milk from the region of Castilla y Léon, this semifirm cheese has a very creamy, sweet, savory flavor all its own. Highly recommended.

roncal

Firm in texture, creamy, with a superb, hazelnutty sweetness woven through its fine, full flavor, Roncal (pronounced Roan-KAHL) is made from sheep's milk exclusively in the Roncal valley in Navarre, on Spain's northern frontier.

swiss mountain fondue

Fondue is one of my wife's favorite foods. Why? After thinking for a minute, she said, "It's like sexy comfort food." That seals the deal in my mind.

Fondue pots are available in most housewares shops. They hold heat well and usually come with small stands and burners to keep the fondue warm at the table. If you've got good cheese, a fondue pot, and a few minutes to stir, preparing fondue isn't much harder than heating up a can of soup.

You can serve fondue with just a green salad and the bread that you'll dip into the hot, bubbly cheese. If the bread is a few days old, it will hold its shape better, which reduces the risk of it falling off the fondue forks.

variations

To make Fondue Comtoise, or the fondue of Franche-Comté, substitute 2 pounds aged Comté cheese for both the Gruyère and the additional mountain cheese.

To make Italian Fonduta, substitute 2 pounds Fontina Val d'Aosta for both the Gruyère and the additional mountain cheese. Add a touch of cream. If it's available, garnish with shavings of white truffle. •

1	pound Gruyère cheese, cut into ¼-inch cubes, at room temperature
1	pound additional mountain cheese such as Emmentaler, Vacherin Fribourgeois, or Appenzeller, cut into ¼-inch cubes, at room temperature
2	tablespoons all-purpose flour
1	garlic clove, peeled and bruised with the side of a knife
3	cups dry white wine, preferably Swiss Fendant
1	tablespoon kirsch
	Freshly ground black pepper to taste
16–24	ounces crusty white country bread for dipping, cut into 1- to 2-inch cubes

In a medium bowl, toss the cheeses with the flour.

Rub the bruised garlic clove over the inside of the fondue pot, then discard the garlic (or reserve for another use). Pour the wine into the fondue pot and bring to a simmer on the stove over medium heat.

Add the cubes of floury cheese, 10 to 12 at a time, stirring gently and constantly. Don't stir too vigorously or you may end up wearing the fondue. When the cheese has melted, add more cubes, stirring gently and constantly. Repeat until all the cheese has been incorporated, about 10 minutes total. The timing will vary depending on the heat level, temperature of the cheese, and your mood.

Stir in the kirsch, remove from the heat, and top with a generous grinding of pepper.

Bring the fondue pot to the table and place it on its stand over a flame.

Using a fondue fork, dip a bread cube into the cheese, turn a few times to coat well, blow on it once or twice so you don't burn your tongue, then eat.

Serve with more of the same wine you used in the fondue.

serves 8 to 10

egg fettuccine with butter, gruyère, and toasted walnuts

We generally don't think of France as a hot spot for pasta, but Provence has a long tradition of eating thin egg noodles. In some spots in southern France, you might find this dish served as often as macaroni and cheese is in the United States. Choose a well-aged Gruyère.

Coarse sea salt to taste
12 ounces egg fettuccine
3 cups coarsely shredded aged Gruyère cheese
2 tablespoons butter, preferably cultured
²/₃ cup walnuts, toasted (see page 31) and chopped
Freshly ground black pepper to taste
Freshly grated Parmigiano-Reggiano cheese for serving (optional)

Bring a large pot of water to a boil. Add salt and the pasta and cook until nearly al dente. While the pasta is cooking, remove ¼ cup of the pasta cooking water and set it aside. Drain the pasta in a colander. Be careful not to overcook.

Working quickly, put the drained pot back on the burner over medium heat, and return the pasta to the pot. Add the reserved ¼ cup cooking water, Gruyère, and butter. Cook, stirring constantly, until the cheese and butter are melted.

Remove from the heat and stir in the walnuts. Add salt and pepper to taste.

Serve in warm bowls with additional salt and pepper available for those who'd like it. If you want, you can sprinkle a bit of grated Parmigiano-Reggiano atop each bowl as well.

serves 4

swiss potatoes and pasta

The only tricky part of this recipe is cooking the pasta and the potatoes so they're done at the same time. If you're unsure of yourself, you can cook them separately, then finish them in the same pot. The onion needs to be slowly caramelized, so start it first, about 20 minutes before the potatoes go into the water.

- 2 tablespoons butter
- 1 large Spanish onion, halved lengthwise, then cut into long, thin slices
- Coarse sea salt
- 1 pound Yukon Gold potatoes (about 3 medium), peeled and cut into cubes roughly the same size as the pasta
- ½ pound ridged pasta (Martelli macaroni works well)
- 1½ cups freshly grated Sbrinz or Parmigiano-Reggiano cheese
- 1½ cups coarsely shredded aged Gruyère cheese
- Freshly ground white pepper to taste
- ⅛ teaspoon grated nutmeg, preferably freshly grated, plus more for serving

In a large heavy-bottomed skillet, melt the butter over medium heat. Add the onion and sauté, stirring occasionally, for 35 to 40 minutes, or until caramelized and golden brown.

Meanwhile, bring a large pot of water to a boil. Add 1 to 2 tablespoons salt and the potatoes and boil for about 5 minutes, or until almost cooked through and still firm.

Add the pasta to the pot and continue boiling until it is al dente and the potatoes are done. Drain, reserving ½ cup of the cooking water.

Return the potatoes and pasta to the pot and stir in the reserved ½ cup water, the cheeses, white pepper, and nutmeg. Cook over low heat for 2 to 3 minutes, or until the cheese has melted. Adjust the seasonings to taste. (By this time, the onion should be caramelized.)

Serve in warm bowls, topped with the caramelized onion. Pass around more white pepper and nutmeg for those who like spicier food.

serves 4 to 6

blue cheeses

More blue cheese probably is sold in America in the form of crumbles than any other way. Bags of them are the basis for almost every commercial blue-cheese dressing you and I have ever had. These crumbles are to the world of blue cheese what green cans of Parmesan are to Parmigiano-Reggiano. When it comes to flavor, authentic versions of the big three blues —Roquefort, Gorgonzola, and Stilton—are at the opposite end of the culinary cosmos.

If Roquefort is the king of blue cheeses, its two crown princes are Gorgonzola from Italy and Stilton from England. Both are widely recognized as some of the world's greatest blue cheeses, with long histories and their own flavors and textures.

what makes blue cheese blue?

Almost certainly the original blue cheeses were created by accident. The legend in Roquefort country—probably offered up in almost every other blue-cheese-making part of the world—is that a shepherd was about to enjoy a bit of bread and some fresh sheep's milk cheese when he spotted an attractive young girl nearby. Setting down his snack on a rock, he headed off to flirt. Noticing the sun setting in the west, he struck out for home, forgetting his food. A few weeks later he returned to the same spot and discovered that a strange bluish green mold had formed on both the bread and the cheese. Although it looked chancy, he sat down and ate it anyway. And, lo and behold, he liked the mold—the cheese had evolved into something really special. The rest, of course, is history.

The blue "veins," collections of caverns, nooks, and crannies, run the color gamut from green to pale blue to indigo. Roquefort is on the green end of the spectrum, Gorgonzola more of a greenish blue, Stilton bluish green, Valdeón from Spain very blue, Maytag from Iowa nearly indigo.

The spots on the map where the big blues are made—France, northern Spain, northern Italy, Britain—offer a clue about the process. Traditionally, blue-cheese making requires a couple of very specific conditions. First, moderate temperatures: Too hot, and the cheese will dry out and the mold won't develop properly. Too cold, and the same problem pops up. Second, plenty of natural moisture: a humid, cool environment is essential for good mold development. For that reason, blues tend to show up in mountainous areas where caverns and caves are the norm. Switzerland, then, is too cold for blue cheese; the Mediterranean basin, too hot; Greece, too dry.

For centuries, it was nature—not science—that dictated the terms of the cheesemaking. Despite the best of efforts, only some cheeses turned blue while others just went bad. Certain cheeses (such as Cheddar or Cheshire) blued when they weren't supposed to; others that usually blued sometimes didn't. Today random selection has pretty much been removed from the process. In almost all cases, the molds that once settled onto the cheese on their own are now actively introduced into the cheesemaking process.

royal blue: real roquefort

Without question, Roquefort has earned a spot on my list of top ten cheeses. It has a seductive softness to its texture—at room temperature it's almost velvety smooth; it will literally melt on your tongue, like a perfect chocolate truffle. Although blue cheeses are often chastised for their pungent aromas, the smell of a soft wedge of ripe Roquefort is enticing: earthy, buttery, exquisite. Most of all, there is the flavor—big, bold, with a hint of butterscotch; the finish is substantial and lingering.

Roquefort is one of the oldest of cheeses. The Romans reveled in it; Pliny wrote about it as early as A.D. 79. King Charles VI of France recognized the rights of the people of Roquefort, and in 1411 he ordered the cheese's production restricted to the area and required it to be aged in the village's caves. In 1666 the Parliament of Toulouse reiterated the earlier royal edicts.

One of the biggest misnomers concerning blue cheese is the belief that it is somehow "injected" with blue mold. The writer of a recent column in the food section of a more than reputable national newspaper reported that she "love[s] blue cheeses, named for the veins caused by molds that are injected for flavoring as the cheeses are made." No Roquefort for her this year! Powdered mold is often added to the milk or to the curd, but the mold is never injected, intravenously or otherwise.

Why do people have this perception? Because of the series of pin-sized holes that mark the exterior of most blue cheeses. These machine-made piercings are just large enough to allow air into the interior, giving the mold spores the oxygen needed to blossom and bloom. So set the record straight in your neighborhood: blue cheeses may show needle marks, but they're never injected.

While almost everyone knows the name, only a handful of Americans have tasted the real thing. Roquefort is frequently confused with lesser alternatives all over the world. Cooks and cookbooks often rather rudely lump it in with other blue cheeses, as if they were all one and the same.

modern-day roquefort making

Roquefort production today is strictly regulated, an effort to protect its reputation from the multitude of lesser likenesses. By law it must be made from fresh unpasteurized milk from local Lacaune sheep. It has to be aged in the caves of Combalou, in the Rouergue region of south-central France. It must be made in, or near, the village of Roquefort, and only during three fourths of the year, from December to late June or early July.

Today—as they have for centuries—Roquefort makers begin their cheesemaking by blending fresh morning milk with that of the previous evening. Starter culture is added to enhance the flavor of the milk's natural enzymes. The bacteria created in the process give off carbon dioxide, which in turn helps to create the all-important crevices and caverns in the curd, aerating the cheese, the better for blue mold to form. Rennet (usually lamb's rennet) is added to begin the formation of the curd.

Two or two and a half hours later, the curd is cut, then slowly, gently stirred for an additional two hours, allowing acidity levels to rise. The curd of the best Roquefort is still stirred by hand—literally. The maker extends his arm down into the kettle and uses his hand to move the curd. After draining off the liquid whey, powdered *Penicillium roqueforti* mold is added. It doesn't take much—a mere two grams is enough to seed the curd of up to four thousand liters of milk. The broken curd is carefully ladled into perforated metal forms (some industrial dairies use plastic, but the old-style metal cools the curd more quickly), from which excess whey drains slowly for three days. The new cheeses are then removed from the molds, rubbed with coarse salt, and turned regularly for an additional five days. To improve the odds of obtaining consistent veining, the cheeses are pierced with stainless-steel needles—the holes provide an effective avenue for air to enter, enhancing mold growth and allowing for more rapid ripening of the cheeses.

spelunking

Eight days after being made, the young cheeses are sent—as they have always been—to the famous limestone caves at Combalou for the most important part of their maturing. Although the name Roquefort means "strong rock," in reality the limestone is cracked and brittle. The porous texture is crucial: it maintains moisture, creating optimal aging conditions in a region that would otherwise likely be too dry. Some people credit the caves—more than the sheep's milk of the region—for Roquefort's greatness. Blessed with a series of natural crevices (known as *fleurines*), the caves allow for relatively rapid air movement around the aging cheeses. The blue mold spores, humidity (over 90 percent), cool temperatures (between 46 and 50 degrees Fahrenheit year-round), and natural airflow all work together to convert the young sheep's milk cheeses into nearly mature Roqueforts in about two to three weeks.

Originally, wheels of Roquefort simply molded at their own speed, taking about five months to finish maturing. But in the nineteenth century, cheesemakers found that they could increase ripening speed and enhance consistency in the bluing of the cheese. Each August thousands of large loaves of rye were baked to serve as a suitable surface for starting new mold growth. Rye was used—with a little wheat added to bind the bread—because it held moisture better, improving the speed of the molding. The crust was partly burned in order to ensure that all bacteria were killed off. To enhance the molding even further, the producers poked holes in the loaves (as for the cheeses) and seeded them with a dose of previously made powdered mold. The loaves molded through in about ten to fifteen days. When they were done, they resembled two-foot-wide black truffles. The crust was then removed, and the rest of the loaf crumbled, dried, ground, and stored for future use. Later it was sprinkled on newly made cheeses, much as sourdough starter is used to build flavor in traditional breads. Papillon, the maker of some of the best Roquefort around, takes great pride in pointing out that it is the only producer that still bakes these traditional loaves to make mold.

Roqueforts are aged standing on edge—not sitting flat as most cheeses are. They spend months upright on damp oak and chestnut boards, some of which are centuries old. The boards assist in the inoculation of new cheeses with mold spores, while also allowing air to pass around the young wheels more effectively than, say, plastic or stainless steel. After another ten to twenty-five days in the caves, the cheeses are wrapped in heavy foil to prevent drying and also to keep them from becoming overly blue. All told, the cheeses mature in the caves for at least three months, from whence they enter very cold, nearly freezing, storage rooms. Throughout, the aging is done in the dark; lights are used only when someone is working in the area. One of the current quality-control men at Papillon says, "The cheeses need to rest and be tranquil."

Since the sheep stop giving milk in the autumn, in centuries past Roquefort was available only seven or eight months a year. But by bringing the maturing process to a halt in cold storage, producers have made Roquefort available year-round. When they're almost ready to ship —between four and twelve months after the wheels are first made—producers retrieve their Roqueforts from cold storage and bring them back to cave temperature. The heavy foil wrapping is removed, revealing a coating of reddish mold, which is scraped off with a curved knife. On occasion, you'll see a bit left on the outside of the wheel.

rising demand, fewer farms

In 1800, 250 tons of Roquefort were made. By 1888, it was up to twenty times that, or about 5,000 tons. To increase productivity, Roquefort kingpins took cheesemaking off the farms and consolidated efforts at central dairies, bringing huge changes to the region. Up until the second half of the nineteenth century, all Roquefort had been made on farms, then brought to

the caves for aging. The establishment of central dairies ended that. By the 1930s, only an infinitesimal amount of Roquefort was still farm-made. By the 1950s, only about twenty Roquefort firms—and no cheesemaking farms—remained. As of 2003, we're down to eight!

While other cheeses continued to descend into the depths of industrial blandness, Roquefort was somehow able to stem the tide and hold on to its integrity. Traditional Roquefort today has a lot more legal protection than most cheeses in France or anywhere else. In 1925 it received the first French cheese *appellation d'origine contrôlée:* by law, milk must arrive at the dairies in metal cans; in order to protect the milk, no tanker trucks can be used. It must be made from pure, raw sheep's milk; no pasteurization is permitted. And, as they have been since 1411, the cheeses must still be aged in the caves at Combalou.

split wheels

Oddly, Roquefort is almost always shipped from France in half wheels. Supposedly the tradition started with Charlemagne, who in 778 stopped off in the region after battling with the Saracens in Spain. Served Roquefort by the local Rouergue abbot, the king took out his knife and began removing the blue veins of the cheese. The abbot gently told him that these blue bits were actually considered the best part. Charlemagne was so taken with the cheese that he immediately asked that he be sent two wagonloads a year. To be sure that he got the bluest cheese, he instructed the abbot to split each wheel in two before shipping. And to this day, most Roquefort still leaves the caves in splits.

Only about one tenth of Roquefort production is exported. The United States imports

roughly 350 tons, much less than a decade or two ago, but this decrease actually signals a heartening change. Although demand for Roquefort as an ingredient in bottled dressings has declined, demand for the best — that which is eaten as table cheese — is increasing and now accounts for about two thirds of American Roquefort imports.

what makes roquefort so expensive?

Real Roquefort isn't cheap. It regularly retails at $18 to $28 per pound. What makes it so pricey? First and foremost, sheep's milk itself is expensive. An average ewe yields only a liter to a liter and a half a day, compared with a cow's yield of about twenty-six liters a day. Additionally, the mandatory use of raw milk, milk-can transport, and extensive aging adds handwork, and hence additional expense, to the making of the cheese.

buying the best roquefort

look for the top four

All Roquefort made according to the guidelines of the Institute National des Appellations d'Origine will be labeled with a red sheep seal, but that seal alone will not assure you of getting a great cheese. While there are a couple dozen brands on the market, there are only eight producers of Roquefort, the largest of which, Société, accounts for about 70 percent of the total. Much of the Roquefort offered in plastic sealed prepacks is certain to be less than great. Cheese that is cut for these packs must be young and firm and has not reached peak creaminess. As with most cheeses, I recommend Roquefort that's been cut to order for you.

In my own tastings and those of others whose palates I respect, the brands of Carles, Papillon,

Crouzat, and Coulet consistently come out on top. Of the group, Carles has become my favorite, with Papillon ranking a solid second. Crouzat's and Coulet's cheeses are also quite good.

CARLES Started in 1928, Carles is the second smallest of the eight Roquefort producers, making a minuscule 1 percent of all the Roquefort produced today. The dairy is located in the tiny village of Martrin, the population of which is about four dozen. Milk is bought from twenty-five to thirty small farms, delivered twice daily in milk cans. The cheese is completely handmade.

PAPILLON Papillon is the second-largest maker of Roquefort. Founded by Paul Alric in 1906, the firm is still family-owned and has nearly two hundred farms producing milk for its cheese. Yet it accounts for only about 11 percent of Roquefort, tiny by the standards of the giant Société. Unlike its much larger competitor, Papillon is purely in the Roquefort business. Its cheeses are made at a neat new facility in the village of Villefranche-de-Panat, about forty-five minutes northwest of Roquefort. The Alrics insist that the mold from the traditional loaves of rye leads to a creamier texture. Over the years, I've regularly found Papillon Roquefort to be good to excellent, almost never excessively salty and almost always well balanced in flavor and creamy in texture. Look for the black foil label bedecked with red, green, and white butterflies. These wheels have the most extensive veining and, from my experience, the most flavor. Additionally, Papillon produces an organic Roquefort that is wrapped in very light green foil.

buy in the fall

Although Roquefort is now available year-round, the best time to eat it is likely to be in the autumn, September through December. These cheeses were made in the late spring and early summer, when the sheep were grazing on the season's fresh growth of grass. They're also likely to be cheeses that have not sat unnecessarily in the cold storage. Although there is no guarantee that what you buy in the United States in autumn will indeed be spring cheese, the odds are higher than at other times of the year.

find a shop with good turnover

This rule of thumb, of course, applies to just about every other cheese as well. But it's even more important for Roquefort, which can suffer if it sits around too long. Roquefort can dry out fairly quickly, and when it does its flavor becomes exceedingly pungent and salty and its texture dry and crumbly instead of moist and mouthwatering.

taste and feel the cheese

The flavor ought to be pronounced, memorable, and distinctive, but never overly strong, bitter, or salty. You should taste a pleasant hint of sheep's milk, perhaps with enjoyable prickles around the edges of your mouth near the finish. Look for a piece that's well veined and moist-looking. Browning near the edges is a bad sign.

Additionally, the cheese should be fairly soft. Roquefort that remains too firm is not ready to be eaten. At its best, the cheese should spread easily with a butter knife.

eating roquefort

Even more so than with most cheeses, be sure to serve Roquefort at room temperature. Its texture should be as soft as warm butter. I like nothing better than to spread a bit of Roquefort on a thick slice of country bread. It's also easy to enjoy on just steamed potatoes—simply crack the potatoes open, brush with a bit of butter or olive oil, then spoon on some soft Roquefort. Salt should be added to taste at the end to balance the tang of the cheese. Crumbled Roquefort on a simple salad of mesclun (baby mixed lettuces) with toasted walnuts is a regular offering at our house. Finally, Roquefort is superb on an after-dinner cheese platter.

gorgonzola: italy's blue

Gorgonzola is *the* blue cheese of Italy. It has been made since the late fourteenth or early fifteenth century. It's a creamy-textured blue, produced from cow's milk in the lush land of Lombardy in the north of Italy, where it's used extensively in all sorts of cooking, an essential ingredient in dozens of dishes. You'll see it on menus everywhere—nearly every Italian pizzeria (at least in the north) offers one pie topped with Gorgonzola. It's liberally used in pasta sauces and risotto. Many people serve a slab of it on the side, next to a hot bowl of polenta. It's very nice with gnocchi. After dinner, it's delightful with ripe pears.

While there is a town of Gorgonzola not far from Milan, today it has little to do with the cheese. The center of Gorgonzola making and maturing is now the town of Novara, which lies farther to the east. Sadly, as best I can tell, there is no longer any farmhouse Gorgonzola being made in Italy today. All of it is produced in dairies, using pasteurized milk. On the upside, there is still some very good Gorgonzola to be had.

Because of its popularity, Gorgonzola is readily available in North America. But as always, there is a wide range in quality. Nine times out of ten, when an American menu lists "Gorgonzola," what you'll usually be served is an indifferent, American-factory facsimile that has little in common with the eminence of the real article from Italy.

getting hold of good gorgonzola

go with gorgonzola *naturale*

I prefer the flavor of Gorgonzola *naturale,* the traditional, drier, longer-aged, more flavorful cheese, to that of the now ubiquitous Gor-

gonzola *dolce.* The latter is a 1940s "innovation" in Gorgonzola making that leaves more moisture in the cheese, creating a "sweeter" product. Mind you, the *dolce* isn't bad cheese. But if you want to taste Gorgonzola as it was meant to be, buy *naturale.*

look for longer-aged gorgonzola

Although there are younger cheeses available, a good Gorgonzola *naturale* will have been aged at least ninety days. Even longer aging — sometimes for more than a year — is also likely to lead to more flavorful cheese. In the old days, the mold for Gorgonzola grew naturally in the environments of the aging rooms. Since the middle of the twentieth century, however, the *Penicillium* has been added directly to the liquid milk at the earliest stages of the cheesemaking to ensure higher levels of consistency. The molds essentially lie dormant until stainless-steel needles pierce the paste of the cheese, generally after about two weeks, allowing air in and thereby activating the molds. This process is repeated at four weeks. The mold gradually works to soften the curd structure of the cheese so that by the time it is six weeks old, it has become surprisingly supple. In order to protect and preserve its drumlike shape as the paste softens, the cheese is wrapped with wooden bands.

How do you know how old the cheese is? You ask.

buy italian

Be wary of American-made Gorgonzola; look closely because most labels will simply say GORGONZOLA without any indication that the cheese was made in the United States, not in Italy. Recommended Italian brands include Ciresa, Cademartori, and Mauri. I'm particularly fond of the extra-aged Gorgonzola from the Fiori family, sold under the brand name Guffanti.

watch out for too much rind

Mishandling by retailers can ruin Gorgonzola. Make sure that the cheese has been allowed to breathe in storage. Otherwise the natural rind, which in ideal circumstances contributes to the quality of the cheese, will become its undoing. Trapped inside plastic wrap, Gorgonzola will develop all sorts of off flavors. Although the rind itself should be ruddy to pink in color, when it encroaches into the paste and lends its color and flavor to the cheese itself, the Gorgonzola is in trouble. Ask for a taste to be sure.

searching for stilton

Stilton is England's best-known blue-veined cheese. Made in the English Midlands, in the counties of Nottingham, Leicester, and Derby, it's been revered, written about, and eaten by cheese lovers, expatriate Englishmen, and assorted Anglophiles around the globe for centuries. Although a staple on English tables year-round, Stilton is as expected a part of British Christmas cuisine as plum pudding.

the story of stilton

Cheese of some sort was certainly made on farms in the area long before there was a town by the name of Stilton. The first written reference to the cheese dates to 1722. The woman

most often credited with inventing Stilton was one Mrs. Elizabeth Scarbrow, who became well known for making a very good early version of it on the estate of Lady Beaumont of Quenby Hall. Later she married a Mr. Orton and continued making the cheese on his nearby farm. Credit for "modern" Stilton is given to Frances Pawlett, who introduced a series of improvements to the old-style farm cheese, including a more consistent weight (about sixteen pounds) and a drum shape. (Some say Pawlett was the daughter of Mrs. Orton; others disagree.) She's also credited with the style of crumbling the curd that's still used to make Stilton today and with the idea of piercing the cheeses with needles to allow in air and enhance mold development.

The town of Stilton was a frequent coach stop for travelers on the road north from London to Edinburgh. Before the era of processed foods and bagged potato chips, coach passengers could pick up a wedge of wrapped Stilton cheese and a pint of ale at the local inns while the coachman hooked up fresh horses. Stilton's distinction as a stopping point ended in the 1840s when the railways came to prominence, but its prestige as a cheese continued to grow.

Until the second half of the nineteenth century, Stilton was strictly a farm-made food, produced exclusively through the handwork of farmwomen, usually at the rate of about a wheel a day. All that changed when the first factory production of Stilton was started in 1875 by Thomas Nuttall in the town of Melton Mowbray. Nuttall's success led the way for other factories and co-ops. In 1910, dozens of Stilton cheesemakers in the English Midlands got together and managed to come to consensus on a technical description of the cheese they all made. Fifty-nine years later, the High Court of Britain formally recognized the guidelines they developed, giving Stilton the legal definition and protection that assures British Stilton buyers of the authenticity of their purchase. Within seventy-five years of the opening of Nuttall's first factory —by the end of World War II—all Stilton was made in commercial dairies. Unfortunately, there is no such thing as farmhouse Stilton today, and production has shrunk to the point at which only half a dozen or so dairies remain, most of them on the larger side.

the signs of great stilton

Not all Stiltons are the same, so here are some signs of greatness.

less blue in the veins

The veining in the best Stiltons is often gentler, more effectively integrated into the cheese and less visually striking than the veins of industrial Stiltons, which are darker blue, almost black. Ernie Wagstaff, the now retired cheesemaker of Colston Bassett Dairy, says the darker blue in the industrial cheese is caused by overuse of *Penicillium*. It looks good to the uninformed consumer because the more extensive veining enhances the visual effect. But for people who love great Stilton, this extra-bold veining is often inversely related to creaminess and flavor. The best Stiltons have veins of many colors and look much like well-weathered marble. Many show far more green than they do blue; others are mottled with delicate dabs of yellow.

creaminess

Ultimately, a creamy texture is probably the most significant sign that you've got a really fine slice of Stilton. The softening begins around the veins and gradually makes its way through the rest of the cheese.

This emphasis on creaminess goes against popular convention, which tells you that blue cheese is for crumbling onto salad, not for spreading on bread. But the best Stiltons should be on the soft side, spreadable at room temperature, with the consistency of good butter and a melt-in-your-mouth, almost velvety smoothness.

rind

Stilton is one of the few big-name blues still sold with its natural rind intact, a powdery brown overcoat that's distinct from that of most any other cheese. Cheesemakers scrape the initial rinds from young Stiltons to ensure proper development later. Colston Bassett smooths the rinds with old kitchen knives. In Thomas Nuttall's day, local cheese lovers considered these scrapings a real delicacy.

The rind—and the area just inside it—is often the best indicator of the quality of a wheel of Stilton. Well-made Stilton should have a powdery light brown rind of medium thickness all around. Many commercial Stiltons—sealed in plastic for easier storage and to minimize weight loss from evaporation—have only a thinnish, flat-looking rind that lacks luster. The cheese inside will almost always fall short in flavor. Too much rind is also a problem. Overripe Stilton has an excessively thick, darkish brown rind. A rind has gone too far when you can taste it in the flavor of the cheese.

superb flavor

In the end, of course, it's the taste that will decide whether a Stilton is superb or so-so. Well rounded, complex, nicely balanced, the flavor of a great piece of Stilton will stay on your tongue long after you've finished eating. Lesser Stiltons will be dry, chalky, flat in flavor, or, alternatively, so overripe that they nearly take your head off.

savoring and serving stilton

British cookbooks will tell you that there are hundreds of ways to cook with Stilton. Stilton soup. Steak with Stilton. Salad with Stilton croutons. Stilton sauce. Stilton scones. But I think that far and away the nicest way to eat Stilton is after dinner, just as it is. Make sure it's at room temperature. Add a handful of biscuits, and maybe a glass of good red wine or perhaps an aged port. Doesn't much matter if you've got a bunch of company or if your only companion is a good book and a baggy sweater. There's a magnificence to it that no other cheese can match.

other blues from britain and ireland

CASHEL BLUE Cashel Blue is made by Jane and Louis Grubb from the milk of a herd of Holstein cows on their farm in County Tipperary in south-central Ireland. The cheese is named for the nearby Rock of Cashel, one of Ireland's most visited and striking sites of natural beauty. The cheese is equally striking. It's very creamy, both in texture and in flavor, with blue veins set into a paste that is the color of well-worn marble and a thin pinkish-reddish rind.

HARBOURNE BLUE Harbourne Blue's cheese-maker, Robin Congdon, is one of the best of the new British cheesemakers dedicated to restoring the honor and character of traditional cheesemaking. The cheese starts with a Roquefort recipe that's been adapted to goat's milk. The cheese is made with the raw milk of the family's goat herd, which grazes on the rich green fields of Congdon's native Devon. It has an alabaster paste, shot through with delicate blue-black veins.

the blues of spain

cabrales

Authentic Cabrales is a walk on the wild side that blue cheese lovers won't want to miss. This cheese is in short supply even in Spain, where it was given a government guarantee of authenticity with its own Denomination of Origin in 1981. Be careful when buying it in this country because a number of other Spanish blue cheeses are sold with tags that say they're Cabrales when they aren't. You can be sure you've got the real thing by checking the wrapping—real Cabrales arrives exclusively in a forest green foil wrap.

Cabrales is often made from a blend of all three major milks: cow's milk gives acidity, goat's milk provides piquancy, and sheep's milk brings butteriness. Handmade in small quantities by farmers in villages around the Arena de Cabrales, on the eastern end of Asturias, Cabrales is one of the last blue cheeses left in the world that is still allowed to "blue" totally on its own. No powdered mold is ever introduced into the milk or the curd of the cheese. Instead, newly made cheeses are matured in caves ventilated by the cold, damp, salty winds coming in off the Bay of Biscay. After its three- to six-month maturing, Cabrales has an off-white paste and plentiful indigo veining.

Real Cabrales is not for those who have mixed feelings about blue cheese. It has a pungent, penetrating aroma and a rustic, robust flavor that hints of the caves and the wildest of

wild mushrooms. Many Spaniards simply spread it on toast. Its strength stands up to grilled steak, over which Spaniards frequently melt it. Serve it with strong honey, with Oloroso sherry, or with Pedro Ximénez, the Spanish dessert wine.

picon

Of late, this blue cheese has become one of my favorites. Picon is produced in the village of the same name in the Liebana region of Cantabria on the north coast of Spain, near the border with France. It's made from raw cow's milk, with, at times, the addition of some sheep's and goat's milk. No mold is added to the milk—the blueing occurs naturally from mold spores circulating in the aging caves. The survival of this ancient, all-natural technique led the cheesemaster Mariano Sanz Pech to call Picon "one of the last of the Mohicans of the blue cheeses in the world." When it's ripe and ready, Picon has an enjoyable buttery texture and a wonderful, fruity flavor, and it finishes with a nice spicy nose. It goes well with fresh fruit and nuts of all sorts.

valdeón

Valdeón is a delicious blue cheese from the slopes of the Picos Mountains in the province of León along Spain's northern coast. It's a close cousin of the better-known Cabrales, which is made nearby. Valdeón is made from pasteurized milk that has *Penicillium* mold spores added to it. Generally it's made from cow's milk, but in spring and summer, it can be a blend of cow's, goat's, and sheep's milk. It's matured in limestone caves or cellars with year-round cool temperatures and high levels of humidity. When fully mature, the wheels are wrapped in maple leaves, then removed from the caves and sent to market. The leaves help the maturers to handle the cheeses without getting sticky fingers. Valdeón has a nice bit of butterscotch in its flavor and is sweeter, mellower, and moister than Cabrales. Valdeón is a good match for a couple of crisp apples and a crusty loaf of country bread. Melt it into a cream sauce and put a dollop on steak or fish. Or serve it on its own, with hard cider or oaky white wine.

four terrific american blues

BINGHAM HILL RUSTIC BLUE A new arrival on the blues scene, this one is made by Kristi and Tom Johnson in Fort Collins, Colorado. The Johnsons don't have their own herd but instead buy BGH-free (without bovine growth hormone) raw milk from a local dairy. They make the cheese the day the milk arrives and add *Penicillium.* The wheels are allowed to form a natural rind, more like a traditional Stilton or Gorgonzola. The cheese is aged for five to six months on poplar shelves, and the natural rind becomes much drier than blue cheeses that are aged in foil, such as Roquefort.

GREAT HILL BLUE An American original that dates to the mid-1990s, Great Hill Blue is made on the shores of Buzzards Bay, about fifty miles south of Boston in the small town of Marion, Massachusetts. Tim and Tina Stone use only the fresh raw milk of Guernsey cows, giving the cheese a very appealing golden hue. To protect the natural flavors of the milk and the texture of the finished cheese, all of the curd is stirred by hand. Aged for about six months, Great Hill takes on a deep, exceptionally sweet blue flavor that will appeal to both novices and those in the know. The flavor can continue to develop for up to ten months.

MAYTAG BLUE Yes, this cheese was—and is—owned by the folks who started the washing machine company. But while they long ago sold off their interest in appliances, the Maytags have held tightly to their cheese. They've been making Maytag Blue in Newton, Iowa, since 1941, when they began working with dairy scientists at Iowa State. Although the Maytags recently sold off their herd of Friesian dairy cows, they continue to use only the finest locally produced unpasteurized milk. The cheese is made into eight-pound wheels, then cave-aged for six months to develop its distinctive blue veining.

Maytag Blue is wonderfully rich and creamy on the tongue, with a sweet, nutty flavor. I like it best on salads, but it's also great on cheeseburgers or with fresh apples or pears.

POINT REYES BLUE Point Reyes is a true farmstead cheese, one of just eight in California and the only blue. It's made by the Giacomini family using the hormone-free raw milk of the family's herd of 250 or so Holsteins. The Giacominis run a "closed herd," meaning that all the animals are bred on their farm, ensuring quality and protecting the animals from external genetic influences. The best of their cheeses to my taste are those made in the spring and summer, when the herd grazes in open pastures on the farm's seven hundred acres overlooking Tomales Bay. The Giacominis make their own starter culture, adding mold spores to the liquid milk during the cheesemaking. The more mature wheels of Point Reyes have a richer, more rounded flavor that I prefer. These aged cheeses have a surprisingly smooth, full flavor. They're great on salad, pasta, potatoes, or polenta and are ideal after dinner at Thanksgiving or Christmas.

vichyssoise with roquefort

This recipe makes a great cold soup for summer or early autumn. The creaminess of the potato puree is an excellent foil for the lively full flavor of the Roquefort.

3 tablespoons butter

4 large leeks, white parts only, cleaned and chopped (about 4 cups)

3 medium Yukon Gold potatoes, peeled and thinly sliced

4 cups water

1 cup whole milk or light cream

Coarse sea salt to taste

Freshly ground black pepper to taste

3–4 ounces Roquefort cheese, at room temperature

Snipped fresh chives for garnish

In a large heavy-bottomed stockpot, melt the butter over medium heat. Add the leeks and stir to coat with the butter. Sauté the leeks until wilted and translucent, taking care not to brown them, about 15 minutes.

Add the potatoes and water and bring to a boil. Reduce the heat to medium and simmer until the potatoes are tender, about 20 minutes.

Remove from the heat and let cool slightly. Pour the soup into a food processor and process, adding the milk or cream a little at a time, until very smooth. Add the salt and pepper.

Serve hot or chill overnight and serve cold with the Roquefort crumbled on top, a few snips of chives, and another grinding of pepper.

serves 4 to 6

salad with peppered pecans

This salad is untraditional but very good. A big hit at holiday time, it's worth making whenever you have Peppered Pecans on hand. It's ideal to serve after a main course because it's got a nice balance of savory and sweet.

4 ounces mesclun or other mixed salad greens (about 8 cups loosely packed)
2 ounces Peppered Pecans (page 330), chopped
1 ounce Stilton cheese, crumbled
2 tablespoons delicate extra virgin olive oil, preferably Ligurian
1 tablespoon aged sherry vinegar
  Freshly ground black pepper to taste

In a large salad bowl, toss together all the ingredients except the pepper. Transfer to individual plates and serve with a generous grinding of pepper on top. **serves 2 as a main course or 4 as a side dish**

roquefort and potato salad

love this dish for its simplicity. The heat of the potatoes should wilt the lettuces a bit and soften the Roquefort as well. It uses one of my favorite vinegars, the hard-to-find but wonderfully flavorful Banyuls from the southwest of France (see page 83). In the summer this salad is an easy main course; all you need to go with it is good bread and something cool to drink.

4	cups very small potatoes, preferably heirloom
4	ounces mesclun or other mixed salad greens (about 8 cups loosely packed)
4	Roma tomatoes, cut into wedges
2	medium cucumbers, peeled and sliced
16	Nyons olives, or other cured black olives
	Coarse sea salt to taste
	Freshly ground black pepper to taste
2–3	ounces Roquefort cheese, at room temperature
½	cup walnut halves, toasted (see page 31)
	Extra virgin olive oil to taste, preferably Provençal
	Banyuls or aged sherry vinegar to taste

Steam the potatoes in their jackets over boiling salted water until very tender, 15 to 20 minutes.

Divide the mesclun among four bowls. Arrange the tomato wedges, cucumber slices, and olives around the rim of the bowls.

Crack the potatoes open and divide them evenly among the bowls. Sprinkle lightly with salt and add a good dose of pepper. Crumble some of the Roquefort over the top of each salad. The heat of the potatoes should soften the cheese. Top each salad with a sprinkling of the toasted walnuts. Dress the salads with olive oil and vinegar. Serve immediately.

serves 4

goat cheeses

If you want to get a sense of how much eating in America has changed in the last twenty years, all you have to do is take a long look at goat cheese. Back in 1982, when Zingerman's opened, goat cheese was pretty darned hard to find. We had a choice of two, Montrachet and Bûcheron. Both came by boat from France. Although neither would win awards by today's much tougher standards, at the time each was considered a gourmet item. In truth, the Montrachet was an unremarkable log of factory-made cheese, often old, rather slimy, and a little bitter. The Bûcheron was bigger, with a white mold rind, which, more often than not, was too soft and overripe. The poor quality of goat cheeses available in America created a bad taste in the mouths of consumers, which took years to turn around.

Two decades down the road, however, goat cheese has gone wild. Today, almost everyone has heard of it, and even former skeptics now sample it regularly. Heck, even kids (the human kind) frequently come in to the deli and ask for it!

what makes goat cheese unique?

The distinctive flavor of the cheese comes from the fact that it's made from goat's milk, not cow's milk. If you expect goat cheese to taste almost the same as cow's milk, you probably won't like it. Goat's milk has a different chemical makeup from cow's milk, and it has different active acids. Instead of lactic acid, goat's milk employs caprylic, caproic, and capric acids. Goat's milk cheese looks different as well: it contains no carotene, so goat cheese is much whiter than most cheese made from cow's milk.

fresh insight: picking the best

"Fresh" is the most accessible avenue for those unfamiliar with goat flavors. Its mildness makes it the obvious choice for inexperienced American palates. All fresh goat cheeses have two things in common: (a) they're fairly fresh (two days to two months old) and (b) they're all made from goat's milk. But that's about it. While consumers and food writers often act as if all fresh goat cheeses are essentially interchangeable, quality levels range widely. There's as much difference between a lousy fresh goat cheese and a great one as there is between a mediocre factory Cheddar and a wonderfully flavorful wedge of cloth-wrapped English Farmhouse. What makes one goat cheese so much better than another? There are three major factors.

1. the quality of the milk

No amount of craft or care on the part of the cheesemaker can ever overcome poor raw material. The sanitation level of the herd, the cleanliness of the milk, and the care with which the milk is handled are imperative. And certainly the impact of the soil, the diet of the herd, the skill of the cheesemaker, and the aging techniques are all as important here as elsewhere in the cheese world.

what's the difference between "chèvre" and "goat cheese"?

There's no difference. *Chèvre* is simply the French word for "goat." Spain, too, makes a wide range of wonderful goat cheeses; Italy, Holland, England, Ireland, Greece, the United States, and Canada do too. And, hey, don't ignore Australia. In France, it's called chèvre. In Italy, it's *formaggio di capra;* in Spain, *queso de cabra.* In America, we go with "goat cheese."

2. hand-ladling of the curd

In making most firm-textured cow's milk cheeses, the curd is cut with knives, heated, and stirred, then cooked, cheddared, milled, or pressed to encourage the expulsion of whey. Fresh goat cheese requires the opposite approach. In fact, the curd for the best fresh goat cheeses is never actually cut at all, but gently broken by the insertion of the ladle. The only pressure applied is that of gravity. Traditionally, when the milk has "solidified" into a tofu-textured curd, the cheesemaker literally spoons it, one ladleful at a time, into the cheese molds. As the curd settles down on itself inside the molds, holes allow the whey to drain naturally. The result of hand-ladling is a noticeably flaky texture. If you pick up a round and bend it back a bit, it "breaks."

Unfortunately, few modern goat cheeses still get such handling. Most curd today is extruded, forced into tubular plastic packages under pressure, much as sausage is squeezed into casings. Extrusion increases production speed and reduces costs, but it also damages the delicate curd, allowing the milk solids to run out, inevitably altering the texture. You can usually spot these extruded cheeses by the way they look in the display case. They're sealed in thick plastic, and the cheese fills the casing without any visible air gaps. Extruded cheeses tend to be gummier—soft, but without structure. If you bend back a piece, it won't break; at best it just crumbles. The paste of extruded cheeses generally oxidizes quickly, often leading to the development of off flavors as the cheese ages.

3. paper wrapping

Like any other well-made cheese, good goat cheese needs to breathe. The best cheeses are those that have ready access to air, which means that a key question is the same one they ask you at the supermarket

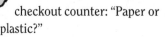

checkout counter: "Paper or plastic?"

Look for fresh goat cheeses that come wrapped in paper, or, better yet, unwrapped altogether, in unsealed wooden crates. Paper-wrapping allows the cheese to develop and mature properly; it will taste quite different at three weeks from how it tasted at one. Cheese that's sealed in heavy plastic suffers from lack of air just as you or I would. It can't breathe, it can't develop, it can't mature as it should. I've yet to taste an extruded, plastic-sealed sample that can come close to the flavor and texture of a well-made, hand-ladled, paper-wrapped goat cheese.

If I had any doubts, a recent tasting at an American Cheese Society conference confirmed the point. In a blind taste test in a room of a hundred cheesemakers, retailers, and writers, almost everyone preferred the hand-ladled cheese.

understanding aged goat cheeses

Although more than 90 percent of the goat cheese currently sold in the United States is soft and spreadable, many goat cheeses are neither. Rather, they are matured for months, even for years, until they attain the same firmness you'd expect from a well-aged cow's milk cheese.

If you stop by a local cheese shop in Selles-sur-Cher, in the Sologne region of central France, you'll be likely to see eight, ten, even twelve versions of the local goat cheese, which is known by the name of the town. Produced by three or four different makers in the area, these cheeses are of various ages, ranging from fresh to mature.

The fresh cheeses are pleasingly plump with moist interiors and the thin coating of gray ash that is mandatory for makers of Selles-sur-Cher. Because they're probably less than a week old, the cheeses have a mild and mellow flavor, barely formed rinds, a mold-free exterior, and a soft and still very spreadable texture.

A little to the right, you'll find a few dozen more rounds of Selles-sur-Cher, all a week or so older. Now the rinds will be more marked, a bit wrinkled, with a few random spots of natural mold. The texture of these disks is drier and denser. While humans often get flabbier as they make their way into middle age, goat cheeses usually get firmer. The flavor of this older cheese is fuller than that of its younger cousin to the left.

Now shift your sights half a foot or so farther to the right. Again you'll see Selles-sur-Cher, but these cheeses are maybe a month old and are probably less than half the volume of the fresh versions you've already viewed. Their flavor is bigger, more determinedly goaty. They're drier, firmer, more compact, almost flaky— more like a long-aged Cheddar in texture.

Off to the side you may see a wicker basket filled with small chalk-hard, very dry disks. These cheeses are simply the same Selles-sur-Cher another few weeks down the road of development. They're the most full-flavored of the lot: intensely piquant and almost peppery, too much for the average American palate but enjoyed by many food lovers in thin slivers alongside a glass of good red wine.

Which is the best version to buy? All are good. The ultimate answer depends solely on your palate and how you plan to use the cheese.

aging gracefully

Contrary to popular belief, goat cheese should not be strongly goaty in flavor: it should never taste as though it were matured in a barn. As with other aged cheeses, however, with maturity comes mold. Lose the mold, and you lose a lot of flavor. One hundred years or so ago, molds on goat cheeses were allowed to form naturally; what appeared on a particular piece of cheese was what was wild and indigenous to the area (or, at least, to the aging rooms) of the *affineur*. Some molds were white, some blue, some gray, some almost orange. Today mold growth on goat cheese is usually managed, much as it is in the case of blue cheeses.

These mold-ripened cheeses can be tricky to make well. Avoid cheeses with saggy rinds that have separated from the paste of the cheese.

Should you eat the rind? Even French connoisseurs don't agree on this topic. So try a taste and see what you think.

how to pick a good goat cheese

1. The cheese should look clean and neat, neither overly dry nor overly wet. Avoid cracked rinds or smooshed pastes.

2. Ask about hand-ladling, the old-fashioned technique that results in the best goat cheeses.

3. Watch the wrapping. Look for cheeses that are unwrapped altogether or those wrapped only in paper. Fresh goat cheeses that are tightly sealed in a thick plastic casing are likely to be of lesser quality. Thinner, unsealed

cling film, although not optimal, is usually less problematic.

4. Be sure that the milk used to make the cheese was "pure" — 100 percent from goats. Some producers cut costs by replacing part of the more expensive goat's milk with cow's milk.

5. Find full flavor that delivers good complexity, appropriate liveliness, balance, and an enjoyable finish. There should be no off flavors. More specifically, good goat cheese should have just the right amount of salt.

recommended fresh and aged goat cheeses

united states

There are literally hundreds of goat cheeses available in the United States today. Here are a few of my personal favorites.

CAPRIOLE FARMS Judy Schad in southern Indiana has developed a whole line of great goat cheeses. She makes everything from fresh cheese to washed-rind to mold-ripened and matured, all worth trying. I'm particularly fond of her Wabash Cannonballs.

COACH FARM Miles Cahn isn't single-handedly responsible for making goat cheese what it is in America today, but he's played a big part. Although it's large by farmstead standards, Coach Farm has been adamant about sticking to tradi-

tional techniques. In fact, Coach Farm has proven itself a far stronger adherent to tradition and top-grade goat cheese than many makers a tenth its size.

Cahn is the man who made Coach Leather into the prestigious luggage company. Back in the mid-1980s, he and his wife, Lillian, decided to sell the firm. And then, unintentionally, as Cahn says, "We sort of retired into the goat cheese business." The Cahns wanted to replicate the kind of farmstead cheese they had eaten in the French countryside.

Coach Farm makes a series of goat cheeses, everything from ultrafresh to mature cheeses that are aged with white molds and some that are seasoned with herbs or peppercorns. All the cheese is made by hand-ladling in Pine Plains, New York, and is wrapped in paper to allow natural breathing.

CYPRESS GROVE CHÈVRE Mary Keehn does just about everything you could ask for in making great fresh and aged goat cheese. Careful hand-ladling of the curd and a creative matur-

ing technique, capped off by great names—how can you resist Humboldt Fog and Bermuda Triangle?—make this northern California cheesemaker one of the best in the country.

VERMONT BUTTER & CHEESE COMPANY'S BONNE-BOUCHE This cheese is one of my top choices among the current crop of American goat cheeses. Made by Allison Hooper and Bob Reese and the staff at Vermont Butter & Cheese, it's a small, white-mold-ripened little button of goat cheese. The curd is all hand-ladled to enhance texture and flavor. The cheese has a thinner layer of mold, which doesn't dominate the flavor and texture, and a delicate goat flavor and nice nutty finish.

france

There are dozens of different goat cheeses made all over France. Among my favorites are Selles-sur-Cher, Valençay, Chevrot Blanc, and Sainte-Maure. But to find the best of these French imports, you really have to shop. As a general rule, the cheeses of the Jacquin family are very good, as are Chèvre Feuille, Picandine, and Sevre et Belle brands. Quality can vary a lot depending on how they've been handled on this side of the Atlantic. There are also a number of small producers whose cheeses arrive in the States without much in the way of labeling, so at the end of the day you have to really talk to your cheese seller and taste before you buy.

cremeux cheeses

Some *affineurs* specialize in maturing goat cheeses into what they refer to as *cremeux*. Just inside a thin, mold-covered crust, which is often bluish gray, you'll find a runny, creamily dense paste that looks a little like that of a ripe Camembert. The aroma tends to be fairly pungent, but don't let that put you off. These cheeses can be truly superb. *Cremeux* cheeses aren't meant for long keeping, so seize the day when you get them.

spain

garrotxa

A traditional cheese from Catalonia, Garrotxa (pronounced Gah-ro-CHA) is rarely seen outside its homeland. In fact it was almost extinct up until the early 1980s, when a few dedicated cheesemakers decided to revive it. Garrotxa should be made from the milk of Murcian goats. It is aged in natural caves to enhance mold development and hence flavor, so don't be put off by its powdery gray rind. This is old-style artisan fare. Garrotxa has a firm texture, ivory interior, and a deep-down, delicious earthy goat flavor. It's great with a loaf of warm crusty country bread, a handful of toasted hazelnuts, and a ripe pear.

majorero

The Canary Islands are known for their beautiful beaches, but cheese lovers might choose to visit just to get their hands on this incredibly good cheese. Majorero (pronounced Ma-ho-RARE-oh) has the semifirm texture of an Italian Fontina, with which it shares a comparable complexity of flavor, including an appealing taste the Spanish call "toasted." I can only assume that the uniqueness of the flavor is due to the topography of the islands and/or to the unique milk of the Majorera goats. Majorero is unlike any other aged goat cheese I've tasted. It has a sweet, discreet goat flavor that makes it an excellent introduction to goat cheese for novices.

queso de vare

From Asturias in northern Spain, this well-made firm-textured aged goat cheese (pronounced KAY-so day Var-AY) will appeal to both amateurs and aficionados. It has a light gray rind with a smattering of whitish pink molds and a pale ivory paste. It's made from the pasteurized high-fat milk of Murcian goats. When young, the cheese has a mild flavor and is impressively creamy. More mature versions are firm-textured, with a nutty, goaty long-lasting finish.

in the kitchen with goat cheese

Fresh goat cheese is as easy to enjoy as cream cheese. You can spread it on bagels; use it to top off your toast; mix it with herbs, such as chives, or almost any other savory spice, then serve as an hors d'oeuvre; add it to cream or tomato sauces; or put it on pizza. You can stuff it into prunes or figs for a party platter. After dinner it's a delicious spread for toasted nut breads.
Aged French-style goat cheeses are great on cheese boards of all sorts. Accompanied by a good loaf of country bread, a little wine, and maybe a bit of fruit or toasted nuts, they're outstanding eaten just as they are. Be sure to let them warm to room temperature before serving.

stuffed piquillo peppers

I've made this appetizer a million times, but I never get tired of it. The spicy smokiness of the Piquillos is a fantastic foil for the creaminess of the goat cheese. Because they arrive already roasted and peeled, the Piquillos are exceptionally easy to work with.

Piquillo peppers grow only in Navarre in the north of Spain, in the mountainous area along the French border. They're small—about two inches long—and triangular. The freshly picked peppers are grilled over beech-wood fires to char their thin red skin, which gives them a sweet woodsy flavor. Then they're peeled by hand without being rinsed, which would deprive them of much of their flavor.

The Spanish savor Piquillos so much that they've regulated the use of the name by getting a Denomination of Origin. Look for it on the jar; pretenders are starting to show up on store shelves, and there really is a difference.

2 jars (12 ounces each) Spanish Piquillo peppers (see note above), drained

1 5-ounce round fresh goat cheese, at room temperature

3 tablespoons extra virgin olive oil, preferably Catalan

1 garlic clove, finely chopped

Coarse sea salt to taste

Coarsely ground black pepper to taste

With your fingers, gently open the stem end of one of the peppers, being careful not to poke through the flesh. With a small spoon or your fingers, carefully stuff about ½ teaspoon goat cheese inside. It should fill the pepper's cavity but should not be falling out. Continue until all the peppers have been filled.

Preheat the broiler to high.

Arrange the peppers in a single layer in a broiler-proof glass baking dish. Pour 1 tablespoon of the olive oil over them. Sprinkle the garlic over the peppers. Broil for 7 to 10 minutes, or until the cheese is soft and bubbly.

To serve, pour the remaining 2 tablespoons olive oil onto a warm white platter. Arrange the peppers so that they look like the spokes of a wheel on the platter. Sprinkle on salt to taste and grind on a bit of black pepper. Serve warm.

makes about 16 to 20 stuffed peppers,
enough to serve 8 as an appetizer

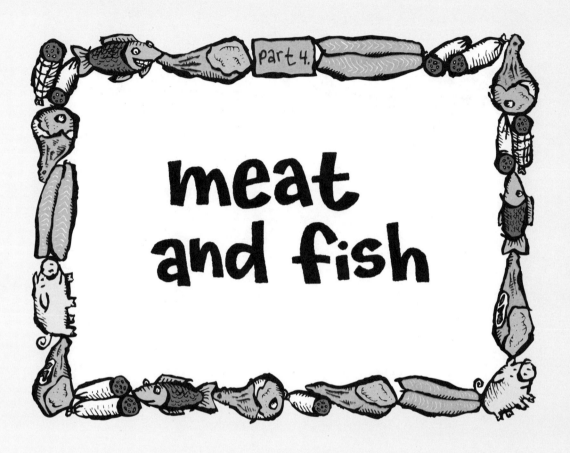

meat
and fish

part 4.

prosciutto

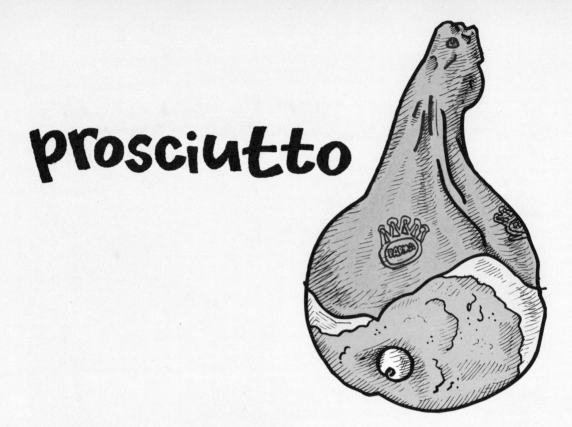

By reputation at least, almost everyone knows about Prosciutto di Parma. For decades (1967–1973 and 1976–1989), government interference blocked it from American tables, enabling a host of feeble copycats to usurp its place. So many imitators created leathery, overly salty, under-aged hams. But take heart: real Prosciutto di Parma is available again in the United States.

Enter any traditional *prosciuttificio,* or prosciutto factory (pronounced pro-shoo-tee-FEE-chee-o), and you'll immediately get a sense of the seriousness with which Italians approach the craft of curing ham. It's a high art that we don't see in the States except in isolated areas in the south, where country ham is king.

home of the parma ham

Located in the flat, lush farmland of the region of Emilia-Romagna in north-central Italy, the heart of prosciutto country, is the town of Langhirano, about twenty-five minutes from the city of Parma. The name *Langhirano* means "Frog's Lake" in English.

At one time the area was a swamp, and although the "lakes" have long since been drained, the soil is still quite moist, enhancing the district's naturally moderate humidity and helping to improve the aging process. As you drive farther from the city, the hills get steadily higher, giving the aging hams access to the sea air coming in from the westerly coasts of Tuscany and Liguria (the Italian Riviera). Invisible as it is, this cool, dry air is credited for the ham's fine flavor.

Parma ham is nothing new, of course. The district has been producing premium pork products for nearly two thousand years. The name *prosciutto* means literally "ham" and is derived from *prosciugare,* meaning "to dry." Originally the term was probably applied to the dry cured meat of any animal — goat, goose, mutton, wild boar, whatever was available. Up until about the fourteenth century, Parma's pigs primarily lived off the local chestnuts and acorns, which enhanced the flavor, and later the reputation, of the hams.

salting the hams

In ancient times, salt was a valuable commodity in the area. Local supplies were limited, but demand — driven by production of ham and Parmigiano cheese — was high. So salt was obtained from the neighboring area of Salsomaggiore. Its high levels of natural boric acid and boric carbonate gave the finished Parma hams a notably bright color and slightly softer texture. Trade also took place with salt suppliers farther afield. In the area of La Spezia in Liguria, Parma cheese was traded for salt, accounting in part for the high use of Parmigiano in Ligurian pesto sauce.

Up until a few hundred years ago, Prosciutto di Parma was just another local cottage industry. Each farm cured the legs of the pigs it slaughtered on-site. Almost all of this prosciutto would have been consumed in the family home, with a small amount traded or sold so the family could acquire products it didn't make itself. Only in the second half of the nineteenth century did Prosciutto di Parma begin the active growth that led to today's large-scale production of roughly 9 million hams a year and international distribution. Ham played such a big role in that part of the world that Langhirano's nineteenth-century city planners designed its streets specifically to allow for the breezes to blow in to help with ham maturing.

In 1963 the Consorzio del Prosciutto di Parma was founded to protect the product from copycats and to assure consumers of minimum quality standards. Originally started with just under two dozen members, the Consorzio has grown nearly tenfold, to include almost two hundred today.

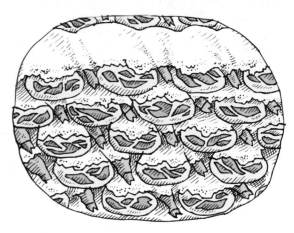

how prosciutto di parma is produced

Nearly a third of all Italian pigs' legs are made into Prosciutto di Parma. By law the pigs used must be a minimum of nine months old and weigh in at between 340 and 420 pounds. More mature pigs, those that are about a year old, are preferable and more costly—their meat is denser and less likely to absorb too much salt. The diet of the animals is dictated by Consorzio standards; they must spend their final four months in north-central Italy, where they eat corn, barley, and whey left behind from the production of Parmigiano-Reggiano. No drugs can be used at all in the weeks before slaughtering. All incoming fresh hams are tattooed with the province, farm, and date of slaughter. The Consorzio inspects the hams for quality; each leg that passes is riveted with a metal insignia proving official Parma certification, then stamped

with the date on which production began.

Up until a decade or so ago, the hams had to come from Parma province. Now all of Italy is eligible, although the Consorzio must approve each of the approximately 5,500 farms. The salting starts shortly after the hams have arrived at the factory. The fresh raw pork is covered with coarse sea salt, then put into cold storage and held at 33 to 39 degrees Fahrenheit. After a week, the residual salt is brushed off and a second salting takes place. This time the ham is held for about eighteen to twenty days. Throughout this period, the hams are stored in quite cold rooms; humidity and temperature are adjusted to encourage the advancement of the salt into the heart of the ham. Only salt can be added. The Consorzio's regulations forbid the use of sugar, spices, or smoke.

Next comes the rest period, in which the salt is still working its way into the ham's center. After roughly sixty days, when the hams are about ninety days old, the salt has made its way through the muscle and reached the bone, and the ham has turned a dull brownish color. The hams are cleaned, trimmed, and rinsed of excess salt. They are then beaten quickly with wooden mallets to tenderize the outer edges of the meat and hung to air for a little less than a week.

From the cold rooms, the legs are moved into a much warmer space (roughly 60 to 68 degrees Fahrenheit) for about four months. Harmful bacteria have been killed, and the ham now no longer needs refrigeration. In this stage, the ham loses about 30 percent of its initial weight, and the natural fermentation of the meat begins. The fermentation is essential, for it is this process that develops the aroma and flavor of the ham. "The greater the fermentation, the greater the flavor," Dr. Luigi Di Vodier, owner of Prosciutto Di Vodier, told me on a recent visit.

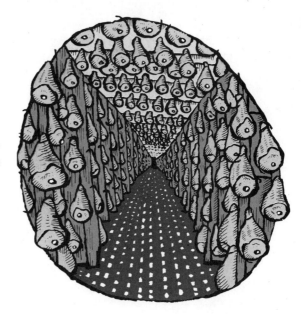

underground treasure

The final aging period starts at about seven months, when the hams are taken to another set of aging rooms, partially underground cellars, where literally thousands of hams hang from weathered wooden racks. The experience of being in one of these rooms always sets my mind reeling. I feel as if I'm in a secret treasure cave. The entire space takes on the color of the hams and is filled with a heavenly golden glow, not unlike the halos with which Renaissance painters adorned their saints. Even Di Vodier, a small producer by commercial standards, has about forty thousand hams hanging, neat and orderly, like rows of elegant suits at an Italian clothier. Fans flutter slowly overhead like helicopters to keep the air moving. The smell in the maturing rooms is enchanting, a singularly special perfume.

The hams hang upside down like giant teardrops. The white ball of the hipbone protrudes from each like the rounded handle of a gearshift. The upper half of the ham wears a natural leather jacket, the golden shiny cured pigskin, which is left intact to protect the ham during the processing. The lower, wider portion of the prosciutto — *la faccia,* or "the face" — is lighter in color. During this stage, the meat returns to its original attractive rose color. Complex proteins are gradually broken down into simple proteins, contributing to the tenderness of the finished prosciutto.

At about seven months, a balm of pork fat, salt, and a touch of ground black pepper is rubbed onto the exposed section of the ham. The fat keeps unwanted air from entering the meat and prevents excessive drying and/or overfermentation. A small sliver of ham is left unsealed, in order to allow for modest movement of air out of the ham. The maturation continues, though at a slower pace, for at least three more months. In total, the Prosciutto di Parma is aged at least ten months, though some go on as long as two years.

The majority of prosciutti sent to the United States have been boned so that they are easier to slice and sell. The maturing and fermentation continue only as long as the bone is left in the meat. So although they wait another three to four months before arriving in a shop, the flavor of "boneless" hams has already been fixed.

crown jewel

At the end of their aging, the hams are checked for quality by the ham master, who pierces the ham in five designated spots using a six-inch-long "needle" carved from the calf bone of a horse. After each penetration, the inspector uses his nose to check for problems. The aroma should be sweet and succulent; off aromas indicate inferior ham. A little over 90 percent of the product will be judged good enough to earn the ducal seal, the Crown of Parma, which is branded onto their sides. The rest of the hams are sold off in other, less prestigious packaging.

sweet pig

"So which prosciutti are the most prized?" I ask Di Vodier.

"Well," he starts out, "a pig is like a woman." Immediately, I feel a sense of panic. There are women — American women, and successful professionals at that — in the room. I consider changing the subject. "You see," he says, "there

are many women in Chicago. But all are not equally beautiful. The prosciutto master's job is to know how to select the right pigs. Commercial producers are much less selective."

Great. Picking pigs for prosciutto is like dating? I think to myself. It's most definitely not the analogy I would have used, but Italy is, well, Italy.

More often than not, fullness of flavor in the finished ham goes hand in hand with size. The bigger the ham, the greater the likelihood that it will end up high on the sweetness scale. And the bigger the ham, the longer it can age without becoming too dry. A few extra months of age on the pig before it goes to slaughter can help the flavor as well. Better producers look for hams from pigs that are eleven to twelve months old; they will be heavier and have bigger hind legs. More mature pigs provide more consistent fiber and better distribution of intramuscular fat, which in turn helps to limit excessive salt absorption, yielding a sweeter, if costlier, ham.

Skillful salting is critical. Bigger producers, with less room for financial error and less skill in the salting room, often use excessive salt to reduce the risk of the ham going bad. Too little salt, and the meat won't cure, leading to spoilage and loss.

Each ham master makes daily decisions about salting, airflow, humidity, or the timing of removing the salt or transferring a ham from one aging room to the next—all of which affect the texture and flavor of the finished product. These decisions are best made when data are paired up with intuitive assessments based upon years of hands-on experience. Maturing a good Parma ham is still a craft, not a science.

buying better-tasting prosciutto

check the age

Ask the age of the ham. If the counter staff can't tell you, ask to see the rivet at the top of the ham's hock. It will show the month (in abbreviated Italian—OTT stands for Ottobre, or "October," for example) and the year the ham was started. Ten months is the minimum. Fifteen to eighteen months is considered optimal, though some experts think longer is even better. The older the ham, the drier its texture and the more intense its flavor.

buy off the bone

Buying prosciutto cut directly from the bone is the easiest way to ensure a better-tasting piece. Unfortunately, bone-in prosciutto is very difficult to find in the United States; roughly 95 percent of the prosciutto shipped here has had the bone removed before leaving the plant in Parma. (Take note that in Italy the percentages are reversed—nearly all the Parma ham sold is sliced by hand!) If you can find bone-in ham, go for it—it will have clocked an extra two to three months of maturation, and its flavor is sure to be fuller.

Buying off the bone sends you home with ham that is closer to what you'd get in Italy. Bone-in hams are always sliced by hand *with* the grain. You can't cut boneless hams with the grain on a machine. Additionally, the heat and friction of a mechanical meat slicer will damage the delicate fat and flavor of the ham; the spinning blade raises the temperature of the meat,

Lardo is one of those truly terrific foods that you still can't get in the United States. If you're going to eat it, you've got to go to Italy. The specialty of the tiny Tuscan hill town of Colonnata, it's pork fat from the rump of the pig, cured for months with rock salt, rosemary, cloves, and some other "secret" herbs in vats of Tuscan marble, then eaten raw. The salt acts to produce a brine during the aging, serving to protect and tenderize the fat. In size, a piece of *lardo* is not unlike a thick slab of bacon.

If you buy a bigger piece of *lardo,* scrape off the salt and seasonings before slicing. But save them — you can use them to season other dishes like fish, meat, or bean stews.

with the result that the fat melts into the meat. While hand-sliced pieces look less glamorous, their flavor and texture remain intact.

smaller slices can be superior

When you look at a leg of Prosciutto di Parma, you'll see two pieces of muscle that come together around the bone. The one that's on the outside — the skin side — will be lighter in color. The one on the inside — where there is no skin to keep the air out — will be rosier. Additionally, the larger of the two will be more generously marbled with fat and will have a sweeter, mellower flavor. The smaller muscle will mature more quickly and may tend to be a bit more intense in flavor, perhaps even a touch saltier.

I should add that the part of the prosciutto up "top," where the slices are smaller and look less luxurious, is generally the most desirable part of the meat. If you want looks, then by all means buy those bigger, longer slices from lower down on the ham. But if you're after fuller, sweeter flavor and more tenderness, take the less appealing looking slices from up top.

keep the fat

Although Americans tend to blanch at the prospect of buying what they perceive to be an unwanted part of the meat, the fat is the source of a lot of flavor. Be sure the store hasn't taken off all of the ham's beautiful white coating, which is actually the most delectable part of the product.

evaluate the producer's experience

In general, one can assess the experience of the *prosciuttificio* by reading the producer's number, which you'll see stamped into the metal rivet near the hoof of the ham. Since the plants were numbered in order of seniority, the lower the plant number, the more established the producer. There are two hundred producers of prosciutto in Italy.

best brands of parma

SALUMIFICIO CIELLE This fairly small, hands-on prosciutto maker in the town of Langhirano on the banks of the Torrente di Parma has excellent access to the all-important winds coming down from the Apennines. The master of the house is Pierluigi Negri, who has over twenty years of experience in making the hams. Prosciutto from this company is available in some specialty shops.

PROSCIUTTIFICIO GALLONI The Gallonis buy their raw pork legs from only a handful of producers, in whom they place great trust. They allow fresh air to circulate through their aging rooms and around their hams, as Parma producers have done for centuries.

prosciutto from other parts of italy

PROSCIUTTO DI SAN DANIELE The town of San Daniele, which lies north of the old city of Trieste, near the border with Slovenia, produces Italy's second most famous ham. San Daniele cures far fewer hams than does Parma—the twenty-seven authorized producers make about 2 million hams per annum. The San Daniele hams are pressed (weighed down to force out excess air during the aging), a technique that local partisans believe intensifies its flavor. The air that blows down from the Alps and up from the Adriatic contributes to the flavor of the ham during the long curing, a minimum of twelve months, often as many as fourteen. In its homeland it's always cured with the hoof on—unlike Parma ham, from which the hoof is removed. Those sent to the States are cured without the hoof because of FDA restrictions.

PROSCIUTTO DI CARPEGNA There's only one producer of this ham, located near the old papal state of San Marino in the Marche region, near the Tuscan border. The prosciutto is a bit more gamy, slightly more intense, than the sweeter hams of Parma and San Daniele. In part the flavor is due to high-altitude aging—the town is about 2,100 feet above sea level. Aging is a minimum of twelve months.

keeping prosciutto

Keep any already sliced prosciutto well wrapped in butcher or wax paper in the refrigerator so that it doesn't dry out and/or pick up aromas from other foods.

what to do with prosciutto di parma

Now that you've gotten your prized prosciutto home, do as the Italians do, and eat it as is. In Parma, prosciutto is an everyday pleasure, one of the little things that make life more livable, never a luxury. It's taken for granted that prosciutto will appear two or three times a week at the beginning of a meal. Of the roughly 9 million hams that the Consorzio certifies each year, nearly 85 percent are still consumed in Italy!

Lay the slices on a plate and enjoy them as a snack, as a light lunch, or before dinner. Accompaniments can be as simple as good bread or olives.

Slices of prosciutto wrapped around wedges of ripe melon or fresh figs are a great appetizer. Chop and sprinkle prosciutto on salads, such as raw fennel, sliced mushroom, and a couple peelings of Parmigiano-Reggiano (use a vegetable peeler) dressed with good olive oil and aged balsamic vinegar. I also like prosciutto on simple sandwiches with a little olive oil, a bit of butter, and some mozzarella or fresh greens. Let the meat come to room temperature before you serve it.

If you're cooking with prosciutto, expose the meat to as little heat as possible. If you're adding prosciutto to a pasta dish, toss it in at the very end.

3 p's sandwich

These sandwiches make a truly tasty picnic lunch. Prepare them an hour or two in advance so the oil has a chance to soak into the bread.

- ¼ cup mellow extra virgin olive oil, preferably Ligurian
- 2 ounces freshly grated Parmigiano-Reggiano cheese (about 1 cup)
  Freshly ground black pepper to taste
- 1 freshly baked baguette, split lengthwise
- 2 ounces Prosciutto di Parma (about 2 slices, each 4–6 inches long and 2–3 inches wide)
- 1 cup loosely packed fresh arugula leaves

In a medium bowl, mix the olive oil, Parmigiano, and pepper until smooth.

Spread the Parmigiano mixture onto one baguette half.

Lay on the prosciutto and arugula, then the top slice of bread. Cut crosswise to make individual sandwiches. Serve.

makes 3 or 4 sandwiches

prosciutto and mozzarella sandwich

This great grilled cheese sandwich is perfect for lunch or dinner, especially when you're eating alone, but you can easily multiply the recipe to feed as many as you'd like. For the fun of it, the red of the pepper, white of the cheese, and green of the arugula approximate the colors of the Italian flag.

2 very thin slices Prosciutto di Parma
2 good-sized slices fresh mozzarella cheese
1 roasted red pepper, cut into strips
6 arugula leaves
2 slices crusty Italian bread
Coarse sea salt to taste
Freshly ground black pepper to taste
1 teaspoon extra virgin olive oil

Place the prosciutto, mozzarella, roasted pepper, and arugula on one slice of bread. Sprinkle with salt and grind on pepper to taste. Place the second slice of bread on top.

In a heavy skillet, heat the olive oil over medium heat.

Place the sandwich in the skillet and weigh it down with a small skillet or a heavy bowl. Fry until golden brown on both sides, about 3 minutes per side. Cut in half and serve immediately.

serves 1

serrano ham

Spain's Serrano ham has only recently appeared in North America. After decades of denial due to bureaucratic blockage, it presents an exciting opportunity for food lovers to enjoy authentic Jamón (pronounced Ha-MON) Serrano without having to fly eight hours to get it. Penelope Casas, the premier writer on the subject of Spanish food, calls cured ham "a national obsession." In Madrid, ham bars specialize in regional fare. Hams of all shapes and sizes hang from the ceilings and walls, and the counters are covered with hams from which skilled slicers serve up small portions, accompanied by glasses of wine or sherry.

Serrano ham is not a second-rate Spanish surrogate for its better-known Italian cousin from Parma. Although each one is a dry-cured ham, ultimately the two are very different products: within the world of dry-cured hams, they're opposites. A good Prosciutto di Parma is meant to be delicate, markedly sweet, soft, succulent. A Serrano is meatier, gutsier, less refined, maybe more interesting to those who like to live on the wilder side. With a good slice of Serrano, you will find a boldness and complexity usually connected with wild game.

Good Serrano is something special. Its aroma is wonderful: sweet, pungent, and subtly spicy. The uneven small slices that slip off the whole ham range from the color of rosé wine to a bouquet of red roses, with a generous bit of white fat marbled into its center and ringing its edges. When all is said and done, there's nothing else quite like it.

hamming it up: a visit to a serrano source

Because there is little regulation in Spain of the label Serrano, the name alone is not enough to guarantee that you're getting your hands on a good ham. Located in the Valencian hill town of Utiel, the firm of Redondo Iglesias is one of the few companies authorized to export Serrano for the American market. The firm has almost a century of experience, which is evident in the flavor of the finished hams.

After arriving at the curing house, the fresh pork is salted. The Redondo family uses only Mediterranean sea salt from the salt beds of the Spanish coast. The hams are stacked in neat rows, then left to sit in cold rooms for ten to eighteen days. The salt is washed off with water, and the hams are sent off to hang in cool drying rooms. Here they are stored at about

45 degrees Fahrenheit and in fairly high humidity, 80 percent, suspended by thick ropes. The goal is to draw out as much moisture as possible.

The aging of Serrano is the opposite of that for Prosciutto di Parma. The exposed section of prosciutto is rubbed with a coating of pork fat to keep it from drying, enhancing the ham's tenderness. In contrast, no fat is put on the face of the Serrano ham, so moisture evaporates, concentrating the flavors in the meat. And while Parma producers work hard to keep mold growth to a minimum, Serrano makers actually encourage it.

When the first stage of the curing has been completed, the hams are moved to the warmer aging rooms, where the temperature is 60 to 65 degrees Fahrenheit. It's in here that the all-important mold begins to bloom. In some rooms, the mold seems greener, while in others it's much whiter. In one room in particular, it seems to border on black. The mold protects the meat inside, while enhancing the flavor. Throughout the aging, the air moving past the pork is also important; the Redondo family purposely built its plant at nearly three thousand feet above sea level, and there's almost always a pleasant breeze.

By the time its aging is over, a good Serrano will have spent a minimum of a year, and often thirteen, fourteen, or fifteen months maturing. In the process it loses a lot of weight—a ham that starts out at twenty-five to thirty pounds will probably finish at about sixteen.

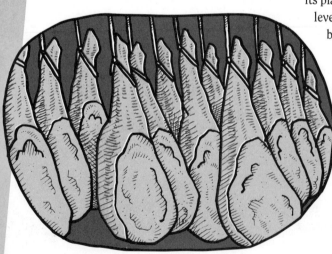

the white fat from my small slice. A Spaniard standing nearby stared at my friend with a look between horror and disgust.

"What's the matter?" I inquired.

"If I am buying jamón from you, and you take away all of this fat," he said, eyeing the knife I had in hand, "I will have to kill you."

BEST BRANDS There are only two Serrano brands on the market in the United States: Redondo Iglesias and Navidul. Redondo hams tend to be bigger in flavor and a bit gamier; Navidul hams are slightly drier and milder.

it ain't pretty

In Spain, Serrano is almost never sold in the long, thin, romantic-looking slices you see in Italian prosciutto ads. Instead it's served in what the Spaniards refer to as *virutas,* which means, literally, "shavings": small, hand-cut, one- to two-inch pieces. Since the best jamón is that which is sliced off the bone by hand—not preboned and cut on an electric slicing machine —these *virutas* are hardly ever attractive by conventional American standards. They're slightly ragged and agreeably inconsistent. Without proper warning on this point, most Americans will go into consumer convulsions.

fat to kill for

The part of the Serrano that Spaniards prize most is the snowy white fat, which surrounds the outside of the sliced meat and marbles the interior. When I was in Spain learning to slice traditional Jamón Serrano, another American in our group suggested I try to trim away more of

three ways to enjoy jamón serrano

Because authentic Spanish Serrano ham is so full-flavored, a little goes a long way. You'll find that you can serve Serrano in satisfying, yet surprisingly small portions. As little as an ounce or so per person is probably enough.

simple snacks

As often as not, jamón is served—and enjoyed —au naturel, as a snack. If you go to one of Spain's renowned tapas bars, you're almost sure to be served a small plateful of Serrano slices that you can eat with your fingers, perhaps with a bowl of Arbequina olives (see page 51), a handful of toasted almonds, a small dish of Piquillo peppers (see page 277), and a glass of chilled fino sherry. It's also excellent with Spanish

white asparagus. Its savory flavor finely counterpoints sweet fruit—try it with some fresh figs. I like it along with Manchego cheese.

sandwiches

In a typical Spanish sandwich offering, Jamón Serrano is ideal sitting atop a piece of Pa amb Tomaquet, the Catalan version of bruschetta (page 114). For a quick lunch or an easy appetizer, rub just toasted slices of farm bread with half of a ripe tomato. Don't be too gentle—you really want to push the juice of the tomato into the bread. Pour on a generous dose of extra virgin olive oil (one from Catalonia if you want to be authentic), sprinkle on a tiny touch of coarse sea salt, and then top with a slice of Serrano. Eat it while it's hot.

soups or salads

Spaniards use a surprising amount of Jamón Serrano in cooking—its flavor is so concentrated that a sprinkling of ham slivers can add interest to all sorts of dishes. A few small cubes can significantly boost the flavor of most any soup, especially hearty vegetable or bean soups. Or you can coarsely cut an ounce of Serrano and sprinkle it over a couple of green salads. The same goes for pasta sauces. Sample it in scrambled eggs, along with a touch of chopped fresh mint leaves. Serrano ham is a fine flavor builder for all sorts of seafood dishes—try adding a bit to sautéed scallops or to a tomato-and-fennel-based seafood stew.

When you use Serrano as an ingredient, cut back on the amount of salt you add. The liquid in the dish pulls the salt from the ham, so taste before you season.

spanish salad with oranges and olive oil

This seemingly strange combination is delicious. I learned it from Mariano Sanz Pech, whose excellent olive oil we've been selling at Zingerman's for many years. It's refreshing and ideal for warm summer days. I love the contrasting colors, textures, and flavors of the orange slices, olive oil, and mint.

You can also serve this salad with a chopped hard-boiled egg. If you're feeling adventurous, it's also excellent topped with soaked and shredded *bacalao* (salt cod).

2	navel oranges, peeled, pith removed, sliced crosswise and quartered, plus 1 navel orange, halved
4–6	large fresh mint leaves, torn
1	ounce Jamón Serrano, cut into slivers
2	tablespoons whole blanched almonds, toasted (see page 31) and coarsely chopped
10	cured black olives, such as Farga Aragon
	Coarse sea salt to taste
	Freshly ground black pepper to taste
1–2	tablespoons extra virgin olive oil, preferably a medium fruity Spanish one

Arrange the orange slices on a small serving platter. Top with the mint, Jamón Serrano, almonds, olives, a sprinkle of sea salt, some pepper, and the olive oil. Squeeze half of the remaining orange over the salads just before serving (reserve the other orange half for another use).

serves 2

miguel's mother's macaroni

I always like to find out how the makers of artisan foods use their products in their own kitchens, which prompted me to ask Miguel Redondo how he likes to eat his ham. "Mostly in sandwiches," he said, "and as an apéritif, for tapas. It's also very good with tomato." (See also Pa amb Tomaquet, page 114). "And," he added, "my mother uses it with macaroni." He described the dish, which is essentially pasta and tomato sauce with Serrano ham.

"What do you call it?" I asked, waiting for some old Spanish name.

"Macaroni," he said.

Don't skimp on the pasta quality.

   6 large tomatoes (3–3½ pounds)
   ½ cup medium-fruity extra virgin olive oil, plus more for serving
   1 medium onion, finely chopped (about 1¼ cups)
   1 garlic clove, peeled and bruised with the side of a knife
   2 cups water
   ¾ teaspoon coarse sea salt, plus more if needed
   1 pound good-quality macaroni
   4 ounces Jamón Serrano, coarsely chopped
   ½ cup coarsely chopped fresh Italian parsley, rinsed and squeezed dry
     Freshly ground black pepper to taste
     Freshly grated Manchego cheese for serving (optional)

Core and halve the tomatoes. Grate the tomatoes on the large-holed side of a box grater into a large bowl. Discard the skins.

In a large saucepan, heat the olive oil over medium-high heat. Add the onion and garlic and sauté until softened, 3 to 4 minutes. Add the grated tomatoes, and bring to a boil over high heat, stirring often. Add the water and stir well. Return to a boil, then reduce the heat to medium-low and simmer until the liquid is reduced by 2 cups, about 30 minutes. Add the ¾ teaspoon salt and stir well.

Add the uncooked pasta to the pan and stir well. Cook until the pasta is nearly al dente, 15 to 20 minutes. Remove from the heat. Add the ham and parsley and stir well. Check the salt and add more if needed.

Serve in warm bowls with a ribbon of olive oil drizzled over the top and a generous grinding of black pepper. You can also sprinkle a bit of grated Manchego cheese over the macaroni if you like.   *serves 4*

trout navarra style

This recipe offers a nice way to get the savor of Jamón Serrano into a main dish.

- 2 tablespoons extra virgin olive oil
- 2 ounces Jamón Serrano, thinly sliced
- 2 whole fresh trout (½ pound each), cleaned
- ½ cup all-purpose flour
- 1 teaspoon coarse sea salt
- 1 teaspoon freshly ground black pepper

In a large skillet, heat 1 tablespoon of the olive oil over medium-high heat. Fry the slices of Jamón Serrano for 1 minute per side, or until golden. Remove the ham from the pan and set it aside. Turn off the heat, but don't wash the skillet.

Place half of the Jamón Serrano into the cavity of each fish. Gently slide a toothpick through the fish to secure the ham.

In a shallow bowl, combine the flour, salt, and pepper. Dredge each fish lightly in the flour mixture.

In the skillet, heat the remaining 1 tablespoon olive oil over medium heat. Gently add the fish to the skillet and reduce the heat to low. Cook until the lower side of the fish appears to become opaque nearly up to the backbone, then flip the fish over and cook it on the other side, about 5 minutes per side. Remove and discard the toothpicks. Serve hot.

serves 4

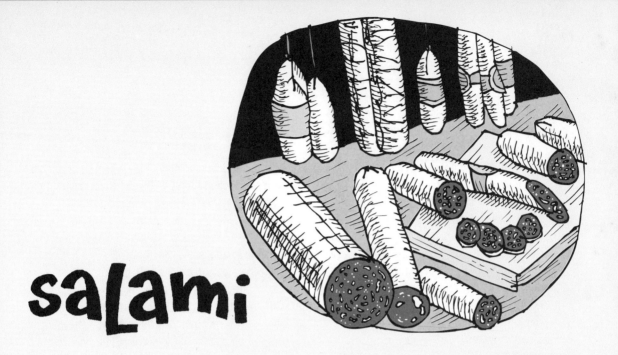

salami

As old as it is and as prevalent a part as it plays in eating in Europe, salami has somehow been skipped over in all the increased attention to good food in North America. What we've ignored or misunderstood ought—by all rights—to be elevated to the same level of culinary esteem as artisan cheese, estate olive oil, hearth-baked bread, and vintage vinegars. Great salami, as you'll soon discover, is something truly special, something that we've allowed the Europeans to hog all for themselves while we've struggled along with Slim Jims and summer sausage sticks.

a visit to a tuscan salami maker

A landmark for knowledgeable food lovers visiting the region, the Macelleria Falorni is located on the central square of the town of Greve-in-Chianti. A forty-minute drive due south of Florence, Greve is one of those great little Tuscan hill towns that thirty or forty years ago was subsumed in poverty. But with the benefit of today's tourist traffic and interest in wine and olive oil, it's become a rather upscale destination. If you make it to Greve, it's easy to find the Falornis' shop. It's the only storefront on the Piazza Matteotti—the main square—that has a two-foot-high stuffed wild boar standing guard by the entrance. (More about the boar later.) At Falorni, I grasped for the first time in twenty years of working with food what great salami is all about.

I knew something was different as I approached the shop, which is brightly lit, alive, in a way I'd never in a million years have imagined a butcher shop could be. It's an attractive space filled to the brim with succulent salami, fresh sausages, pancetta, and whole legs of cured ham. Standing inside on a rainy Saturday night, there were consistently five, ten, even fifteen people lined up at the single cash register to pay for shopping baskets full of nothing but pork products. I was almost as impressed by the shop's aromas as I was by the overall ambiance. The Falornis' shop smells sweet but not in a cloying, syrupy way. Rather, it has a soft, deep earthy perfume that welcomes you and beckons you to buy.

As in most great food shops, there's almost always an owner on-site at the Macelleria. Shortly after arriving, I'm introduced to Stefano Bencista, who represents something like the eighth generation of the Falorni family to make salami. Tall, with combed-back black hair, a pair of elegant, egg-shaped wire-rimmed glasses, and a big, blustery handlebar mustache, Bencista carries himself with the air of a successful nineteenth-century count, a statuesque sovereign of superior salami.

anatomy of a great salami

"What makes a great salami?" I ask.

"Aroma," Bencista begins thoughtfully. He pauses. I wait. He ponders. "Flavor," he continues, but then stops again.

"Industrial salamis," he says, "use all sorts of things that you won't find in a traditional salami: soy protein, flour, water, artificial colors, sugar, dry milk, MSG, preservatives. All those additions," Bencista adds, pursing his lips behind his mustache and shaking his head unhappily, "leave a bad taste in the mouth."

Bencista picks up a salami sitting nearby and holds it up to the light. It has a soft, downy coat of white mold. He picks up a knife from the wooden butcher's block nearby and slices the salami in half. "It should look fresh," he says. Indeed, the interior is glowing and alive, like the rosy cheeks of a healthy child. "Its color should be even, consistent throughout. The color should be pink. Not too red—that would be a sign of artificial coloring. Too pale isn't good either," he adds. "It's a sign of poor processing." He squeezes the salami between his thumb and forefinger. "It should have some suppleness . . . feel full in its casing.

"Of course," Bencista goes on, "you can't have a salami without mold." The mold acts as a natural antioxidant and protects the fat inside from rancidity. The flavor of the meat will continue to develop as long as the mold is present. How long that is depends on the size of the salami, the amount of moisture in the meat, and the conditions in the aging rooms. Essentially, the mold will stay alive as long as there is enough moisture in the meat to support it. Hence, bigger salamis can be cured for a longer time and develop a fuller flavor.

the magic of mold

Bencista suggests we take a quick trip to the Falornis' maturing rooms, a few minutes' drive down the road. Thousands of salamis hang from hooks in various stages of blooming. The temperature is cool, not cold. The humidity is lower than it would be for most cheeses, but the space definitely isn't dry. As the salamis mature, they are moved into other rooms, which get gradually cooler and drier. Each has just the right environment to encourage appropriate levels of mold growth. Ample room is essential so that the air can move around the meat. The aging rooms smell sweetly of mold and also of ammonia. The latter is a natural byproduct of the mold and the maturing, as it is with many types of cheese.

The mold begins to appear within three to four days of entry into the aging rooms. At the end of one week, a soft white coat forms. As the salami matures, the mold growth builds. At fourteen days, the moisture in the meat starts to lessen, concentrating its natural flavors. At three weeks, the mold is a powdery bluish white — you can actually blow it off at this point. Bencista demonstrates by bringing a salami close to his lips and quickly sending a small cloud of white mold spores into the air, where they join thousands of their invisible cousins hovering overhead. The Falornis' salamis are ready at five to seven weeks, at which point they are covered with a generous grayish white powdery coating.

Although it's essential to the maturation of the meat, you don't actually eat the mold. Instead, you peel off the casing — and with it, the mold — and eat the meat inside.

the meat makes the salami

To back up a bit, it's important to understand that a finished salami will never be superior to the fresh meat from which it was made. The animals themselves — their breed and their diet — are an essential component of the quality.

The fat that goes into a salami is just as important as the meat. Although Americans tend to fear the fat, it's responsible for much of the distinctive flavor of the best salamis. Pigs have a layer of very hard fat on their shoulders — known as "the shield" — a vestige of prehistoric pigs' habit of charging through thick bushes and brush. The best salamis start with this firm-textured fat rather than the softer, more plentiful fat from other parts of the pig.

With a thin-bladed knife, Bencista takes a few slices off a salami. The texture is soft. Slowly the flavor opens up in my mouth: full, sweet, succulent, and well balanced, with an uncommonly pleasant finish. Without question, it's much meatier than any salami I've eaten at home. In comparison, standard American products seem almost flavorless. Supermarket salami doesn't taste of meat but of spices, too much garlic, hot pepper, fennel. Salami in the United States is usually chewy, often stringy, and greasy. But at Falorni, the texture is different. The fat is in balance with the meat, and it doesn't leave my mouth feeling oily, but refreshed.

As I'm marveling at the full flavor, I note that the salami Bencista has sliced comes from the counter, not the refrigerator. As with fine cheese, the flavor of superior salami shines when it's brought to room temperature instead of being served straight from the cooler at 35 degrees Fahrenheit.

slaughtering

The Falornis bring the pigs to their slaughterhouse in truck pens, ten pigs to a truck. More than ten won't work because if the pigs are packed in too tightly, their stress levels rise. Conversely, fewer than ten means that the animals will be bumped around en route, also causing stress. Stressed pigs have a higher pH, and hence a higher rate of salt absorption, which will adversely affect the flavor of the cured meat.

"From the time of the slaughter," Stefano Bencista says, "you have only thirty minutes to butcher the animal." The quality of the butchering work also has an enormous impact. The best salami must be made from meat that's been carefully hand-cut in order to pull out all the sinews and tough tendons. Less careful butchering leads to all the white particles of sinew you see in poor-quality salami.

Bencista pulls open the door of a cooler to show off the freshly cut meat: twenty or so tubs, each filled with a different cut. The meat looks fresh and smells clean. All the cuts stay in the cooler overnight so that moisture can evaporate; excess water enhances weight but diminishes flavor. Each type of salami will be made by mixing specific cuts in prescribed portions by hand. Careful trimming and cutting prevent the fat from being emulsified into the meat and preserve the independent flavors and textures that are so important to a good salami. Good salami is never greasy.

The Falornis' commitment to quality carries through as well into their seasonings. They use only wild fennel seeds; their black peppercorns are big and plump; the garlic never overwhelms the flavor of the meat. The care continues in the use of old-style natural casings, which allow the salami to breathe and mature properly, the way a good rind does on a cheese. "The casing," one traditional producer told me, "is to the salami maker what the cask is to the winemaker." Natural casing adds significantly to the cost of the salami, but it also adds enormously to the fullness of the flavor.

maturing

Once in the casings, the salamis must be matured. Properly cured meat goes through two stages of fermentation. In the first, the natural glycogen in the meat and any sugar ferment. This stage lasts about a week, during which the meat releases its natural moisture. At the same time, nitrates and nitrites naturally convert into nitrous oxide, a gas that moves through the

Probably the most prestigious regional specialty salami of Spain, *salchichón* is the pride of the small Catalan town of Vic, a little more than an hour northwest of Barcelona. Casa Riera Ordeix is one of the oldest and best producers of this salami.

The traditional production for *salchichón* starts on Saint Martin's Day in early November. Fresh pork is allowed to rest for a few days, then hand-trimmed of fat and sinews. The meat is chopped, mixed with pork belly for fat, and then seasoned with salt and black pepper. After a couple of days of marinating, the meat mixture is stuffed into natural pork casings and hung on wooden racks in the upper floors of special curing houses. There the mountain mists and the native white molds transform the sausage over a period of five to six months. From there the salamis are shifted into cooler cellars for another few months. The finished *salchichón* are marvelously meaty, full-flavored, and surprisingly sweet.

meat, killing unwanted bacteria and fixing the meat's naturally reddish color. Proper curing at moderate temperatures (around 80 degrees Fahrenheit) over the course of a week will ensure that only traces of nitrates and nitrites in the meat remain. Often derided in this country as "bad for you," these substances have been used as preservatives in cured meats for thousands of years. Without them, salt would have to be used at such high levels as to make a salami inedible to our modern palates.

During the second phase of the maturing, the natural enzymes in the meat and mold convert the meat's low-flavor proteins into high-flavor amino acids. In the process, moisture leaves the meat, the flavor develops, and the salami takes on character. All told, it takes roughly three weeks for the smallest salami to ripen. Midsized salami will take about five to six weeks, and the biggest of the bunch can go for a good two months. During the aging, the salami will likely lose about one third of its original weight. And in the process, the natural enzymes in the meat will build up the flavor and enhance the texture of the finished salami.

Maturing cured meats is a complex craft. "The question is, 'How does it taste?' No machine can tell you this. You have to get harmony," says Bencista.

signs of superior salami

check the ingredients list

Generally, the shorter the ingredients list, the more likely the salami is to be good. Shy away from water, corn syrup, nonfat dry milk (except in a San Francisco–style salami such as Molinari, in which nonfat dry milk is expected), MSG, or excessive amounts of sugar. Stay away from starches or wheat flour, thickeners used in place of proper maturing.

choose pork

U.S. producers usually use beef to keep costs down. But unless you're looking for a kosher or kosher-style salami, you should opt for pure pork, which has a superior aroma and fuller flavor.

look it over

The best-tasting salamis are usually those with a healthy coat of whitish gray mold. A good salami will also be pleasantly plump, filling its casing. A salami that looks flat, oil-stained, or blotchy has passed its peak. The coarser the cut of the meat, the fuller the flavor.

smell it

The aroma should be sweet, succulent, appealing.

check the blade when you slice it

The salami should never leave a greasy trail on the knife or slicer blade.

taste it!

The meat should be the most dominant flavor. Garlic and spices should generally play supporting roles.

great regional salamis

Every region of Europe has its own style of salami. And because the locals in each area are partisans of their particular product, you'll never get a consensus about which is the "best." I treat salami like cheese—I try to serve an array in order to highlight their contrasting flavors and textures.

italy

American law doesn't permit cured salami to be imported from Italy. Happily, high-quality versions are being made here. I'm partial to the Ticino label made with Niman Ranch pork under the guidance of Francois Vecchio.

felino

Known as the king of Italian salami, it features hand-sorted meats and fats stuffed into a thick natural pork casing. In Italy, Felino salami is so special that it's earned its own Denomination of Origin.

finocchiona

Salami in the style of Florence, it's made with large pieces of coarsely ground pork scented with the sweetness of fennel seeds.

soppressata

The name *soppressata* is used in a number of Italian regions, but it's best known as the traditional salami of the Veneto. It's composed of hand-trimmed shoulder meat and pure pork fat coarsely cut, then spiced with pepper, garlic, and red wine.

toscano

The well-known Tuscan-style salami consists of finely chopped lean pork blended with pieces of flavorful pork fat. It's great on antipasto platters, with eggs, or paired with Pecorino cheese.

varzi

A big, bold, coarse-cut country-style salami from the fertile Po valley, between Milan and the

Swiss border, Varzi salami undergoes six months of maturing and a long, slow fermentation process. It's typically served in slices as an accompaniment to polenta.

france

rosette de lyon

Probably the most prestigious salami in France, Rosette is made in the style of the city of Lyon, the country's charcuterie capital. It is made of hand-cut pure pork, stuffed into old-style, all-natural pork casings. It has a rich, winy flavor and a long finish. It's excellent with a selection of great French cheeses and wines.

Of late, a very good and fairly authentic French salami has been given approval for importation into the United States. It's sold under the label of Jean de France.

spain

chorizo

The name *chorizo* is well known in the United States, but the sausage itself is little understood. Americans often confuse—or even worse, substitute—Mexican chorizo for Spanish, or vice versa. While the names are the same, the substitutes couldn't be more inappropriate. Mexican chorizo is a fresh, spicy sausage that needs to be thoroughly cooked before eating. Spanish chorizo is cured and ready to eat, made from coarsely chopped pork and pork fat that's spiced with garlic and plenty of good Spanish paprika. Note too that rather than one universal Spanish chorizo (as is often implied), there are actually dozens of variations.

Happily, the forty-plus-year-old firm of Palacios now exports chorizo to the United States.

serving good salami

The authentic salami experience is far removed from the American practice of serving it on subs with lettuce and tomato. In Europe—and I hope soon in the United States—great salami is served up in small portions, eaten for its full flavor to accompany a salad, a wedge of hearth-baked bread, some pasta, or even fruit.

Like good cheese and wine, salami is best served at room temperature. When serving top-quality salami, break yourself of the "thinly sliced" habit. Slice it thick. You want to taste the meat.

tuscan scrambled eggs

wild-fennel pollen

Available at some food shops, wild-fennel pollen is a specialty of Tuscany. It's incredibly aromatic but far subtler than fennel seed. Tuscans use it often on roasted pork, but it's also great sprinkled on simple dishes like this one.

Salami and eggs was a regular dinner dish when I was a kid. As an adult I got to thinking how good it would be with really good salami. If you've got wild-fennel pollen, a sprinkling of it on the finished dish will turn it into something special. You can make this recipe in a matter of minutes and enjoy it for breakfast, lunch, or dinner.

You can serve spoonfuls of the scrambled eggs topped with the fennel pollen on small slices of bruschetta for an outstanding appetizer.

6 large eggs

3 tablespoons whole milk

2 tablespoons very fruity extra virgin olive oil

3 ounces fennel salami, cut into ¼-inch cubes

Coarse sea salt to taste

Freshly ground black pepper to taste

Wild-fennel pollen to taste (optional)

In a medium bowl, beat the eggs gently. Add the milk and olive oil.

Add the egg mixture to the top of a double boiler or a skillet. (If you're using a double boiler, keep the water bath at a gentle boil; the upper pan should not touch the water. If you're using a skillet, be sure you are working over low heat.) Cook, stirring occasionally, gently moving the slightly set bits of egg from the hottest spots in the pan to the cooler edges until the eggs are thickened and no visible liquid remains.

Remove the pan from the heat and stir in the salami.

Serve with a sprinkling of salt and pepper and fennel pollen, if using.

serves 4

salami and butter baguette

When you combine great bread, superb salami, and really good butter, what seems like a simple recipe becomes a truly sumptuous sandwich.

1 6-inch-long piece of freshly baked baguette
Cultured butter, at room temperature

6–7 slices good-quality salami, preferably a larger salami, such as Varzi, or a well-aged soppressata, at room temperature

Split the baguette piece lengthwise. Spread a liberal amount of butter on each open half. Place the salami slices on the bottom half and replace the top half of the baguette. Press together and serve. serves 1

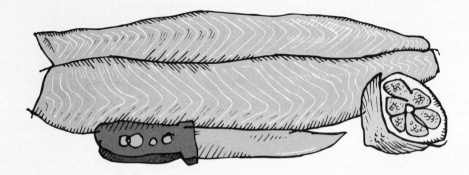

smoked salmon

Our family knows smoked fish. My great-grandfather Bzalel Persowitz (Perlis after he passed through Ellis Island) was a fishmonger in his native Belorussia. Every Saturday night after the Sabbath ended, he'd hitch up his wagon and pull it from his hometown of Volkovisk to the port. There he'd bargain and buy from the fishermen, then load up for home. He'd arrive back in Volkovisk on Wednesday evening, and on Thursday would set up to sell fresh fish to Jewish households preparing for the weekly Sabbath meal. When he arrived in Chicago near the end of World War I, Bzalel became "Charles" and went to work smoking fish on the city's West Side. At the end of the week, he'd come home with a big bag of it. My great-grandfather remained in the fish busi-

ness until he was well into his seventies and was still at it until about six months before he died.

Long before the days of Bzalel Persowitz, fishermen in both the Old and New Worlds had used various forms of smoke to preserve their salmon for thousands of years. Because fresh salmon ran upstream only in the late summer and early fall, if you wanted to set some aside for the winter, you had a handful of options: salt brine, rock salt, smoke, or a combination of the three. Before the advent of refrigeration, these preservatives had to be applied with a heavy hand. Salmon smoking stayed pretty much the same until the middle of the nineteenth century, when new and faster methods of transportation, such as trains, made it possible to ship fresh fish inland in a matter of days instead of weeks or months. That meant that the smoke and salt could be minimized.

Now that salmon smoking is a matter of taste rather than necessity, the discriminating consumer confronts a range of choices unimaginable in my great-grandfather's day. Wild or farmed salmon? Atlantic or Pacific? Hot-smoked or cold-smoked? Smoked salmon or lox?

a salmon story

Before mechanical refrigeration became widely available in the early twentieth century, most fish had seasons, just like other natural products.

Salmon is what's known in aquatic circles as *anadromous* — from the Greek word meaning "running upward." The fish migrate from fresh water out to sea and then several years later return to the same body of water to spawn. The scent of the river in which they were born is chemically imprinted on the brain of the young salmon so they can make their way back to their birthplace. Arching themselves and thrusting against the current, the salmon go home in order to lay their eggs sometime around August.

Despite its present-day prominence as a luxury item, salmon was a mundane meal up until the twentieth century. In North America, it was very much a staple of the Colonial diet, along with salt pork, corn, and wheat. It was so common that farmers used it to fertilize their cornfields. In the nineteenth century, well-meaning American legislators looking out for house-hold help actually set legal limits on the number of times salmon could be fed to servants.

wild versus farmed

It's safe to say that to my great-grandfather, the entire idea of "farming fish" would have been in and of itself pretty darned wild. As recently as twenty-five years ago, all smoked salmon started with wild fish — that's all there was. Today, by contrast, you'll be hard-pressed to find smoked Atlantic wild salmon — the most prized of smoked salmons — in the market. Pollution and overfishing have radically reduced the stocks. Strict regulation today protects the remaining fish but has severely limited the supply for smokers.

On the Pacific coast, the situation isn't quite so grim, but nevertheless dams have radically inhibited the salmon's ability to get back to its spawning grounds, and the fish is clearly in danger. In thirteenth-century England, salmon was regarded with such reverence that the Magna Carta forbade dams on rivers where it spawned.

But today in the Pacific Northwest, each new dam we build diminishes the salmon run further, and from 1938 to 1975 eight federal dams were constructed on the Lower Columbia River and the Snake River.

Nearly every side or slice of Atlantic smoked salmon starts on the "farm." Although you won't see much of it from the highway, fish farming—more formally known as "aquaculture"—is one of the world's fastest-growing industries. There are records of fish being "raised" that date back to Roman times, but the modern industry has its roots in the middle of the 1960s. A group of Norwegians began experimenting in dammed-up fjords through which seawater was pushed and salmon eggs were hatched. A decade later, in the mid-1970s, the farms moved out of the fjords and into free-floating cages at sea, a system that is still in use today. How much growth is there in aquaculture? In 1976 Norwegian farms produced about 2,000 metric tons. In 1989 Norwegian production was up to 120,000!

Aquaculture's proponents—of whom there are many—say fish farming offers greater consistency and increased variety and does less long-term damage to the environment than the uncontrolled depletion of wild ocean stocks we've seen in the last hundred years. While the spawning cycle of wild fish limits salmon catches to the summer months, fish farming has made the "harvesting" of fresh salmon possible almost every day of the year. As supplies have grown, prices have fallen; farmed fresh salmon can now be bought for roughly a quarter of what we paid for fish twenty years ago.

As successful as it's been, farmed fish is on the verge of becoming one of the world's most controversial sources of food. Its opponents argue that aquaculture is unnecessarily polluting the oceans and that excessive quantities of uneaten feed collect on the sea floor, depleting the ocean's natural oxygen levels. Farm fish often escape the pens and breed with wild fish, diluting the natural gene pool. Many farms employ antibiotics to keep salmon healthy. And now infectious salmon anemia—a disease believed either to have been started or rapidly spread by the farm environment—is ravaging fish farms and even appearing in wild fish as well.

When it comes to taste and texture, smoked wild salmon and smoked farmed salmon are two very different animals. While the wild fish are "grazing" out at sea—the salmon equivalent of unplowed mountain meadows in dairying—their farm-raised cousins are fed with factory-made pellets. Exercise contributes as well—while wild salmon are out swimming, farm fish are veritable couch potatoes, living their whole lives in pens. Time plays a big role too: to reach fifteen pounds, a wild salmon would have to live to be about five or six years old. A farmed salmon, by contrast, grows to the same size in a little over a year, so its flesh has far less chance to develop the desirable depth of flavor.

The question of whether to choose farmed or wild salmon presents an ethical dilemma. On the one hand, wild salmon is scarce. But it's also far more flavorful. At the end of the day, there's a place for both in the deli case.

How can you tell if a salmon is wild? Farmed salmon have a series of thick white lines running through their flesh, which you won't see in wild fish. Because they swim freely, wild salmon are often marked with bruises and blemishes that would be unlikely to appear in the world of aquaculture. These often deepen during the smoking process. Hence smoked wild salmon may actually look the worse for wear than smoked farmed fish.

If you taste the two side by side, the difference will be very much in evidence. On its own, the smoked farmed salmon is fine. But sample one after the other and—shock—the wild stuff tastes more . . . like salmon; much meatier, richer, and *a lot* more interesting in flavor. Farmed smoked fish tastes flat by comparison.

atlantic versus pacific salmon

These are two different species, and each brings its own attributes to the smokehouse.

salmo salar

The most prestigious salmon for smoking is the Atlantic *Salmo salar*. The name means "salmon the leaper." Native to both Europe and North America, this species is actually a closer kin to trout than to wild Pacific salmon. It can grow to be over five feet long and over a hundred pounds. When people on the East Coast of North America or in Scotland, Ireland, or the rest of Europe say "smoked salmon," they mean *Salmo salar*. Atlantic salmon is particularly good for smoking because of its natural high fat content and full but delicate flavor.

oncorhynchus

Not surprisingly, Pacific Northwesterners are partial to their native *Oncorhynchus* species. West Coast salmon are significantly more plentiful than *Salmo salar*, and about 90 percent of them come from Alaska. Listed in order of my preference, Pacific salmon include:

king

The king is the biggest Pacific species, growing to be nearly forty pounds. It's also commonly known as the "chinook." Shoppers love the look of king salmon because it's such a sumptuous bright orange color. It's also got the biggest, wildest flavor of the Pacific family. King salmon born in the largest rivers are said to be the most flavorful (look for fish from the Columbia River in Washington or the Copper River in Alaska). Because the fish stop feeding when they get to fresh water, those that have the farthest to go at sea will likely be the fattest and hence the tastiest. A king's natural oil content can be as high as 15 percent. Unfortunately, the king now accounts for only a tiny percentage of wild Pacific salmon.

silver

Silver salmon weigh in at a fifth of the king's size, somewhere between six and twelve pounds. They're a lot less fatty and usually less flavorful than king. The oil content varies from as low as 2 percent on up to 12 percent.

chum

Also known by the less than appealing name of "dog salmon," chum have a bright silver skin and deep orange flesh. (In the old days, so many king salmon had been caught by the time the chums came in that the chums were usually fed to the dogs, hence the nickname.) Inland, chums were often the only salmon to choose from because other fish frequently failed to make it back up the rivers.

coho

The coho is a native Pacific species that's now quite common in places as disparate and distant as Chile and the Great Lakes. Under ten pounds in size, wild cohos are available in some places in the early fall, and farmed fish can be found during the rest of the year.

flavor factors

Just as the quality and variety of what cows eat will affect the meat's flavor, so, too, the fish's food plays a part in their flavor. The best farmed salmon are fed a diet designed to duplicate the more varied feeding patterns the fish would seek out in the wild. Since the feed accounts for over half the cost of a farm-raised fish, there's plenty of incentive for the grower to get by with a lesser product.

The amount of water movement in the pens matters too. Strong natural tidal flows are best, forcing the fish to fight the currents, building muscle tone, keeping them healthier, creating a better balance of fat and muscle. Generally, colder water means more flavorful fish and better muscle tone. The Bay of Fundy, off the coast of Maine and New Brunswick, is often said to produce the best fish because tidal movement is strong, with consistently cold temperatures. Chilean salmon are less tasty because they live in a nearly constant water temperature.

The fish's fat content, often related to water temperature, is also important. More isn't always better, but too little and too lean make for dry and bland smoked salmon. Sockeye salmon, for example, are beautiful fish, but their fat content is a third that of North Atlantic salmon, making them too lean and dry for the smokers. Off the coast of New England, even farmed fish live in colder temperatures in the winter months so they have a far higher fat content.

And of course, the more quickly the fish are moved from the water to the smokehouse and the more effectively they're refrigerated en route, the better the quality.

at the smokehouse

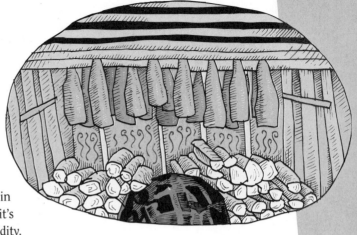

To quote Frank Hederman of Hederman Smoked Salmon in County Cork, one of Ireland's top salmon smokers, "If you give the same farm fish to four different people, you'll end up with four distinct products." Quite simply, there are a multitude of factors that must be managed in relation to one another: the time in the smoke, the type of wood and the way it's prepared, the temperature, and the humidity.

curing and drying

It all starts with the fish coming in off the boats. Most smokers like to wait a couple of days for the fish to go through rigor mortis, which softens the flesh. Good smokers will move quickly either to brine their fish or, if they're dry-curing it, to hand-rub it with salt. If they wait too long, the cells of the fish start to break apart and decay.

Curing may also include sugar or other spices. Some smokers rub in rum or whiskey. The curing can be done with a wet brine or, alternatively, a dry rub. The difference in texture between the two is akin to that of hams that are dry-cured versus those that are brined—after smoking, the former are generally drier and a bit more intensely flavored; the latter are softer in texture, a bit milder.

In the case of wet curing—the technique used for what most of us know as "Nova smoked salmon"—the salt is pulled into the flesh of the fish while it sits in a brine solution. A dry rub can be more difficult to do well, because the salt sits directly on the fish and is less forgiving than the liquid. Dry salting takes about 10 percent of

the moisture off the fish and lasts eight to ten hours. Some smokers use both techniques in tandem. In either case, the total curing time is contingent on the size of the salmon. The thicker the fish, the longer the curing time required. Where the fillet is biggest, more salt is needed. The thinner tail gets the least. Sloppy salting can result in an oversalted tail.

As for those ingredients other than salt, some swear by them, others swear at them. "If it's good fish, what are you trying to cover up?" says Simon Krassman, a Nova Scotia smoker at Fisherman's Market.

After the brining work has been done, the best smokers hold the fish for a day or so to dry them. This step enhances the flavor and improves texture. If the fish is too wet or too dry, the salmon won't smoke properly.

smoking

Smoke isn't simple stuff; it has "upwards of two hundred components," according to the scientist Harold McGee, writing in *On Food and Cooking*. Smoke adds enormous complexity to the flavor of the foods on which it's been used, and that flavor is dependent on a number of variables.

which wood was used?

Smokers choose their woods with the same sort of care that coffee roasters employ to buy their green beans or winemakers their grapes. Because each wood contributes its own flavor and aroma, deciding which to use is one of the most important choices a smoker will make. For every smoker who advocates oak, there's another who opposes it. About the only thing that most salmon smokers seem to agree on is that hickory is too strong for the fish. Regional preferences come into play in the choice. Irish and Scottish salmon smokers traditionally swear by oak. But even in those countries, there are dissenters. Frank Hederman opts for beech, which he prefers for its sweetness and subtlety. At Loch Fyne in Scotland, salmon are smoked over shavings of barrels that were originally used for aging bourbon, sherry, and whiskey, before finally being cut to fire the smokebox.

Simon Krassman uses native Nova Scotia hardwoods, ground juniper, and a little apple too. Ducktrap Farms in Lincolnville, Maine, uses a mix of four woods to smoke the salmon —the fruitwoods cherry and apple, and the hardwoods maple and red oak—according to the founder, Des Fitzgerald. West Coast salmon smokers rely heavily on alder, which has a strong, sweet smell. If you grew up in the Pacific Northwest, this flavor is almost certainly the one you associate with smoked salmon.

The form of the wood is also an issue. Salmon smokers all insist on sawdust because it burns more evenly and more slowly than whole logs, a good thing because the goal is to make smoke, not fire. But even this choice is not straightforward. "What's important is that you don't have too coarse a sawdust," says Simon Krassman. "It should be almost like wood flour."

hot-smoked or cold-smoked?

Hot-smoking is done at temperatures in the range of 120 to 200 degrees Fahrenheit for up to twelve hours. The heat essentially bakes the fish, while the smoke contributes flavor. If you're from the West Coast, the smoked salmon you eat has probably been hot-smoked. This salmon is flakier than cold-smoked, with the texture of smoked bluefish or mackerel. You can break it up and serve it on bagels or add it to salads or eggs or just about anything else. On the East Coast, hot-smoked salmon is also referred to as "kippered" salmon (not to be confused with "kippers," which are hot-smoked herring).

Cold-smoked salmon is done at temperatures below 75 degrees Fahrenheit. The salt and the smoke act as natural preservatives, but the fish is never actually cooked. Its texture should never be flaky but rather supple, like a nice slice of prosciutto.

The longer the salmon is in the smoker, the smokier the taste. Hot-smoked Pacific salmon, usually smoked over alder wood, is very smoky. Atlantic salmon should have a much subtler smoke. Some salmon is so lightly smoked that it seems as if the fish simply waved at the smoker on the way to the packing room. The Scottish salmon from Loch Fyne Oyster Company is in the kiln for eighteen hours; H. Forman and Son, an English smoked salmon supplier, keeps it in for twenty-four.

seven secrets to buying the best smoked salmon

From the smokehouse, the fish is shipped off to a series of distributors or retail shops. When I asked one fish smoker how a caring consumer can be sure to get a good slice of smoked salmon, he said, "Find a retailer you can trust."

Here's what I look for.

1. freshness

It doesn't take an expert to state with a fair bit of certainty that the age of the fish is a huge issue. The question isn't "When did the smoked salmon come into the shop?" That's essentially irrelevant. The keys are:

- When did it leave the water?
- If it was frozen (as wild fish must be if they

are to be smoked in the off-season), how quickly was it chilled to proper storage temperature?
- How soon after that did it leave the smokehouse?

If you catch a whiff of ammonia and there's that little bit of acidic bite in the fish, it's headed downhill. Vacuum packing and code dating can give people the illusion that smoked salmon lasts forever, which it most certainly does not.

2. few ingredients

The best-quality smoked salmon should have nothing in it but salt and fish: no nitrates, nitrites, or artificial colorings. Occasionally, smokers use a touch of sugar or other spices. Some suppliers extend the shelf life of their salmon to eight, nine, even ten weeks, with nitrates. That's way too long for top-notch smoked fish. If you see nitrates on the ingredients list, the salmon is not of the finest quality.

3. eye appeal

Good smoked salmon looks good: lustrous, with a pink, glistening, fresh, moist appearance. The color shouldn't look flat, nor should the flesh be laced with cavernous cracks. Remember that wild salmon will usually show signs of natural bruising or discoloration—these are actually hallmarks of quality.

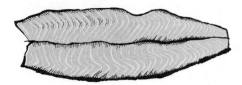

4. fat

Willy Krauch, an old-time salmon smoker from Nova Scotia, once said, "Never smoke a skinny salmon." As with corned beef or prosciutto, the flavor starts with the fat. I shake my head when a well-meaning customer demands that we take off all the fatty gray flesh that runs along the salmon's skin.

The size of the fish will affect the fat ratio as well; too small, and the smoked side will be too dry and not so velvety. Too large, and the fish are very fatty and tend toward mushiness.

5. hand-slicing

The vast majority of smoked salmon you'll see these days is unfortunately sold sliced in Cryovac prepacks. But if you can find a store that sells it freshly sliced to order from a whole side, you have a couple of advantages. For openers, you can taste before you buy. Ultimately, that's the only way to tell if you're going to like it before you invest your hard-earned money. Additionally, you'll be better able to assess the appearance of the whole fish, something you can't do when it's inside a plastic pouch. Then there's freshness: Because the fish in the prepack was sliced at the plant before being shipped, it's been exposed to air for much longer and its fat will likely oxidize very quickly, adversely affecting flavor. A whole side of salmon will stay fresher longer. Finally, when you slice smoked salmon, you release a lot of the oil, which can make salmon packed in Cryovac greasy.

If you do find a shop that's still slicing salmon off the side, you can specify a particular cut. People like me who prefer the fattier fish will want it from the area right behind the dorsal fin (where the fat reaches its highest level) or toward the head. Those who prefer their fish on the lean side will want it sliced from the tail.

6. thick slices

To my taste, smoked salmon is at its best when it's sliced significantly thicker than most of us are used to. This sounds counterintuitive, because we're used to paper-thin slices. Without doubt, I know that if my grandmother were still here to do her shopping, she'd want ultrathin. I've sliced for folks who hover over my shoulder chanting, "Thin! Thin! Thinner!" over and over again as if they were at a pep rally. If you like it that way, so be it.

But here's the thing. In Ireland (which I've been fortunate enough to visit many times now), I found that most everyone slices smoked salmon at two or three times the thickness we do. Don't panic. I'm not talking T-bone steaks here, just thicker than very, very thin slices. And you know what? It tastes better! Much meatier and more meaningful. With a thicker slice, you get more of a sense of the flavor and texture of the fish.

7. taste

Until you put the salmon in your mouth, you won't really know what you've got. Whenever possible, taste before you buy.

The best smoked salmon should be meaty, marvelous. The smoke and the salmon should be in balance. It should have a clean, complex flavor and a long, lingering aftertaste that makes you want to go back for more. Too much salt is a problem. Unless the fish is extremely oversalted, it usually won't make its presence felt until a minute or two after you've swallowed. Too little salt isn't really right either. Beware of off flavors. With its naturally high fat content, salmon is a

magnet for other flavors and aromas. Store an unwrapped smoked salmon next to a cut onion for a few hours, and you'll be serving up onion-flavored fish. Even worse, old fish will start to smell or taste of ammonia.

salmon styles

There are no bad choices but, rather, different styles of salmon curing that result in significantly different products.

lox versus nova

I'm sure there was a time when most consumers knew the difference between Nova and lox, but those days are definitely over. Let me set the smoked-fish record straight. Despite the fact that the terms are often used interchangeably, lox is not, nor has it ever been, the same as smoked salmon. In the United States, lox has its origins in the practice of shipping large quantities of salmon from the West Coast back to the eastern seaboard. To survive the journey in an era when there was no refrigeration, the salmon were packed in barrels filled with heavily salted brine. En route, the salmon cured, and when they arrived in New York they were sold as lox: salt-brine-cured salmon.

To this day, lox is always made from Pacific salmon. It isn't smoked, just cured in brine. To most modern palates, lox will be too salty. Die-hard traditionalists or people who grew up on the East Coast love it. But after twenty years of selling smoked fish, I can confidently say that nine out of ten people who order lox actually want Nova.

Which brings me to Nova, which is short for "Nova Scotia," or, more appropriately in most cases, "Nova Scotia–style," smoked salmon. Nova is cold-smoked Atlantic salmon. Typically the salmon has been cured first in a wet brine of water, sugar, and salt and then smoked.

Lox is salty, and Nova is not. And Nova is smoked, lox isn't. Got it?

euro salmon versus nova

Traditional European versions begin with Atlantic salmon. They are usually dry-cured —that is, rubbed with salt or, at most, a cure of salt and some sugar. Unlike traditional Nova, the fish never goes into a wet brine cure. After being rubbed down with salt, the fish are cold-smoked. A number of smaller American fish smokers like Ducktrap use this style of cure, as does nearly every smoker in Ireland or Scotland. Generally this style of curing yields a drier, more intensely flavorful salmon.

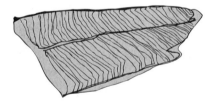

what to do with smoked salmon

Eat it! The best thing to do with smoked salmon is merely to serve it with good bread and good butter or cream cheese (see page 208) and eat it as is. Be sure to serve it at room temperature so you can get the full flavor of the fish. I'm a big fan of serving salmon with Irish brown bread, spread with lots of butter.

BEST BRANDS For a European-style, dry-cured smoked Atlantic salmon, I like the fish I've had from Ducktrap River Fish Farm in Maine, as well as that of Fisherman's Market in Nova Scotia. In Ann Arbor, Michigan, T. R. Durham does a very nice job of smoking farm-raised salmon. The folks at Stonington Sea Products in Stonington, Maine, also smoke some very fine farmed Atlantic salmon.

For wild Atlantic salmon, Forman's of London does excellent work. I can actively recommend three Irish producers who smoke very fine wild salmon in County Cork—Frank Hederman's Hederman Smoked Salmon, Sally Barnes's Woodcock Smokery, and Anthony Creswell's Ummera Smoked Products.

Marshall's Smoked Fish and Acme Smoked Fish both produce consistently good wet-cured Nova-style smoked salmon in Brooklyn, New York.

leo

lox, eggs, and onions

This old-time deli classic makes a great breakfast or a light supper. Despite the name, my version calls for smoked salmon because it's less salty, but if you like, use lox and skip the salt at the end. Serve with hot buttered rye toast.

2 tablespoons butter

¼ cup finely chopped onion

6 large eggs

¼ cup heavy cream or whole milk

Freshly ground black pepper to taste

4 ounces cold-smoked salmon, thinly sliced and cut into ¼-inch-wide strips

Coarse sea salt to taste

In a large heavy skillet, melt the butter over medium heat. Add the onion and sauté until soft and lightly golden, 3 to 4 minutes.

Meanwhile, in a medium bowl, lightly beat together the eggs and the cream or milk. Add a twist or two of black pepper.

Slowly add the eggs to the skillet and cook, stirring gently with a spatula, until they start to set, 2 to 3 minutes. Be careful not to over-cook. When the eggs are almost done, fold in the smoked salmon and warm through. Transfer the eggs to plates and serve immediately, passing salt and pepper at the table.

serves 2 or 3

kedgeree

This popular British breakfast dish (pronounced KED-jur-ree) is— like curry and chutney—the result of Britain's many years in India. It was once restricted to Anglo-Indian cooking in country clubs, but over the years it's become everyday fare in Britain. You can whip it up any time you have a little leftover smoked fish. Many Brits use finnan haddie (smoked haddock), but I like it best with hot-smoked (kippered) salmon. Still, you can substitute any smoked fish, and left-over cooked fish will work well too. You can adjust the butter and pepper levels up or down depending on your preferences. Most people I know in England serve it with chutney.

3 tablespoons butter
1/4 cup sliced scallions (white and green parts)
2 cups cooked long-grain white rice
1/2 pound hot-smoked salmon, flaked
2 anchovy fillets
Hot red pepper flakes, preferably Marash (see page 58), to taste
Coarse sea salt to taste
Freshly ground black pepper to taste
2 large hard-boiled eggs, chopped
Chutney for serving (optional)

In a large skillet, melt the butter over medium heat. Add the scallions and sauté until soft, about 3 minutes. Add the rice, salmon, anchovies, red pepper flakes, salt, and pepper. Cook, stirring frequently, until heated through.

Remove from the heat, add the hard-boiled eggs, and mix quickly. Serve immediately, with a couple of spoonfuls of chutney on the side, if you like.

serves 2 as a main course or 4 as a side dish

part 5.

seasonings

pepper

> "Pepper ready-ground becomes completely meaningless once you have started using the pepper mill."
> ● **Isabelle Vischer,**
> *Now to the Banquet*

If you were to alter one routine in your everyday eating from reading this book, it ought to be choosing better pepper or switching to sea salt. If forced to choose, I think I'd probably recommend pepper. Big though it is, the flavor gap between iodized commercial salt and good sea salt is small in comparison with the veritable continental divide that you'll find between that old bottle of preground pepper you bought at the supermarket six years ago and a spoonful of freshly ground Tellicherry peppercorns. Once you

make the move, I doubt you'll go back. I know I haven't.

I can't say with total certainty that good pepper can do as much for you as it has for me. I'm a self-confessed pepper addict. You won't see me in a twelve-step program for pepper abusers any time soon.

Surprisingly, my penchant for pepper has become a particular problem for me when I go to Europe. Although there are many, many great advantages to eating on the Continent, one thing that makes me crazy is the near impossibility of getting good black pepper in a European restaurant. In Italy and Spain you *might*, if you're lucky, get some preground black pepper in a small cut-glass shaker. More often than not, though, the holes are so small that about the only thing I ever manage to extract is frustration. In other countries, France in particular, you won't get any pepper at all. At best you'll be offered a small shaker filled with preground, often stale, white pepper.

twist and shout

Regardless of the quality of the peppercorns themselves, grinding fresh is guaranteed to be better than buying ground pepper from a tin or bottle. The difference is so great that the two should almost be classified as different products.

Pick up a pinch of old, preground black pepper. The staler the better. Rub it between your fingers. It feels flat, powdery, like a dry day on the Kansas dust bowl. Take a smell. Its bouquet is negligible. Even if the can has only recently been opened, great gobs of flavor and aroma have already been assimilated into the atmosphere.

Now get your pepper grinder. Grinding whole black pepper is an exceptional sensory experience in almost every way. Pull out a packet of peppercorns. Before you fill the grinder, look them over: you'll see wrinkled, charcoal-colored little rounds. Pour them in, close up the grinder, give it a good twist, pause, then give it another. Freshly ground pepper is alive; you can hear the peppercorns crunch and crackle as you shift the gears. Then, almost immediately, there's the aroma. Freshly ground pepper doesn't just make you sneeze—it perfumes the entire room. Pick up a bit and rub it between your thumb and forefinger. You should be able to feel the essential oils as you move it back and forth. Then adjust the grind to meet your needs. If you're looking for a more pronounced flavor, keep it coarse.

If you want just a hint to blend in with other flavors, keep it fine.

Last, take a taste. Big! Bold! Beautiful!

just say yes to better pepper

I'm really not kidding about good pepper being a lot like a drug. The more you use, the more you want. Going without is hard. There's more to this craving than meets the eye—or the nose.

Pepper does contain an alkaloid called piperine, which is indeed a stimulant. People in search of added energy can get a pick-me-up from pepper oil rubbed vigorously onto the soles of their feet. Alternatively, you can catch a dose of pepper power by taking any number of supplements that sport pepper high up on their ingredients lists. Supposedly pepper raises your body temperature and helps you lose weight. Be careful: in the nineteenth century, the health-conscious Sylvester Graham (who invented the graham cracker) claimed that excessive use of pepper could make you crazy.

pepper power

Exotic, intriguing, enticing, and potentially addictive, pepper came to us first from India's west coast, where it was probably cultivated by about 1000 B.C. It's mentioned in three-thousand-year-old Sanskrit texts. Later it was carried by boat to Malaysia and Indonesia. Black peppercorns were one of the first Asian spices to be shipped to Europe, arriving in about the fourth century B.C. in the hands of Arab traders.

Pepper's fortunes in the West rose and then fell with those of Rome. Originally, Europeans used pepper more as a medicine than as a spice. But the Romans took peppercorns into the kitchen with a vengeance, adding them to seemingly every dish in the imperial repertoire. By the first century A.D., they had figured out how to sail to India, returning with boatloads of peppercorns and other spices. When Rome finally fell, the Visigoths demanded comparable amounts of both gold and peppercorns (about two and a half tons of each, if you're wondering). When the Roman Empire collapsed for good, so, too, did the spice trade, and for hundreds of years European cuisine became bland and basically pepperless.

Spices again became a major element of European eating during medieval times. Pepper was so costly that it was often sold by the piece, counted out a single corn at a time. When pepper was to be sold already ground, purveyors shut their windows before weighing it, for fear that a sudden draft would blow away the profits. Like gold and silver—with which it was roughly at par—pepper often became a medium of exchange as well as itself an item of trade, with people paying for purchases in peppercorns instead of coins. During the Renaissance, Venice grew to become the major pepper port of Europe, and from the twelfth to the sixteenth centuries, the pepper trade helped to build the city-state into an international power. At its zenith, Europe was consuming about 6.5 million pounds of pepper per year.

Keeping up with the Joneses in medieval Europe meant offering your guests prodigious quantities of pepper, and the rich were derisively referred to as "pepper sacks." Ever vigilant about possible theft, the British required the dock porters who handled pepper to sew their pockets shut.

In the fifteenth century, the lack of speedy transportation and the short supply led to huge increases in the price of pepper. Demand was so high that pepper became the driving force behind European expansionism, the explorers assuming the role of drug dealers intent on providing Europe with its fix. In fact, when Vasco da Gama stepped onto Indian soil for the first time in 1498, he reputedly stood up and exclaimed, "For Christ and for spices!"

When the Portuguese finally succeeded in

finding the route to India by sea, they established new trade routes and therefore more plentiful supplies of pepper. Slowly but surely, pepper prices fell. By the end of the seventeenth century, spices lost their supremacy in world trade. Gradually pepper became more affordable and more readily available to the middle classes. The culinary spotlight then shifted from spices to chocolate, coffee, and tea.

Soon the United States picked up an important role in the pepper trade. In 1791 it re-exported 500 pounds of pepper. In 1805 the figure had shot up to 7.5 million pounds. Strangely, it was the witch-trial town of Salem, Massachusetts, that became the center of the North American pepper trade. Elihu Yale was one of the most successful American pepper traders in Salem. He made a small fortune in the spice field, some of which he later donated to found the university that bears his name.

a peppery predicament

If you're dining in North America, the odds are about even that your waiter will swing by with one of those three-foot-long grinders — better than what I've come to expect in Europe but miles from what good pepper service could be. Have you ever had a waiter inquire whether you'd prefer the pepper to be ground fine or coarse? In all my years of dining out, I don't think anyone's ever asked me! Not only that, but the pepper grinders are offered only for salad service and pasta. You're in trouble if you want to have a little pepper on your pompano or your baked potato. While other accompaniments come throughout the meal, pepper arrives only once. More iced tea? Terrific. More bread? Of course. More water? Why not. But more pepper? Perish the thought.

So what's the problem? The standard restaurant-industry refrain is that if you risk putting out pepper grinders, they'll have "walked out" by the end of the night. Still, there's got to be a better way. Maybe we could chain the grinders to the middle of the table? Or how about if the host hands you one when you're seated and asks for a $10 deposit? Or maybe I could lobby my congresswoman for national pepper mill insurance.

black, white, and green: the colors of the peppercorn rainbow

Black pepper is a berry whose botanical name is *Piper nigrum*. It grows ten to twenty degrees on either side of the equator, where it can get needed heat and a long rainy season as well as some shade. India, Indonesia, and Malaysia are the most prominent producers. Like vanilla, the pepper plant is a vine and, also like vanilla, it is often planted at the base of "tutor trees" on which it can climb. The tutors need to have rough-textured bark so that the tendrils can take hold: mango, silver oak, rosewood, white teak, and coffee trees all have "second jobs" guiding the growth of the pepper plants. A more modern technique is to put the plants next to simple wooden posts hammered into the ground. Allowed to grow unchecked, the plants can reach heights of nearly two hundred feet, but most modern vines are trained to stay between nine and twelve feet for easier access at harvest time.

Pepper isn't a quick cash crop. From the time of planting, a grower must wait two to five years before the vines bear fruit. From that point on,

they can expect another twelve to twenty-five years of productive activity. In March, the pepper plant puts out a series of small blossoms. Later in the spring, pollinated flowers produce three-inch-long spikes, each of which holds about fifty to a hundred small greenish berries, about a quarter of an inch across. Inside each berry is a single seed, which, after curing, will become—about nine months later—the dried peppercorn.

As they mature, the berries move from yellow to orange and finally, when fully ripe, to red. The peppercorn's natural heat develops early in the ripening process and remains pretty much as is, regardless of harvest time. One of the challenges to the grower is that while the berry's flavor increases the longer it's on the vine, so too does the risk of autumn rains ruining the crop. The safe bet is to harvest earlier and produce less flavorful pepper. In India, pickers traditionally scale the trees on long bamboo poles that have had shorter bamboo pieces lashed across them for rungs. With cloth sacks tied around their waists, they work to collect the pepper berries from the plants when about one third of the berries have turned red. Despite pepper's prominence in the spice trade, pepper growing is still pretty much the province of small farmers who till plots not much larger than a good-sized home garden as a supplement to their incomes. A single family's effort may produce only a pound or two of pepper per year!

black beauty

Black pepper is, far and away, the biggest part of the pepper crop. To produce it, the berries are plucked when they have attained their full size but are still greenish, just turning to yellow. At this point the fruit is not yet actually ripe.

These are actually not peppercorns at all, but the pinkish red berries of another bush, *Schinus molle.* Though they may not know it, many Americans are already familiar with their flavor, which contributes to the spicy taste of Teaberry chewing gum.

Because the berries ripen at different rates (even on the same plant), the harvest may continue for weeks.

Although we refer to whole, freshly ground peppercorns as "fresh pepper," the reality is that it's not fresh at all but dried. The just picked berries are removed from the stems, then laid out on bamboo mats in uncovered courtyards where the tropical sun has its way with them. Some estates now dip the freshly picked peppercorns in boiling water first, which speeds the maturing process. After three to seven days, the sun has shrunk the berries into their well-recognized wrinkled state and turned their outer skin a flat black color. The peppercorns are then cleaned of the usual stones, stems, sticks, and other assorted agricultural debris. Later, the peppercorns are sorted by traders who run them through a series of screens, then sort and pack them into sacks of roughly 150 pounds for shipment.

a whiter shade of pale

Ancient peoples often wrongly assumed that white and black pepper came from two different plants, an inaccuracy that was widely accepted up until the fourteenth century. In fact, they come from the same plant, just as green and black olives come from the same tree. True white pepper is made from ripe yellow or orange berries, picked a week or so later than those for black pepper. Bags of these ripe berries are left submerged in streams—or now in man-made vats—for a week to ten days. This unusual underwater cure essentially rots away the outer skin of the fruit, which would otherwise turn black during curing. After drying, what's left is the cream-colored core, which is what we know as white pepper.

White pepper has a subtler flavor than black. It's used most often when you want the pepper to be a subtle blip on your spice screen. Visually, of course, it's well suited to lighter-colored sauces. It's better to grind black pepper just before you use it, and the same goes for white pepper.

Strangely, a great deal of commercial white pepper today is made by merely taking the outer skin off black peppercorns that have been harvested at the earlier stage. This kind of white pepper may look similar to the traditional sort, but the flavor is more like a mild black pepper than the subtler, authentic version.

Some of the best white peppercorns come from the Indonesian island of Bangka and are sold under the name of Muntok. The Sarawak

white peppercorns from Malaysia are also excellent.

go green

Green peppercorns are simply the fresh, undried version of black pepper. They have a fruity, slightly sweet pungency. They're excellent with beef, chicken, or fish and very good with fresh goat cheese as well.

The unripe berries are harvested a few weeks before those for black pepper would be picked. At this stage, the core of the fruit isn't fully developed, and the young berries are not cured in the sun. They have a pleasantly crunchy texture, a flavor that hints of green fruit and eucalyptus, and a commensurately short shelf life. In India, they're sold soft enough to be mashed into a paste.

Because they were traditionally consumed only in their fresh state, green peppercorns were essentially unheard of in the West until the middle of the twentieth century. Today, for export purposes, they're either freeze-dried or packed in brine to keep them from turning black. It's easy to use green peppercorns in either form. In France, it's quite common to mix dried green peppercorns with black pepper in one's grinder for a varied set of flavors. You can crush them lightly with a mortar and pestle. Because their flavor is far less pungent than that of their cured black cousins, they're excellent in cream sauces or with fresh fish.

how to pick a pepper

the look

With pepper in particular, cleanliness is a big issue. Consistency in size and color is a sign that the pepper was handled carefully by people who take pride in their product.

Black pepper should be dark brown to black without any, or very few, light berries. White spots on the pepper—a sign of fungus—are undesirable.

White peppercorns should be creamy white to beige and should have few discolored corns. The best white pepper comes from places where farmers have freshwater springs for soaking. In standing water, the dark color of the outer layer of the peppercorn leaches into the core of the berry and leaves the berry gray instead of creamy white.

cracking quality

Pepper quality can, at least in part, be judged by the way it cracks. "Good dry pepper should be brittle," says Anandan Adnan Abdullah of the Malaysian Pepper Board. "And," he adds, "it should break cleanly into two or more particles when cracked between the teeth." Good pepper

should not crumble into a powder when you press on it, a sign that it has been overdried or is old.

aroma

Because it sits on mats for so long during the curing process, poorly handled pepper is vulnerable to contamination and off aromas. Beware of the smell of mold or must, either of which is a sure sign of poor handling.

the source

india: tellicherry and malabar

The two best-known names for quality in Indian black pepper are Tellicherry and Malabar, two different grade sizes from the same regional pool of pepper. The town of Tellicherry, now known in India as Thalassery, is located on the southwest coast in the state of Kerala in the Malabar region and was one of the earliest and best-known ports of the thriving pepper trade. Most often, the Tellicherry peppercorns are those taken from the top of the vine, where the berries ripen more quickly and grow larger. Because they're often picked somewhat earlier, you may find a slightly reddish undertone when you grind.

Malabar peppercorns, often from the lower portions of the pepper vine, tend to ripen a bit more slowly, may be a bit smaller, and hence may have a greenish undertone.

I prefer the Tellicherry. The peppercorns are likely to be higher in piperine—the active ingredient in peppercorns—and a bit more aromatic.

peppered pecans

We make this treat at Zingerman's during the holidays, but it's great year-round. You can eat it for a snack or an hors d'oeuvre. Or you can use it as an ingredient in salads (see page 267). You can halve the recipe if you like.

- 12 tablespoons butter, at room temperature
- 2¼ cups sugar
- 3 tablespoons freshly ground black pepper
- 1¼ teaspoons fine sea salt
- 2 tablespoons ground cinnamon
- 1¼ teaspoons ground allspice
- 1¼ teaspoons ground cloves
- ¼ teaspoon ground ginger
- Pinch ground cardamom
- 2 large egg whites
- 2 pounds raw pecan halves

Preheat the oven to 325°F.

In a large bowl, stir together the butter, sugar, pepper, salt, and spices. Add the egg whites and mix well. Add the pecans and mix thoroughly to coat well.

Spread the spice-coated nuts in a large roasting pan. Roast for 18 to 25 minutes, or until they are toasted through, turning every 5 minutes or so with a spatula.

Remove from the oven and continue turning every 5 minutes until the nuts reach room temperature.

The peppered pecans will keep in airtight containers for 4 to 6 weeks.

makes 8 to 10 cups

black, white, and green peppercorn mulligatawny soup

This soup was usually prepared for wealthy Anglo-Indians during the British raj. *Mulliga* means "pepper," and *thani* means "water," so the name translates literally as "pepper water." Lakshmi Shetty, who used to work at Zingerman's and grew up in southern India, remembers having it as a little girl at Anglo-oriented restaurants, or when British business contacts came to dinner. Despite its hybrid origins, it's easy to prepare and very tasty.

I make mulligatawny with a mix of peppercorns—ground and whole; black, green, and white—to give it a nice contrast of spicy flavors. (It's typical to use only black.) The soup is even more flavorful if you make it a day or two ahead and then reheat it before serving, when it can be a first course or the main event.

2	garlic cloves, chopped
1	1-inch piece fresh ginger, peeled and chopped
3	tablespoons clarified butter or vegetable oil
1	medium onion, coarsely chopped (about 1 cup)
¼	teaspoon whole black peppercorns
¼	teaspoon whole white peppercorns
¼	teaspoon whole dried green peppercorns
1½	teaspoons garam masala
½	teaspoon freshly ground black pepper, plus more for serving
¼	teaspoon ground coriander
¾–1	pound boneless lamb, cut into ¾-inch cubes
2	medium tomatoes, coarsely chopped (about 1½ cups)
4	cups water or chicken broth
2	tablespoons uncooked basmati rice
	Coarse sea salt to taste
	Chopped fresh cilantro for garnish (optional)

Mash the garlic and ginger into a smooth paste using a mortar and pestle or with 2 tablespoons water in a food processor. Set aside.

In a large saucepan, heat the butter or oil over medium heat. Add the onion and sauté until soft, about 5 minutes. Add the garlic-ginger paste and sauté for 1 to 2 minutes more. Add the whole black and white peppercorns and cook for 1 minute. Stir in the garam masala, ground pepper, and ground coriander and cook for 2 to 3 minutes more, or until it's incorporated.

Increase the heat to medium-high, add the lamb, and cook, stirring frequently, until lightly browned, 5 to 7 minutes.

Add the tomatoes and water or broth and bring to a boil. Reduce the heat to medium-low and stir in the rice. Simmer for 30 minutes, or until the flavors have melded. Season to taste with salt, a generous dose of freshly ground black pepper, and a bit of cilantro, if you like, and serve.

serves 4 to 6

pasta with pepper and pecorino

This recipe comes from the pasta-making Cavalieri family (see page 131). It's one of my favorite dinners to prepare after a long day of work when I don't have much time or energy. Using the best possible pasta, Pecorino cheese, and Tellicherry pepper is essential. To quote my colleague Jenny Tubbs, "This is so good you don't need to garnish it with anything but a fork!"

2	ounces Pecorino Romano cheese, grated (about 1 cup), plus more for serving (optional)
2	teaspoons freshly ground Tellicherry black pepper
1–2	tablespoons coarse sea salt
½	pound pasta (I prefer Cavalieri linguine, but any cut will work well)

In a small bowl, combine the Pecorino and pepper and set aside.

Bring a large pot of water to a boil. Add the salt and the pasta and stir well. Cook until almost al dente. Drain the pasta, reserving ¼ cup of the cooking water.

Return the pasta to the pot along with the reserved water. Over low heat, quickly stir in the Pecorino mixture and cook for 1 to 2 minutes, or until the cheese is hot. Serve with additional grated Pecorino, if you like.

serves 2

dried figs with black pepper

Joyce Goldstein, the cookbook author and restaurateur, told me about this Greek recipe. It makes a fine after-dinner course in the winter months when good fresh fruit isn't readily available. It's also a nice addition to an hors d'oeuvre buffet. As always, the flavor of the figs will make a big difference, and the pepper needs to be freshly cracked. Greek sheep's milk Manouri cheese is a good accompaniment. Note that you'll need to make this recipe five days in advance of serving.

    2 dozen moist dried figs
    ¼ cup freshly cracked black pepper
   12 dried bay leaves

Trim the stems from the figs and roll them in the pepper. Place the figs in a container with the bay leaves, alternating layers of figs and leaves. Press down and then cover tightly with plastic wrap. Store for at least 5 days before serving so that the flavors will meld. The figs should last for a month at room temperature.

makes 3 to 4 cups, enough to serve 6 to 8

sea salt

Salt is an essential element of good eating. We use it on almost everything. Without it, we fail to unfurl the flavors of our food. To most of us—myself included until about ten years ago—salt is salt. But the truth of the matter is that salt is anything but simple. Different salts have different flavors. And, more important, better salt brings out the best in other foods.

In doing my salt homework, I was amazed to discover that I was — literally — sitting atop one of the largest salt mines in the world. Not far up the road from Zingerman's, about a quarter mile below the surface of the city of Detroit, is a 390-million-year-old salt deposit. The source is a huge prehistoric sea that once covered the entire region.

The mines were started in 1906, eleven years after salt was discovered there, and Michigan became the leading producer of salt in the United States during most of the first half of the twentieth century. Huge trucks with seven-foot-high wheels used to move the salt around the mine's fifty miles of roads, past fifty-foot-wide rooms with twenty-five-foot-high ceilings. Supposedly there's enough salt in these mines to last the next 70 million years. But in 1985, the mines, no longer economically viable, were closed. Ontario and Ohio mines still work the same vein to the east and south of the original Detroit sources.

the search for salt

What we take for granted in the modern world was, for most of human history, a rare and wonderful treasure. Salt was gathered from the sea or the earth with the same passion people later put into searching for precious metals. In fact, there were times when it traded for twice the price of gold.

Salt has always played an important role in ritual, religion, and government. In the Book of Leviticus, the ancient Hebrews were directed, "With all your offerings you shall offer salt." In many societies, parents rubbed their newborn babies with salt for good luck. Ancient Germanic tribes were convinced that the gods would be more attentive to their prayers if they were delivered in a salt mine. Roman soldiers were paid a special allowance to purchase salt — a *salarium* — the source of our current "salary." Ancient Tibetans used salt cakes stamped with the imperial seal of the emperor Kublai Khan as their money. To this day, a basket of bread and salt is an esteemed welcome gift in central Europe.

In earlier eras, salt was believed to ward off evil demons. Much the way modern urbanites sport pepper spray, ancient townsfolk flung a handful of salt into the eyes of an attacker (accompanied by the appropriate incantation), rendering him helpless. The most binding pledge of loyalty for a man was to have "eaten another's salt." When in doubt about a rival's allegiance, a ruler would offer him some salt. If he ate it, a truce was called. Jewish folklore dictated that eating foods sprinkled with salt ensured wisdom and good health.

In 1458 the duke of Savoy created what came to be known as the *gabelle,* or salt tax. The *gabelle* probably did more to provoke the resentment of the French peasantry than the British tea tax did to incite the Boston Tea Party. The tax was so severe that most people were unable to afford salt for cooking or curing. By 1630 the *gabelle* set the price of salt at roughly fourteen times its cost. By 1710, it was 140 times the cost of the actual salt! The salt tax wasn't repealed until 1790, and traces of it remained in place until just after World War II.

Salt was heavily taxed in England as well, at the exorbitant rate of about £30 per ton. In 1785, the earl of Dundonald wrote that every year in Britain, "10,000 people are seized for salt smuggling." In 1930, when Gandhi kicked off the campaign for the Indian Declaration of Independence, he sought an issue around which to rally his people. He chose the salt tax and began by leading a two-hundred-mile march to the sea

The now famous slogan "When it rains, it pours" is the legacy of the Morton salt people in the late nineteenth and early twentieth centuries. That's when most American salt was still sold in cloth bags. When it rained or when humidity was very high, the salt solidified. Commercial cooks commonly carried hammers to help break it up. In 1907 the Morton folks figured out that by adding magnesium carbonate to standard salt, they could keep it from clumping. The catch phrase, hammered out by some clever sloganeers, first appeared in an ad in *Good Housekeeping* in 1914.

to make his salt the old-fashioned way — from seawater — a peaceful act of defiance against the British-imposed tax.

essential salt

Until recently, salt was the world's primary preservative, and it remains an essential element in proper flavor development. The list of foods that would be unpalatable without salt is so long that it's not worth printing here. Even cookies, pastries, pancakes, and pies rely on salt to help pull their flavors together. Caramels made without salt won't taste right. Salt in cooking water keeps the natural mineral salts in the vegetables and fixes their color. Humans need salt for reasons of health as well as for flavor enhancement. Each of us consumes about eight to ten grams a day (in medieval times consumption was probably twice that), and we carry around an internal inventory of about three and a half ounces each at all times.

The flavor of salt started to suffer with the success of the Industrial Revolution, as did many foods. In the 1920s, American health authorities decided to add iodine to salt to combat goiter, one of the most dreaded diseases of the day. By the 1950s, roughly three quarters of the country's salt was iodized, improving health but adding bitterness to the flavor of our food.

where salt comes from

Rock salt is usually crystalline and white or, at times, tinged with pink from iron. It occurs in underground deposits, believed to have been formed by the drying up of ancient seas. In this sense, all salt is — or I should say was — originally sea salt. Traditionally it was mined, much like other minerals, taken in rock form from underground sources.

Commercial producers today make standard kitchen salt by piping water into salt-bearing underground rock, then pumping back up the newly salinated brine solution. The liquid is dried, leaving behind rock salt. Grind-

sea salt

ing the rock down to a fine consistency produces standard table salt. Iodine is added, and starch or phosphates may be blended in to keep the salt running freely so that "when it rains, it pours."

step up to sea salt

Do a little informal tasting, and I think you'll find commercial salt rather one-dimensional. It's certainly salty but at best bland; at its worst it can be off-puttingly bitter. Switching to almost any sort of sea salt will improve the flavor of your food.

While all salts are composed primarily of sodium chloride, their other elements vary. Natural sea salt is about 83 percent sodium chloride; the remaining 17 percent is composed of residual moisture and other minerals like magnesium, iron, sulfur, and zinc, which add to the distinctive flavor. Commercially processed table salt is nearly 98 percent sodium chloride, making it purer but less interesting in flavor.

Sea salt is made in almost every country with a coastline. I've sampled good ones from France, England, Portugal, and Sicily, and there are dozens of others, each with its own distinct flavor profile. Many are available in either coarse or fine form. For most foods, I prefer coarse salt, which looks like coarse sugar crystals. Using coarse salt allows you to taste it as an independent ingredient instead of just a background note. I like the texture it adds, the way the salt set-

tles onto my tongue and spreads slowly outward in little ripples. Finely ground sea salt, on the other hand, is best for dishes where you want smooth texture and more even distribution.

industrial sea salt versus sun-dried

If you want to take your eating one step beyond sea-salt basics, start by differentiating between mechanically harvested, refined sea salt and the kind that is naturally sun-dried. The refined salt has less character and complexity; the sun-dried salt tastes wild, natural, and of the sea.

There are significant differences in the way the two are gathered. The traditional work is done in much smaller ponds; the industrial action takes place on large three-thousand-foot flats. Traditional methods call for removing salt from the flats every few weeks, while industrial producers allow it to build up over the entire summer and take it off only once a year in the autumn. The artisans rely on old-style wooden rakes; industrial-scale salt gathering is done with bulldozers.

Artisan sea salts are dried naturally in the sun for five to six days, then packed as is. By contrast, industrial salt undergoes additional processing. Because it turns grayish yellow from the natural sediments that build up at the bottom of the salt pans, it's usually washed, run through large high-heat driers, rewashed, ground, and in some cases bleached or painted to attain the bright white color that consumers expect. Many producers add a series of chemical anticaking agents. Some also add iodine. The washing removes all of the natural micronutrients that are found in the seawater and leaves industrial salt lacking in the depth of flavor that you find in traditionally harvested salts.

I will warn you that there are two disadvantages to seasoning your food with better salt. Once you get accustomed to its exceptional flavor, standard salt just won't cut it anymore. The other "problem" is that it's impossible to use the more coarsely textured sea salt in a saltshaker. The crystals are too big and also quite damp. To serve traditional sea salt, you pass it in a small bowl and let people take a pinch between their thumb and forefinger.

an array of traditional sea salts

The best way I know to take advantage of the more interesting flavors of good sea salt is to use it much as you would the best extra virgin olive oil, as a condiment added at the end of a dish. Sprinkle a few coarse grains onto pasta, salad, freshly sliced tomatoes, or bruschetta.

Traditional salt is produced in three spots on France's Atlantic coast: in the ancient Breton walled town of Guérande and on the offshore islands of Île de Noirmoutier and Île de Ré, where sea salt has been the most highly prized local product for centuries. The other big salt-producing areas of France are the Mediterranean coast and the mountain region of the Franche-Comté, where salt brines were boiled to make salt.

Traditional sea salt harvesting is seasonal. It takes place only in the summer, when the sun is strong, the winds steady, and rain minimal. The first step in the process is to capture seawater by allowing it to flow naturally into shallow trenches dug along the coastline a couple of times a month at high tide. The art of the salt gatherer is to design, dig, and maintain these mazelike channels to keep the water gliding slowly through, neither too fast (which would inhibit evaporation) nor too slow (which could cause stagnation). The shallower the channel, the more the sun and the wind can work their evaporative magic, and the closer the salt is to harvest. The process ends in small pools known as *oeillets*, only an inch or two deep. A full-time salt worker harvests from about sixty of these pools per season and can take in roughly three tons of salt in a good year.

Here are a few of my favorite salts.

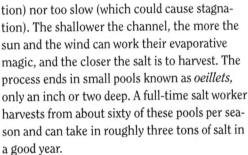

Fleur de Sel de l'Île de Noirmoutier

queen of salts: france's fleur de sel

The queen of French salts is fleur de sel. It is the first formation of the salt on the seawater's surface. Supply is inconsistent because the formation of the salt is irregular. Some seasons you see it, some you don't. Locals say that on the days when fleur de sel is being formed, you can see it sparkling in the water as the afternoon sun hits.

At about $9 per 8-ounce package, it is expensive, but you can tell it's something special just by looking at it. Whereas other sea salt generally takes the form of flakes or grains, fleur de sel is composed of small, snowflake-like crystals. Put a pinch in the palm of your hand, take it outside, and hold it up to the light; the fleur de sel sparkles in the sun. Its aroma is said to be reminiscent of violets. (Unfortunately the aroma lasts for only a few days after the salt has been taken from the sea, so you have to go to the source to experience it.) In fact, the scent is the origin of the name: *fleur,* as in "flower." Drop a few grains on your tongue and taste it. Its texture is exceptionally delicate. It melts in a matter of seconds. It really does taste remarkable.

Try a bit of fleur de sel on toasted country bread sprinkled with a generous dose of good French olive oil. Drop a few flakes on slices of freshly made mozzarella, then add olive oil and freshly ground black pepper.

breton gray salt

Underneath the fleur de sel is what is known as *sel gris,* or "gray salt," which makes up the majority of sea salt harvested on the Atlantic coast of France. The gray color comes from natural clay at the bottom of the ponds. Fleur de sel, by contrast, is snow-white because it forms on the top of the pools and never touches the ocean floor.

Although it's slightly less sparkling in flavor, gray salt is no slouch. Despite its bleak-sounding name, it's one of the most flavorful of salts. Its complex mineral makeup and high levels of residual seawater give it a flavor so bold that I've come to view it as the Tuscan oil of the salt world. It has a big, bold taste-of-the-sea flavor. It's also affordable enough for everyday eating. Gray salt is great for beef, lamb, or poultry dishes because its full flavor can hold its own with meat.

maldon salt: special salt from southern england

In the southeast corner of England, a modern-minded salt maker uses almost outdated techniques to make salt that's so good it's sought after by a growing number of *au courant* cooks and chefs. In fact, you'll find a small saucer full of Maldon salt on the tables of almost every upscale London eatery. This particularly special salt is so prized that demand easily exceeds supply.

The small building that houses the Maldon Crystal Salt Company sits on the south side of the Blackwater River estuary, a few hundred yards in from the coast in the county of Essex in southeastern England. Essex is the driest district in Britain and is well suited to salt production. At one time, salt making was a thriving industry in the area; the Domesday Book — written in the eleventh century — notes the existence of nearly fifty salt pans in the area.

Although Maldon salt has attained an international reputation, the company has been very much a small family business since 1919 when it was bought by the grandmother and step-grandfather of Clive Osborne, who currently owns and runs it.

The higher the salt content of the estuary, the easier it is to make salt. The Osbornes regularly monitor weather reports and keep close tabs on the direction of the winds and the level of the tides. If the natural salt levels in the seawater are too low, the production won't take.

With a grant from the Winston Churchill Foundation, David Lea-Wilson and his wife, Alison, did research on salt and a few years later reestablished the old Welsh tradition of salt making on the Isle of Anglesey off the northwest coast of Wales. The Lea-Wilsons have been selling their salt since 1997.

The process of salt making in Wales is much the same as that at the Maldon saltworks on the opposite coast of Great Britain. Like Maldon, Halen Môn sea salt forms naturally into beautiful pyramid-shaped translucent white crystals. The salt has a marvelous, mellow, slightly sweet flavor. It's also certified organic.

Rain—and the resulting reduction in salt levels in the estuary—can be a serious setback. In order to minimize impurities, the seawater is taken off rising tides only so that any land-based contaminants are reduced instead of pulled into the Maldon tanks.

Once the water has been drawn, it's left to stand for a few days, allowing sediments to settle to the bottom. After this natural decanting process is complete, the seawater is filtered and stored in underground tanks until it's needed for salt making. From there, it's pumped up into one of four metal tanks squeezed into a small space inside the old Maldon building. Roughly twelve feet square, each tank holds a few thousand gallons and will yield approximately 200 to 400 pounds of salt, depending on the salinity of the water. The liquid is brought to a boil for about a quarter of an hour, at which point it shows a significant layer of scum on top. This foam, known as the "lees," is skimmed off and discarded. The cooking temperature is turned down a touch, then held at a steady simmer just below the boiling point. The exact "cooking" temperature is determined only after taking into account the salinity of the water and the weather.

The longer the seawater simmers, the lower the water level gets in the pans. At a certain point, the salt begins to crystallize, forming tiny inverted pyramids that come to the surface. The pyramids float, gently bumping into one another as they move. As the hours pass, the crystals get larger; if you look closely, you can see the bands of varying shades of white in the bigger pyramids.

After about fifteen to sixteen hours of simmering, the crystal formation has reached such a significant level that the salt is raked to the side of the pans and then shoveled into hoppers. Mass-produced commercial sea salts are dried at high heat in a matter of hours. At Maldon the process moves much more slowly. It takes days of natural drying for most of the remaining liquid to evaporate. The

final step is a few hours of gentle heat in an electric "oven."

Within each box of Maldon salt, you'll find a few dozen pyramids totally intact; imagine a miniature dome made out of salt. Pour a pile into your palm, and it shimmers and shines like a handful of fresh snow held up to the sunlight.

But more important is the way Maldon salt tastes. Take a pinch and sprinkle it onto any dish, or taste it on its own. It's completely lacking in the bitterness that mars commercial table salt. It's far whiter in color and much mellower, sweeter, and softer in flavor than the gray salt from France's Atlantic coast, making it particularly well suited for more delicate dishes like fish or light salads.

portuguese flor da sal

A southern European version of Brittany's beloved fleur de sel, this exceptionally delicate and delicious sea salt is made by a small group of environmentally conscious traditionalists in the National Park of Ria Formosa on the southern coast of Portugal. Led by João Navalho, a Mozambique-born Portuguese student of marine biology, the group has recently revived traditional Portuguese sea salt production.

The Algarve has produced and exported salt since at least the eleventh century. Once Portuguese salt was considered the best in Europe, but in the past century the area's production fell prey to the efficiencies of the modern makers who switched to mechanical drying and industrial production. Navalho and his peers have worked to relearn the Portuguese salt traditions of centuries past. They located and restored the old wooden hand rakes and other tools used in flor da sal's production. Their work has also helped restore the local ecosystem, aiding in keeping the area's birds—egrets, herons, and others—alive and active.

In comparison to the French fleur de sel, the Portuguese product is lighter, the flakes a touch smaller. It contains no artificial ingredients or other additives. Like its French counterpart, the Portuguese flor da sal is best sprinkled onto foods just before serving. Try it on broiled fish, grilled octopus, sautéed vegetables, or toasted bread drizzled with extra virgin olive oil.

Navalho's group also harvests the sea salt from below the

Certainly one of the most
eye-catching salts, this
Hawaiian specialty is reddish
orange. Its color comes from
an iron-rich red mountain
clay, and its mineral content
imparts a slightly earthy flavor. The salt, which has a
sweet finish, is costly, in the
same price range as fleur de
sel. Alaea salt is very good on
fish dishes.

flor da sal. Unlike the French gray salt, it contains no
sediment from the bottom of the pools. As a result, it
is much whiter than its French counterpart,
more akin to flor da sal, and more delicate in
flavor than gray salt. This more affordable option is sold as Portuguese traditional sea salt.

sicilian sea salt

This traditional salt is gathered by hand near the
town of Menfi off the southwest coast of Sicily. It's raked into small
mounds just offshore, then allowed to dry in the hot Sicilian sun. It
comes in lovely round grains, like couscous, and has a subtle, nearly
sweet flavor and none of the bitterness of standard table salt. It brings
out the best in fish, vegetables, tomatoes, and salads.

salt and pepper croutons

These croutons taste good—they rely on the quality of the bread, olive oil, salt, and pepper that you use rather than the overabundance of dried herbs or garlic that dominates the flavor of most commercial offerings. They're excellent on salads, but they also make a great snack. Eat them warm right out of the oven or try them on cold gazpacho or a green salad.

variation

To make delicious toasted bread crumbs, put the croutons in a small sealed bag and crush them. You can also grate them in a hand-held rotary cheese grater.

8–12	ounces two- to seven-day-old crusty white country bread
1	garlic clove, peeled and bruised with the side of a knife
3–4	tablespoons medium fruity extra virgin olive oil
1	rounded teaspoon coarse sea salt
1	rounded teaspoon freshly ground Tellicherry black pepper

Preheat the oven to 275°F.

Meanwhile, cut the bread into ¾-inch cubes. Spread the cubes on a large sheet pan. Dry the bread in the oven for 8 minutes. Remove the bread from the oven, then increase the oven temperature to 325°F.

Rub the inside of a large roasting pan with the bruised garlic, then discard the garlic. Toss the bread cubes, olive oil, salt, and pepper in the roasting pan and let stand for 10 minutes. Bake for 15 minutes, or until crunchy and golden.

Let cool before storing in a covered container. The croutons will keep for 3 to 4 weeks.

makes 6 to 8 cups

irish roasties

first had these potatoes in Ireland three years ago, and I've never forgotten them. The key to good roasties is cooking at high heat for a good long time, then making sure they're amply salted.

Floury potatoes like russets or Yukon Golds work best. You can substitute rendered duck or chicken fat for the olive oil if you're feeling extravagant.

3 tablespoons extra virgin olive oil
1 teaspoon coarse sea salt
   Freshly ground black pepper to taste
1 pound small Yukon Gold potatoes, uniform in size

Preheat the oven to 450°F.

In a small bowl, mix the olive oil, salt, and pepper together. Set aside. Halve the potatoes and put them in a large roasting pan. Pour the oil mixture over and toss until the potatoes are thoroughly coated. Spread the potatoes in a single layer (they shouldn't be piled up or they'll steam). Roast on the middle rack, stirring every 10 to 15 minutes, for 50 minutes, or until the potatoes have a light golden, gently crisp crust. When you cut into one, the inside should be very soft. Serve hot.

serves 4 as a side dish

variation

To make roasted potatoes with rosemary and olive oil, prepare them as in the Irish Roasties recipe but add to the roasting pan 4 garlic cloves, peeled, halved, and bruised with the side of a knife, along with one 6-inch sprig fresh rosemary, broken into 1-inch pieces. These potatoes are a delicious accompaniment to almost any sort of meat or poultry. Remove and discard the rosemary before serving.

potatoes baked in sea salt

These potatoes make a great side dish with meat. The salt forms a crust that leaves them exceptionally tender and tasty. For a buffet gathering, serve them right from the roasting pan.

   3   pounds coarse sea salt
   1½ pounds very small potatoes (the more interesting the
         variety, the better)

Preheat the oven to 400°F.

Place a 1-inch layer of salt in a roasting pan or 9-x-13-inch baking dish. Place the potatoes on the salt in a single layer. Pour the remaining salt over the potatoes to cover, then gently pat down the surface.

Bake for 1 hour. A salt crust should form over the potatoes. If you're serving from the kitchen, gently crack the crust and remove the potatoes with a spoon. Be careful not to break the skins. Brush off the excess salt and serve hot. If you're using them as a buffet dish, bring the whole pan to the table and crack the crust for all to see.

serves 4 to 6 as a side dish

fish baked in sea salt

The salt forms a crust around the fish, keeping the flesh moist and juicy. The finished fish is not at all salty.

1   2-pound sea bass or porgy, cleaned but not scaled
4   pounds coarse sea salt

Preheat the oven to 400°F.

Rinse the fish and pat it dry. In a casserole dish large enough to hold the length of the fish and all the salt, make a 2-inch layer of salt, using about half the salt.

Lay the fish atop the salt and then pour the remaining salt around and over the fish so it's completely covered. Pat the salt down around the fish.

Bake for 30 minutes. Gently tap the salt to break the crust that's formed. Pull off as much of the salt as you can to keep it from getting into the fish. Serve immediately.

serves 2

beef baked in sea salt

This tasty dinner for guests doesn't require a lot of effort; the salt seals in the beef's natural juices. Breton gray salt works very well for this recipe. When the beef is done, it should still be pink in the center. If you can find beef that's raised on a good diet and in good conditions, such as that from Niman Ranch, the dish will be far more flavorful.

> 1   3-pound boneless rib-eye roast
> 1   teaspoon freshly ground black pepper
> 5   cups coarse sea salt
> ½   cup all-purpose flour
> 1½   cups cold water

Preheat the oven to 350°F.

Rub the entire roast with the pepper and set aside.

In a large bowl, combine the salt, flour, and water. You should end up with a thick mortarlike consistency.

On the bottom of a roasting pan, pat a ½-inch layer of the salt mixture into a rectangular shape 1 inch larger on all sides than the roast. Center the roast on the rectangle and pack the rest of the mixture onto the beef until it's completely covered. It's a bit tricky to get the salt mixture to stay on sometimes, but if you keep patting it, it will cover the roast. If just a little falls off as you place it in the oven, don't panic, the recipe will still work well.

Roast the beef for about 80 minutes, or until a meat thermometer inserted into the thickest part reads 140°F for rare to medium-rare.

Remove from the oven and let stand for a few minutes. Gently tap the salt to break the crust that's formed. I like to serve the beef right in the roasting pan atop the pieces of salt crust so my guests can enjoy the full visual impact.

Carve and serve immediately.

serves 6 to 8

saffron

There's something about the way the food world deals with saffron that sets me on edge. Almost every article on the subject starts out by stating that "saffron is the world's most expensive spice." The portrayal of saffron as beyond the reach of normal people is enough to make novices not want to get anywhere near it. Which, really, is the home cook's loss.

Saffron is infinitely more accessible than it's made out to be. Anyone who can handle opening and heating a can of soup has a good shot at being able to cook successfully with saffron. It's about that easy—and that affordable.

mad about saffron: a history

Probably native to Asia Minor, saffron is mentioned in the Song of Solomon in the Bible and in ancient Egyptian scrolls as well. Greek mythology held that the god Hermes threw a discus at his friend Crocus, accidentally killing him. Three drops of the boy's blood fell onto a nearby flower, which became the first saffron crocus, with its three red stigmas.

The Phoenicians brought saffron to Britain three thousand years ago, when they traded it for Cornish tin. Growing saffron was a significant agricultural activity in England from the fourteenth to the eighteenth centuries.

In fourteenth-century Florence, it's said to have been quicker to obtain a bank loan using saffron as collateral than it was using coins. In that same century, the Swiss started a war over saffron—when eight bags of it were stolen in Basel, an army was raised to chase the thieves, leading to the so-called Saffron War.

William Woys Weaver, an authority on the subject, writes that German Jews brought it to America at the end of the eighteenth century. Eventually saffron bulbs were planted in Pennsylvania. Today, saffron is still used in many Pennsylvania Dutch recipes, primarily in chicken and noodle dishes, soups, and sauces.

seeing the saffron harvest

I make the drive from Toledo, Spain, to La Mancha to see my first saffron harvest with my wife on a misty morning. Off to the sides of the road, we see farm fields, small villages, and assorted castles. This is the countryside Don Quixote passed through, though he traveled on horseback, not by minivan. My wife senses my excitement. Embarrassed, I try to downplay my enthusiasm. "Come on," she says, "you've been waiting for this for three years."

Six hours later, my eyes light on a once-in-a-lifetime sight: seven pounds of saffron sitting on someone's kitchen table. But what hits me first is the aroma. It saturates the space—dense, almost erotic, ethereal. The color is even more bewitching than the bouquet. It isn't a color you see in everyday life. A vivid, intense crimson, it's almost supernatural.

The mistress of the house stands back, arms folded, smiling at my obvious fascination. In La Mancha, saffron may be the best way to impress someone.

field of dreams

Just outside the village of Madridejos, an hour south of the town of Toledo, Antonio García, president of the Denomination of Origin for La Mancha saffron, veers off the main road onto a small dirt track to show us the saffron fields. Expecting to be overwhelmed by a heady rush of purple flowers, I see only a bunch of idle construction equipment sitting in a dry, pale brown field and a few scraggly grassy spots in the dirt.

In contrast, García seems so excited that I wonder if I've made a mistake in coming. We approach and I spot a few crocus flowers growing in the grassy shoots. They're beautiful, to be sure, but tiny. And I'm less bothered by the size than by the infrequency with which they appear. On this twenty-by-fifty-yard plot, I see, at most, only fifty flowers, instead of the enormous fields stretching across the horizon that I'd imagined.

In the saffron world, even the word *harvest* overstates things a bit. A more appropriate word would be "gathering," as in "gathering vegetables from your garden."

saffron: from bulb to stigma

Despite its otherworldly aroma, saffron starts as a simple plant that goes by the scientific name *Crocus sativus.* Like its crocus cousins, saffron grows from corms, small spherical bulbs that are about an inch in diameter. Though saffron can be seen growing in small quantities in dozens of rather surprising places, like Pennsylvania, the vast majority of it is planted in the Mediterranean and the Middle East.

The plant does best at moderate altitudes and in cool, loose, sandy soils. In the high altitudes of La Mancha, the flowers have to fight hard to survive the significant climatic swings of the year. "This is part of what makes La Mancha saffron so special," Antonio García notes proudly. "We have very cold temperatures close to freezing in the winter, and very hot temperatures in the summer."

Although the saffron-gathering season lasts only a few weeks, growing the flower requires year-round activity. After the crop has been gathered in the autumn, the surface of the soil must be loosened with a special rake. In March the plots must be cleaned and prepared for planting. In the spring the bulbs from the fields are dug up, then replanted during the summer. Hand-weeding goes on throughout the year. Unlike most other crocus family members, saffron blooms in the autumn and is collected from late October through the first week of November, roughly three weeks in total. The local saying "Saint Teresa's Day, saffron on the table" refers to the October 15 holiday.

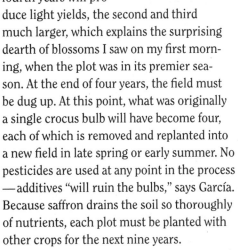

Although the cured saffron will keep almost indefinitely, saffron plots have a life of only four years. Typically the first and fourth years will produce light yields, the second and third much larger, which explains the surprising dearth of blossoms I saw on my first morning, when the plot was in its premier season. At the end of four years, the field must be dug up. At this point, what was originally a single crocus bulb will have become four, each of which is removed and replanted into a new field in late spring or early summer. No pesticides are used at any point in the process —additives "will ruin the bulbs," says García. Because saffron drains the soil so thoroughly of nutrients, each plot must be planted with other crops for the next nine years.

Standard wisdom in saffron literature is that flowers will wilt and be lost if not picked by late morning, but according to García, they last all day. They do start to wilt when the sun goes down, but they can be gathered all the way into early evening.

The second plot we come upon—a flat landscape ringed by low mountains—is more impressive than the first, though still not exactly overwhelming. It may contain fifteen to five hundred blooms at any given point. To put that in context, to make the seven pounds of saffron I saw on that kitchen table, roughly three quarters of a million flowers were hand-harvested and their stigmas hand-plucked.

On their own, the flowers are both beautiful and aromatic. Even if I knew nothing about saffron, I'd be thankful to receive a bouquet. Most have six pale purple petals, about an inch or at most two inches high. In the center of each blossom are three yellow stamens, of no value for cooking, and three crimson-colored stigmas, which will become saffron.

culling the crocus

Despite some efforts in Israel and Spain to mechanize the process, harvesting is still done completely by hand, as it has been for thousands of years. Gathering saffron is very much a family affair. City dwellers often return to the countryside to help with the labor-intensive work. Because both time and hands are hard to come by when the crocuses are in bloom, everyone contributes. Some work in the fields; others stay home to take the stigmas from the flowers. Kids are trained to gather the blossoms as soon as they're old enough to carry small baskets into the fields. Older folks work the fields well into their sixties and seventies before they "retire" to plucking the stigmas at home.

As they move down the rows, pickers pull wide-mouthed wicker baskets along with them. The stems of the saffron crocus are delicate so the flowers can be removed simply by the action of a thumbnail against a forefinger. Pickers pull ten or twelve flowers at a time, before turning to drop them into the baskets. The wicker is woven with wide gaps to allow the air to circulate so that the dew on the flowers can evaporate naturally.

Thirty rows, each roughly fifty yards long, will take two people three to four hours. "Of course," García adds with a smile, "it would take *you* all day." A plot that's been thoroughly picked by the end of the day on Monday will be ready for action again Tuesday morning. The *mondare,* or "pluckers," pick every day and are paid in kind. They get to keep one third of their take. "Nobody lives off saffron alone," García says.

at home with the strippers

For every hour spent gathering the flowers in the field, it takes two to three more to prepare the saffron for sale. In town, Antonio García leads us to one of the many well-kept homes on the block and introduces us to the woman of the household, Gregoria Carrasco Sánchez, a *mondadara,* or "stripper." Her fingers are almost blue, the mark of many hours of handling the flowers. While we mill around the kitchen, the family—four generations strong—continues

tight box for storage. From this point on, it's handled as little as possible. Surprisingly, the saffron actually has less aroma and flavor right after roasting. "It's a lot more intense a day or so after the toasting has been completed," says García.

lunch with the man of la mancha

Over lunch—saffron-seasoned squash soup, Spanish rice in saffron broth, hare with saffron, and saffron-scented cheesecake—García shares some personal history. "My grandparents grew saffron, so I was raised with it from the time I was a boy," he explains. "Later there was a crisis here because there was a lot of saffron being repackaged as Spanish that was coming from elsewhere." The people who produced the authentic saffron couldn't compete with the low prices of the imported product. To save the local culture, García helped to establish the Denomination of Origin for La Mancha saffron. In fact, he even designed the logo—a violet-blue saffron crocus. (You can see the DO's guarantee of authenticity by looking for the numbered seal it attaches to each packet or jar of saffron.)

stripping. There are still thousands of blossoms spread out on the tablecloth.

toasting

Off to the side, stigmas that have already been picked are toasting over a low flame in shallow, cloth-lined wooden baskets that look a lot like Chinese bamboo steamers. To ensure even heat, the saffron is turned over once in the thirty-minute toasting period. "It doesn't *look* complicated," explains García, "but you have to toast the threads just right."

The drying must eliminate 80 percent of the saffron's natural moisture, a step essential for proper preservation. Overdo it, and the saffron will scorch. Undertoast, and moisture may lead to mold or spoilage. Once toasted, the saffron is shaken out onto pages of the local newspaper to cool, after which it is transferred to an air-

cooking with saffron

Saffron in food is aromatic, enticing, alluring, subtly sweet. It's an essential ingredient in risotto alla Milanese, French bouillabaisse, and many paellas. Saffron goes really well with citrus and with honey.

To release its natural oil, which is called

two utensils to avoid

Stay away from whisks when you're working with saffron—the threads will cling to the wires, and you'll have to pull them off and put them back into the pot. Similarly, avoid wooden spoons; the wood absorbs the saffron and will be stained yellow.

safranal, saffron must be heated. You can steep it in a small amount of liquid or toast it in a pan.

steep it

To steep, simply place your saffron threads into a small bowl of just boiled water, cover it, and set it aside until you're ready to cook.

The longer you leave the saffron in the liquid, the more flavor you'll get. The color comes out quickly, but the flavor takes longer, a good twelve to twenty-four hours for full extraction.

When you set to work to make your sauce or soup, simply add this small bowl of "saffron starter."

toast it

To toast, place the saffron in a dry pan for thirty seconds or so. Be careful not to burn it, or the saffron will become very bitter. Crush it with a stone mortar and pestle or the back of a metal spoon. Avoid working saffron with a wooden pestle, which will absorb the spice's oils.

saffron superstitions skewered!

myth #1: price

It's true that when priced by the pound, saffron is an expensive spice: $600 isn't exactly pocket change. But when will you use an entire pound? For something like a dollar's investment, a tiny bit of saffron can turn mashed potatoes into something truly special, or make your standard soup into an extraordinary saffron chicken broth — all for less than you'd pay for a liter of Diet Coke. By modern-day spending standards, saffron is a bargain. And, as far as exotic flavors go, saffron is practically a steal.

myth #2: adulteration

Every single saffron essay I've ever read dwells on dishonest traders who tamper with saffron. By the time I'm finished reading one, I'm inclined to believe that the president should appoint a national commission to combat saffron swindling. But I have to say that while I've seen plenty of misrepresented products in my twenty years of working in the food business, I've never seen or bought suspect saffron in a professional setting here in the United States. (I won't make the same claim for the street markets in the Mediterranean, where caution in purchasing is advisable.)

If you're anxious about authenticity, there are more worthwhile ways to direct your obsessions. Worry about whether that inexpensive olive oil you saw at the store was actually made in Italy or merely bottled there. Worry when you buy pregrated "imported Parmesan." But don't lose sleep over saffron. Spend your five bucks and have some fun in the kitchen.

getting good saffron

Saffron is sold in both thread form and powder form. The latter is ground saffron threads and just as flavorful.

saffron threads

If you're buying whole threads, look first at the label. It should show you the coloring strength, the crop year, the country of origin, and the moisture content. Cut, color, and aroma should also be factors in your selection.

coloring strength

Higher coloring strength will ensure that what you're buying hasn't been adulterated and that it will provide full flavor, a lot of aroma, and a rich color. The international standard for top-grade saffron specifies a minimum coloring strength of 190. The Denomination of Origin for La Mancha saffron sets its minimum at a level of 200 and is said to have some samples that have registered over 300.

crop year

Properly stored, saffron can last for years. Given a choice, though, buy the most recent harvest.

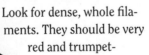

cut and color

Look for dense, whole filaments. They should be very red and trumpet-shaped. Threads that are white, orange, or yellow are stamens or styles of the flower, which add weight but no flavor, and hence are signs of a less desirable product. The best saffron is that which is cut very short, $3/8$ to $1/2$ inch, so that all of the flower's style is removed. Longer saffron threads look nice but actually contain more of the flavorless style.

moisture

The moisture content of saffron can vary from about 2 percent to over 20 percent; lower is better. Residual moisture adds weight and hence cost. It also can lead to mustiness. "If you crush the best saffron between your fingers, it will crack," says the longtime importer Juan San Mames.

aroma

The smell of the saffron should be strong when you open the jar. Fluff it a bit with dry fingers and smell again. The scent should be even stronger, clean and fresh, not musty or earthy.

country of origin

Spain, Greece, Kashmir, Italy, and Iran are all potentially sound choices. Each country has its own variations. And each is adamant that its saffron is the best.

Spain is the most well-known producer of saffron, but today a majority of the world's crop actually arrives from Iran. Greece is in second place in the saffron standings, with Morocco and Kashmir tied for third. Spain comes in fourth. Italy, England, Switzerland, the United States, and a few other countries produce small quantities as well.

saffron powder

Buy from a reputable source or grind your own. The latter takes all of about twenty seconds with a stone mortar and pestle. If you're in a hurry, using powder is by far and away the best alternative. All you have to do is drop some into your sauce, soup, or sauté, and you're well on your way to saffron success.

Good saffron powder should be the same deep crimson you'd expect to see in threads. The ultimate measure of quality is coloring strength. To check authenticity, you can drop a bit into cold water, which should release some color and aroma. At first you should see red dots, then an appealing yellow glow should spread through the liquid. Aroma is also a very good indicator. Saffron substitutes rarely have any at all. If the powder sticks together in a lump, it has probably been exposed to too much moisture.

buying better saffron

iran

Of all the saffrons I've tasted, Sargol from Iran is by far the sweetest. Its very short, very red threads have a lab-tested coloring strength of 230 to 255 and a low, low moisture content of about 2 percent. It's imported by Vanilla, Saffron Imports in San Francisco, which has successfully worked with saffron for decades. If you order powder, the company grinds itto order. Good flavor, easy to use, and very affordable.

spain

Be sure that Spanish labels carry the Denomination of Origin seal to ensure authenticity. Take note that the Azafrán de la Mancha DO doesn't allow powdered saffron to be sold with its seal. (The saffron of Antonio García is sold in the United States under the Cefran label.)

greece

I've collected completely conflicting views on the subject of Greek saffron. Ellen Szita, an expert on the subject, notes that it is important to buy Greek saffron from the cooperative in Krokus, which carefully regulates the quality of what's sold under its label: Greek Red Saffron, Krokos Kozanis.

united states

In the long-standing saffron tradition of the Pennsylvania Dutch, Martin Keen, who sells his saffron under the Greider's label, harvests by hand. He uses a small dehydrator, not the Spanish toasting method. Production is very small.

saffron chicken broth

You can use this broth for Gregoria's Saffron Meatballs (page 358) and for braising chicken and cooking rice, pasta, potatoes, risotto, and much more. I like to make a big batch, cool it, then pour it into quart-sized containers and freeze it.

> 2 tablespoons extra virgin olive oil
> 1 large onion, coarsely chopped (about 2 cups)
> 2 garlic cloves, peeled and bruised with the side of a knife
> 2 medium tomatoes, chopped (about 1 cup)
> ½ teaspoon saffron threads, soaked in ¼ cup boiling water for at least several hours
> 12 cups chicken broth, preferably homemade
> Coarse sea salt to taste

In a large heavy-bottomed saucepan, heat the olive oil over medium-high heat. Add the onion and garlic and sauté gently until the onion is soft, about 5 minutes. Do not brown. Stir in the tomatoes, saffron, and the saffron soaking water. Cook for 1 minute more. Stir in the chicken broth. Simmer, partially covered, for 45 to 60 minutes, or until the flavors have melded. Add salt and simmer for a few minutes more. (Or omit the salt at this point and add it when you reheat the broth at a later date.)

Strain the broth through a fine sieve and discard the solids. Cool and store the broth in the refrigerator for up to 1 week, or freeze it for up to 3 months.

makes 9 to 10 cups

gregoria's saffron meatballs

This dish is a specialty of La Mancha's saffron-growing areas. You can serve it as an appetizer or as a main dish with Spanish rice on the side. Gregoria Carrasco Sánchez inspired this recipe. Her meatballs are said to be so good that they can "raise the dead."

 6 ounces ground pork
 5 ounces ground beef
 5 ounces ground veal
 $\frac{1}{2}$ cup bread crumbs (see page 119)
 $\frac{1}{2}$ cup minced onion
 $\frac{1}{4}$ cup finely chopped Italian parsley, rinsed and squeezed dry
 2 garlic cloves, minced
 $\frac{3}{4}$ teaspoon coarse sea salt
 1 teaspoon freshly ground black pepper
 $\frac{1}{4}$ cup plus 2 tablespoons full-flavored extra virgin olive oil, preferably Spanish
 1 large egg
 3 cups Saffron Chicken Broth (page 357)
 3 tablespoons all-purpose flour
 Saffron threads for garnish (optional)

In a large bowl, gently combine the pork, beef, veal, bread crumbs, onion, parsley, garlic, salt, pepper, $\frac{1}{4}$ cup olive oil, and the egg. Form the mixture into small meatballs, about $1\frac{1}{2}$ inches across. You should have about 30 meatballs.

In a large heavy-bottomed skillet, heat the remaining 2 tablespoons olive oil over medium heat. Add the meatballs about 10 at a time, so as not to overcrowd the pan. Turn the meatballs with a spoon so that they brown evenly on all sides, 15 to 20 minutes. Remove from the skillet and repeat until all the meatballs have been browned.

Meanwhile, in a large saucepan, bring the broth to a boil.

Return the browned meatballs to the skillet and pour the boiling broth over them. Simmer over medium heat for 25 minutes. Reduce the heat to medium-low and transfer the meatballs with a slotted spoon to a serving dish, covering them to keep them warm. Keep the broth simmering.

In a small bowl, mix the flour with 1 cup of the hot broth from the skillet to make a paste. Stir the paste back into the simmering broth, and simmer slowly, stirring constantly, until thickened, about 5 minutes.

Pour the sauce over the meatballs in the serving dish. If you'd like, you can add a few saffron threads to garnish the dish.

serves 4 to 6 as a main course or 10 as an appetizer

saffron fish broth

This broth is the base for all sorts of great dishes. You can use it for paella, bouillabaisse, or Saffron Fish Chowder (opposite).

  2 tablespoons extra virgin olive oil, preferably Catalan
  1 large onion, chopped (about 2 cups)
  2 garlic cloves, peeled and bruised with the side of a knife
  2 medium tomatoes, chopped (about 1 cup)
  1 teaspoon whole fennel seeds, toasted (see page 54)
$\frac{1}{2}$ teaspoon saffron threads, soaked in $\frac{1}{4}$ cup boiling water for at least several hours
12 cups water
  4 pounds white fish frames (bones and heads)
     Coarse sea salt to taste
  1 sprig fresh thyme (about 4 inches)

In a large pot, heat the olive oil over medium-high heat. Add the onion and garlic and sauté until the onion is soft, about 5 minutes. Stir in the tomatoes, toasted fennel seeds, saffron, and the saffron soaking water, and sauté for 1 to 2 minutes more. Add the 12 cups water and fish trimmings and bring to a boil. Reduce the heat to medium-low. Simmer, partially covered, for 45 to 60 minutes, or longer for a stronger broth. Add salt and thyme and simmer for a few minutes more. (Or omit the salt at this point and add it when you reheat the broth at a later date.)

Strain the broth through a fine sieve and discard the solids. Cool and store the broth in the refrigerator for up to 3 days, or freeze it for up to 3 months.

makes 9 to 10 cups

saffron fish chowder

The only time-consuming part of this soup is making the broth. The rest is easy, and the soup is elegant and delicious.

variation

If you're up for something fancier, serve the chowder with a dollop of frothed milk in the middle (from your espresso machine if you've got one at home), topped with a few saffron threads.

2 tablespoons delicate extra virgin olive oil, preferably Ligurian

1 large onion, diced (about 1½ cups)

3 garlic cloves, finely chopped

1 teaspoon hot red pepper flakes, preferably Marash (see page 58)

½ teaspoon dried thyme

8 cups Saffron Fish Broth (page 360)

5 Roma tomatoes, skinned, seeded, and chopped, or about 1½ cups canned tomatoes, drained and chopped

¾ cup Italian rice, preferably Arborio or Vialone Nano

3 tablespoons butter

3 tablespoons all-purpose flour

1 pound firm white fish fillets, such as silver hake, halibut, haddock, swordfish, monkfish, cod, snapper, or bass, cut into bite-sized pieces

½ cup half-and-half

Coarse sea salt to taste

Freshly ground black pepper to taste

1 tablespoon finely chopped Italian parsley, rinsed and squeezed dry

In a large pot, heat the olive oil over medium heat. Add the onion, garlic, pepper flakes, and thyme. Increase the heat to medium-high and sauté, stirring occasionally, until the onion is transparent, 7 to 9 minutes. Don't brown.

Add the broth, tomatoes, and rice. Bring to a boil, reduce the heat to medium-low, and simmer until the rice is al dente, about 15 minutes.

When the rice is halfway done, in a small saucepan, melt the butter over medium heat. Slowly stir in the flour. Cook, stirring constantly, until it thickens but is still pourable, 2 to 3 minutes. Slowly stir the roux into the simmering soup. Simmer for 5 minutes, then stir in the fish and simmer for 5 minutes more. Remove from the heat and let stand for 5 minutes to cool slightly. Add the half-and-half. Add salt and pepper to taste. Serve in warm bowls, garnished with parsley.

serves 6

vegetarian saffron broth

H ere's a vegetarian broth for saffron-scented soups and sauces.

- 2 tablespoons extra virgin olive oil
- 1 large onion, coarsely chopped (about 2 cups)
- 2 garlic cloves, peeled and bruised with the side of a knife
- 2 teaspoons fennel seeds, toasted (see page 54)
- 4 medium tomatoes, chopped (about 2 cups)
- ½ teaspoon saffron threads, soaked in ¼ cup boiling water for at least several hours
- 10 cups water

  Coarse sea salt to taste

- 2 tablespoons Pernod (optional)

In a large heavy-bottomed saucepan, heat the olive oil over medium-high heat. Add the onion, garlic, and fennel seeds, and sauté until the onion is soft, about 5 minutes. Do not brown.

Stir in the tomatoes, saffron, and saffron soaking water. Cook for a minute more, then stir in the 10 cups water. Simmer, partially covered, for 45 to 60 minutes, or until the flavors have melded. Add the salt and simmer for a few minutes more. (Or omit the salt at this point and add it when you reheat the broth at a later date.)

Strain the broth through a fine sieve and discard the solids. Return the strained broth to the pot and add the Pernod, if using. Simmer gently for 5 minutes.

Cool and store in the refrigerator for up to 1 week, or freeze it for up to 12 months.

makes 8 to 9 cups

part 6.

honey, vanilla, chocolate, and tea

honey

"Unvarying flavor and perfect clarity should be as disquieting in honey as in wine."

● Edward Behr

Let a thousand flowers bloom." So said Mao Tse-tung as he kicked off the Cultural Revolution. It's a phrase that would fit well into the vocabulary of every honey lover around the world.

The best honeys are gathered from single floral sources. Beekeepers follow the flowers from field to field as the seasons change, like Grateful Dead groupies touring with the band. As with good wine or good olive oil, each of these varietals has its own unique flavor, aroma, and texture. When you get a good honey, you get a mosaic of marvelous, hard-to-describe flavors, you get seasonal and geographic variations, and you get to taste the honey the way you would have eaten it a few hundred years ago, before pasteurization and other industrial "improvements." By contrast, the plastic bear labeled *honey* is like a bottle of table wine, a blend lacking character and charisma, mixed for consistent color and flavor so it will look and taste the same year in and year out.

honey history

The first honey that humans ate was made by wild bees. Neolithic cave drawings in Spain show honey gatherers clearing hives twelve thousand years ago. From there, humans progressed to making their own hives in hollow logs or pots. By baiting the inside of these artificial hives with a bit of honey, they coaxed the bees into stopping there instead of their original wilder haunts. Somewhere along the line, someone learned that you could lull bees to sleep with smoke, a technique still used today. In 1851, the Reverend Lorenzo Langstroth discovered that bees do best when they work in a passageway exactly three eighths of an inch wide, a distance known to this day as "bee space." With this breakthrough, the good reverend developed the modern beehive—a set of boxes that can be stacked one on top of the other. Within each box, ten or so frames hang three eighths of an inch apart. On these frames the bees make their comb. The bottom of each bee box is kept free for the hive's queen to lay her eggs, to the tune of about one hundred thousand a year.

Honeybees arrived in the Americas with the early European settlers, and then went, well, wild. American honey hunters took down wild hives, then traded the combs they found inside for food and other necessities. It took bees a couple of hundred years to make it all the way across the continent to the West Coast. Along with maple sugar, honey was the dominant sweetener until the eighteenth century, when colonial plantations in the Caribbean finally made sugar cheap enough for everyone to eat.

Although good honey is a completely natural product, made with a minimum of human interference, the kind we eat today is the output of domesticated bees that live in man-made hives. We have learned how to arrange the bees' living patterns so they can produce more honey than they themselves need to eat. Bees pollinate roughly 85 percent of the nation's food crops. In this way, the honeybee is indirectly responsible for about two thirds of what we eat in the United States.

a bee's-eye view of honey making

Honey starts with the nectar—a watery solution of sugars, with traces of other substances—found naturally in flowers. It attracts the worker bees, who suck it from the flowers and store it in their nectar sac, then depart for the next flower with bits of pollen on their legs, thereby ensuring pollination of the plant species. A bee has to visit two hundred to three hundred flowers to collect a full load. By the end of the day, a good bee will have brought in a grand total of .03 grams of nectar, for which it will have traveled an impressive one and a half miles.

The bee's body starts concentrating and purifying the nectar even before it returns home. The workers make a beeline to the hive, trans-

Roughly twenty-one pounds of honey go into a single pound of beeswax. To make it, the worker bees stuff themselves with honey, then sit still for twenty-four hours while the wax forms inside their bodies. It emerges a day later in the form of small plates from wax pockets on the underside of their body. Each pound of wax is enough to make something like thirty-five thousand honeycomb cells.

fering the honey to one of the "house bees" that in turn passes it, drop by drop, to another bee on its tongue. They beat their wings to dry and concentrate the nectar further. About fifteen to twenty minutes later, the finished honey goes into the comb. To make a pound of honey, eighty thousand bee-loads of nectar are needed. At the end of a season, a well-managed hive, with roughly 250 drones, a single queen, and 50,000 workers—should have produced about sixty to eighty pounds.

what makes one honey different from another?

Although most people think of honey as a homogenous substance, there are more than three hundred varieties in the world. Every blossom, so to speak, begets its own "brand," a honey that's based on the floral source in the same way that wines depend on the grapes they're made from. Rosemary, blueberry, blackberry, fireweed . . . each makes a distinct honey that comes from the nectar gathered by the bees from its blossoms. Take note, though, that very few honeys actually taste like the flower or fruit—blueberry honey, for instance, does not taste like blueberries.

Geography plays a part in the taste of the honey as well. The same type of blossom in two different parts of the world will yield honeys of varied texture and flavor. The vintage also makes a difference. Like every other natural food, varietal honey will be different each year, depending on changing climatic conditions.

The variety of the flower the bees are feeding on has a lot to do with the honey's texture. Honey is primarily made up of relatively equal parts glucose and fructose. The more glucose (and the less fructose), the more likely the honey is to have a naturally crystalline, nearly opaque texture.

The majority of good varietal honeys are cloudy and naturally crystallized; thick to almost solid, often completely opaque. In much

Don't make the mistake of
confusing authentic varietal
honeys with commercial
clover honey that has been
flavored. Most of the time
Blueberry Honey Creme on a
store shelf is made by bees
that have never seen a blueberry blossom. It's nothing
more than standard-issue
honey with a dose of blueberry extract. Products like
this are to the world of great
honey what hazelnut-mocha-
mint is to fine coffee. They
have nothing at all to do with
authentic blueberry honey,
which is gathered after the
bees have been feeding on
blueberry blossoms.

of Europe, these honeys are the preferred model. Good lavender honey can be creamy white. Chestnut honey can be the color of fudge, opaque all the way through. These are the honeys I love, for their granular texture, their smoothness in the mouth, their fullness of flavor. (These naturally crystalline honeys are not the same as commercially "spun" or "creamed" honeys, which are created by breaking down the natural crystals in the honey to form a softer, creamier spread, the equivalent of soft-spread margarine.) A few varietal honeys—those that are high in fructose—flow more freely. Thyme honey from Greece, for example, is the color of light maple syrup and about as runny. Light golden acacia is another naturally clear honey. Black button sage, fireweed, and tupelo—three of this country's most interesting indigenous honeys—will rarely crystallize. The honey in the plastic bear, on the other hand, is clear primarily because it's been processed: after harvesting, it is heated to melt the naturally occurring crystals and filtered to remove any solid particles that might lead to recrystallization. These treatments also remove much of the flavor.

what to look for in honey— and what to avoid

The less the honey is handled after it's been taken from the hive, the higher the quality is likely to be. Other than a very gentle warming used to loosen and remove honey from the hive, most other heat is likely to be harmful. There should be no added fruit flavors or colors, no additives of any sort.

There's no bee consortium to certify that the blossoms the bees visited are the ones on the label. Fortunately, though, bees tend to stick to a single nectar source until it's been used up, so you can feel fairly confident that the majority of the flowers they've visited have been of the same sort. There are, though, hundreds of naturally occurring blends that come together when more than one type of flower is in bloom in the same area at the same time.

Ultimately, you really have to taste honey before you buy to see if you like it. Because it is so variable from year to year, buying by brand assures some degree of continuity but not an identical product. Taste before you take anything home.

great varietal honeys

Here are just a few of the many versions of varietal honey worth seeking out.

acacia

One of the palest and clearest of honeys, acacia has a delicate flavor. It's not one of my favorites, but it's high in fructose so it stays clear under almost any circumstances and is very popular.

basswood

A favorite in the southeastern United States, this honey is light in color but strong in flavor, with a subtle hint of mint. In Europe it's know as lime, or linden, honey.

buckwheat

Dark in color with a robust, full flavor, buckwheat honey is not for the faint of heart. At Zingerman's we take advantage of its depth in our honey cake, which we make religiously each autumn to help mark the Jewish New Year.

carob

Perhaps my favorite honey in the last few years, this one from Sicily is hard to find but exceptionally delicious. A late-season honey, gathered around Christmastime, it's very costly because bees are torpid and move slowly at this point in the year, and the yields are always low. Dark in color, very thick and granular in texture, this honey is caramelly, slightly mentholated, very aromatic, and not too sweet.

chestnut

Very popular in Italy, this honey is harvested in mid to late summer. It has a slightly bitter, sensually smoky flavor. It's strong stuff, so not everyone will like it as much as I do. Good chestnut honey is a deep, dark, mysterious brown, the color of freshly brewed coffee; it has an exceptional taste with a pleasant touch of bitterness. It makes a fabulous honey ice cream, and it's great on Gorgonzola cheese.

corbezzolo

Made from the nectar of the corbezzolo, otherwise known as the strawberry tree, or arbutus, found mostly on the Italian island of Sardinia, this honey is produced in very small quantities high in the wild central mountains of the island. It's made in the late autumn and early winter. Yields are always low because the bees must work so hard to produce it.

eucalyptus

This honey offers a wide variety of flavors and aromas, depending on where in the world and which variety of eucalyptus the bees visited.

fir tree

Known in France as *sapin,* this honey has a dark caramel color and a lovely hint of anise in its flavor. I've also had an excellent creamy fir tree honey from Greece.

fireweed

Native to the Pacific Northwest, fireweed honey is known as the "champagne of honeys" for its elegant flavor and delicate nose, according to one longtime beekeeper. It has a satiny texture and a surprisingly fruity flavor. It's hard to find but is worth seeking out if you like honeys with lighter flavors.

lavender

Primarily from Provence in southeast France, this one is highly perfumed, highly prized, and relatively hard to get. The French lavender honeys are high in glucose and hence quite crystalline in texture.

The lavender honey from Spain is also excellent and very different from the French. It's clear, with a thick, almost chewy texture that leaves a lovely coating on your lips. Not too sweet, it has a wonderful bouquet, with a flavor that hints of golden raisins and a delicate bit of pepperiness at the finish. California produces good lavender honey as well.

leatherwood

Just after New Year's, the leatherwood trees in the rain forests of western Tasmania burst forth with white filigree flowers. The honey is the color of medium amber maple syrup and has an enticingly piquant aroma and a delicate licorice flavor.

lehua blossom

This white, creamy honey comes only from Hawaii, where it's gathered from the blossoms of the lehua tree. It crystallizes so rapidly that it has to be removed from the hive very quickly. The honey has a wonderful flavor with a brown sugar–perfumed richness.

lemon blossom

A coarsely textured honey the color of almond shells, with a lovely, sweet citrus flavor, lemon blossom honey is delicious with tea and toast. The best I've had has been from eastern Spain.

manuka

From New Zealand, this slightly bitter honey has subtle licorice undertones.

orange blossom

This heavily scented, light liquid honey has a hint of orange perfume.

raspberry blossom

This light, clear, golden honey has a floral aroma.

rosemary

I've had exquisite rosemary honey from Spain that's high in fructose and free-flowing. And I've had rosemary honey from France that is high in glucose, coarse-textured, and crystalline. It's darker in color and slightly bitter.

scottish heather

This honey has a rich, buttery, candied taste and appearance and a toffee perfume. There are excellent heather honeys from Sardinia, Corsica, or anywhere that heather grows in profusion.

sunflower

Bright golden orange in color, this honey has a beautiful bitterness that underlies its natural sweetness.

thyme

Greek honeys are generally thick; the plentiful sunshine dries the honey and reduces its natu-ral moisture content. The best known is the wild thyme honey made from late-spring flowers. Dark amber in color, slightly bitter, beautifully aromatic, it can be almost chewy. Because herbs grow so well in the wild in almost all of Greece, versions of thyme honey abound.

tupelo

One of America's rarest and tastiest honeys, it's gathered only in northern Florida and southern Georgia along the Apalachicola River basin, where bees feed on the pale green flowers of the Ogeechee tupelo, a small shrubby tree that grows knee-deep in the swamps. The hives are mounted on fourteen-foot-high platforms, and the honey is hand-harvested each spring by bee-keepers on barges. It's a clear golden color, with a complex flavor that hints of anise.

wildflower

Gathered anywhere that unplowed fields of flowers grow uncorrupted by modern agriculture, wildflower honey varies in flavor from area to area depending on the type of flowers and herbs in the meadows. Italians often refer to these honeys as *millefiori*, or "thousand flowers."

yellow star thistle

Yellow star thistle is a California wildflower that yields a lemon-colored honey with a sweet, candylike flavor. (But beware: different flowers share the same or similar names in various parts of the country but are quite different in flavor. Star thistle in Michigan is actually knapweed, and in my experience the honey's not particularly tasty.)

what do you do with varietal honey?

I'm all for simply spreading it on hot toast—the heat of the bread warms the honey and releases its fragrance and flavor. Varietal honeys are also delicious with fresh ricotta cheese—spread a slice of lightly buttered toast with ricotta and then spoon on a generous dose of the honey of your choice. Gorgonzola goes especially well with good honey, as do most fresh cheeses. In Spain I've enjoyed slices of Manchego cheese drizzled with honey, a great way to end a meal.

Honey is also an excellent base for marinades because it clings to meat and mixes well with other seasonings. The combination of sweet and savory works well. With meat, I prefer to use more strongly flavored honeys because their flavors don't get overwhelmed as easily. Try rubbing a leg of lamb with a blend of Scottish heather honey and apple cider. Roast a chicken that's been dressed in a coat of thyme honey.

You can also bake with

good honey. Honey cakes (see Buckwheat Honey Cake, page 381) stay soft instead of drying out like most baked goods because honey attracts moisture. In fact, many honey-based baked goods are better a few days after you make them. You can substitute honey for sugar in baking, but because it contains more liquid, it will alter the chemistry of your cakes or cookies. As a general guideline, you can experiment by substituting honey for sugar one to one in a recipe; but you must reduce other liquids by $1/4$ cup for each cup of honey. You'll also want to reduce the baking temperature by 25 degrees Fahrenheit because honey browns faster than sugar.

honey butter

Honey butter is a simple way to enjoy the flavors of good honey and good butter. I like this spread melted onto almost anything warm, from toast to pancakes to just cooked wild rice. The variety of honey you use depends on your personal preferences.

4   tablespoons butter, at room temperature
3½   teaspoons varietal honey, at room temperature

Place the butter in a medium bowl, and pour the honey over it. Using the back of a wooden spoon, slowly blend the honey into the butter.

You can keep the honey butter, covered, in the refrigerator or at room temperature for up to 2 weeks. During the hot summer months, leave it in the refrigerator.

serves 4 as a spread

olive oil and honey with bread

variation

This recipe is equally excellent with walnut or hazelnut oil instead of olive oil. You can replace the pine nuts with chopped walnuts or hazelnuts.

I learned of this combination not long ago from my friend Janet Campbell, who told me that she and her Moroccan-born boyfriend, Hicham, eat it regularly for breakfast. I wondered why I'd never heard of it or come up with it on my own long ago. Great olive oil and great honey—what could be bad? It's as good as it sounds, maybe even better —perfect for breakfast and excellent after dinner or as a snack.

First, set out a white plate. (It has to be white to give you the full visual effect. It shouldn't be cold, or it will dull the flavors of the oil and honey.)

Open a bottle of good varietal honey. Take your pick; any good honey will work. Put a nice dollop in the middle of the plate.

Pour a bit of one of your favorite extra virgin olive oils on the plate around the honey. Not a huge amount—the idea is that the oil will edge its way up to the honey but not go over it. For garnish, if you have a few untoasted pine nuts, drop them onto the honey.

Now set out some good crusty white bread. If you're not in a hurry, warm it in the oven for 10 minutes. Tear off a chunk of the bread and push it through the oil and honey so you get some of each. The combination of sweet honey and savory oil is excellent—sort of a Mediterranean honey butter.

grilled tuscan pecorino cheese

Although Pecorino Romano is certainly the best known of Italy's sheep's milk cheeses, when it comes to eating as is, I tend to turn to the less-renowned cheeses of Tuscany. To my taste, the Tuscan cheeses are more complexly flavored, gentler and less salty, worthy of consideration among the best anywhere. In particular, I'm partial to the Pecorino di Pienza, from the southeast corner of the region. Chestnut honey works well in this dish and is common in Tuscany, but any good, full-flavored honey will do. Serve for lunch with a green salad or for dessert.

Full-flavored extra virgin olive oil, preferably Tuscan
8 ounces Pecorino di Pienza cheese (with rind)
1–2 tablespoons full-flavored honey

Preheat an outdoor grill and lightly oil the grate.

Leaving the rind on, cut the cheese into ½-inch-thick, 3-inch-long slices. It should be thick enough to grill on each side without having the cheese melt and slip right through the grill grate.

Grill the cheese until it is bubbly and lightly golden, then flip and grill on the other side.

Transfer the cheese to a warm serving plate, top with a drizzle of honey, and serve immediately. I leave the rinds on to keep the slices intact, then let the guests trim them off on the plate as they eat.

serves 6 to 8

zingerman's cheese blintzes

These blintzes have been a big hit at Zingerman's for over twenty years. You can make them a day ahead and fry them up right before you eat. Serve with good preserves or sour cream. They're great for brunch, but you can enjoy them at any time of the day.

CREPE BATTER

- 1½ cups all-purpose flour
- ½ teaspoon fine sea salt
- 2 cups whole milk
- 2 large eggs, lightly beaten

FILLING

- 2 vanilla beans
- 8 ounces farmer cheese
- 8 ounces cream cheese (preferably natural—without vegetable gum, see page 208), at room temperature
- 2 tablespoons full-flavored honey, preferably chestnut
- ½ tablespoon butter, at room temperature
- 1 large egg yolk
- ½ teaspoon fine sea salt

Butter for pans

Make the batter: Sift the flour and salt into a medium bowl. Make a well in the center. Pour in the milk and eggs and stir slowly until well blended. There will be a few lumps. Cover with plastic wrap and let stand while you make the filling.

Make the filling: With a sharp knife, split the vanilla beans lengthwise. Using the tip of a spoon, gently scrape the seeds into a medium bowl. Reserve the pods for another use (such as Vanilla Sugar, page 394). Add the farmer cheese, cream cheese, honey, and butter to the bowl and mix until well blended. Gently stir in the egg yolk and salt. Mix well again and set aside.

Make the crepes: Heat a 7-inch crepe pan over medium heat. When a little water splashed onto the skillet dances and evaporates, it is ready. Grease the pan lightly with butter, regulating the heat so it does not burn.

Lift the pan from the heat and ladle ¼ cup batter into the center of the pan, then tilt the pan in a circular motion to coat the cooking surface with a thin, even layer. Cook until the bubbles disappear and the underside is golden, 1 to 2 minutes. Transfer to a clean dishtowel and keep covered. Repeat until all the crepes are done, lightly buttering the pan before each. You should have 12 or 13 crepes.

Make and cook the blintzes: Place 2 slightly rounded tablespoons of filling onto the uncooked side of the crepe. Fold it closed to make a rectangular package, folding in the top and bottom first, then the sides. Each blintz will look a bit like a nicely folded envelope.

In a large skillet, melt 2 tablespoons butter over medium heat. Working in batches so as not to overcrowd the skillet, add the blintzes seam side down. Cook until the underside is golden brown, about 2 minutes. Flip and cook for 1 minute more, or until the other side is golden brown as well. Serve immediately. serves 4 to 6

rosemary, saffron, and honey lamb stew

This stew brings together a medieval combination of Spanish flavors. The aroma released as it's cooking will assure perfect attendance at the dinner table. Better-quality lamb will make a difference: those from Niman Ranch and Jamison Farms are consistently very good.

- 2 tablespoons all-purpose flour
- ½ teaspoon coarse sea salt, plus more to taste
- ½ teaspoon freshly ground black pepper, plus more to taste
- ¾ pound lamb loin, cut into ¾-inch cubes
- ¼ cup extra virgin olive oil, preferably from southern Spain, plus more for serving
- 1 large onion, chopped (about 2 cups)
- 1 garlic clove, chopped
- 4 medium Yukon Gold potatoes (about 1¼ pounds), peeled and cubed
- 6 cups chicken broth
- ½ teaspoon saffron threads, soaked in ½ cup boiling water for at least several hours or up to 1 day
- 1 generous tablespoon savory honey, preferably rosemary
- 1 small sprig fresh rosemary (about 3 inches)
- 2 dried bay leaves
- 2 teaspoons Champagne vinegar or white wine vinegar
- 2 teaspoons fresh orange juice

In a large shallow plate, mix the flour, ½ teaspoon salt, and ½ teaspoon pepper. Add the lamb and toss until well coated.

In a large stockpot, heat the ¼ cup olive oil over medium heat. Add the onion and garlic and sauté until soft, about 7 minutes.

Increase the heat to medium-high, add the lamb, and cook, stirring occasionally, until browned. Add the potatoes and cook for 10 minutes, stirring frequently.

Slowly stir in the broth. Stir in the saffron and its soaking liquid, the honey, rosemary sprig, and bay leaves and bring to a boil. Reduce the heat to medium-low and simmer until the potatoes are soft and the stew is thickened, about 25 minutes.

Add the vinegar and orange juice, stir well, and simmer for 5 minutes more. Add additional salt and pepper to taste. Remove and discard the rosemary sprig and bay leaves. Serve in warm bowls, garnished with a ribbon of olive oil across the top.   serves 4 to 6

honey and black pepper pork

The blending of sweet honey with spicy black pepper has its roots in medieval times. One key to the flavor of the dish is the quality of the pork: start with free-range meat from suppliers like Niman Ranch and you'll end up with a much tastier meal. I like it with lots of black pepper, but you can cut back on the amount if you prefer less heat.

4 teaspoons coarse sea salt
2 tablespoons coarsely ground black pepper
⅓ cup full-flavored honey
1 boneless pork loin (about 3 pounds)

Preheat the oven to 350°F.

Mix the salt and pepper in a small bowl. Untie the roast, then rub the honey evenly over the surface of the pork and coat it with the salt and pepper. Retie the roast.

Place the pork in a roasting pan and roast, uncovered, in the middle of the oven until a meat thermometer inserted into the thickest part of the pork reads 140°F, about 1 hour 10 minutes. The cooking time will vary depending on the density of the meat and on your oven, so use the thermometer, not the clock, as your guide. The meat should be slightly pink inside. Remove from the oven and let rest for 10 to 15 minutes before carving and serving.

serves 4 to 6

buckwheat honey cake

Lekach, or honey cake, is an annual added incentive to celebrate the Jewish New Year. We use this recipe at Zingerman's Bakehouse, based on what Michael London (of Mrs. London's in Saratoga Springs, New York) learned in the Jewish bakeries of New York City many moons ago. It's made from a long list of luscious ingredients, including a healthy helping of buckwheat honey, which has a bold flavor that stands up to all the other ingredients. The quality of the honey will significantly affect the flavor of the cake. While we typically bake this honey cake for the Jewish New Year, it's delicious year-round. The cake is best after it's had a few days for the flavors to blend. It will last for a week or two.

1	tablespoon Earl Grey tea leaves
1/2	cup boiling water
1 1/3	cups rye flour
3/4	teaspoon baking soda
1/4	teaspoon fine sea salt
1/4	generous teaspoon ground cinnamon
	Pinch ground cloves
	Pinch ground ginger
	Pinch freshly ground nutmeg
3	tablespoons butter, at room temperature
1/3	cup plus 2 teaspoons firmly packed muscovado or dark brown sugar
1	large egg
2/3	cup buckwheat honey
1	tablespoon grated orange zest
2	teaspoons grated lemon zest
1/3	cup golden raisins
5	tablespoons sliced almonds, toasted (see page 31)

Preheat the oven to 325°F. Lightly grease a 6-cup bundt pan.

In a small bowl, steep the tea leaves in the boiling water for 5 minutes, then strain, discarding the leaves. Set aside.

In a medium bowl, combine the rye flour, baking soda, salt, and spices. Set aside.

In a large bowl, cream the butter and sugar. Stir in the egg and mix well. Stir in the honey, tea, and zests until well combined. Slowly stir in the dry ingredients until well combined. Fold in the raisins and 3 tablespoons of the almonds.

Sprinkle the remaining 2 tablespoons almonds evenly over the bottom of the prepared pan. Slowly pour in the batter. Bake for 40 minutes, or until a toothpick inserted in the center comes out clean.

Transfer the pan to a cooling rack and let stand for 10 minutes. Carefully invert the pan and remove the cake. Cover with a clean dishtowel and let rest for at least 24 hours before slicing and serving. *serves 8*

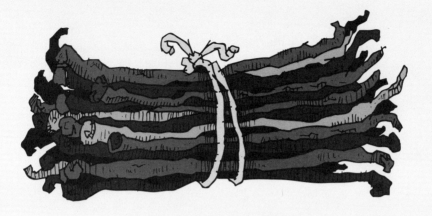

vanilla

There's nothing ordinary about "plain vanilla." It's a mysterious, magical product, unlike any other food.

Although the United States is now the single largest consumer of vanilla in the world, most Americans eat far more lab-produced artificial vanillin than they do real vanilla. Switching from the substitute to the authentic article is a major move forward, like listening to music in stereo instead of on an old transistor radio.

the story of real vanilla: a visit to veracruz

When I visited the original capital of the ancient vanilla world, the town of Papantla on the Gulf Coast of Mexico, it was spring, the season when the annual pollination of the plants takes place. About a four-hour drive north of Veracruz, Papantla is the birthplace of vanilla.

The surrounding countryside is a strange blend of Alps and Amazon. There are plenty of well-trimmed green hills, many of which play host to grazing cattle. But round the bend, and you find yourself face to face with near jungle conditions. The weather is generally hot and humid all year, with a dry season in the winter and a wet, rainy spring and summer. The standard small farm in the area is broken into four sections: one each for oranges, corn, and plantains, and a fourth for herbs and spices used for medicinal and culinary purposes. This last area is where vanilla vines are traditionally found.

aztec exotic

Although much about vanilla is cryptic, most botanists do seem to agree that it's native to Mexico, probably the area along the Gulf Coast north of Veracruz, where it was "discovered" by the local Totonac peoples. Vanilla was definitely well known to the ancient Aztecs; in the middle of the fifteenth century, they took control of the Totonac lands and demanded vanilla as part of an annual tribute.

Europeans first came into contact with vanilla in 1519, when Cortés and his crew arrived in the Americas. Our word *vanilla* is derived from the Spanish *vainilla,* which is derived from the root *vaina,* or "sheath," an approximate description of the bean's appearance. Within a short time, vanilla was on its way back across the Atlantic. Originally it was reserved for use by European royalty in the chocolate drink that Cortés had co-opted from the Aztecs, and also as a perfume, a role it retains to this day in primitive production settings in Mexico as well as in the most sophisticated scent shops of Paris. Vanilla's big breakthrough in Europe came in 1602 when Hugh Morgan, apothecary to Elizabeth I of England, suggested it as a flavoring for other foods besides chocolate.

From the Continent, vanilla was planted throughout Europe's colonial holdings in the tropics. In 1793 the French brought vanilla to their Indian Ocean island of Réunion, known then as Île de Bourbon. The Dutch planted it in Indonesia, and the British brought it to India. Reportedly, Thomas Jefferson introduced North America to vanilla, having traveled all the way to Paris for this native New World novelty. It remained largely unknown in the United States until vanilla ice cream gained prominence in the middle of the eighteenth century.

botanical vanilla

The vanilla vine is a member of the orchid family, the only one of over thirty-five thousand orchids that produces anything edible. It grows in a band 25 or so degrees north or south of the equator. Optimal growing temperatures range from about 68 degrees to 90 degrees Fahrenheit. While it can handle lows down to about 40 degrees for short periods, too much cold will kill the plant; an occasional, unexpected frost has put many small growers out of the vanilla business over the years. Although in Papantla, the plant grows pretty close to sea level, it can survive at altitudes of up to a few thousand feet. Whatever the location, the vine needs about fifteen to twenty millimeters of rain per year, although it also requires a six- to eight-week dry spell after the harvest to accommodate its curing.

The vanilla orchid is a social climber. The vine can't grow well without the close company of "tutor" trees that provide a natural trellis to which the plant can attach itself. The tutors need a two-year head start in order to provide an infrastructure for the orchids. Shade trees are equally essential; they create the critical balance of sun and shadow. Getting the right ratio is more difficult than you might think. Essentially it's akin to trying to set a camera's exposure without the benefit of a light meter. Too much sun causes burning in the vine's delicate leaves; too little stunts the plants' growth.

One of the vanilla farmer's primary responsibilities is to protect the plants' fragile roots, which barely go below ground and are easily stepped on or damaged. To cover them, the farmers build up small mounds of earth and other organic materials around the base of the vines. As in any tropical setting, small plants spring up quickly all around the roots. Farmers hack offenders with machetes, then carefully lay the newly cut organic matter at the feet of the vanilla vines to protect the roots and also to fertilize the plants and enhance flowering.

Ironically, although vanilla beans are the seedpods of the plant, the vines are not planted from seed. Rather, they are reproduced from two-and-a-half- to three-foot-long cuttings from mature models. It takes about two years for a new cutting to attain its optimum height of six to eight feet, and another year before it begins to bear fruit. Left on its own, the plant will continue to grow as high as the tutor will take it. In the wild, for example, a vanilla vine can creep as high as a four-story building. Under cultivation, though, the vines are regularly trimmed and trained to make it easier for the pickers and pollinators, who work on ladders, to reach the flowers in their jungly, hilly habitat.

the pollination

The actual act of pollination is probably the strangest part of the vanilla process. It's done completely by hand. The workers go on foot from plant to plant looking for newly opened blossoms. When they find a flower that looks right to their experienced eyes, they take hold of the base with one hand, then gently push open its petals with the other. Using a small, sharpened stick the size of a stylus, they scrape pollen from the male anther, then stroke the stick over the curved female stigma. Some of the workers still insist that their thumbnail is more effective than the stick, in which case the process takes place without any tools whatsoever. Nine months after pollination, the plant has produced a ready-to-pick, raw vanilla bean. That the pollination almost never happens on its own is incredible to me — the

stigmas and anthers are at most a couple of millimeters apart. Yet the reality is that without the conscious effort of humans, the plant remains celibate.

In the French world of vanilla, the pollination process is still known by its nineteenth-century label, *le mariage de vanille.* Today, a skilled, modern-day "priest" can perform 1,500 to 2,000 "marriages" a day. The process is exceedingly labor-intensive and, without question, limits production and keeps costs high.

The vanilla blossoms, which are almost completely devoid of fragrance, begin to open in late March and continue to do so through April and May. They appear on the plant in clusters, ten or twelve buds per bunch. The modern approach is to pollinate at most only four flowers per cluster, then to cut off the rest of the buds in order to direct the plant's resources toward the emerging pods.

In addition to the difficulties of operating in tropical heat and often on uneven ground, there is an urgency to the pollination. Vanilla flowers open before dawn, usually at about four or five in the morning. Of the 150 or so blossoms produced on a vine every year, only a few open on any given day. Hence the growers must go back day after day during the season to check for new flowers. And that's only half the challenge: from the time the blossoms unfold, workers have only eight to ten hours to pollinate them. If they haven't been fertilized by early afternoon on the day they open, the blooms fall off.

Flowers that have been pollinated will stay on the vine all the way through the growing season until the uncured vanilla beans are harvested in late autumn. Between the just pollinated flower and the vine's green stem is an inch-long ovary, which gradually grows into a raw vanilla bean. At the time of harvest, the pods that hang down from the vines will be somewhere between three and eight inches long, looking not unlike a fresh green bean you might buy at your local produce market. The best beans are those allowed to mature fully on the vine. Picking early in the season saves time but usually yields smaller, less flavorful beans. Workers go from plant to plant, plucking those that are ready. The harvesting is still done entirely by hand; workers press their thumbnails down against the top of their forefingers to sever the beans from the stems. It's something of a minor miracle that anyone actually discovered that you could turn these tasteless fresh green seedpods into the blackened, deeply perfumed, aromatic item we now know as vanilla beans.

benefit plan

Once the beans have been gathered, they're left in the hands of those who do the drying. People in Papantla insist on the Spanish term *beneficiar,* meaning "to benefit." The person who does the curing—a *beneficiador*—takes an essentially flavorless, aromaless green pod and turns it into one of the most amazing and expensive foods in the world.

The process is an old one, having changed very little in the last hundred years. The first step is to "murder" the pods, either by heating them quickly in an oven, as is done in Mexico, or by dipping them momentarily into near boiling water, as they do in the former French colonies. The heat ends the active life of the plant matter, allowing the release of the essential oils inside. The pods are then laid out in the tropical sun until they're so hot they can't be picked up with bare hands. In the evening, the beans are wrapped in thick blankets and brought inside to sweat out the night. The next day, they're brought back into the sun, then back in for more sweating the following evening. The process is repeated for weeks, like some sort of medieval torture. All told, a properly cured bean must go through two dozen of these slow sweats before the curing is complete and they shrivel and turn the familiar deep brown-black that bakers know and love.

Because the curing ends at about the same time that the new buds are beginning to emerge, mid-March brings something of a war of wishes over the weather. The *beneficiador* is happy when there is no rain; hot, dry weather makes it much easier to complete the curing. The grower, on other hand, is rooting for rain, hoping to hasten the arrival of the spring's forthcoming flowering.

If it's sunny straight through the season, curing can be done in under a month. But with clouds or rain or cool weather, it takes longer. Eventually, if the weather fails to cooperate, modern curers will resort to the use of ovens to complete the drying. All the producers I spoke with, however, are adamant that sun-cured beans are better.

When the sun treatment ends, the vanilla is stored to age for an additional month or two to make sure it's been properly cured. If the beans' moisture has not been sufficiently removed, they will mold and be ruined, so they must be watched carefully for trouble signs during this period. Finally, three months or so after being plucked from the vine, the vanilla is reduced to one fifth its original weight. And nearly a year after the season's first blossoms arrive, the new crop of cured vanilla beans is ready to ship.

varieties of vanilla

Although there are actually more than four dozen species of vanilla orchid, only three varieties are used commercially today. Each has its own flavor and character. The two major types in production are grown in different parts of the world. Tahitian vanilla, which is both a variety and a geographical source, is grown only on the island of Tahiti. Almost all the other vanilla commercially available is of the *planifolia* type.

planifolia

This is the most prominent name in the vanilla world. Grown in Madagascar, the Indian Ocean islands of Réunion and the Comoros, Indonesia, and Mexico, the *planifolia* plant accounts for the vast majority of vanilla bought and sold in the United States.

bourbon *planifolia*

Most of this vanilla comes from Madagascar (which accounts for nearly 80 percent of production), with lesser quantities from the Comoros (about 18 percent), and the remainder from the island of Réunion. When you see the term "Bourbon vanilla," it means that the vanilla originated in one of those three former French colonies. All of these islands grow the *planifolia* type. Madagascar vanilla is smooth and rich. Réunion vanilla is said to be sweeter, with a bit more spice in its finish.

indonesian *planifolia*

Although meaningful quantities are being produced, Indonesian is generally regarded as the least desirable source of vanilla. Indonesian beans are cured over wood fires for only a few weeks instead of the long sun-curing used in Mexico and Madagascar. Early picking is also said to contribute to lower quality.

mexican *planifolia*

Mexico is the homeland of vanilla, and Mexican *planifolia* is my personal favorite. Although in the United States it has had a less stellar reputation than Madagascan vanilla, those in the know have long considered it one of the most prized. To my taste, it has a spicy note that's absent in other vanillas.

pompona

Although its rapid rate of reproduction makes *pompona* of interest to agronomists, its low levels of vanillin make it less than appealing to anyone interested in flavor. Little of it is sold in the United States.

tahitian

Tahitian vanilla is a different variety of the vanilla bean. Many food professionals whose opinions I respect hold Tahitian vanilla in high regard. The vine was first brought to this former French colony in 1848, via the Philippines, and Tahitian growers gradually developed a cross between *pompona* and *planifolia,* the results of which have created a botanically different species. Tahitian vanilla has a different chemical makeup than the other two; it contains less vanillin and more heliotropin than the more popular *planifolia* beans. Visually, Tahitian beans are fatter, with thicker skin. They have a more flowery aroma and a noticeable musky note in their flavor, with a somewhat lower seed count.

I can't tell you how many times good customers have come into the store, proudly boasting about the "great deal" they got on vanilla in Mexico. "A big bottle for three dollars!" they exclaim.

What's in those inexpensive bottles is *not* vanilla. As Heriberto Larios, a Papantla *beneficiador,* said, "The labels say vanilla, but it has nothing to do with the plant." Mexican labeling laws, it seems, are rather liberal.

If what's inside isn't vanilla, what is it? While the liquid may exhibit a vanilla-like aroma, it's actually made from coumarin, which is extracted from toxic tonka beans. Smell again and you may notice a somewhat coconutty aroma as well. Taste it and you'll find little that resembles real vanilla. Coumarin is cloying and unpleasant. Those bargain bottles, I'm sorry to say, don't contain anything close to the real McCoy.

vanilla extract

Vanilla extract is an authentic way to bring the best of the bean's flavor into an easily usable liquid form. Invented in 1837 by the American Joseph Burnett, the technique involves running an alcohol and water solution over coarsely chopped vanilla until all the beans' precious flavor has been coaxed into the liquid. Vanilla extracts are graded into folds. A single fold means that 13.35 ounces of vanilla beans have been used for a gallon of extract. A two-fold vanilla has twice that; three-fold triple; four-fold quadruple. By law, pure vanilla extract in the United States must have a minimum 35 percent alcohol by volume.

The quality of the extract depends on the caliber of the raw beans and the care in processing them. Low-temperature extraction protects the fragile flavors; higher heat speeds the process but damages flavor. Neilsen-Massey, a nearly hundred-year-old family-owned firm whose extracts have long been among the quality leaders in this country, uses a cold-extraction process that limits heat levels to a constant 72 degrees Fahrenheit, but working in this cooler climate takes weeks instead of days. A batch of two-fold vanilla made in this manner takes three weeks to make; a four-fold batch takes five weeks.

If the liquid has less than 35 percent alcohol, U.S. labeling laws prohibit the use of the term "extract." There are those, though, who actually prefer less alcohol, in the belief that the alcohol masks some of the flavor of the actual vanilla. Bottles containing less than the approved amount are sold as vanilla essence.

why beans are better

Although extract is far more commonly used in North America, I've become a big believer in working with the whole beans rather than the commercially prepared liquids. When you buy whole vanilla pods, you're more likely to be getting something special—the best beans are generally not the ones that get chopped and blended up with the alcohol for extract. And because a significant proportion of the flavor of extract is alcohol, sticking to the whole beans is more likely to assure a truer vanilla flavor in your food. Using beans requires slightly more effort than pouring ready-to-use extract from a bottle, but it's well worth it.

beananza: buying the best vanilla beans

aroma

There's something magnetic about vanilla's scent. Its aroma is almost addictive. Sniff the bean and you can't help but notice the intensity, the swarthy scent of the tropics. It's no wonder that vanilla's been a key ingredient in the perfume world for so long. A kilo of cured vanilla in my suitcase filled an entire airplane with its sensuous smell every time I opened the overhead bin.

The first way to judge a bean is to hold it up to your nose. The aroma ought to announce itself as soon as you open the package. It should be clean, delicate, sweet-smelling.

vanilla storage

Store whole vanilla beans in a tightly sealed bottle away from exposure to direct sunlight. Properly put away, they should keep easily for a year, probably much longer. Although they won't go bad, the flavor and aroma will slowly dissipate over time. If they do dry out, you can use them to good advantage in Vanilla Sugar (page 394).

Handling the beans for even a matter of minutes leaves your hands smelling sweetly hours later. (Minimal aroma is likely to mean minimal flavor.) The scent carries well from bean to finished baked goods and is one of the surest signs that you've gotten hold of better-quality cakes, cookies, and pastries.

flexibility

Despite the fact that a well-cured bean has lost over four fifths of its original moisture, the best beans are quite soft. You should be able to tie a well-cured bean around your finger without cracking or breaking it.

size

Generally, comparing the size of beans that are the same variety is an indicator of quality: larger is better (remember that Tahitian vanilla is a different variety and naturally tends toward greater girth across its midsection).

a higher percentage of natural vanillin

Of the 250 or so flavor components that combine to make natural vanilla, vanillin is the single largest contributor. (It's also what commercial producers synthesize in labs and later use as imitation vanilla.) Vanillin content will usually be apparent only in the final flavor of your food. But in some instances the vanillin will naturally, if inexplicably, form tiny white crystals on the outside of the bean. The French call this *givre,* or "frost." The *givre* forms only on Mexican or Bourbon beans (*Vanilla planifolia*); you won't see it at all on Tahitian beans. It's generally considered a sign of superior vanilla.

more oil, more seeds

The best vanilla beans have more oil, which creates a resinous dry stickiness, and oil-rich beans will almost stick to your hands. The seeds are the real power behind the flavor of the vanilla bean. When you slice a bean in half, it should be filled with soft, almost spreadable seeds.

synthetic vanillin: wood pulp and coal tar

Driven by the high cost of cured beans and encouraged by the momentum of the Industrial Revolution, which promised to bring just about anything under the control of modern science, nineteenth-century scientists were able to synthesize vanillin in laboratories. In its natural state, vanillin is the single largest flavor component of real vanilla, accounting for about 30 percent of the perceptible flavor of the bean. Unfortunately, there are another 249 flavor components in vanilla in addition to vanillin.

Infinitely less costly and far less laborious to produce, artificial vanillin is used in the majority of commercial baked goods all over the world. Today it's made in large quantities, mostly from wood. You read that right — wood. When mills make paper, they start by cleaning the pulp of coniferous trees. The sulfite solution that comes from the cleaning process is run through a series of chemical extractions to remove what's known as lignin, which in turn is chemically purified, resulting in what's known in the trade as "USP [United States Pharmacopoeia] lignin vanilla." Another artificial alternative is ethyl vanillin, which is significantly stronger than lignin vanilla. This one is made from guaiacol, which is a coal tar derivative. How's that for luscious label copy?

The cost differential is enormous — a four-ounce bottle of pure vanilla extract costs more than $9.50. An equal amount of artificial vanillin can be had for a mere $1.39.

vanilla beans in the kitchen

Here are three simple techniques that let you use real vanilla beans to enhance the flavor of your food.

1. slit and scrape

Simply slit the bean lengthwise with a sharp knife until it separates into halves. Inside you'll see a surfeit of tiny seeds. Using the tip of a small spoon or the point of a paring knife, scrape the seeds from the inside of the pod. Mix them into anything you're making—cheesecake filling, cookie dough, custard.

2. make vanilla sugar

You can make vanilla sugar in two ways. Scrape the seeds into white sugar (see the recipe on page 394 for exact proportions) and let stand for a few days, then use the vanilla sugar instead of standard white sugar in coffee, in French toast batter, or in sweets.

Or, alternatively, if you're scraping beans for other items, you can let the leftover scraped pods dry a bit, then run them through your mini-processor until they're finely chopped. Mix with sugar and let stand a few days.

3. use them as they are

"In Veracruz," the Latin American cooking authority Maricel Presilla told me, "cooks use the whole bean, and they chop it up like any dried fruit and add it to tamales, to stews, to baked goods. You can do anything with them that you'd do with prunes and raisins."

You can add an inch or so of a whole bean to all sorts of sauces (and remove it before serving). Alternatively you can dice the whole pods finely and then cook them right into the food. Bits of bean will simply add flavor and texture to jam and chutneys.

In a savory dish, vanilla can round out flavors, much as half a cup of cognac can complete a cream sauce or the addition of a few anchovies can add enormous depth to a southern Italian fish stew. Diners won't necessarily be able to identify the vanilla in the dish, but they'll enjoy the fullness of flavor that will add enormously to the eating experience.

vanilla sugar

Use vanilla sugar as an ingredient in other dishes, or simply for spooning over French toast or into coffee.

4 vanilla beans
2 pounds sugar

Split the beans lengthwise with a small, sharp knife. With the tip of a small spoon, scrape out the seeds and drop them into a bowl with the sugar. Add the scraped pods to the sugar. Mix the sugar and vanilla well. Store in a sealed glass jar at least 4 days before using. The longer you leave the vanilla in the sugar, the more intense the flavor will become.

makes 2 pounds

vanilla syrup

Vanilla syrup is a good way to take advantage of the flavor of fine vanilla beans. Its uses are almost endless. Some of my favorites include drizzling it over fresh fruit salad, making homemade vanilla egg creams or cream soda, pouring it onto French toast or pancakes instead of maple syrup, and adding it to coffee, tea, or cappuccino.

3 cups sugar
6 vanilla beans
4 cups water

Put the sugar in a large saucepan.

Split the beans lengthwise with a small, sharp knife. With the tip of a small spoon, scrape the seeds into the sugar and mix well. Drop the pods in and add the water.

Bring to a boil, stirring occasionally. Reduce the heat to medium-low and simmer rapidly for 20 minutes, or until the syrup has the consistency of warm maple syrup.

Remove from the heat and let cool to room temperature. Strain the syrup, discarding the solids.

Stored covered in the refrigerator, it will last for 4 months.

makes about 4 cups

mashed sweet potatoes with vanilla

Here's an all-American if somewhat exotic way to make mashed potatoes.

variation

You can remove the potato pulp carefully, then restuff the skins with the potato mixture.

    4 large sweet potatoes (about 3³/4 pounds)
    5 vanilla beans
    4 tablespoons butter, at room temperature
    2 tablespoons chopped pecans, toasted (see page 31)
       Coarse sea salt to taste
       Freshly ground black pepper to taste (optional)
  ³/4 teaspoon maple sugar (optional)

Preheat the oven to 400°F.

Poke the sweet potatoes a few times with the tines of a fork. Bake them until very tender, 45 to 60 minutes. Let stand until cool enough to handle.

Meanwhile, split the vanilla beans lengthwise with a small, sharp knife. Place the butter in a small bowl. With the tip of a small spoon, scrape the seeds into the butter and mash (reserve the pods for another use).

Slit the sweet potatoes open and scoop the pulp into a medium bowl.

Mash the butter mixture into the sweet potato pulp. Stir in the toasted pecans and add salt to taste.

Serve with pepper or a sprinkling of maple sugar, if you like.

serves 4 to 6

allison's excellent pear butter

Allison Schraf, who's worked wonders at the deli for many years, developed this recipe. It's great on toast.

3 vanilla beans
8 ripe Bartlett pears (about 4 pounds), cored and chopped
¼ teaspoon fine sea salt
½ cup water
  Fresh lemon juice to taste (optional)
  Sugar to taste (optional)

Split the vanilla beans lengthwise with a small, sharp knife.

In a large nonreactive pot, combine the pears, salt, and water. With the tip of a small spoon, scrape the vanilla seeds into the pot and add the pods. Bring to a boil, stirring frequently. Reduce the heat to medium-low, and simmer until the pears are very soft, about 30 minutes.

Remove the vanilla pods and strain the mixture through the fine disk of a food mill or a medium-fine sieve.

Return the pulp to the pan. Simmer, stirring almost constantly, until thickened, 10 to 15 minutes. It's ready when a spoonful of the pear butter set on a small plate releases very little juice.

After it's cooled, adjust the sweet-tart ratio with lemon juice or sugar, if you like.

Store in an airtight container for up to a month in the refrigerator.

makes about 3 cups

zingerman's vanilla bean rice pudding

This pudding has been a favorite at the deli for so long now that I can't remember when we first started to make it. It's a great way to highlight good vanilla. We use the wonderful Carolina Gold rice from South Carolina. It's an old variety that makes for a particularly flavorful pudding.

4	cups water
1¼	cups long-grain white rice, preferably Carolina Gold
¼	teaspoon fine sea salt
4	cups whole milk
2	vanilla beans
1	cup dark raisins (preferably Red Flames)
¾	cup firmly packed muscovado or dark brown sugar
1½	teaspoons ground cinnamon
1	rounded teaspoon orange zest
	Pinch freshly grated nutmeg
1	cup heavy cream, plus more for serving

In a large saucepan, bring the water to a boil. Stir in the rice and salt. Reduce the heat to medium, cover, and cook until almost all the water is absorbed, 15 to 20 minutes.

Add the milk, stir, and simmer, uncovered, until the rice is very tender, almost all the milk is absorbed, and the mixture is creamy, about 20 minutes.

Meanwhile, split the vanilla beans lengthwise with a small, sharp knife.

Remove the rice from the heat. With the tip of a small spoon, scrape the seeds into the rice (reserve the pods for another use). Add the raisins, sugar, cinnamon, orange zest, and nutmeg. Stir well. Add the cream a little at a time and mix thoroughly.

Pour into a shallow dish and cool in the refrigerator. Serve chilled but not ice-cold. If you're feeling lavish, offer additional cream on the side to pour over the top of the pudding.

serves 6 to 8

chocolate

So many people speak so passionately about their love for chocolate that I'm wary of getting into the subject. It's not good to mess with people's passions. And it is true that great chocolate is amazing to eat. The thing is, though, that many of us have never had the chance to eat truly great chocolate.

Try this test. Buy a piece of your favorite dark chocolate. To get at the full flavor of the cacao beans in their purest form, you've got to start with the dark stuff. To taste the chocolate properly, you'll need to chew a couple of times to release its flavor components, then stop for a few seconds to give the chocolate a chance to melt in your mouth. (If the chocolate started out cold, this procedure may take a minute or two, so don't rush.)

You can start by noticing the texture, which should be smooth, not grainy or coarse, as the chocolate moves sensually across the top of your tongue and then slowly onto the sides of your mouth.

From there, you can assess the flavor. If the chocolate is well made, there will be some sweetness, but not an excessive amount. Similarly, you should notice a bit of bitterness. Because bitter is a flavor for which we have to develop our taste (as with beer or coffee), those who aren't accustomed to eating good dark chocolate may balk when they detect this bitterness for the first time. But bitterness is a big part of what makes great chocolate great. You may also catch a hint of tartness or wininess, something that novices will never have noticed in a Nestlé Crunch bar. After you swallow, hold off a minute or two before you eat any more. The best chocolates deliver long, enjoyable finishes that stay with you after you're through eating them.

In a well-made chocolate, the sweetness should highlight the cacao's natural complexity and bitterness the way it can when you add small amounts to a cup of good espresso. Excessive amounts of sugar will bring a big burst of sweetness and then . . . nothing. This hollowness is what makes the lack of flavor in low-grade chocolate so glaringly apparent. No wonder people eat whole bars of bad chocolate in a manner of minutes.

getting to know your chocolate

Although we buy it from store shelves, fine chocolate is not a standardized product. It varies from batch to batch, based on all the same sorts of particulars that can influence the flavor of coffee or olive oil. Chocolate is one of the most complex products we purchase. There are a host of factors, some easily identifiable to a consumer, some less so, that contribute to its quality.

Gather together a few friends and do a little chocolate tasting. For $20 or less, you can taste four chocolates of very high quality. For a few dollars more, you can add an equal number of low-grade choices for comparison's sake. As you taste, take notes. In a month or two (or less, if you love chocolate), try it again. I'm always amazed by the differences among various brands and by the very apparent variations in a single brand of chocolate from one batch to the next.

what kind of cacao beans is it made from?

Better stuff always starts with better raw material, which in this case means better varieties of cacao beans. The best chocolates use the highest percentages of Criollo (pronounced kree-O-yo) and Trinitario beans. Criollos are likely to be the closest living relative of the original wild cacao tree, certainly the oldest variety still widely grown. The name, from the Spanish, means "native." Like old seed varieties of other sorts, Criollos are more vulnerable to disease, produce smaller annual harvests, and are generally considered more difficult to grow. But like other old seed varieties, Criollos are also far more flavorful than modern hybrids. Criollos (or Criollo variants) grow primarily in Venezuela, Ecuador, Colombia, Indonesia, on a few of the islands of the Caribbean, and in assorted pockets of Central America.

Forastero (the name means "foreigner") is easier to grow and higher-yielding. It makes up 90 percent of the annual cacao crop world-wide. Consequently, the majority of the world's chocolate is from these beans. Most African and Brazilian cacao is Forastero. While Forastero beans cost less than Criollo, their flavor is coarser and not nearly so complex.

A third variety, Trinitario, accounts for only about 8 percent of the world's cacao, but like the Criollo, it plays a prominent role in the development of the world's most flavorful chocolates. Named for the island of Trinidad, where it originated, Trinitario is a hybrid dating to the eighteenth century. When most of the island's Criollo beans were destroyed by a natural disaster, Forasteros were imported. The new beans were bred with the remaining Criollos, yielding a hybrid that combined the flavor of the Criollo with the durability of the Forastero. Today Trinitario beans are grown in Indonesia, Sri Lanka, South America, and the Caribbean islands.

Although Criollo and Trinitario together account for only about 10 percent of the world's annual cacao crop, they are the beans of choice for any chocolate maker whose primary objective is flavor. Because they sell for more than twice the going rate of Forastero beans, better-tasting chocolates are almost always more expensive.

where did the beans come from?

As with every other agricultural product, the flavor of cacao begins in the soil. Every cacao-producing country (and region within that country) lends a distinctive character and quality to its beans. As with wine, there is no easy way to say, unequivocally, that one region is best. On the contrary, each has its supporters and its critics. And as with wine, there will always be variations within a given area. No country has exclusively good or bad beans. That said, my experience is that more often than not you can count on the fact that chocolate makers who identify the geographical source and variety of their beans are likely to be devoted to developing a more flavorful finished product.

Just as with coffee, many chocolate makers will actively work to blend a series of beans from different sources in order to bring out the best in each. These makers roast each type individually, then mix them. Most guard their blends jealously.

cocoa more / less / lighter / darker / chocolate

what's the cacao content?

This characteristic is increasingly easy for consumers to identify. More and more, good chocolate makers take care to list the specific percentage of chocolate on the label. Higher percentages of chocolate are often indicators of increased chocolate flavor. These percentages are helpful because American legal minimums are much lower than their European counterparts. American milk chocolate, for example, may contain as little as 10 percent cacao; in Europe, the minimum is three times as much. Similarly, a semisweet chocolate in the United States needs only 35 percent cacao. In Europe it must have more than 50 percent. As the cacao content goes up, the percentage of the other major contributor to finished chocolate — sugar — goes down.

Don't assume that all chocolate bars with, say, 60 percent cacao will be essentially identical. The percentage tells you only the volume of cacao that went into the chocolate. What it doesn't tell you is how much of that 60 percent is made up of cocoa butter and how much is cocoa solids (see "Going Dutch or Not," page 410). If you find that one brand of 60-percent chocolate feels creamier on your tongue, it's

likely that the maker uses a mix slightly higher in cocoa butter.

is it made with real vanilla or artificial vanillin?

Happily, a consumer can tell from the label. In my experience, the best chocolates are those made with real vanilla. Vanilla is a natural product with hundreds of different flavor components; vanillin is synthesized from wood pulp to replicate the flavor of natural vanilla's single largest flavor constituent (see page 391). Vanillin hides flavor defects in inferior cacao.

where does the chocolatiers' chocolate come from?

There are thousands of small local chocolatiers who "make their own chocolates," but only a handful of companies left in the world who turn cacao beans into chocolate. Most are big multinational corporations. The small chocolatiers buy their materials in the form of big blocks of chocolate known in the trade as couverture.

As in almost every agricultural industry, the increasing domination of the market by multinationals like Callebaut and Nestlé make it harder and harder for small, quality-oriented growers and independent producers to survive.

blooms without flowers

There are two sorts of chocolate bloom, one not so good, the other serious. The not-so-good kind is cocoa butter bloom, which is generally caused by poor tempering (a process that ensures uniform crystallization) during the making of the chocolate or by uncontrolled temperature changes during storage. The cocoa butter crystals come to the surface and then recrystallize. You can still save this chocolate by melting it down and retempering it, in which case its flavor should be fine.

The second sort of bloom is the result of sugar crystals that have recrystallized on the surface. If you're into home science experiments, you may be able to create this type of bloom by keeping chocolate at very cold temperatures and then bringing it immediately out into a warm, humid room. The condensation will cause the sugar to dissolve and then appear on the surface. This chocolate will look a lot like an opaque window in winter in Michigan, coated with ice crystals. Unfortunately sugar-bloomed chocolate is not salvageable.

Smaller players like Venezuela's El Rey, France's Michel Cluizel, and San Francisco's Scharffen Berger are making concerted efforts to crack their way into this market.

Couverture from chocolate manufacturers comes in dozens of different formulations. Callebaut from Belgium offers dozens of different versions of its couverture. Cacao Barry (now merged with Callebaut) from France and Valrhona offer similarly varied selections. So, too, do big names like Peter's Gibraltar (Nestlé) and Van Leer (recently bought by Callebaut).

Small chocolatiers will experiment with various combinations of couverture to develop their own blend. The process is much the same as any recipe development work. You cook—or in this case melt—you taste, you test, you revise. Eventually you settle on a recipe, which you stick with until a change in one of your suppliers' products or your own palate causes you to reconsider.

"we'd like to buy some bonbons. were they hand-dipped?"

Industrially produced bonbons are made using an enrobing machine: flavored fillings are run through the machine, which then coats ("enrobes") them with liquid chocolate. While the machine increases production speed, chocolate traditionalists are adamant that the best bonbons are those that are hand-dipped, which means exactly what it sounds like. Someone grasps the firm center between his thumb and first two fingers and then dips it—often up to three or four times—into liquid chocolate. The result is a crisper and more delicate shell.

how good are the additional ingredients?

Lots of chocolate bars or bonbons contain almonds or other nuts. But just as all chocolates aren't the same, neither are nuts. Generally, European almonds and hazelnuts have lower moisture and hence more flavor than their American counterparts. Similarly if someone is using liquor, you'll want to know if it's Grand Marnier or merely an anonymous orange brandy.

how fresh is the chocolate?

While chocolate bars are essentially shelf-stable, their age does play a part in their flavor. The best chocolates are living products, and their

flavor will continue to change long after they are packed. If you were to pull three bars from the same batch of chocolate, eat one the day it's made, another six months later, and another after one year, there would be differences in flavor. Dark chocolates are at their best about six months after being made. Many say that the maturing time rounds out the flavor and mellows any sharpness. After that the flavor will begin to diminish very slightly, until, at about twelve to eighteen months, the quality of the chocolate begins to degrade and lose liveliness, luster, and complexity.

Buyers will note that European chocolate bars are stamped with sell-by dates. They can be helpful, though take them with a grain of salt. Some makers choose dates that are so far ahead that stores often leave the bars on the shelf well after freshness has fallen off. Others set the dates so soon after production that perfectly good chocolates appear suspect.

With bonbons, shelf life is much shorter. In general, freshly made chocolates have more butteriness and are far livelier in flavor. But their flavors start to deteriorate within as little as two weeks. Boxed chocolates are made to last longer, but they often lack the liveliness of their fresh counterparts.

how does it look?

Good chocolate should have a high-gloss sheen. A dull, flat finish is undesirable. With bonbons, beware of sunken centers, which can indicate excessive age.

An obvious flaw is what's known in the chocolate world as "bloom" (see page 403). You'll know it by sight—instead of a shiny,

smooth, evenly colored brown, the chocolate will look blotchy, uneven, almost dusty, and gray. Chocolate in its bloomed state tastes different because its physical structure has been altered. It won't be harmful to eat, but it certainly won't have the flavor or texture that you'd expect from fine chocolate that's been properly handled.

how does it feel?

Unlike M&M's, good chocolate should melt in your hand. Because it starts to soften at about 95 degrees Fahrenheit, or just below body temperature, chocolate with a high cocoa content will begin to coat your fingers in less than a minute. If a chocolate doesn't start to soften in your hands, you've either got one that's quite low in cocoa or very high in stabilizers. Either way, it's not what you want.

how does it sound?

Crack a corner off a well-made chocolate bar in a quiet room and you should hear a solid snap, which is caused by the crystalline structure of the cocoa butter.

an annotated history of chocolate

sixth century A.D. The Mayans begin cultivating cacao on the Yucatán Peninsula.

1200 The Aztecs take over Mayan society. Mayan growers send cacao beans to the Aztec court in Tenochtitlán, where they are roasted, coarsely ground, and mixed with hot water, ground chiles, and toasted cornmeal (as a thickener) and consumed by the cupful. Consumption at court is estimated at about two thousand pitchers per day.

1494 Columbus returns from Spain, carrying the first cacao beans to Europe. Nobody knows what to do with them.

1502 On his fourth voyage to the Americas, Columbus becomes the first European to experience the taste of cacao, most likely in what we now know as Honduras. Focused on his search for pepper, he pays scant attention to the little brown beans.

1519 Cortés and his crew of Spanish conquistadors come to the Aztec court of Montezuma, where they discover that cacao beans are used as currency (possibly the first recorded instance of money growing on trees). Cortés seizes Mexico and brings cacao back to Europe in 1528.

1580 The first European factories for roasting and grinding cacao are built in Spain.

c. 1600 Spaniards discover Criollo cacao in Venezuela. Although the plant travels poorly and is rarely transplanted with success outside the area, cacao production booms.

1615 The fourteen-year-old Anna of Austria, daughter of King Philip of Spain, marries the fourteen-year-old Louis XIII of France and moves from Madrid to Paris. With her comes the Spanish custom of drinking cups of chocolate. Chocolate quickly becomes the drink of the European aristocracy. The most decadent among them drink it only in the boudoir and preferably in bed.

1620 The Catholic Church opposes the introduction of chocolate. One French cleric writes that chocolate is the "damnable agent of necromancers and sorcerers." Inevitably this denunciation only increases interest in the exotic beverage.

c. 1625 The bishop of Chiapas Real in Mexico orders the excommunication of anyone caught drinking chocolate within church walls. Local chocolate-loving women then boycott the church until the bishop mysteriously takes ill and dies from drinking poisoned chocolate. This case of death by chocolate is never solved.

1628 The Englishman Thomas Gage provides the first written records of chocolates given as gifts. A long and sweet tradition takes hold.

1662 The renowned English physician Henry Stubbe claims that one ounce of chocolate contains more fat and nourishment than a pound of meat; he begins writing medical prescriptions for chocolate.

Samuel Pepys recommends drinking chocolate as a cure for hangover.

Cardinal Brancaccio of Rome pronounces that drinking chocolate does not violate fasting for Lent or other religious observances.

1684 Records show 167 cacao plantations with 450,000 trees in the Spanish territory of Venezuela. A small number of families, only 172, control them. Spain has a monopoly on cacao production.

c. 1700 In South America, cacao growing spreads to new territories. Brazil and Peru contribute good-sized quantities. In Europe, the use of spices in drinking chocolate subsides. In

England, Hans Sloane, physician to Queen Anne, begins to brew the beverage with milk instead of water.

1712 A Boston apothecary offers chocolate for sale.

1728 The first water-powered mill for grinding cacao is set up in England by Walter Churchman.

c. 1745 Still the principal exporter of cacao, Venezuela now boasts more than 1,500 plantations. About 20 percent of cacao production in the area is controlled by the Catholic Church.

In Europe, high taxes on chocolate lead to smuggling and adulteration. Chocolate is often cut with cornmeal, brick dust, ground seashells, and other unsavory substances. In England, chocolate smuggling is made punishable by a year in prison and a fine of £500.

c. 1750 In Paris, an aging Voltaire popularizes the now famous combination of hot chocolate and hot coffee.

1755 The first direct cacao trade takes place between South and North America.

1765 Dr. James Baker of Massachusetts sets up the first chocolate factory in North America. Later he went on to develop Baker's Chocolate (a sweet dark German-style chocolate).

1786 New York City boasts a mere three chocolate makers.

1810 Venezuela still accounts for half of the world's cacao production.

1819 François-Louis Cailler opens Switzerland's first chocolate factory.

1822 Britain imports 230 tons of cacao.

1824 John Cadbury opens his first tea and coffee shop in Birmingham, England.

1828 Using a large wooden screw press, a Dutchman named Coenraad Van Houten invents a method to separate cocoa butter from cocoa solids, making what we now know as cocoa powder. This discovery leads to the development of eating chocolate as we know it today.

1830 Britain imports 400 tons of cacao, nearly double the amount imported only eight years earlier. Over half is held for use by the Royal Navy as an easy-to-store, nutritious way to help keep men at sea healthy.

1832 Franz Sacher, the Viennese hotelier, invents the Sacher torte, one of Europe's most famous chocolate cakes.

1847 The firm of Fry and Sons in Bristol, England, introduces the first eating chocolate.

1849 In Europe, people shift from drinking chocolate to eating it. Cadbury sells eating chocolate in England.

Domingo Ghirardelli, an Italian confectioner, comes to California looking for gold. By 1885 Ghirardelli's company imports about 200 tons of cacao.

1850 Britain imports 1,400 tons of cacao, three and a half times the total of twenty years earlier.

1851 The British medical journal *Lancet* reports that more than 90 percent of cocoas on the market are adulterated.

1860 Etienne Guittard leaves France for San Francisco, where he starts his chocolate company.

1876 In Switzerland, Daniel Peter invents solid milk chocolate with the help of Henri Nestlé's powdered milk.

1879 While trying to make the perfect chocolate bar in Switzerland, Rodolphe Lindt invents the conching machine. Conching breaks down the sharp sugar crystals and coarse grains of ground cacao to make an ultrasmooth paste.

1893 At the World's Columbian Exposition in Chicago, Milton Hershey buys newly available chocolate equipment. The following year he introduces the Hershey's Milk Chocolate Bar, and in

1905 he opens his new factory in Pennsylvania.

1900 World cacao production reaches 75,000 tons.

1907 Hershey's Kisses are introduced, copied, it's said, from Mr. Hershey's competitor, Wilbur's Buds.

1910 Chocolate bars are introduced to United States Army rations.

1912 Nabisco introduces Oreo cookies.

1920 The Baby Ruth, named for the daughter of former President Grover Cleveland, is introduced in Chicago.

1921 Hershey's adds little paper streamers to its Kisses.

1923 The Milky Way bar is introduced in Chicago. In Pennsylvania, H. B. Reese, an ex—Hershey employee, introduces his Reese's Peanut Butter Cups.

1925 Valrhona begins making chocolate in France.

1930 The chocolate chip cookie debuts at the Toll House Inn on the outskirts of Whitman, Massachusetts.

1941 Forrest Mars introduces M&M's to Americans.

1990 World cacao production reaches 1.5 million tons. Venezuela, once the dominant player in the world market, now accounts for less than 1 percent of production.

1997 Scharffen Berger Chocolate starts production in San Francisco.

turning beans into bars: how chocolate is made

the harvest

Cacao trees grow in a band of tropical rain forests, from 20 degrees north to 20 degrees south of the equator. The tree looks unusual, with blossoms and fruit that jut straight out from the trunk and the larger branches. The tree yields fruit four or five years after planting, is mature at eight years, and continues to produce effectively until it is about thirty.

At full size, the fruit, also known as a cacao pod, looks a bit like a tropical melon; Europeans might say it looks like a rugby ball. As the pods ripen, they pass from green to gold to reddish brown. Ripe pods—about five to ten inches long and four to five inches wide—are harvested from the trees by pickers working with machetes. The fruit is filled with a pinkish white mucilage (called the "baba"), which surrounds about twenty to forty individual cacao beans. A good tree yields about thirty to forty fruit each year, or about twelve hundred beans per year, enough to make a half pound or so of finished chocolate.

the fermentation

Small groups of workers armed with machetes sit cross-legged on cement in front of piles of newly harvested multicolored pods. Picking up a pod in one hand, they heft the machete in the other and hack into it. The beans are removed from the pods, then brought indoors to begin the process of fermentation, which eliminates their natural rawness and bitterness and begins to unlock the flavors of the cacao.

As the beans are exposed to the light and air, fermentation begins, enhanced by the sugars in the mucilage. Naturally occurring yeasts and bacteria in the air transform the sugars into alcohol, which is in turn transformed into acetic acid. During the early stages of the fermentation, the temperature in the piles of the beans rises and a strong vinegary smell fills the rooms. The germ of the cacao seed is killed, leaving the bean ready for the complex series of changes to come. As fermentation proceeds, the beans are moved regularly from one wooden bin to another to keep them from overheating and to maintain the appropriate amount of air movement. The temperature is kept at about 120 degrees Fahrenheit.

At this point, the beans begin to develop their distinctive flavor. Better and more consistent fermentation leads to much bigger, better flavor in the cacao. By the end of the process, the mucilage has liquefied and drained off, leaving the beans darker and wrinkled and looking a bit like deep brown oversized almonds. Good Criollos (the best beans) take forty-eight to ninety-six hours to ferment; less flavorful Forastero beans generally take only six to seven hours.

drying, storing, and shipping

After fermentation, the now naked beans are spread on enormous slatted wooden trays in the sun to dry for five to seven days, during which time they are raked regularly. At night, the trays of beans are rolled indoors (or simply covered) to protect them. During the drying, the beans get darker and deeper in color and their moisture content is reduced from about 60 percent to 8 percent of their total weight. Once dried, the beans can be stored and then shipped to producers, the best of whom have historically been located in Europe.

During storage and shipping, the beans must be well aerated. If they're kept in areas with poor air circulation, they can turn moldy and musky.

roasting, winnowing, and grinding

Everyone knows that the skill of the coffee roaster is essential in producing a better-tasting cup. With cacao, it's the same, but many more steps are involved.

While all chocolate makers roast their cacao, the details of the process vary based on the machinery they use and the size of the batch. The beans are cleaned, then roasted at low heat for thirty to sixty minutes. In contrast to coffee, which is roasted at temperatures that exceed 400 degrees Fahrenheit, cacao is usually heated to between 220 and 250 degrees. Roasting enhances cacao's flavors, bringing out the sweetness and some of the complex floral or caramel notes.

Producers who buy lower-grade cacao may overroast to mask a lack of complexity. Underroasting is equally problematic because it fails to maximize the beans' flavor and leaves an unpleasant hint of green.

After roasting, the beans are shifted to a winnowing machine, in which two narrowly spaced rollers crack the outside of the shell, mixing pieces of it with the nib, or the core, of the cacao. Air then pulls the lighter-weight shells and chaff up while the heavier nibs fall. The nibs are sorted with screens, then sent along to the grinding room. At this stage, the nibs resemble broken-up nutmeats and contain about 53 percent cocoa butter.

Newly freed from their shells, the nibs are milled into a dark brown, gritty, viscous paste that's known as "chocolate liquor" (the term indicates no connection to alcohol, only to the fact that the mixture is a liquid). During the grinding, the nibs liquefy. As they are crushed, the natural fat (the cocoa butter) is released. The heat from the friction of the grinding works the mass into a thick paste of cacao solids and cocoa butter. While it's warm, chocolate liquor remains in a liquid state; allowed to cool, it solidifies and becomes "unsweetened chocolate liquor."

making eating chocolate

To make finished eating chocolate, sugar and more cocoa butter are added to the chocolate liquor. The best chocolates also contain pure vanilla. A bit of lecithin, a natural stabilizing agent, is usually added as well. The higher the percentage of cacao used, the darker the finished chocolate. Conversely, the more sugar you add, the sweeter and less chocolatey the chocolate.

To make milk chocolate, powdered milk is added to the mixture as well. The quality of a milk chocolate depends on the ratio of chocolate liquor to sugar and milk, the quality of the milk, and the quality of the chocolate liquor itself.

conching, tempering, and molding

Invented by Rodolfe Lindt in Switzerland in 1879, conching gives finished chocolate its melt-in-the-mouth smoothness. Prior to Lindt's invention, chocolate was much grittier and coarser. In addition to smoothing texture, conching (chocolate makers pronounce the "ch") also helps to mellow the flavor by releasing volatile acids.

To conch chocolate, stainless-steel rollers move back and forth through the liquid chocolate, much like a kneader for bread dough. Many producers also add back some cocoa butter at this stage for a more richly textured chocolate. Longer conching generally produces a smoother, silkier texture, while too little can cause the high notes to take over, creating an overly intense winy flavor. New equipment is making it possible to reduce conching time while still producing very high-quality chocolate.

By alternately raising and then lowering the temperature of the chocolate, chocolate makers "temper" it, a process designed to cause the cocoa butter molecules to crystallize uniformly for consistent storage and shelf life. In the process, tempering protects the chocolate's texture, gives it sheen, and adds snap to the finished product.

Once the chocolate has reached the right level of smoothness, it is poured into molds. After a gentle cooling period, the chocolate is unmolded, then wrapped and packed, ready to ship worldwide.

going dutch or not?

To make cocoa powder, producers use a technique patented by the Dutchman Coenraad Van Houten in 1828. Chocolate liquor is subjected to high pressure, forcing out the cocoa butter. The solids that remain after the cocoa butter has been removed resemble a dry cake, which is then ground into powder. The "Dutch process" adds alkaline salts (potassium or sodium carbonates), leaving the powder darker in color.

The more alkali used, the darker the color of the cocoa and the less pronounced its flavor. The dark color often misleads consumers, who believe the dutched cocoa will be richer than undutched, when in fact it will taste less so. The cocoa powder used in Oreos, for example, is nearly black but (nostalgia aside) the amount of actual chocolate flavor it delivers is negligible. Dutch processing has been said to mellow the flavors of cacao, but many in the industry argue that it actually masks the defects of lower-quality beans.

Robert Steinberg, one of the founders of Scharffen Berger Chocolate, who spent many months researching, tasting, and testing dozens of cocoas, is one of those who challenges the assumption that the best cocoa powder is made using the Dutch process. In addition, he says, many producers make cocoa powder from lower-cost, poorly fermented beans that they wouldn't be willing to use for better-quality chocolate for eating or baking. As a result, many cocoas are bland or, worse still, harsh, metallic, bitter, or slightly salty, with little real chocolate flavor.

By using the most flavorful, well-handled, properly fermented beans, Scharffen Berger has been able to bring all the positive characteristics of the best eating chocolates to its cocoa powder. There is a real difference in the delicacy, aroma, complexity, and balance of its cocoa powder, which is noticeable in cakes and other baked goods.

best cocoa brands

Scharffen Berger's cocoa powder is very good.

Valrhona cocoa powder is dutched, but consistently very flavorful. Like Valrhona, Pernigotti cocoa powder from Italy is dutched but has a good, deep cocoa flavor.

best brands

valrhona chocolates from france

If you like your chocolate dark, dense, and intense, Valrhona is for you. The firm was founded in 1925, but for most of its first sixty years, it sold its chocolates only to other manufacturers and chocolatiers. In 1986 Valrhona began to market to consumers, and the quality of life of chocolate lovers everywhere has been better ever since. Although it was bought by a large multinational a few years back, the quality of the chocolate continues to be excellent.

Valrhona pioneered many of the trends toward better chocolate that have now become accepted as the norm, including clearly labeling the cacao content in its bars and marketing single-origin cacaos. The firm uses only real vanilla in its chocolate. Valrhona produces more than a dozen different bars. Here are a few of my favorites.

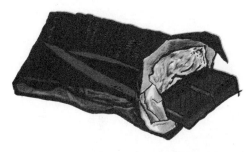

LE NOIR AMER More than 70 percent cacao makes for a chocolate bar with bold, dark, flavors that aren't hidden behind the sweetness of sugar. There's just enough sugar to bring out the complex, winy flavors of the top-quality cacao beans that Valrhona relies on. If you like dark chocolate, this is the standard against which to judge all others. It's well balanced, with a long finish and very full flavor.

GUANAJA DARK CHOCOLATE Made with a 70 percent cacao, this chocolate is made exclusively from beans grown on the island of Guanaja, which Columbus encountered in 1502 on his fourth voyage to the Americas. Valrhona Guanaja has an exceptionally long finish and hints of nuts and coffee.

MANJARI With 64 percent cacao, this varietal Indonesian chocolate has a notable fruitiness, a smooth texture, and a light copper color that's characteristic of Criollo beans from the Indian Ocean.

LE NOIR VALRHONA At 56 percent cacao, this chocolate falls in the middle of the Valrhona range. Made with cacao that comes from the Caribbean and Southeast Asia, it has deep nutty notes and a nice wininess that take a minute or two to emerge.

LE LACTÉ One of the most flavorful milk chocolates on the market, it's made with a minimum of sugar, 41 percent cacao, and a touch of vanilla. (By contrast, commercial American milk chocolate can have a cacao content as low as 15 percent.) It has a caramelly flavor.

el rey from venezuela

Cacao and chocolate have a long history in Venezuela: the area south of Lake Maracaibo is probably the source of the original Criollo cacao trees. Venezuela once supplied half of the world's chocolate, but with the discovery of oil off the Venezuelan coast in the early twentieth century, cacao lost much of its cachet and economic importance. Today Venezuela supplies less than 1 percent of the world's cacao, but the

flavorful beans it does produce are highly prized.

Thanks to the efforts of the seventy-year-old family firm El Rey, Venezuelan Criollo cacao is now attaining some well-deserved attention. El Rey is the first South American firm to follow quality cacao production all the way through from beans to finished chocolate bars, bringing state-of-the-art equipment and a commitment to quality to Venezuelan chocolate making. Its chocolate is made exclusively with Criollo cacao, yielding chocolate bars with a complex character and a fine, lingering finish. The company uses only real vanilla and makes its own cocoa butter, ensuring maximum flavor. Long conching ensures smoothness and creamy mouth-feel.

El Rey lists its cacao content on the label. Each of the following chocolates is named for one of the typical shade trees that shelter the cacao in Venezuela.

APAMATE DARK CHOCOLATE High in cocoa butter, this bar has a very creamy mouth-feel, a delicately fruity aroma, and a nice finish. It contains 73.5 percent cacao.

GRAN SAMAN EXTRA BITTER At 70 percent cacao, this bar is dark, mysterious, and much less bitter than comparable European-made chocolates I've tried. There's some fruitiness in the finish, along with an array of interesting high notes. Dark-chocolate lovers won't want to miss it.

MIJAO DARK CHOCOLATE At 61 percent cacao, Mijao is a well-balanced dark chocolate. It hints of dried stone fruits such as plums and possibly apricots. It's not as sweet as Apamate or Gran Saman, and it melts more easily and has a silkier mouth-feel.

BUCARE BITTERSWEET To my taste, Bucare, at just 58.5 percent cacao, is the most distinctive of the bunch, with lovely fruit flavors that fill the mouth. It has a wonderful aroma and appealingly toasty finish.

CAOBA DARK MILK I'm not by nature a milk chocolate lover, but El Rey's Caoba Dark Milk is delicious. With a much higher cacao content, 41 percent, than most milk chocolate, it has a creamy texture, a flavor filled with caramel and toffee notes, and a notably fruity finish.

scharffen berger from the united states

Scharffen Berger is something of a study in American ingenuity, a solid symbol of our national move toward better-quality food. The first American chocolate-making company to be founded since the middle of the

White chocolate is not technically chocolate — it is made from cocoa butter, milk, sugar, and vanilla but no cacao solids. At its best, it is a delicious confection. Unfortunately most white chocolate is not great. Many manufacturers treat cocoa butter with heat, leaving richness but removing flavor. El Rey's Icoa is made with 100 percent natural cocoa butter taken from pure Venezuelan cacao beans. Icoa may be the most fragrant, delicious white chocolate I've ever tasted.

twentieth century, the firm is the brainchild of John Scharffenberger and Robert Steinberg. Since they founded the company in 1997 in San Francisco, the two have been relentless in their pursuit of bringing a quality American-made chocolate bar onto the market.

The company buys only top-grade beans, uses only real Tahitian vanilla, stone-grinds its beans, and conches with great care to produce the finished bars. The chocolate is equally excellent for eating and baking.

michel cluizel from france

Michel Cluizel is one of the only family-owned chocolate makers in France that still makes its own chocolate couverture. The company got its start just after World War II in southern Normandy when Marc Cluizel, a retired pastry chef,

converted his laundry room into a chocolate workshop. Working with varietal beans from its own farms in nearly every producing region in the world — Sumatra, Venezuela, Ghana, Java, Ivory Coast, among others — Michel Cluizel creates some of the most interesting chocolates around. The company is also (to my knowledge) the first commercial chocolate maker to produce bars without any added lecithin. Michel Cluizel uses only real vanilla. Visit the shop on the rue Saint-Honoré if you head to Paris.

Here's a list of some of the firm's best chocolate bars.

AMER 85% CACAO If you truly love the beautifully bitter, barely-a-hint-of-sweetness sensation of really, really dark chocolate, this one's for you. It has very interesting spicy notes, with a touch of cinnamon in the finish.

AMER 72% CACAO This dark and mysterious bar has surprising high notes and a toastiness reminiscent of light roasted coffee. Of course, it contains real vanilla. Made without lecithin, it has an exceptionally creamy mouth-feel.

AMER 60% CACAO This bar has a long finish and very creamy mouth-feel and is one of the first to be made without the lecithin stabilizer.

AMER AU GRUÉ A bar of delicious dark — though delicate — chocolate, Amer au Grué contains 60 percent cacao and is loaded with crunchy cacao nibs.

JAVA MILK BAR Named for the island from which these cacao beans come, the Java Milk Bar has a 50 percent cacao content, making it one of the chocolatiest on the market and much less sweet than most any other milk chocolate. Javanese beans give it a dark toasty flavor.

storing superior chocolate

Air and light are the enemies of finished chocolate. Store chocolate away from direct sunlight. Keeping air out is best done with a dual wrap of aluminum foil and then plastic — direct contact with the plastic for any length of time can alter the aroma and even the flavor of the finished chocolate.

Storing at 60 to 68 degrees Fahrenheit is optimal. Temperature swings of any sort are undesirable.

Plain chocolate won't actually spoil, so you're never in danger of harming anyone by serving old chocolate. But it is generally agreed that milk chocolate will begin to lose flavor after nine to twelve months, and dark chocolate after twelve to eighteen.

chocolate sandwich

This treat is truly a delicious dessert or afternoon snack. Some chocolate fiends even fry it up for breakfast. I like it with dark chocolate, but you can certainly make it with any good milk or white chocolate as well.

- 1 tablespoon butter, at room temperature
- 2 ½-inch-thick slices sourdough bread
- 1 ounce (2 large squares) dark (bittersweet) chocolate

Butter each slice of bread on one side. Sandwich the chocolate between the nonbuttered sides.

Heat a small skillet over medium heat. When the skillet is hot, place the sandwich in the center. Set a bowl or plate on the sandwich to weigh it down. Cook until the bottom of the bread is lightly browned, about 3 minutes. Turn the sandwich over and brown the other side, about 3 minutes more. Serve warm so the chocolate can drip down your wrists as you eat.

serves 1

food dance café's double chocolate pudding

Kalamazoo, Michigan, isn't on many travel itineraries, but any time you're driving along I-94 between Detroit and Chicago, you should make time to stop at Julie Stanley's excellent Food Dance Café. Her chocolate pudding is incredible. Cacao nibs, the intensely flavored, crunchy nutmeats of cacao beans, are sold in specialty shops.

1	vanilla bean
4½	cups whole milk
1	cup sugar
⅓	cup dark unsweetened cocoa powder, preferably Scharffen Berger or Valrhona, sifted
¼	cup all-purpose flour
⅛	teaspoon fine sea salt
2	large eggs
4	large egg yolks
10	ounces dark (bittersweet) chocolate, broken into small pieces
4	tablespoons butter
½	cup cacao nibs, toasted (optional)

Split the vanilla bean lengthwise with a small, sharp knife.

In a medium saucepan, combine 4 cups of the milk and ½ cup of the sugar. With the tip of a small knife, scrape out the seeds from the vanilla bean pod into the saucepan. Add the seedless pod too. Heat over low heat, stirring. As soon as the mixture starts to simmer, remove from the heat. Let it stand for 10 minutes, then discard the vanilla pod.

Meanwhile, in a medium bowl, combine the remaining ½ cup sugar with the cocoa powder, flour, and salt. Whisk in the remaining ½ cup milk until you have a smooth paste.

Whisk ¼ cup of the warm milk-vanilla mixture into the cocoa mixture until well blended. Pour this mixture back into the saucepan and whisk well to combine. Bring to a simmer over low heat and cook, stirring frequently, until fairly thick, about 5 minutes.

Meanwhile, in a small bowl, whisk the eggs and yolks together until well blended.

Very slowly whisk 1 cup of the warm chocolate mixture into the eggs until well combined and smooth.

Slowly stir this mixture back into the saucepan, whisking constantly until it thickens, 3 to 5 minutes. Do not allow it to boil.

Remove from the heat and place on a wooden cutting board or other heatproof surface. Add the chocolate and butter to the saucepan and whisk until smooth.

Pour the pudding into eight custard cups or small bowls. Refrigerate for 2 to 3 hours, or until the pudding is set.

For added chocolate intensity and textural contrast, serve the pudding garnished with the cacao nibs if you like. **serves 8**

dark chocolate granita

While this recipe takes some kitchen time, it's a great dessert, especially in warm weather. The proportions are set to keep the chocolate flavor intense and the finished granita not overly sweet.

- 5 tablespoons dark unsweetened cocoa powder, such as Scharffen Berger or Valrhona
- ¼ cup sugar
- 2 vanilla beans
- 2 cups boiling water
- ½ cup whipping cream (preferably not ultrapasteurized) for serving

In a medium heatproof and freezerproof glass or metal bowl, combine the cocoa and sugar. Split the vanilla beans lengthwise with a small, sharp knife. With the tip of a small spoon, scrape out the seeds and stir them into the cocoa-sugar mixture. (Reserve the pods for another use.)

Slowly stir in the boiling water, ¼ cup at a time, stirring well each time you add more liquid and taking care to dissolve any lumps that form.

Place the container in the freezer, uncovered. Every 40 minutes or so, stir vigorously. Continue until the mixture has reached the consistency of chipped ice, 3 to 4 hours. If it gets too hard, take the container out of the freezer to thaw a little, checking it often.

When you're ready to serve the granita, whip the cream in a chilled metal bowl until soft peaks form.

Serve the granita in four chilled dessert cups with a dollop of whipped cream on top.

serves 4

zingerman's funky chunky dark chocolate cookies

We bake these cookies in four-inch rounds, but you can just as easily portion them into smaller sizes. They are on the firmer end of the chocolate-chip-cookie spectrum, as opposed to the very soft fudgy cookies some prefer. Muscovado sugar—traditional-process unrefined brown sugar—brings out the best in these cookies.

variations

You can play with chocolate varieties almost endlessly, using darker, lighter, or milkier versions to fit your taste. Or, to tantalize your guests, you can use two different chocolates in the same batch. You can also alter the nuts—try pecans or hazelnuts.

$1^2/_3$ cups all-purpose flour

$3/_4$ teaspoon baking soda

$3/_4$ teaspoon fine sea salt

2   vanilla beans

8   tablespoons butter, at room temperature

$1/_2$ cup firmly packed muscovado or dark brown sugar

$1/_4$ cup plus 2 tablespoons sugar

1   large egg

8   ounces dark (bittersweet) chocolate, broken or chopped into bite-sized pieces

4   ounces walnut halves and pieces, toasted

Preheat the oven to 350°F.

In a small bowl, whisk together the flour, baking soda, and salt.

Split the vanilla beans lengthwise with a small, sharp knife. With the tip of a small spoon, scrape out the seeds into a large bowl (reserve the pods for another use). Add the butter and mix together. Stir in the sugars and egg until creamy. Gradually stir the flour mixture into the butter mixture. When thoroughly combined, stir in the chocolate pieces and nuts. Chill the dough for 10 minutes in the refrigerator.

Line two baking sheets with parchment paper. For each cookie, scoop out $1/_4$ cup of the dough and roll it into a ball, then press out on the cookie sheet into a $3^1/_2$-inch round, about $1/_4$ inch thick. Place the rounds of cookie dough about $1^1/_2$ inches apart on the baking sheets.

Bake on the middle rack, one sheet at a time, for 7 to 10 minutes, or until the cookies are golden brown and baked through. Cool on the baking sheet for 1 minute, then transfer to a rack.

Serve hot or cool and store for up to 2 weeks, although to keep them that long you may have to hide them well.   *makes 12 large cookies*

tea

Sometimes seemingly simple, everyday items can be the most difficult to track down if you're determined to buy and enjoy the best. Take tea: twenty years ago when I started my search, I headed from booth to booth at a huge trade show in New York, hoping to hear something substantive about the teas on display. One by one, I'd ask each purveyor what made his tea so terrific. With each stop I grew increasingly frustrated. Nine times out of ten my inquiries were met with something simplistic along the lines of

"Well, ours is fresher and better quality."

The frustration didn't stop at the show. The deeper I dug, the more clear it became that the industry had essentially made it as tough as possible for the average consumer to learn how to assess its products. Sure, every teashop had shelves filled with fancy packages, plastered with lovely little bits of tea-drinking lore about dragons, kings, queens, emperors, and the like. But if you actually wanted to know what distinguishes a great Darjeeling from a mediocre one, you'd be in trouble. The more I learned, the more I realized that while there was great tea to be had, it wasn't being had by anyone I knew. Most teas on the market were sold with fine-sounding names that meant absolutely nothing. Though the situation has improved somewhat, it's still far from ideal.

tea ball of confusion

Consider the well-known Orange Pekoe, for instance. Since it's emblazoned on millions of tea bags, you might imagine it as a badge of quality. Even worse, you might be—as I was for years—fooled into thinking it was orange-flavored tea. Both assumptions are wrong.

Orange Pekoe is, in fact, a leaf size, one of many grades used by tea growers in countries that were once part of the British Empire. The name is derived from the House of Orange, Holland's royal family. Although they get little recognition for it today, the Dutch were leaders in bringing tea to Europe in the early years. And when the first teas were presented at court in the Netherlands, someone had the idea of naming them after the royal house. "Pekoe" comes from *pek-ho,* or *bai hao,* a Chinese word meaning "white down" because the tea buds are covered with a faint white fuzz. The term is moderately meaningful to tea merchants because it's frequently associated with other, more material issues connected to quality. But for the purpose of trying to purchase better-tasting tea, Orange Pekoe is as helpful as the adjective "round" would be in relation to cheese.

Writing in the 1930s, William H. Ukers, author of the tea industry standard *All About Tea,* stated, "Through unfortunate advertising, many consumers, especially those in the United States, have come to regard the term 'Orange Pekoe' as a synonym for excellence of quality." And he went on, "In no sense is the term a description of quality." So what is it doing on all those labels? Beats me.

Although the name Darjeeling at least tells the consumer where the tea was grown, the quality can vary widely, depending on when it was grown and more specifically where, and whether it's been blended with filler.

Tea is a subject to which one could easily devote one's life. But given that most folks have other things to do, the following pages will provide you with a workable guide that will help you purchase, prepare, sip, and savor a truly exceptional pot of freshly brewed hot tea. All you need is a clean kettle, cold fresh water, a good teapot, some great tea to put in it, and a willingness to learn.

what is tea?

The first step toward tastier tea is getting a few facts straight. The term *tea* is misused and abused more than the speed limit on the interstate highway system, seemingly (and incorrectly) applied to almost any hot beverage that isn't coffee or hot chocolate. For our purposes, let's agree that tea will mean the stuff that comes from the tea plant—known scientifically as *Camellia sinensis.*

Mind you, there are a number of other very nice beverages you can brew up from dried leaves: chamomile, mint, mugwort, and the like

can be very good, but because they don't come from the tea plant, they aren't tea. The French refer to these herbal beverages as *tisanes,* giving them their own identity.

Native to China and northeastern India, the tea plant is an evergreen, requiring relatively warm, humid climates with eighty to ninety inches of rain a year. Left to its own devices, the Chinese version can grow to be fifteen feet tall, the Assam variety as high as sixty feet. Trees take roughly three to five years to produce leaves good enough for processing. Each spring delicate white flowers—about an inch across—appear, followed by a small fruit, which surrounds a nutmeglike seed (or two or three).

Other than water, tea is the most widely enjoyed beverage in the world. There are a few thousand varieties of it growing in about two dozen countries around the globe. Most are in Asia and Africa, though of late there's an ever increasing amount of tea being grown in Argentina as well. And there's even a small bit grown in South Carolina.

opiate of the people?

Any book about tea will tell you that it's one of the oldest beverages in the world. Tea was already being widely consumed in China by the fourth century A.D. Although the three schools of tea brewing that emerged in China—boiling, whipping, and steeping—sound like ancient tortures, these techniques were about pleasure, not pain. It was during the Tang Dynasty, from 618 to 907, that the esteemed poet Lu Yu wrote the *Cha Ching,* the first book about tea. At that time, it was almost exclusively a drink for the

The little lift we get from a cup
of tea has certainly been part
of its attraction to tea drinkers
over the centuries. All natural
teas have some caffeine. Black
teas have a caffeine content of
3 percent (about half that of a
cup of black coffee), green teas
1 percent, white slightly higher
than that. Oolongs lie somewhere in between, at about 2
percent. The caffeine in tea is
believed to be absorbed more
slowly than that of coffee but
may stay in the system longer.

As with decaffeinated cof-
fees, decaffeinated teas tend
to lose substantial flavor and
character during the decaf-
feination process. The best of
the lot are decaffeinated using
pressurized carbon dioxide
(ask your supplier which
method was used). As with decaffeinated coffee, decaf tea
retains a bit of its original caffeine content.

upper echelon of society, prepared by boiling the leaves, often in conjunction with salt, rice, spices, or citrus.

During the Song Dynasty, from about 960 to 1279, tea was often
pressed into bricks and used as currency. The beverage was prepared by
whipping the powdered leaves into a froth in hot water. Spices ceased to
be added to tea, replaced instead by the gentler jasmine and lotus blossom. (The Song-era style of whipping is thought to be the source of
today's Japanese tea ceremony.)

During the third era, that of the Ming Dynasty, from 1368 to 1644,
the three major methods of tea-leaf preparation—black, green, and oolong—came to prominence. By this time the Chinese were steeping tea
leaves in hot water, though they brewed it in tiny pots, in a much more
concentrated form than today. Because Europe discovered tea at the
end of this era, steeping is the style of tea brewing we have adopted in
the West.

Nearly all of the tea available in its first years in Europe was green,
the predominant form in China at that time. It first arrived on the Continent in the Netherlands in 1610. The tsar of Russia received his first
tea leaves in 1618, a gift from his Chinese counterpart. From the end of
the eighteenth century to the beginning of the twentieth, when the
Trans-Siberian railway was built, tea was shipped to St. Petersburg by
camel caravan, a trip that usually took nearly a year and a half to make.
(Tea was so popular that the Russian Empire imported about six thousand camel-loads a year. Strangely, the aromas that the scent-sensitive
teas picked up from the camels are likely the origin of the flavor profile
for much of the tea sold today as "Russian Caravan.")

Tea made it to France in 1636 and arrived in North America before it
got to Britain. Only in 1650 did it make its way there, and by that time
coffee had established a strong following. Tea was expensive, certainly not a commoner's cup. By the end of the
seventeenth century, the cost of a pound of poor-quality
tea in England was the equivalent of almost a week's
wages. Adulteration was rampant. Because green tea was
easier to doctor than black, people gradually switched to
the latter, hoping to ensure authenticity in their purchases. (This shift was so strong that Westerners still
consume mostly black tea, in contrast with the Chinese,
who drink far more green.) In the eighteenth century, tea
gained new popularity when it began to become the British
breakfast beverage of choice, replacing ale.

CHINA

Tea bags are . . . a convenience. If you're in a spot
where convenience counts
more than flavor, then by all
means use them. There are a
few bags on the market that
have better tea in them. But
not that much better.

The big problem with tea
bags isn't the bags. It's that
the tea that goes into them is
rarely the most interesting.
Additionally, bags are best
suited to broken-leaf teas,
which are usually inferior, or
teas that infuse more quickly
but lack complexity, character, and balance.

If you want good tea, you
have to brew it from loose
leaves. It takes just as long to
boil water for a tea bag as it
does for a pot of really good
tea leaves.

By the late eighteenth and early nineteenth centuries, the British had become so dependent on tea that the empire was steadily going broke trading silver to get it from the Chinese. In an effort to stem the cash flow, the British brought Chinese tea plants to India in 1834 and proceeded to grow them over much of the colony. (Ironically, eleven years earlier tea was discovered in the wild in Assam on the edge of the Himalayas.) Over the next century, Indian tea exports dramatically increased, and the British dependence on the Chinese offerings was reduced. In a further effort to overcome their shortage of hard currency, the British began to trade Indian opium to the Chinese for chests of tea.

Ultimately, tea's connection with colonial status and its link with unjust British taxes led to its rapid decline in popularity in the United States, with coffee taking its place.

In 1857 tea was brought to Ceylon, now Sri Lanka. After the island's coffee plants were devastated by a blight in 1880, Sir Thomas Lipton, a globetrotting Scotsman, moved aggressively to replace coffee with tea, then went on to build the Lipton brand of Ceylon tea into the giant of the Western tea world. In 1909, a New York tea trader named Thomas Sullivan inadvertently invented the tea bag when he sent out tea samples in small silk sachets. He intended for his customers to empty the tea into pots and brew it as they always had. But some misguided souls poured the water directly onto the sachets, altering tea history forever.

a guide to great tea

Getting great tea from the plant and into the pot is complex, which I suppose is why many of us revert to the low-stress solution of accepting a mediocre tea bag when we could have so much more.

Hundreds of factors can contribute to the flavor of a tea. Although tea comes from the opposite end of the globe from wine (grape production and tea growing require completely different climatic conditions), the topography, language, and images of wine are a good guide to follow when it comes to getting a handle on the nuances of great tea. In each case, one basic plant produces thousands of wonderfully complex flavors. The altitude and soil in which it was grown, the time of year it was picked, the care and handling of the leaves, the method of processing, and about a hundred other issues come into play.

green, black, white, or oolong?

A couple of thousand years ago, freshly plucked tea leaves were boiled as is, straight from the bush. But what we're accustomed to today are leaves that have been processed primarily in one of four ways, resulting in green, black, white, or oolong teas. Contrary to popular misconceptions, all four come from the same plant.

processing tea

All four types of tea start out similarly on their path from bush to brewing. The best producers get the leaves from field to factory in a matter of hours. The first step in the process is called "withering." While the technique varies from one area to the next, the concept is essentially the same everywhere. Heat is used to soften the leaves and reduce the moisture content from their natural level

of 75 to 80 percent. Withering prepares the leaves for further processing and softens them so they can be rolled without breaking into pieces. Great care has to be taken not to let the leaves get too hot; if temperatures rise above 85 degrees Fahrenheit, quality will suffer. If the leaves have been handled carefully during the harvest, they should remain green after withering. Poorly handled leaves will often discolor and turn brown in the same way that apples will if you bruise them.

When the withering has been completed, the leaves are then rolled. Many of the best teas are still rolled by hand. The rolling crushes the cell walls of the leaf, releasing its essential enzymes and natural flavor. Rolling styles are often unique to particular teas. Some are left loose, others are twisted very tightly, while still others are rolled into small round balls. In general, the tighter the rolling, the longer the tea will have to infuse during brewing, and the longer its shelf life is likely to be.

After rolling, the leaves for green tea are quickly heated, or fired, putting a stop to any enzymatic activity or advanced levels of oxidation. The tea leaves are then dried, protecting them for storage. Most of the world's consumption—centered in Asia—is of green tea. A cup of green tea tastes literally greener, hinting of everything from garden herbs to freshly mown grass and a thousand fine flavors in between.

Black teas take the process one step further.

Instead of immediately firing the leaves to stop their development, producers allow oxidation to turn the leaves the familiar dark brown-black that most of us in the West associate with tea. (In China, black teas are often referred to as "red teas" because of the color of the liquor they produce when brewed.) The process releases new and interesting flavors from the leaves by allowing the naturally occurring polyphenolic flavonols to combine with oxygen in the air. (The oxidation process is often referred to in the tea world as "fermentation.") In general, the shorter the oxidation, the lighter the color of the leaves and the lighter the liquor will be after brewing. When the oxidation has reached the optimal point, the leaves are fired to put a stop to the process. Some of the heat from the firing causes the natural sugars in the leaves to caramelize, adding to the flavor of the finished tea.

Oolongs lie somewhere between green and black teas. They're partially oxidized (but not as long as black teas are), then fired. They're almost always made from the largest of tea leaves (known now as "souchong"), which you'll recognize distinctly in the pot even after you brew them. Because the amount of oxidation varies, you can find oolongs that are almost green, on up to those that are very nearly black, and pretty much anything in between. The greener oolongs have a big following in Asia. They're excellent after meals. The darker oolongs tend to be more popular in the West.

Little known in the West, white teas are the "simplest" of teas since the leaves are merely packed, withered, and carefully dried to kill the plant's natural active enzymes and to prevent oxidation. Unlike green, black, or oolong, white tea leaves are rarely rolled at all. Further enhancing their delicacy, many are plucked before the new spring buds even open. The dry leaves generally have a pale, silvery appearance, hence the name "white tea."

how does it look?

In and of itself, leaf size is rarely a major factor in quality, but it's often a good indicator. Since the whole-leaf teas are generally those that have been handled least, they are likely to be better. Also, because they will have less surface area exposed to the water, their flavors tend to be more delicate. Broken-leaf teas, on the other hand, are generally from the lower end of the quality spectrum. They will, however, give a stronger infusion due to the high ratio of leaf surface exposed to the water.

In any case, when you're buying tea, the leaf should be consistent in size, a sign of careful sorting.

where was it grown?

Once you know whether you're buying green, black, white, or oolong, the next thing to find out is the origin of the tea. And although the answer to that question probably ought to be simple, it isn't.

For openers, if you ask folks what sort of tea they like, they may well tell you "English tea." Certainly their favorite brand may have been blended in Britain. It may even have a nice Union Jack or a profile of the queen on the package. But neither of those things really tells you much about its quality or flavor. The tea may have been processed in England, but it's been picked elsewhere. (For more on English tea, see page 437.) What you need to know is where the tea was actually grown. China, India, Taiwan, Sri Lanka (Ceylon), and Japan are the big names I look for (though you can watch out for interesting teas that may arrive from Kenya or other spots in Africa).

You also need to know in which region of each country the tea was grown in. Just as France's Bordeaux and Burgundy have their own identities, flavors, and aromas, so too do India's Darjeeling and Assam.

how was it picked?

To quote from the classic *Tea Growing,* by C. R. Harler, "To make fine teas, fine leaf must be harvested." In the tea world, that generally means leaves taken only from the end of each branch on a bush, the most tender and flavorful growth on the plant. The best leaves are picked by hand, plucked with a downward movement of the thumb and then dropped into cloth bags or baskets. By contrast, the mechanical picking done now in many places often gathers tea by stripping the entire bush rather than just the tender leaves, resulting in inferior tea.

when was it picked?

To assess the appeal of a tea, I want to know both the season and the year in which it was harvested. One without the other is helpful, but on

its own neither can really give you the background you need.

Let's start with the year. For openers, good tea, like wine or olive oil, varies from year to year. A few years are great, others all right, some so-so. On occasion one year may not be acceptable at all. To me, this variability is one of the beauties of great tea.

If you're considering a purchase, the merchant ought to be able to tell you what year's harvest the tea in question came from. Having been properly processed, even low-quality tea won't really ever spoil. But tea does lose life as it ages. (Pu-erh teas from mainland China are an exception, since they're actually made to be aged for years.) Modern packaging techniques have made freshness less of an issue. Many tea products are now vacuum-packed, so shelf lives are longer. In general, black teas hold their life longer than greens, so be more careful about buying the latter. But the general rule of thumb is that ideally you should buy teas from the current crop year.

In which season was the tea harvested? Unlike so many agricultural products that have one primary harvest season, tea leaves are plucked many times during the year. In some areas there could be up to twenty or even thirty pickings, known in the tea trade as "flushes," in a single year.

Remember that the tea plant is an evergreen; in subtropical climates, as in Sri Lanka, southern India, or East Africa, it may continue to produce new leaves almost year-round. And much to the frustration of anyone who wants a black-and-white answer to the question of which tea to try, the same bushes on the same estate picked at two different times of the year can—and will—yield different-tasting teas. In cooler climates, where the temperature range between winter and summer is more than 20 degrees Fahrenheit, the plant will have a dormant period in winter, as is the case in most of China, northern India, or Japan, where leaves begin to emerge anew each spring after the annual hibernation period. As a general rule, many of the most interesting teas will come from this first new season's growth, known in the trade as the "first flush." Why? Because the plant has had all winter to store up its resources; by definition, the enzymatic makeup of the leaves will be special when they first emerge in the spring.

Teas from the second picking are also, more often than not, among the best. They're usually more in balance than the first-flush teas. While they may lack a few of the wilder high notes you get in a first picking, they tend to be rounder, bigger, and weightier in flavor. So in many cases, these teas are considered the standards against which others are judged. In some instances, the third picking will be very good as well. After that, complexity and flavor tend to drop off significantly.

Take one of my favorites, Darjeeling. During the cool winter months, the tea plants are basically dormant; no new leaf growth emerges. When the buds begin to appear in the spring, the fresh shoots are particularly flavorful. Hence, the best teas from this special district in northeast India are picked from either the first growth of new leaves each spring (the first flush), or the second, late-spring picking (the second flush) six weeks or so later.

Similar patterns are found in every producing region. Certain seasons are associated with the most flavorful teas. In Assam, also in northeast India, it's the second-flush teas that are considered best because they have more body and weight than the first picking. In Taiwan, the winter-season teas taken from the November and December harvest are considered the most flavorful. On Sri Lanka, tea is gathered almost year-round. On the east side of the island, in the Uva district, the best teas are harvested at the end of our

summer. On the west side, in Dimbula, the premier pluckings are in February and March. In Japan, where there are usually three or four main harvests a year, the first picking of the season — generally early in May — yields the leaves that go into making the best teas for Gyokuro (see page 436) and for the ceremonial tea, known as *tencha,* or *hiki-cha.* The second harvest produces leaves for Sencha tea (see page 437), which ranges from good to superb.

How can you spot old tea? First, test the dry leaves before you buy. They should have some spring when you squeeze them. Next, test the leaves after you brew. Again, the leaves of old teas will quickly lose their spring after steeping. Fresher leaves, on the other hand, will bounce back much better, like a lively bread dough. Finally, taste-test. This instruction is hard to follow if you don't know tea at all. But the more you drink, the easier it is to tell when you've got old tea in the pot. Fresher teas will have a certain sparkle, a notable liveliness, while older teas will lack luster.

shortcut to a great tea: find a great supplier

The easiest way to get consistently great tea is to familiarize yourself with your own tastes and put yourself in the hands of a good tea merchant. You may have to buy through the mail. How do you know who's reliable? A good tea dealer should stand behind his tea. If you want a taste, ask for a sample. If you don't like what you bought, return it.

my favorite teas

As much as I've learned over the years, I still feel like a novice in the tea world, where aficionados have done nothing but study the subject for longer than I've been alive. There are other exceptional teas beyond the ones on this list so don't feel limited by it. Anyone who's adamant about tea quality will probably be happy to share a list as well.

Let me introduce my favorites by confessing to being a tea purist. My preference is to stick with what in the nineteenth century were known as "straights" and are now called "classics," or "self-drinkers." To my mind, these teas, which have been enjoyed for ages and likely will be for ages to come, are the greats. Although this traditionalist approach rules out a lot of the fancy-sounding blends and trade-name teas, there's still more than enough variety to keep your palate pleasantly entertained for a couple of lifetimes. You won't come across many flavored teas like Earl Grey on my list, but that doesn't mean you shouldn't be drinking them.

In buying teas, it's helpful to know the following:

1. Type: green, black, oolong, or white.

2. Country of origin: China, India, Japan, Sri Lanka, etc.

3. Region in which the tea was produced (if possible).

4. Name of the variety: Wu Yi, for instance, is a wonderful oolong tea from China. The name refers both to the region in which the tea is grown and to the variety.

5. Brand name: of value only if you know and trust the taste of the people who run the company.

honey, vanilla, chocolate, and tea

india

In India, teas are generally sold by referring first to the region in which they're produced, most prominently the areas of Darjeeling, Nilgiri, and Assam. Nearly all the tea produced in India is black.

first-flush darjeeling

Most passionate tea drinkers have one or two types of tea that they return to over and over again for enjoyment. For me, that tea is Darjeeling.

Darjeelings are a good example of both the best and the worst of the tea world. Unfortunately, most of what's out on the market is mediocre. But when you find the best, you're drinking exceptional tea. If you've never had a truly great Darjeeling, I can't suggest it strongly enough. If you're not sure if you've ever had a great Darjeeling, it's safe to say that either you haven't had one or you don't like Darjeeling. Either is certainly possible. Exceptional Darjeelings make up only a small percentage of the tea sold with DARJEELING on its label. And Darjeeling flavors—especially those of first-flush teas—aren't for everyone.

Wedged among the ancient kingdoms of Sikkim, Nepal, and Bhutan, Darjeeling sits in the foothills of the Himalayas. The rajah of Sikkim ceded the area to the British in return for protection against neighboring Nepal. The name means "Land of the Thunderbolt." The town itself faces Kanchenjunga ("Five Magnificent Snow Treasures"), the third highest mountain in the world, roughly 28,000 feet tall.

Tea growing in Darjeeling is a relatively recent phenomenon, dating to the middle of the nineteenth century. At the time, the town itself was tiny, used as a resort by the well-to-do. The mean temperature of the area is only a couple of degrees higher than it is London, but there's a broad range in temperature as you move through the seasons and up into the mountains. The terrain makes planting and picking exceptionally difficult, adding a lot to the cost of Darjeeling in comparison to tea grown on more level ground. Using the all-important orthodox hand-plucking method, which takes only the newest two leaves and the bud, you need about 11,000 shoots to make a pound of good tea.

In Darjeeling, tea grows at altitudes ranging from 2,000 to nearly 10,000 feet. Generally, but not always, the higher the altitude, the better the tea. Four thousand feet is considered an im-

the cost of fine tea

Tea is one of the most affordable luxuries in the world. At your first exposure to the price of great tea, you may think it a bit expensive. But even a rare first-flush Darjeeling with the seemingly sky-high price of $80 per pound breaks down to less than 40 cents a cup! It's amazing that so much tea pleasure can be had for such a good price.

portant milestone in this regard. Equally or more important than altitude is the skill of the person who guides the work and decides when to pluck, how long to wither, how tightly to roll, how heavily to oxidize, and how hot to fire. The impact of the estate manager on tea quality is probably higher in Darjeeling than anywhere else.

First-flush Darjeeling is often referred to as the "Beaujolais Nouveau" of tea. Harvested in March or April, they are the first leaves of the new season. The dry leaf will be thoroughly tinged with green leaves, with plenty of gold and brown flecks. How much green shows in each tea is a function of the level of oxidation that's chosen by the estate manager. Any given garden may have a hundred different first-flush teas to offer from the same year: variability in plucking, oxidation, and altitude means that each is different. Some are good, some so-so, some superb.

Once brewed, a good first-flush should be a light amber—not deep red like many Chinese or African black teas. Good first-flush Darjeelings have a high flavor profile; they can be light and almondy, with a flowery scent that suggests fresh apricots. They also have a distinctive puckery mouth-feel from naturally high tannin levels.

second-flush darjeeling

When the first-flush season ends in late April or early May, the tea bushes are trimmed back sharply, then allowed a few weeks to recover. When the buds reemerge in late May or early June, the second-flush season is under way.

Second-flush Darjeeling should provide greater balance and more bottom, or bass, in its flavor than the first flush, which tends to be dominated by its high notes. The cup may be a bit darker in color with a more rounded Muscat flavor that is reminiscent of freshly cut mangoes. Second-flush Darjeelings can be very complex teas with all sorts of interesting characteristics: nuttiness, a bit of menthol, fruity pineapple. The flavor will be smoother, with a longer finish. In fact, long finish is one of the distinguishing characteristics of a good Darjeeling. If the finish is lacking, it's often a sign that the tea may have been blended; a particularly dark cup may have had Assam leaves added to cut costs and bulk up flavor.

There's usually a correlation between complexity of color in the dry leaf and the flavor of the brewed tea. When you're buying Darjeeling, if you see reds, golds, and greens mixed in with brownish black tea leaves, you are likely to have found a great tea. Generally speaking, with Darjeeling, the larger leaves are also more complexly flavored.

Both first- and second-flush Darjeelings are taken from single-source gardens (also referred to as estates). Like farmhouse cheeses, these teas have been planted and produced by a single grower, the equivalent of a great estate wine.

Although an estate name alone is not a guarantee, it's an indication that the tea will be good. There are roughly one hundred gardens within the Darjeeling district, with names like Selimbong, Makaibari, Gielle, Poobong, and Namring.

I'd like to tell you that three or four of these gardens consistently produce the best teas, but in my experience, each year's crop is quite different. Even within a single garden there will be wide variations in flavor. I've tasted ten different samples of first-flush Darjeeling all from the same year on the same estate, and each has its own flavor and character. (My picks each year are sold under the Zingerman's Universe O' Tea label.)

After the second-flush season comes the rainy season. With so much precipitation, the plant's growth accelerates and leaves are picked roughly once a week. Though it comes from the same plants as the exceptional first- and second-flush teas, it has little flavor and even less character. Unfortunately, this rainy-season tea makes up the majority of the Darjeeling harvested each year. Sip a cup of an estate Darjeeling from the second flush next to one from the rainy season and you'll barely know the two were from the same country, let alone the same garden.

Following the rainy season come autumnal flushes. Although tea writers consistently credit these teas with being of good quality, I've rarely come across any that get me excited.

The best Darjeelings are never inexpensive. Demand is high, especially in Germany and Japan, and yields are low. Top quality and low grade combined, Darjeeling teas account for less than 3 percent of what's grown in India. And of the more than 22 million pounds of Darjeeling produced each year, only about 10 percent is from the first picking and another 10 percent from the second. One industry expert estimated that only a quarter of that is exceptional, meaning that a mere 5 percent of the tea grown in the region in a given year is actually going to be top-quality.

nilgiri

Darjeeling isn't all there is in the Indian world of tea. Of late I've come upon a line of outstanding teas from Nilgiri in the Blue Mountains of southern India. These teas have set a whole new standard for the region. They're sold under the Bespoke label by the tea writer James Norwood Pratt and the Nilgiri native and tea seller Devan Shah. Pratt and Shah sell four single-estate teas picked in January, when temperatures drop to right above freezing at night, and the first buds of the season are newly emerged on the tea plants. All of the estates are at a high altitude (roughly 6,500 feet), and the teas are excellent. Tea from the Havukal estate has been my favorite of the four.

assam

Assams from northeast India can also be excellent. As with all teas, you should avoid the low-grade, broken-leaf, mass-market Assam whose flavor is of little interest. Stick to whole-leaf single-estate teas. The second flush — usually picked from mid-May to mid-June — is traditionally the most highly valued in the tea world and offers the highest complexity of flavor.

china

While Indian teas are generally labeled according to the region in which they're produced, China teas are usually classified by type — green, black, oolong, white, scented, or the rare and unusual Pu-erh. China teas also often have names that are associated both with particular styles of preparation (how tightly the leaves are rolled, how long the leaves are fired) and with the region in which that style of tea is prepared. If that sounds confusing, it is.

China teas can be particularly challenging to buy in the United States, in part because of the translation of names from the original Chinese into English, varied pronunciations, and less-than-straight paths to sourcing them. Happily, premium-quality China teas are now becoming more available, due to the dedication of a few importers who buy direct from the gardens rather than the brokers. Ultimately your best bet is to work with a source you trust, use the information you've gathered, taste a lot (especially comparable teas from different sources), take notes, and enjoy the exploration process.

People like Joshua Kaiser at Rishi Tea, David Lee Hoffman at Silk Road Tea, and Sebastian Beckwith at In Pursuit of Tea know what's happening in the many tea-producing districts of China and have traveled extensively within the country to identify reliable sources.

What follows are just a few of the China teas that have tickled my fancy of late.

oolong

If you want to study the flavors and aromas of fine tea in depth, oolong is the place to start. There are so many great teas in this category, from greener, lightly oxidized, and flowery, to fuller-bodied teas with rich flavors and complex aromas, ranging from toasted chestnut to nectarine to wildflower. Oolong teas are classic accompaniments to Asian cuisine.

Wu Yi tea comes from the mountainous region of the same name in the northern districts of the Fujian province of China, which gained international attention as the location of the film *Crouching Tiger, Hidden Dragon*. Oolong tea processing—semi-oxidation and the techniques of special firing, shaping, manipulating, and drying of the tea leaves—began here in the middle of the eighteenth century. The region's mineral-rich, rocky cliffs and constant mist contribute to the signature flavor and aroma of the authentically processed tea. The finest of these teas come from exceptionally old trees, some more than a hundred years old, and have a superb rich flavor, which can range from slightly earthy with subtle toasty notes to concentrated accents of wildflowers and stone fruits. Some of the best of the region's tea is the Wu Yi Yan Cha, or Wu Yi "Rock-Cliff" tea.

Ti Kuan Yin, or Iron Goddess of Mercy, is another excellent oolong. It's from the famous tea city of Anxi, in the southern area of Fujian. Superior grades have a baked-grain or toasted-chestnut flavor with a light golden to amber cup and a deliciously drinkable, full flavor.

Known as the "champagne of teas," Formosa (Taiwan) oolong, at its best, is truly incredible. Known also as Dong Feng Mei Ren, or Oriental Beauty, it has an amazing aroma of fresh wildflowers and a deliciously delicate flavor almost devoid of astringency. The best grades will present a lingering finish suggestive of nectarines or peaches. Bai Hao, or White Tip, Formosa is an easier-to-find grade of the rare Oriental Beauty.

china green

Lung Ching, or Dragon Well, is the classic name in China greens, and when it's good, it's really good. It's got a pleasant bittersweet green intensity with a flowery and toasted-chestnut aroma. Rishi Tea's organic special-harvest Dragon Well has been excellent. Another on my list of favorites has been Yellow Mountain Mao Feng from the famous Huang Shan tea district in the Anhui province. This classic China green has a mild pine-needle and toasted-grain nose with a flowery and savory finish.

china black

Black teas are known in China as "red teas" for the color of the brewed liquor (as opposed to the color of the dry leaf). Yunnan has long been one of my favorite ways to start the day. It comes from a mountainous region in southwest China called Kunming near the borders with Vietnam, Myanmar (formerly Burma), and Laos, an area that many believe to be the birthplace of the tea plant. At its best, Yunnan is full-bodied, rich, and almost creamy, with a wispy smokiness and a hint of pepperiness that creep across your tongue. It's one of the rare teas that combine aroma with interesting flavors and solid strength. Rishi Tea's organic Golden Needle from Yunnan has been very good.

Another worthwhile China black is Keemun. Typically strong, full-bodied and fragrant, Keemuns are often rather romantically referred to as the "Burgundies of China" teas. Unfortunately, as is so often the case in the tea world, the romance frequently exceeds the taste. Rishi Tea has had some excellent Keemun that it sells as Special Reserve. Good Mao Feng ("hair point") Keemun is an even more finely twisted leaf and has a balanced flavor with notes of roasted sugar cane, chocolate, pine, and red wine. If you can find top-grade Hao Ya Keemun, that, too, can be very good—choose the A grade (rather than B). It can be delicate, complex, and slightly sweet with a touch of smoky pine.

china white

Only recently gaining recognition in North America, white teas are gentle, complex, and sweet. They can be quite refreshing in the summer because they're low in caffeine, and they're great in the evening and go well with delicate foods.

Bai Mu Dan is from the Fujian province, located along the coast south of Shanghai. The name means "white peony." It has lots of silver needle tips with a lively aroma and smooth taste with hints of nuts and bamboo. Yin Zhen, also from Fujian, is a rare tea that consists of only hand-selected, silvery, down-covered needlelike buds. Brewed, it yields a crystalline pale liquor with a subtle, fresh fragrance and savory, sweet finish. Rishi Tea's Organic Snow Buds from Fujian province are superb, mellow, and surprisingly savory with a finish that's almost chestnutty.

scented teas

I don't like most flavored teas, jasmine teas excepted. The best, in my experience, are those that are blended with natural flowers rather than sprayed with flower-scented essences. After the scenting, the petals are removed, and the finished tea is left with a fine aroma and delicate flavor.

Yin Hao jasmine, long, thin, well-twisted leaves of lightly oxidized oolong, is made with real jasmine petals, picked early in the day before they open. The petals are then piled next to the tea leaves. At night, the petals open, and their aroma is absorbed by the tea. The leaves are removed the following morning. For the best jasmines, the process is repeated seven times with new jasmine petals each time. Jasmine Dragon Phoenix Pearl is one of the most beautiful teas I've ever seen; jasmine-scented tea leaves are hand-rolled into tiny bundles that look like ancient Egyptian scarabs made from fine green-gold thread. The leaves unfurl like dragons, then rise like phoenixes, as they steep. It has a soft, sensual jasmine flavor with none of the jarring, overpowering perfume of lesser-quality jasmine teas. (Rishi Tea has developed the first and at this point the only certified organic Jasmine Pearl.)

japan

Almost all the tea produced in Japan is green.

Gyokuro (the name means "precious jade dew" or "pearl dew") is the top of the line of Japanese green teas, one of the few great low-grown ones. Gyokuro is costly but quite special. It accounts for less than 1 percent of Japanese tea production. It's one of the mellowest of the green teas, made from the first picking of shade-grown tender leaves and buds and cultivated in the area near Mount Fuji. The bushes spend their final three weeks shaded by mats, which protect the leaves and filter out 90 percent of the sun's rays, increasing the tea's chlorophyll

china pu-erh tea

Pu-erh is to the tea world what balsamic is to the realm of vinegar. A rare, long-aged offering, it's known outside Asia only to a small circle of aficionados. Not everyone likes Pu-erh tea. It has an earthiness that can be likened to a walk through the forest during a spring thaw.

Pu-erh originated in the Xishuangbanna district of Yunnan in southwest China. Authentic Pu-erh owes its uniqueness to a fascinating symbiotic relationship between a specific variety of tea and a pair of wild yeast strains that live in the Yunnan.

A properly made Pu-erh tastes pleasantly full-bodied with an elemental earthy and distinct camphor aroma. The most prized are aged for many decades and can carry prices as high as $200 a pound, but there are some well-made teas that are only a few years old, affordable, and very good. Pu-erh teas stand up beautifully to spicy meat dishes or rich sauces.

Like balsamic vinegar, Pu-erh appears in many less-than-authentic forms at far lower prices than what the real thing might cost. Some poorly made teas that have only one yeast have an overly musty or sometimes downright moldy aroma. Even the best Pu-erh can spoil due to improper storage. Know thy source!

level and keeping its tannin content to a minimum. The tea is picked in mid-May, then steamed, shaped, dried, and aged for six months to one year before the final processing. The Gyokuro, released in October, is particularly flavorful, so I drink as much as I can while it's at its peak.

For the majority of tea drinkers in Japan, Gyokuro is a special, often seasonal treat. What they drink through the year is Sencha tea. The best Sencha teas are rolled by machines that duplicate the exact hand movements of the master tea producers. These teas have clean, green, refreshing flavors.

Kukicha is a mellow but complexly flavored tea made from early-season tea leaves and broken twigs. Rishi Tea's Kukicha Hatsukura Supreme has been excellent.

tea for the british and irish palate

I spent a solid ten to twelve years trying to figure out why the tea we carried at Zingerman's failed over and over again to meet the expectations of visiting English men and women. I'd search and sample, then offer up the tea, only to meet with further rejection. I fared no better with Irish visitors. I'd serve some of the best estate Darjeeling, and they'd send it back wailing that it was "weak." I'd order in expensive Assams, said to be the basis of all good English Breakfast blends, and they, too, were turned away. I tried Ceylons. No luck.

I was on the verge of giving up when Mike Spillane, a longtime tea merchant in San Fran-

cisco, mentioned a type of tea I'd never heard of. The answer, he said, was CTC.

Although hardly any tea drinker has ever heard the term, CTC tea is what most people in the Western world drink today. In the same way that you could study baking for ten years without ever coming across any information on Hostess Twinkies, I'd been looking in the wrong direction. I'd assumed that I must not be buying good enough tea, so I kept trying to buy better. But to replicate the roughness that British and Irish tea lovers are generally looking for, you have to go down — not up — the quality ladder.

CTC stands for "crush-tear-curl." Introduced in the early 1930s, it refers to the machine processing of tea leaves. The plucking of the best teas, by contrast, is referred to as "orthodox" manufacture, picking primarily by hand and processing so as to preserve and protect the structure of the leaf. In contrast to the understated elegance of handpicked and traditionally prepared tea leaves, CTC tea comes out looking something like little brown Grape-Nuts.

Ultimately, anyone who wants to buy really good tea can start by asking for leaves that come from "orthodox" production. That means that they were handpicked, taking at most the newest two leaves and the bud off the end of each branch, and that the processing did not use CTC methods. In and of itself, orthodoxy doesn't guarantee quality, but it is a likely indicator that what you've got is good. This is not just an issue of aesthetics. No old-time tea connoisseur will argue that you can make a great cup out of CTC leaves. Once it's been machine-processed, the leaf basically becomes a different product. As the use of more cost-effective machine techniques continues to grow, orthodox manufacturing is becoming as endangered as farmhouse cheese. If we're not careful, we will lose the opportunity to enjoy traditional teas as we have known them. But just as consumer interest has helped to support a return to traditional cheesemaking and artisan bread baking, so, too, can our efforts help to support the work of those who stick with orthodox tea production.

CTC processing alters the flavor and, more important, the mouth-feel of the finished tea. It brews up quickly to give impatient tea drinkers color and strength in minutes. And it gives the tea that really big, bold, high-tannin (often referred to in the tea world as "creamy") mouth-feel that Anglo-Irish tea drinkers insist on. Only CTC tea is thick enough in the cup to stand up to a dose of milk and sugar. Its quick-brew, quick-to-color attributes have pushed CTC to a dominant position in the market.

Within the world of CTC teas, there are huge differences in quality from one cup to the next. My personal pick in this Anglo-Irish tea world is an old family-run company in the city of Cork in Ireland called Barry's Tea. If CTC tea is what you're after, Barry's is the one to buy.

brewing tea

Whatever kind of tea you buy, make good brewing a habit. Badly brewed tea can be almost undrinkable.

You'll need a teakettle or something similar for boiling your water. The water you use will make a difference in the flavor of what you brew. If you take tea leaves with you from Pittsburgh to Portland, your tea will taste different in each location, unless you use the same brand of bottled water. Ideally, the water should be as neutral as possible, neither too hard nor too soft. If your local source has high levels of minerals such as magnesium or chlorine, consider buying bottled water. Either way, make sure the water is cold and freshly drawn.

To some degree, the teapot you choose is a matter of personal preference. Make sure that it's made from a nonporous material. I like to use a clear glass teapot, so that I can see the tea in all its glory. When the water's been poured, you'll see the leaves unfurling and pirouetting like snowflakes in an amber sky.

As for the ratio of tea to water, I use about 3 level teaspoons of leaves in my pot, which holds 3 pints of water. The old British standby is 1 spoonful per cup, plus 1 for the pot, but my experience is that fine tea requires less. (See the table on the opposite page.)

Don't use a stainless-steel tea ball—it doesn't allow for an adequate flow of water over the leaves. I like to let my tea leaves float free in the pot until the water has been infused, then pour the liquor through a simple strainer into the cup. The cloth or paper tea filters available in some stores work well.

ready, set, brew!

1. Bring the cold water to a boil. Turn the water off as soon as it starts to boil. Extended boiling cooks all the life out of the water, and the flavor of your tea is likely to be flat.

2. Pour a bit of the hot water into the pot to warm it. Pour it off. Place your tea in the pot (for suggested amounts, see the table below). Pour the just boiled water over the tea. (Never — I repeat, never — put the tea into the water. The difference in flavor is remarkable.)

3. For best brewing results, check the temperature of the water to make sure it's correct before you pour.

4. Let the tea steep. How long you steep it is partly a matter of personal preference and depends on the type of tea you choose.

5. Pour yourself a cup. (Find a cup you like — again, I prefer clear glass.) In a couple of minutes, the tea is cool enough to drink.

6. Sip. Savor. Enjoy.

Tea Variety	Water Temperature	Infusion Time	Amount of Tea per 12-Ounce Cup or Pot
White	175°F–180°F	3–4 minutes	1 tablespoon
China green	180°F	3 minutes	1 tablespoon
Japan green	175°F–180°F	2 minutes	1 teaspoon
Oolong large shape	205°F	3–4 minutes	1 tablespoon
Oolong small shape	205°F	3 minutes	1 teaspoon
Most black	205°F	5 minutes	1 teaspoon
China black	205°F	3–4 minutes	1 tablespoon
Darjeeling first-flush	195°F	3–4 minutes	1 teaspoon
Darjeeling second-flush	200°F	3–5 minutes	1 teaspoon
Pu-erh*	205°F	3–4 minutes	1 tablespoon

* Steep for 20 seconds, then pour off the liquid to wash the leaves. Pour new water over the moist leaves, then steep for no more than 1 minute. Good Pu-erh tea can be resteeped 4 to 6 times.

the traditional chinese technique for brewing

Although this technique is unfamiliar to most Americans, it is one of the most popular ways to brew tea in China. *Gong fu* brewing of tea will set your sense of tea preparation completely on its ear. Forget the three to five minutes of steeping, forget the spoonful of tea for each cup, forget the teapot you love.

This distinctive brewing method was formalized in Fujian province in the sixteenth century. Special tiny clay teapots, no bigger than the palm of your hand, and cups the size of shot glasses are used. The pot is warmed with hot water, drained, then filled halfway with dry tea leaves. Hot water is poured over the leaves and immediately drained to wash the leaves and remove their natural bitterness. The pot is again filled with hot water, allowed to steep for ninety seconds at most, and poured into cups to drink. The process is repeated with the same leaves in the pot at least four or five times.

The best pots to use for *gong fu* brewing are known as Yixing, made from the clay found in the vicinity of the Chinese town of the same name. They can cost more than $100 each. Because the clay is porous, it's seasoned by the type of tea you use, so you'll need a dedicated Yixing pot for each type of tea. I recommend those from Rishi Tea.

honey, vanilla, chocolate, and tea

tasting tea

You bought, you brewed. Now it's time to taste. Because it's hard to get the full flavor when it's really hot, let the newly brewed tea cool down a bit. Check the aroma first—tea has more than five hundred different elements in its scent. Then check the color. It should look bright. It should beckon.

Now take a taste. Note the different flavors as they register in different parts of your mouth. A lively tea should sparkle, with sweetness up front, tannins on the sides, and any bitterness all the way in the back. Astringency can be pronounced in some teas—particularly Indian teas —as a result of high natural tannin content. Most Formosa oolongs, on the other hand, will have almost none. Note the finish as well. Just as you'd expect with good wine, better tea tastes good long after you've swallowed it.

The best way to learn about the relative quality levels of teas is to brew more than one at a time. Better yet, set a cup of supermarket tea-bag tea next to a cup of fine Darjeeling. The latter's explosion of complex flavors will put the wide world of tea into terrific perspective.

Ultimately, of course, the truest test comes down to what you like or don't like. No one but you can decide.

three chai recipes

The best teas in India are exported, so most people there drink chai, strong tea boiled with spices, sugar, and milk. Here are three variations on the theme that Vikram and Meeru Vij serve at their excellent restaurant, Vij's, in Vancouver, British Columbia.

Feel free to experiment with other spices. You can adjust the ratios of milk, water, and sugar to suit your own preferences. The black cardamom can be hard to find, but it adds a nice subtly spicy complexity to the flavor. These recipes won't work well unless you've got strong machine-processed CTC tea (see page 437).

strong spiced chai

This is the tea equivalent of a latte," Meeru Vij explains, "served with lots of spices in it." It's stronger and sweeter than some other versions. The staff at Vij drink this chai daily, usually at midmorning to tide them over until lunch, and then again at about 4:00.

    1   black cardamom pod
  2¹/₂   cups cold water
    2   tea bags, preferably Barry's Irish or other CTC tea
    4   teaspoons sugar (more or less depending on your preference)
   10   green cardamom pods, lightly pounded
    2   vanilla bean pods (seeds scraped out and reserved for
        another purpose)
    2   4-inch cinnamon sticks
  ¹/₄   teaspoon fennel seeds
  1³/₄   cups whole milk

Husk the black cardamom pod. Remove the seeds and discard the pod. In a heavy-bottomed pot over a low flame, lightly toast the black cardamom seeds. When the seeds are toasted, add all the other ingredients except the milk to the pot. Bring to a boil for 2 to 3 minutes. Add the milk, mix well, bring back to a boil, and remove from the heat. Pour through a strainer, and serve in four warm mugs.

serves 4

city chai

This chai is the lightest and least sweet of the three.

4½ cups cold water
8 green cardamom pods, lightly pounded
4 tea bags, preferably Barry's Irish or other CTC tea
½ cup whole milk
   Sugar to taste

In a large pot, bring the water and the cardamom pods to a boil for 1 minute. Add the tea and boil for 1 more minute. Remove the tea bags, stir in the milk, and return to a boil. Remove from the heat, pour through a strainer, and serve in four warm mugs, with sugar on the side.

serves 4

vij's chai

This chai is ideal when company is coming. Vikram and Meeru Vij vary the spices according to their mood or the market, and you may want to do the same.

- 1 black cardamom pod (optional)
- 7 cups cold water
- 4 tea bags, preferably Barry's Irish or other CTC tea
- 16 green cardamom pods, lightly pounded
- 3 tablespoons sugar
- 1 vanilla bean pod (seeds scraped out and reserved for another purpose)
- 1 4-inch cinnamon stick
- 10 black peppercorns, lightly toasted, then cracked
- 2 whole cloves (optional)
- 3/4 cup whole milk

Husk the black cardamom pod. Remove the seeds and discard the pod. Lightly toast the seeds in a heavy-bottomed pot. When the seeds are toasted, add all the other ingredients except the milk to the pot. Bring to a boil. Reduce the heat to low and then simmer for 2 to 10 minutes, depending how strong you'd like the chai.

Remove the tea bags, stir in the milk, and return to a boil. Remove from the heat, pour through a strainer, and serve in eight warm mugs.

serves 8

mail-order sources ▨

for further reading ▥

indexes ◉

mail-order sources

If you aren't able to find some of the foods I've written about in your local shops, you can take solace in knowing that with the rapid growth of the mail-order food business and almost universal access to the Internet, getting your hands on good food is easier than ever. Happily, what once required a trip to the big city can now be done with a couple of phone calls or some quick on-line activity.

general sources

The following mail-order sources carry wide selections of specialty foods from all over the world.

zingerman's mail order

I hope it's not a surprise that I've put our own mail-order business at the top of the list. The same twenty years of research, tasting, and testing that have gone into gathering the in-formation for this book have gone into refining the selection at Zingerman's Mail Order. We ship breads from Zingerman's Bakehouse, traditional cheeses from Zingerman's Cream-ery and from all over the world, as well as tra-ditionally made olive oils, olives, vinegars, pasta, polenta, Italian and Spanish rice (and paella pans), really wild wild rice, dry-cured ham, salami, smoked salmon, black pepper, sea salt, saffron, honey, vanilla, chocolate, tea (including Barry's Tea from Ireland), and every other variety of traditional food dis-cussed in this book. What appears in the Zingerman's Mail Order catalog represents only a small portion of what is available. Please call and ask if you're looking for some-thing specific but haven't seen it represented in Zingerman's mailers or on our Web site.

Zingerman's Mail Order
422 Detroit Street
Ann Arbor, MI 48104
www.zingermans.com
(888) 636-8162

a. g. ferrari foods

4001 Piedmont Avenue
Oakland, CA 94611
www.agferrari.com
(510) 547-7222

A West Coast mail-order source for very good food from Italy, including estate olive oils, olives, aged vinegars, pasta, Italian rice, polenta, cheeses, dry-cured ham, salami, sea salt, honey, and more.

dean and deluca

560 Broadway (Prince Street)
New York, NY 10012
www.deandeluca.com
(212) 226-6800

A longtime New York institution whose mail-order operation stocks good-quality olive oils, olives, vinegars, pasta, rice, really wild wild rice, polenta, cheeses, dry-cured ham, salami, smoked salmon, black pepper, sea salt, saffron, vanilla, chocolate, and tea.

esperya usa

1715 West Farms Road
Bronx, NY 10460
www.esperya.com/usa
(877) 907-2525

A very nice selection of traditional Italian foods, including olive oils, vinegars, pasta, Italian rice, cheeses, dry-cured ham, salami, sea salt, honey, chocolate, and more.

formaggio kitchen

244 Huron Avenue
Cambridge, MA 02138
www.formaggiokitchen.com
(617) 354-4750

This small shop has a fine offering of olive oils, olives, vinegars, pasta, rice, cheeses (including many that are in the company's cave), polenta, dry-cured ham, salami, smoked salmon, sea salt, saffron, honey, vanilla, chocolate, and other good things to eat.

the spanish table

1427 Western Avenue
Seattle, WA 98101
www.spanishtable.com
(206) 682-2827

The Spanish Table stocks only foods from Spain and Portugal, including fine olive oils, olives, vinegars, pasta, rice (and paella pans), cheeses, sausage, Serrano ham, sea salt, saffron, honey, chocolate, tea, and more.

additional sources

These sources specialize in one particular product or product area.

olive oil

KATZ AND COMPANY
Mail-Order Department
101 South Coombs, Y-3
Napa, CA 94559
www.katzandco.com
(800) 676-7176

A very nice selection of California olive oils.

olives

HELLAS INTERNATIONAL
35 Congress Street
Salem, MA 01970
www.hellasintl.com
(800) 274-1233

Handpicked, traditionally cured Greek olives, as well as olive oils, vinegars, and honeys.

balsamic vinegar and wine vinegars

VINEGAR CONNOISSEURS INTERNATIONAL
P.O. Box 41
104 West Carlton Avenue
Roslyn, SD 57261
www.vinegarman.com
(800) 342-4519

A wide selection of interesting vinegars from all over the world.

bread

These bakeries regularly ship their bread around the United States.

AMY'S BREAD
75 Ninth Avenue
New York, NY 10011
www.amysbread.com
(212) 462-4338

IGGY'S
205-4 Arlington Street
Watertown, MA 02472
www.iggysbread.com
(617) 924-0949

METROPOLITAN BAKERY
Rittenhouse Square
262 S. 19th Street
Philadelphia, PA 19103
www.metropolitanbakery.com
(215) 545-6655

POILÂNE
8 Rue du Cherce-Midi
75006 Paris, France
www.poilane.com
(33) 1-44-39-20-94

Poilâne ships the loaves from its renowned Paris bakery by mail. Poilâne's breads are also available through Zingerman's Mail Order.

Stop by these excellent bakeries for
artisan bread when you're in any of these cities.

ACME BREAD COMPANY
1601 San Pablo Avenue
Berkeley, CA 94702
(510) 524-1021

BOULANGERIE BAY BREAD
2325 Pine Street
San Francisco, CA 94115-2714
(415) 440-0356

BREAD & COMPANY
2525 West End Avenue
Nashville, TN 37203
(615) 329-1400

BREAD LINE
1751 Pennsylvania Avenue NW
Washington, D.C. 20006
(202) 822-8900

EMPIRE BAKING COMPANY
5450 West Lovers Lane
Dallas, TX 75209
(214) 350-0007

GRAND CENTRAL BAKING COMPANY
Pioneer Square
214 1st Avenue South
Seattle, WA 98104
www.grandcentralbakery.com
(206) 622-3644

HI-RISE BREAD COMPANY
208 Concord Avenue
Cambridge, MA 01238
(617) 876-8766

LA BREA BAKERY
624 South La Brea Avenue
Los Angeles, CA 90036
www.labreabakery.com
(323) 939-6813

MRS. LONDON'S
464 Broadway
Saratoga Springs, NY 12866
www.mrslondons.com
(518) 581-1652

SEMIFREDDI'S BAKERY
4242 Hollis Street
Emeryville, CA 94608
(510) 596-9934

SULLIVAN STREET BAKERY
Soho
73 Sullivan Street
New York, NY 10012
www.sullivanstreetbakery.com
(866) 551-3905

polenta

1922-C Gervais Street
Columbia, SC 29201
www.ansonmills.com
(803) 467-4122

An excellent American-made option.

REALLY WILD wild rice

510 SE 11th Street
Grand Rapids, MN 55744
www.greyowlfoods.com
(800) 527-0172

Wild rice harvested by First Nations people
of Saskatchewan.

422 Pine Avenue
Grand Rapids, MN 55744
(800) 882-4902

A range of genuine wild rices (as well as cultivated paddy rice from Minnesota, so be sure
to ask for the real wild stuff).

cheddar cheeses

P.O. Box 87
Grafton, VT 05146
www.graftonvillagecheese.com
(800) 472-3866

Full-flavored traditional Cheddar made from
the milk of Jersey cows.

1611 Harbor Road
Shelburne, VT 05482
www.shelburnefarms.org
(802) 985-8686

Handmade Cheddar from the farm's own
herd of Brown Swiss cows.

goat cheeses

P.O. Box 117
10329 Newcut Road
Greenville, IN 47124
www.capriolegoatcheese.com
(812) 923-9408

Fresh and aged goat cheeses made by hand
in southern Indiana.

4600 Dows Prairie Road
McKinleyville, CA 95519
www.cypressgrovechevre.com
(707) 839-3168

A range of goat cheeses made by hand in
northern California.

free range beef, pork, and lamb

1025 East 12th Street
Oakland, CA 94606
www.nimanranch.com

Top-quality beef, pork, and lamb from
humanely treated herds.

salami

JOHN VOLPI AND COMPANY
5250-58 Daggett Avenue
St. Louis, MO 63110
www.volpifoods.com
(800) 288-3439

Good-quality Italian-style salamis made in St. Louis.

LA ESPAÑOLA MEATS, INC.
25020 Doble Avenue
Harbor City, CA 90710
www.donajuana.com
(310) 539-0455

A wide selection of Spanish-style sausages made in the United States.

smoked salmon

The following four firms will ship smoked wild Atlantic salmon directly from Europe to the United States.

HEDERMAN SMOKED SALMON
Belvelly Smoke House
Cobh, County Cork
Ireland
(353) 21 811089

A longtime smoker of wild salmon.

H. FORMAN AND SON
30 Marshgate Lane
London E15 2NH
U.K.
www.formans.co.uk
(44) 20 8221 3900

This London fish smoker, established in the early twentieth century, specializes in smoked wild salmon.

UMMERA SMOKED PRODUCTS LTD.
Inchybridge, Timoleague, County Cork
Ireland
www.ummera.com
(353) 23 46644

One of the few smokehouses still specializing in wild salmon.

WOODCOCK SMOKERY
Sally Barnes
Castletownsend, County Cork
Ireland
(353) 28 36232

Smoked wild salmon from the far west coast of Ireland.

The following companies are good sources for smoked farmed Atlantic salmon.

DUCKTRAP
57 Little River Drive
Belfast, ME 04915
www.ducktrap.com
(800) 828-3825

One of the longtime leaders in smoking fine farmed salmon.

DURHAM'S TRACKLEMENTS
212 E. Kingsley Street in Kerrytown
Ann Arbor, MI 48104
www.tracklements.com
(800) 844-7853

A small smokehouse that's steadily gaining national recognition for its smoked farmed salmon.

FISHERMAN'S MARKET
607 Bedford Highway
Halifax, Nova Scotia
Canada B3M 206
www.fishermansmarket.ca
(902) 443-3474

Dry-cured smoked farmed salmon from Nova Scotia.

STONINGTON SEA PRODUCTS
P.O. Box 100
Stonington, ME 04681
www.stoningtonseafood.com
(888) 402-2729

Good farmed salmon dry-cured and smoked over cherry and hickory.

pepper

PENZEYS SPICES
P.O. Box 924
Brookfield, WI 53008
www.penzeys.com
(800) 741-7787

This leading mail-order spice house offers Tellicherry black pepper as well as a range of other peppercorns.

saffron

GREIDER'S PENNSYLVANIA SAFFRON
5253 Main Street
East Petersburg, PA 17520
www.pageneralstore.com
(800) 545-4891

Offers limited amounts of Pennsylvania saffron.

PENZEYS SPICES
P.O. Box 924
Brookfield, WI 53008
www.penzeys.com
(800) 741-7787

A range of saffron from Spain and Kashmir.

VANILLA, SAFFRON IMPORTS
949 Valencia Street
San Francisco, CA 94110
www.saffron.com
(415) 648-8990

Longtime specialists in saffron, with offerings from Spain, Iran, and Greece.

honey

AMERICAN SPOON FOODS
1668 Clarion Avenue
P.O. Box 566
Petoskey, MI 49770
www.americanspoon.com
(888) 735-6700

This company bottles some very nice Michigan varietal honeys.

BEE HIVE PRODUCTS
10 Jay Street, Suite 201
Brooklyn, NY 11201
(718) 834-1518

A good selection of American varietal honeys.

KATZ AND COMPANY
Mail-Order Department
101 South Coombs, Y-3
Napa, CA 94559
www.katzandco.com
(800) 676-7176

Excellent California honeys.

MOONSHINE TRADING COMPANY
1250-A Harter Avenue
Woodland, CA 95776
www.moonshinetrading.com
(800) 678-1226

A long-standing, high-integrity U.S. honey supplier.

vanilla

NIELSEN-MASSEY VANILLAS, INC.
1550 Shields Drive
Waukegan, IL 60085
www.nielsenmassey.com
(800) 525-7873

The leading name in vanilla, this company's extract has long been the market leader in the United States.

VANILLA, SAFFRON IMPORTS
949 Valencia Street
San Francisco, CA 94110
www.saffron.com
(415) 648-8990

Longtime importer of top-quality vanilla beans from around the world.

chocolate

The following companies all offer their own top-quality hand-dipped truffles and bonbons by mail.

FRAN'S
2504 NE University Village
Seattle, WA 98105
www.franschocolates.com
(800) 422-3726

A longtime maker of top-quality chocolates.

L. A. BURDICK
P.O. Box 593
Main Street
Walpole, NH 03608
www.burdickchocolate.com
(800) 229-2419

A small, quality-oriented chocolatier.

LA MAISON DU CHOCOLAT
1018 Madison Avenue
New York, NY 10021
www.lamaisonduchocolat.com
(212) 744-7117

Makers of some of the best bonbons you'll buy anywhere.

RECCHIUTI CONFECTIONS
1 Ferry Building
Market Shop 30
San Francisco, CA 94111
www.recchiuticonfections.com
(800) 500-3396

Top-notch artisan chocolates.

VOSGES

520 North Michigan Avenue
Chicago, IL 60611
www.vosgeschocolate.com
(312) 644-9450

Known for its handmade chocolate truffles
spiced with an array of exotic flavors.

tea

IN PURSUIT OF TEA

224 Roebling Street
Brooklyn, NY 11211
www.inpursuitoftea.com
(866) 878-3832

Fine teas from all over the world.

KYELA TEAS

4057 Esplanade
Montreal, Quebec H2W 1S9
Canada
www.kyelateas.com
(514) 499-0068

A strong selection of special Darjeeling teas.

RISHI TEA COMPANY

207 East Buffalo Street
Milwaukee, WI 53202
www.rishi-tea.com
(800) 342-7767

Outstanding teas from all over the world,
plus Yixing clay pots and other tea-brewing
equipment.

TEA SOCIETY

1629 Date Street
Montebello, CA 90640
www.teasociety.org
(877) 832-5263

One of the few sources for Nilgiri tea, this
company is also an excellent source for other
Bespoke Teas.

UPTON TEA

34-A Hayden Rowe Street
Hopkinton, MA 01748
www.uptontea.com
(800) 234-8327

A broad range of top-notch teas from every
producing region.

for further reading

books

Alford, Jeffrey, and Naomi Duguid. *Seductions of Rice: A Cookbook*. New York: Artisan, 1998.

Anderson, Burton. *Treasures of the Italian Table: Italy's Celebrated Foods and the Artisans Who Make Them*. New York: William Morrow, 1994.

Androuët, Pierre. *The Complete Encyclopedia of French Cheese (and Many Other Continental Varieties)*. Translated by John Githens. New York: Harper's Magazine Press, 1973.

Barrett, Judith, and Norma Wasserman. *Risotto*. New York: Scribner, 1987.

Behr, Edward. *The Artful Eater: A Gourmet Investigates the Ingredients of Great Food*. New York: Atlantic Monthly Press, 1992.

Blofeld, John Eaton Calthorpe. *The Chinese Art of Tea*. New York: Random House, 1985.

Casas, Penelope. *Paella*. New York: Henry Holt, 1999.

Clayton, Bernard. *Bernard Clayton's New Complete Book of Breads: Revised and Expanded*. New York: Simon and Schuster, 2003.

Diggs, Lawrence J. *Vinegar: The User-Friendly Standard Text, Reference, and Guide to Appreciating, Making, and Enjoying Vinegar*. San Francisco: Quiet Storm Trading Company, 1989.

Dupaigne, Bernard. *The History of Bread*. Translated by Antonio and Sylvie Roder. New York: Harry N. Abrams, 1999.

Field, Carol. *The Italian Baker*. New York: Harper and Row, 1985.

Fletcher, Janet. *The Cheese Course: Enjoying the World's Best Cheeses at Your Table*. San Francisco: Chronicle Books, 2000.

Fussell, Betty. *The Story of Corn*. New York: Knopf, 1992.

Garavini, Daniella. *Pigs and Pork: History, Folklore, Ancient Recipes*. Translated by Isabel Varea. Cologne: Könemann, 1999.

Goldstein, Joyce. *Kitchen Conversations: Robust Recipes and Lessons in Flavor from One of America's Most Innovative Chefs*. New York: William Morrow, 1996.

Greenstein, George. *Secrets of a Jewish Baker: Authentic Jewish Rye and Other Breads*. Freedom, Calif.: Crossing Press, 1993.

Harrison, Jim. *The Raw and the Cooked: Adventures of a Roving Gourmand.* New York: Grove Press, 2001.

Hauser, Susan Carol. *Wild Rice Cooking.* New York: Lyons Press, 2000.

Hess, Karen. *The Carolina Rice Kitchen: The African Connection.* Columbia: University of South Carolina Press, 1992.

Humphries, John. *The Essential Saffron Companion.* Berkeley, Calif.: Ten Speed Press, 1996.

Jenkins, Nancy Harmon. *Flavors of Tuscany: Traditional Recipes from the Tuscan Countryside.* New York: Broadway Books, 1998.

———. *The Mediterranean Diet Cookbook: A Delicious Alternative for Lifelong Health.* New York: Bantam Books, 1994.

Jenkins, Steven. *Cheese Primer.* New York: Workman Publishing, 1996.

Johns, Pamela Sheldon. *Italian Food Artisans: Traditions and Recipes.* San Francisco: Chronicle Books, 2000.

Jordan, Michele Anna. *Polenta: 100 Innovative Recipes, from Appetizers to Desserts.* New York: Broadway Books, 1997.

———. *Salt and Pepper: 135 Perfectly Seasoned Recipes.* New York: Broadway Books, 1999.

Kasper, Lynne Rossetto. *The Splendid Table: Recipes from Emilia-Romagna, the Heartland of Northern Italian Food.* New York: William Morrow, 1992.

Knickerbocker, Peggy. *Olive Oil: From Tree to Table.* San Francisco: Chronicle Books, 1997.

Kummer, Corby. *The Pleasures of Slow Food: Celebrating Authentic Traditions, Flavors, and Recipes.* San Francisco: Chronicle Books, 2002.

Kurlansky, Mark. *Salt: A World History.* London: Jonathan Cape, 2002.

Lambert, Paula. *The Cheese Lover's Cookbook and Guide: Over 150 Recipes with Instructions on How to Buy, Store, and Serve All Your Favorite Cheeses.* New York: Simon and Schuster, 2000.

Laszlo, Pierre. *Salt: Grain of Life.* Translated by Mary Beth Mader. New York: Columbia University Press, 2001.

Luongo, Pino. *A Tuscan in the Kitchen: Recipes and Tales from My Home.* New York: Clarkson Potter, 1988.

Lu Yu. *The Classic of Tea.* Translated by Francis Ross Carpenter. Boston: Little, Brown, 1974.

McCalman, Max, and David Gibbons. *The Cheese Plate.* New York: Clarkson Potter, 2002.

McGee, Harold. *On Food and Cooking: The Science and Lore of the Kitchen.* New York: Collier Books, 1988, 1984.

Northrup, Jim. *The Rez Road Follies: Canoes, Casinos, Computers, and Birch Bark Baskets.* New York: Kodansha International, 1997.

Opton, Gene. *Honey: A Connoisseur's Guide with Recipes.* Berkeley, Calif.: Ten Speed Press, 2000.

Ortiz, Joe. *The Village Baker: Classic Regional Breads from Europe and America.* Berkeley, Calif.: Ten Speed Press, 1993.

Plotkin, Fred. *The Authentic Pasta Book.* New York: Simon and Schuster, 1985.

Pratt, James Norwood. *James Norwood Pratt's Tea Lover's Treasury.* Santa Rosa, Calif.: Cole Group, 1995.

Presilla, Maricel E. *The New Taste of Chocolate: A Cultural and Natural History of Cacao with Recipes.* Berkeley, Calif.: Ten Speed Press, 2001.

Rain, Patricia. *Vanilla Cookbook.* Berkeley, Calif.: Celestial Arts, 1986.

Rance, Patrick. *The Great British Cheese Book.* London: Macmillan, 1982.

Rosenblum, Mort. *Olives: The Life and Lore of a Noble Fruit.* New York: North Point Press, 1996.

Sardo, Piero, with Gigi Piumatti and Roberto Rubino. *Italian Cheese: Two Hundred Traditional Types: A Guide to Their Discovery and Appreciation.* Slow Food International, August 2001.

Schivelbusch, Wolfgang. *Tastes of Paradise: A Social History of Spices, Stimulants, and Intoxi-*

cants. Translated by David Jacobson. New York: Pantheon Books, 1992.

Silverton, Nancy. *Breads from the La Brea Bakery.* New York: Villard Books, 1996.

Steingarten, Jeffrey. *The Man Who Ate Everything: And Other Gastronomic Feats, Disputes, and Pleasurable Pursuits.* New York: Knopf, 1997.

Szita, Ellen. *Wild About Saffron: A Contemporary Guide to an Ancient Spice.* Daly City, Calif.: Saffron Rose, 1987.

Taylor, Judith M. *The Olive in California: History of an Immigrant Tree.* Berkeley, Calif.: Ten Speed Press, 2000.

Thorne, John. *Simple Cooking.* New York: Penguin, 1989, 1987.

Ukers, William H. *All About Tea.* New York: Tea and Coffee Trade Journal Company, 1935.

Vennum, Thomas, Jr. *Wild Rice and the Ojibway People.* St. Paul: Minnesota Historical Society Press, 1988.

Werlin, Laura. *The New American Cheese: Profiles of America's Greatest Cheesemakers and Recipes for Cooking with Cheese.* New York: Stewart, Tabori & Chang, 2000.

Willard, Pat. *Secrets of Saffron: The Vagabond Life of the World's Most Seductive Spice.* Boston: Beacon Press, 2001.

Wolfert, Paula. *Paula Wolfert's World of Food: A Collection of Recipes from Her Kitchen, Travels, and Friends.* New York: Harper & Row, 1988.

newsletters

The Art of Eating. Quarterly by Ed Behr.
P.O. Box 242, Peacham, VT 05862
www.artofeating.com
(800) 495-3944

Simple Cooking. A Food Letter by John and Matt Thorne.
P.O. Box 778, Northampton, MA 01061
www.outlawcook.com

general index

Balsamic condiment, 76, 77–78
Balsamic vinegar, 69–78
    affordable alternative to, 76, 77–78
    aging of, 72–74
    aroma of, 73
    authentic (traditional), 68, 69, 71–77
    flavor of, 76–77
    identifying real, 71
    levels of certification for, 74
    mass-produced (industrial), 71, 77, 78
    production of, 71–72
    source for, 448
    tasting, xv, 68, 75–76
    uses of, 77
Banyuls wine vinegar, 83
Baramendi, Rolando, 143
Barbieri, Erika, 76–77
Baricelli Inn cheese, 211
Barnes, Sally, 318, 451
Barrels
    for balsamic vinegar production, 72–74
    for sherry vinegar production, 81
Barry's Tea, 438
Basswood honey, 368
Bavarian Blue cheese, 262
Beaufort cheese, 237, 244–245
Beckwith, Sebastian, 434
Bee Hive Products, 452
Beeswax, 366
Bellon, Henri, 21
Bencista, Stefano, 300, 301
Berzemino grapes, 72
Bespoke tea, 433, 454
Bingham Hill Rustic Blue cheese, 264
Bistecca sanremasca, 110
Black button sage honey, 367
Black olives, 45. *See also* Olives
    in cans, 45
Black pepper, 326–327
Black tea, 424, 426, 427, 428, 435
Bleached flour, 101
Bloom, on chocolate, 403, 404

"Blue Bries," 262
Blue cheese, 252–268
    aging of, 255–256
    American, 264–265
    double-cream, 262
    Gorgonzola, 253, 258–260
    mold in, 252–253, 254, 259, 261
    piercing of, 254, 259
    production of, 253, 254–255
    product recommendations for, 257–258, 260,
        263, 264–265
    Roquefort. *See* Roquefort cheese
    Spanish, 263–264
    Stilton, 253, 260–262
    tasting, 258
Boeri olive oil, 20
Bomba rice, 179–180
Bonbons, 403–404
Boulangerie Bay Bread, 97, 449
Bourbon vanilla, 388, 391
B. R. Cohn raspberry vinegar, 80
Bread, 94–111, 114–122
    aroma of, 100, 108
    artisan, 97
    baguettes, 99, 107–108
    bruschetta and, 109–111
    color of, 96
    country, 98, 103, 104
    crust of, 97–98, 99, 108
    evaluating, 97–103
    flavor of, 98, 100, 107, 108
    hearth-baked, 98–99
    heating, 108, 109
    history of, 95–96
    holes in, 102–103
    ingredients in, 100–101
    misconceptions about, 102
    production of, 101–102
    pumpernickel, 104
    recipes using, 114–121
    rye, 102, 104–107
    soft, 96–97, 99

Bread (*continued*)
sources for, 448–449
sourdough, 104, 106–107
squeezing, 98–99
storing, 108–109
tasting, 103
texture of, 108
toasting, 110
Bread & Company, 449
Bread Line, 97, 99, 449
Breton gray salt, 340
Brine curing of olives, 46–47
Bromated flour, 101
Bruschetta, 109–111
Buckwheat honey, 368
Burnett, Joseph, 389

C

Cabernet vinegar, 84
Cabrales cheese, 263–264
Cacao Barry chocolate, 403
Cacao beans
drying, storing, and shipping of, 408
fermentation of, 408
grinding of, 409
harvesting of, 407
nibs of, 416
origin of, 401
roasting of, 408–409
varieties of, 400–401
winnowing of, 409
Cademartori Gorgonzola cheese, 260
Cahn, Miles and Lillian, 274
Calasparra rice, 178–179, 179, 180
Callebaut chocolate, 402, 403
Cambazola cheese, 262
Campbell, Janet, 374
Cannelloni, 133
Capers, 53
Capezzana olive oil, 17

Cappellini, 133
Capriole goat cheese, 274, 450
Carles Roquefort cheese, 257
Carnaroli rice, 160–161
Carob honey, 368
Carpegna prosciutto, 287
Carrasco Sánchez, Gregoria, 352, 358
Carr Valley Cheese, 232
Casarecci, 133
Casa Riera Ordeix, 303
Casas, Penelope, 291
Cashel Blue cheese, 263
Castello della Paneretta olive oil, 18
Castello di Cacchiano olive oil, 17–18
Castello rice, 162
Catalan Cuisine (Andrews), 114
Cavalieri, Benedetto, 131, 333
Cavalieri pasta, 131
Cavalli, Roberto and Giovanni, 72, 75, 76, 78
Cavalli balsamic condiment, 78
Cavalli vinegar works, 72–74
Cava vinegar, 84
Cefran saffron, 356
Cerignola olives, 50
Chai recipes, 442–444
Chardonnay vinegar, 84
Cheddar cheese, 226–235
aging of, 229–230
English versus American, 229–232
history of, 226–227
production of, 227–229
product recommendations for, 230–232
recipes using, 233–235
sources for, 450
Cheese, 202–214. *See also specific types of cheese*
age of, 210
aging of, 210–211
animals' diets and, 206–207
for cheese course, 213–214
choosing, 205–213
climate and, 204
cutting of, 212

flavor of, 205, 206–207, 207, 208–209

milk quality and, 208–209, 270, 274

mountain. *See* Mountain cheeses; *specific cheeses*

price of, 207

producer of, 206

raw-milk, 209–210

raw versus pasteurized milk for, 209–210

region of production of, 206

rind of, 221, 262, 273, 212

seasonal factors affecting, 203

starter cultures for, 204–205

storage of, 212

tasting before buying, 213

temperature for eating, 212

topography and, 203–204

type of animal providing milk for, 207–208

Chestnut honey, 367, 368

Chèvre. *See* Goat cheese

Chèvre Feuille, 275

Chevrot Blanc goat cheese, 275

Chinook salmon, 311–312

Chironi, Umberto and Sarah, 23

Chocolate, 399–420

bloom on, 403, 404

cacao beans and, 401–402, 407–409

cacao content of, 402

conching of, 409

couverture, 402–403

evaluating, 400–404

freshness of, 403–404

hand-dipping, 403

history of, 405–407

melting of, 414

milk, 409

molding of, 409

production of, 407–409

product recommendations for, 411–414

recipes using, 415–420

sources for, 453

storing, 414

tasting, 399–400

tempering of, 409

texture of, 399

vanilla in, 402

white, 413

Chorizo, 184, 305

Chum, 312

Cider vinegar, apple, 85

Ciresa Gorgonzola cheese, 260

Cluizel, Marc, 413

Coach Farm goat cheese, 274

Cocoa powder, 410

Coho, 312

Colavita olive oil, 9, 25

Cold-pressed olive oil, 5–6, 14

Colonna, Maria, 19, 42

Colonna olive oil, 19

Colston Bassett Stilton cheese, 262

Columbia River salmon, 312

Comté cheese, 237, 244

Conchiglie, 133

Congdon, Robin, 263

Consorzio del Formaggio Parmigiano-Reggiano, 216, 221

Consorzio del Prosciutto di Parma, 282

Consorzio di Tutela e Valorizzazione delle Varietà Tipiche di Riso Italiano e delle Sue Tradizioni, 161–162

Consorzio fra Produttori di Aceto Balsamico Tradizionale di Reggio Emilia, 72

Consorzio Produttori Aceto Balsamico Tradizionale di Modena, 75, 76

Cooperativa del Campo Virgen de la Esperanza, 179, 180

Copper River salmon, 312

Coratina olives, 8

Corbezzolo honey, 368

Corn, for polenta, 149

Cornicabra olives, 22

Corzetti, 133

Coulet Roquefort cheese, 257

Couverture, 402–403

Cow's milk, cheese produced from, 207

Harbourne Blue cheese, 263
Harler, C. R., 428
Harper, Dennis, 192
Hazan, Marcella, 134
Hazelnut oil, 62
Hederman, Frank, 313, 314
Hederman Smoked Salmon, 313, 318, 451
Hellas International, 47, 49–50, 448
Herb vinegars, 83
Hess, Karen, 96
H. Forman and Son, 315, 318, 451
Hidalgo Solera Reserva Manzanilla sherry
    vinegar, 83
Hi-Rise Bread Company, 97, 449
History of Bread, The (Dupaigne), 96, 455
Hobz biz-zejt, 110
Hoffman, David Lee, 434
Hojiblanca olives, 22
Hondroelia olives, 49
Honey, 364–382
    choosing, 367
    commercially flavored, 367
    history of, 365
    production of, 365–366
    recipes using, 373–382
    sources for, 452
    storing, 371
    substituting for sugar, 372
    uses of, 371–372
    varieties of, 366–367, 368–371
Hooper, Allison, 275
Huile d'Olives des Treilles, 21
Huilerie Leblanc, 60

i

Idiazábal cheese, 246
Iggy's, 448
Il Mongetto tomato sauce, 144
Il Nobile olive oil, 23
Indonesian vanilla, 388

In Nonna's Kitchen (Field), 150
In Pursuit of Tea, 434, 454
Institute National des Appellations d'Origine, 257
Iron Goddess of Mercy tea, 434
Italian rice, 158–174
    choosing, 160–162
    cooking, 164–167
    growing of, 162–164
    harvesting of, 164
    history of, 159–160
    labeling of, 161–162
    product recommendations for, 167
    recipes using, 168–174
    varieties of, 160–161

j

Jacquin family French cheeses, 275
Jamison Farms lamb, 378
Jamón Serrano. *See* Serrano ham
Jasmine Dragon Phoenix Pearl tea, 436
Jasmine tea, 436
Jean de France salami, 305
Jewish rye bread, 102, 104–107
Johnson, Kristi and Tom, 264
John Volpi and Company, 450
José Páez Lobato sherry vinegar, 82

k

Kaiser, Joshua, 434
Kalamata olives, 45, 46, 49
Kasper, Lynne Rossetto, 70
Katz and Company, 448, 452
Keehn, Mary, 274
Keemun tea, 435
Keen, Martin, 356
Keen's Farm Cheddar cheese, 230, 231
Kimberley Wine Vinegars, 85

King salmon, 311–312
Kleiman, Evan, 157
Krassman, Simon, 313, 314
Krauch, Willy, 316
Krokos Kozanis, 356
Kukicha tea, 437
Kyela Teas, 454

London, Michael, 98, 100, 101, 106, 381
Loriva nut oils, 61
Lox, 317
Lucedio rice, 162–164, 167
Lumache, 133
Lung Ching tea, 435
Lye curing of olives, 47

l

La Brea Bakery, 97, 449
L. A. Burdick, 453
La Española Meats, Inc., 450
La Lodigiana rice, 162
La Maison du Chocolat, 453
Lamb, product recommendations for, 378
Lambrusco grapes, 72
Lardo, xxi, 286
Lasagne, 133
Lasagnotte, 133
La Spineta olive oil, 20
Latini, Carlo and Carla, 131
Latini pasta, 131
Laudemio olive oil, 12, 18
Lavender honey, 367, 369
Leatherwood honey, 369
Lea-Wilson, David and Alison, 341
Leblanc, Jean-Charles, 60
Leccino olives, 8
Lehua blossom honey, 369
Lemon blossom honey, 369
Lemon olive oil, 24
Leonardi balsamic condiment, 78
L'Estornel olive oil, 22
L'Etivaz cheese, 238–241
Ligurian olives, 45
Limonato, 24
Lindt, Rodolfe, 409
Linguine, 133
Lipton, Thomas, 425
Loch Fyne Oyster Company, 315

m

Maccheroncini di Campofilone, 134
Maccheroni, 133
Macelleria Falorni, 299–303
McEvoy, Nan, 23
McEvoy Ranch olive oil, 23
McGee, Harold, 313
McGlynn, Colleen, 23
Madagascar vanilla, 388
Mahnomen wild rice, 195
Maille herb vinegars, 83
Mail-order sources, 446–454
Majorero cheese, 276
Malabar pepper, 329
Maldon salt, 340–342
Malloreddus, 133
Mantecatura, 167
Manuka honey, 370
Manzanilla Cacareña olives, 22
Manzanilla olives, 51
Manzanilla sherry, 83
Marash red pepper flakes, 58
Mariano's olive oil, 22
Marino, Felice, 146
Marino, Ferdinando, 146
Marino, Flavio, 146, 148
Marino polenta, 146–148, 149, 150
Marshall's Smoked Fish, 318
Martelli, Chiara, 130
Martelli, Dino, 128–129, 130
Martelli, Valentina, 130
Martelli pasta, 128–130

aging of, 283–284
aroma of, 284
bone-in, 285
choosing, 285–286
flavor of, 284–285, 286
production of, 282–285
product recommendations for, 287
recipes using, 289–290
salting of, 281–282, 285
storing, 287
uses of, 288
Prosciutto Di Vodier, 283
Pu-erh tea, 428, 436
Puig, Josep, 84
Pumpernickel bread, 104
Pumpkin seed oil, 62

q

Quadrucci, 135
Quality of ingredients, xviii, xx, xxii
Queso de cabra. *See* Goat cheese
Queso de vare, 276

r

Rao's tomato sauce, 144
Raspberry blossom honey, 370
Raspberry vinegar, 80
Raw-milk cheeses, 209–210
Reblochon cheese, 245–246
Rechiutti Confections, 453
Red label balsamic vinegar, 74, 75
Redondo, Miguel, 296
Redondo Iglesias Serrano ham, 292, 293
Red pepper flakes, Marash, 58
Red tea, 427, 435
Reese, Bob, 275
Réunion vanilla, 388
Rez Road Follies, The (Northrup), 189, 195, 456

Rice. *See* Italian rice; Spanish rice; Wild rice
Ricotta cheese, 210
Rioja vinegar, 84
Riseria di Lenta rice, 162
Riseria Ferron rice, 162
Riseria La Gallinella rice, 162
Rishi Tea Company, 434, 435, 436, 440, 454
Risi e bisi, 161
Riso in bianco, 166
Risotto, 158, 159, 164–167. *See also* Italian rice
Robert Rothschild Farm raspberry vinegar, 80
Robinson, Ruth and Larry, 85
Rock Hill Bakehouse, 98
Rock salt, 337–338
Roi olive oil, 20
Romana, Jeannotte, 37
Roncal cheese, 247
Roquefort cheese, 253–258
    aging of, 255–256
    choosing, 257–258
    declining number of farms producing, 256
    eating, 258
    price of, 257
    production of, 254
    product recommendations for, 257–258
    splitting wheels of, 256–257
    tasting, 258
Rosemary honey, 370
Rosenblum, Mort, 21
Rosette de Lyon salami, 305
Ruiz Egea, José, 179
Rustichella pasta, 132
Rustichella tomato sauce, 144
Rye bread, 102, 104–107
    in Roquefort cheese production, 255

s

Saffron, 349–362
    authenticity of, 354
    choosing, 355–356

V

Z

recipe index